LUMINESCENCE

SHEDDING LIGHT ON THE CREATIVE PROCESS WITH DJAMILA KNOPF

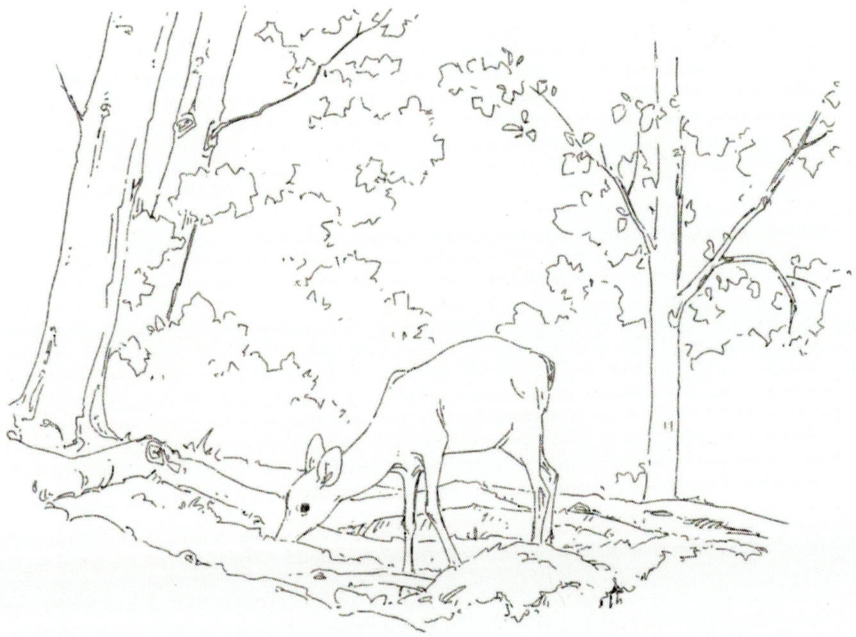

3dtotalPublishing

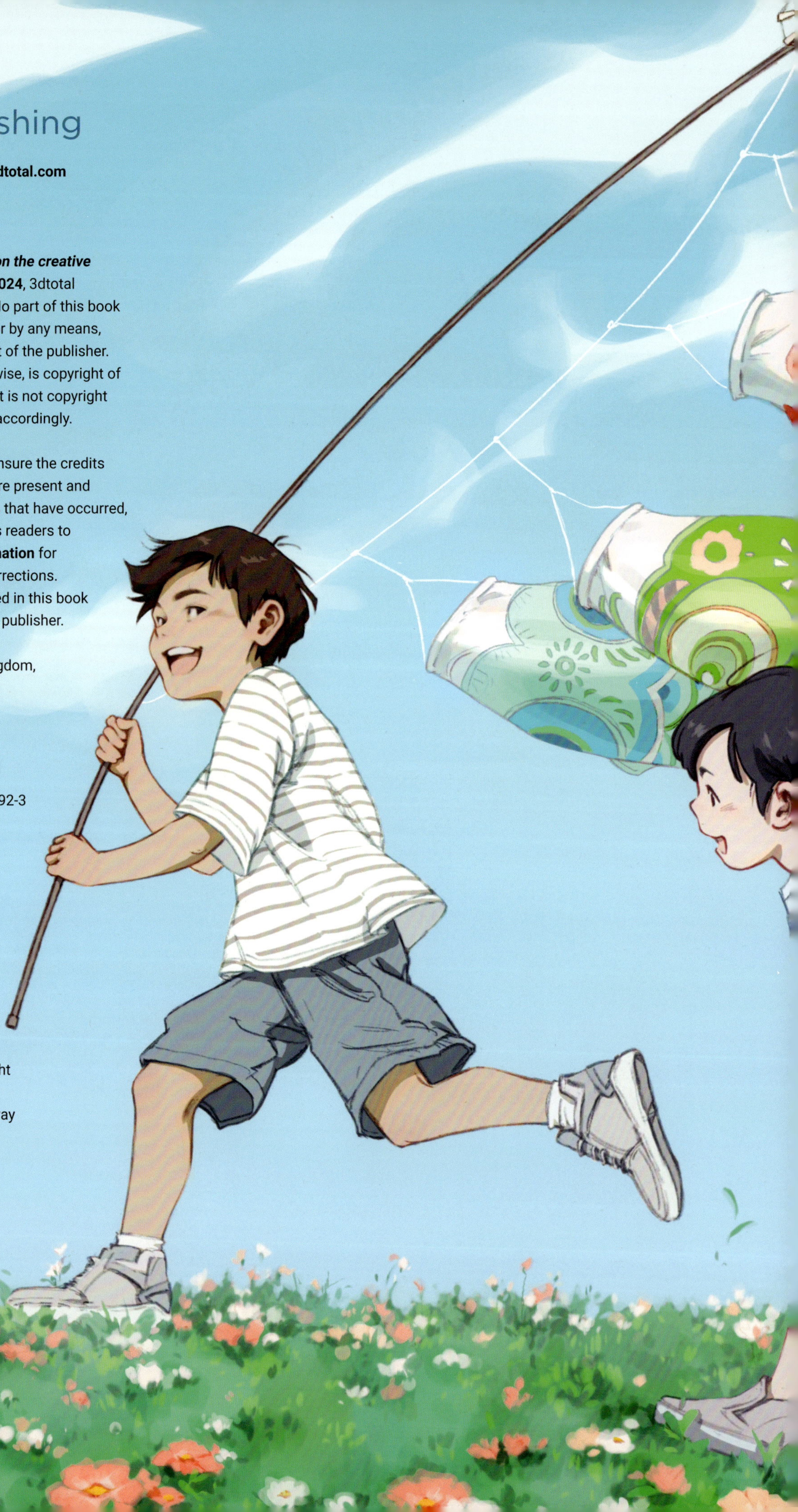

3dtotal Publishing

Correspondence: **publishing@3dtotal.com**

Website: **store.3dtotal.com**

First published in the United Kingdom, 2024, by 3dtotal Publishing.

Address: 3dtotal.com Ltd,
29 Foregate Street, Worcester,
WR1 1DS, United Kingdom.
Hard cover ISBN: 978-1-912843-92-3

Printed and bound in China
by C&C Offset Printing Co., Ltd

Visit **store.3dtotal.com**
for a complete list of
available book titles.

Editorial Project Manager:
Rhiannon Joseph
Lead Editor: Samantha Rigby
Lead Designer: Joseph Cartwright
Studio Manager: Simon Morse
Managing Director: Tom Greenway

FSC www.fsc.org MIX Paper | Supporting responsible forestry FSC® C008047

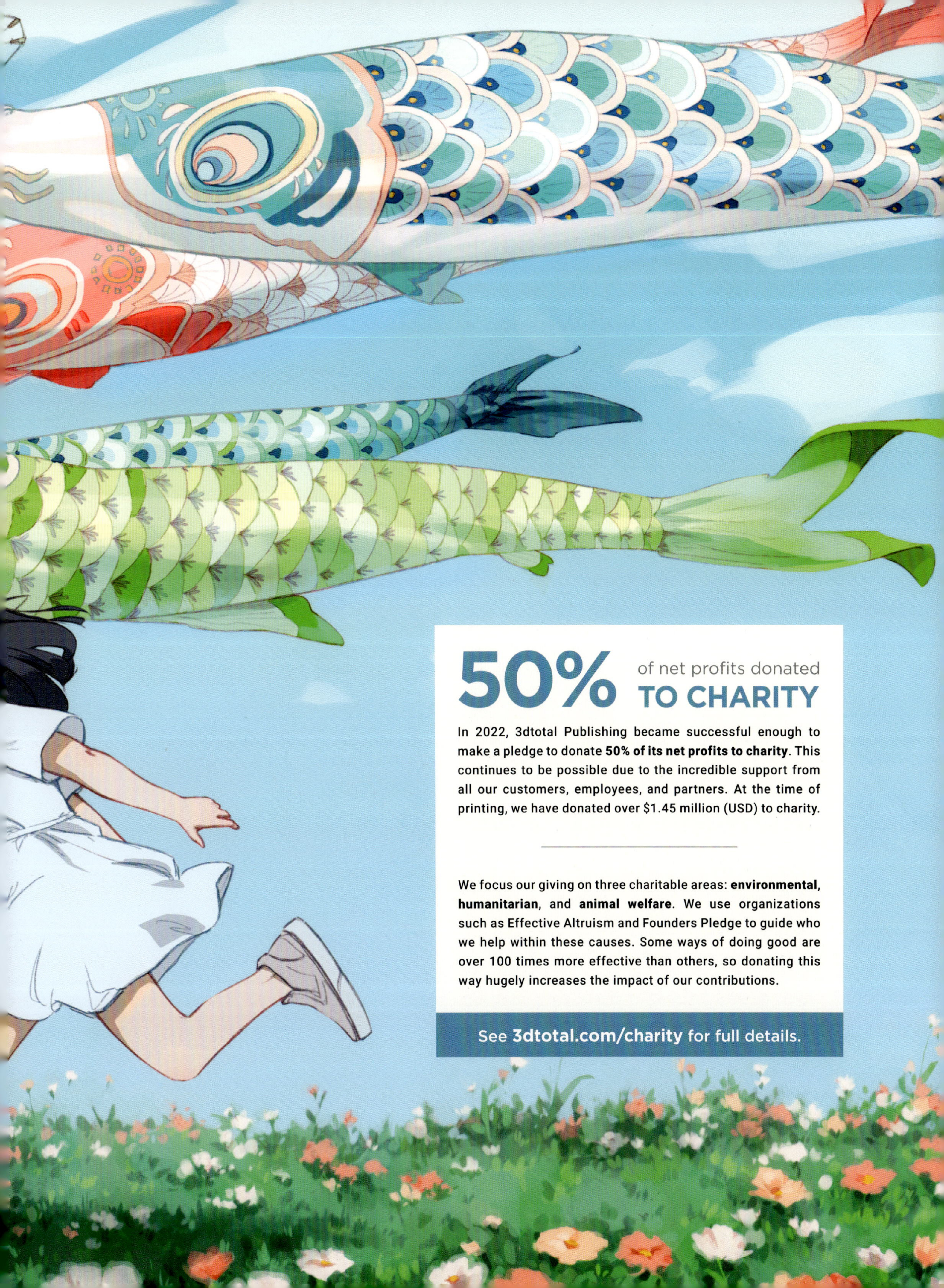

50% of net profits donated TO CHARITY

In 2022, 3dtotal Publishing became successful enough to make a pledge to donate **50% of its net profits to charity**. This continues to be possible due to the incredible support from all our customers, employees, and partners. At the time of printing, we have donated over $1.45 million (USD) to charity.

We focus our giving on three charitable areas: **environmental**, **humanitarian**, and **animal welfare**. We use organizations such as Effective Altruism and Founders Pledge to guide who we help within these causes. Some ways of doing good are over 100 times more effective than others, so donating this way hugely increases the impact of our contributions.

See **3dtotal.com/charity** for full details.

CONTENTS

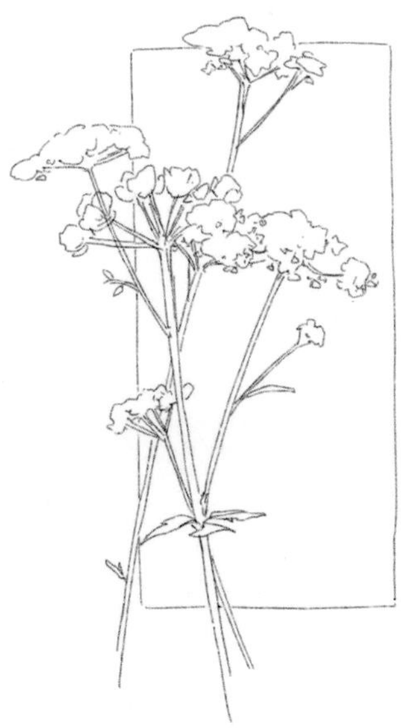

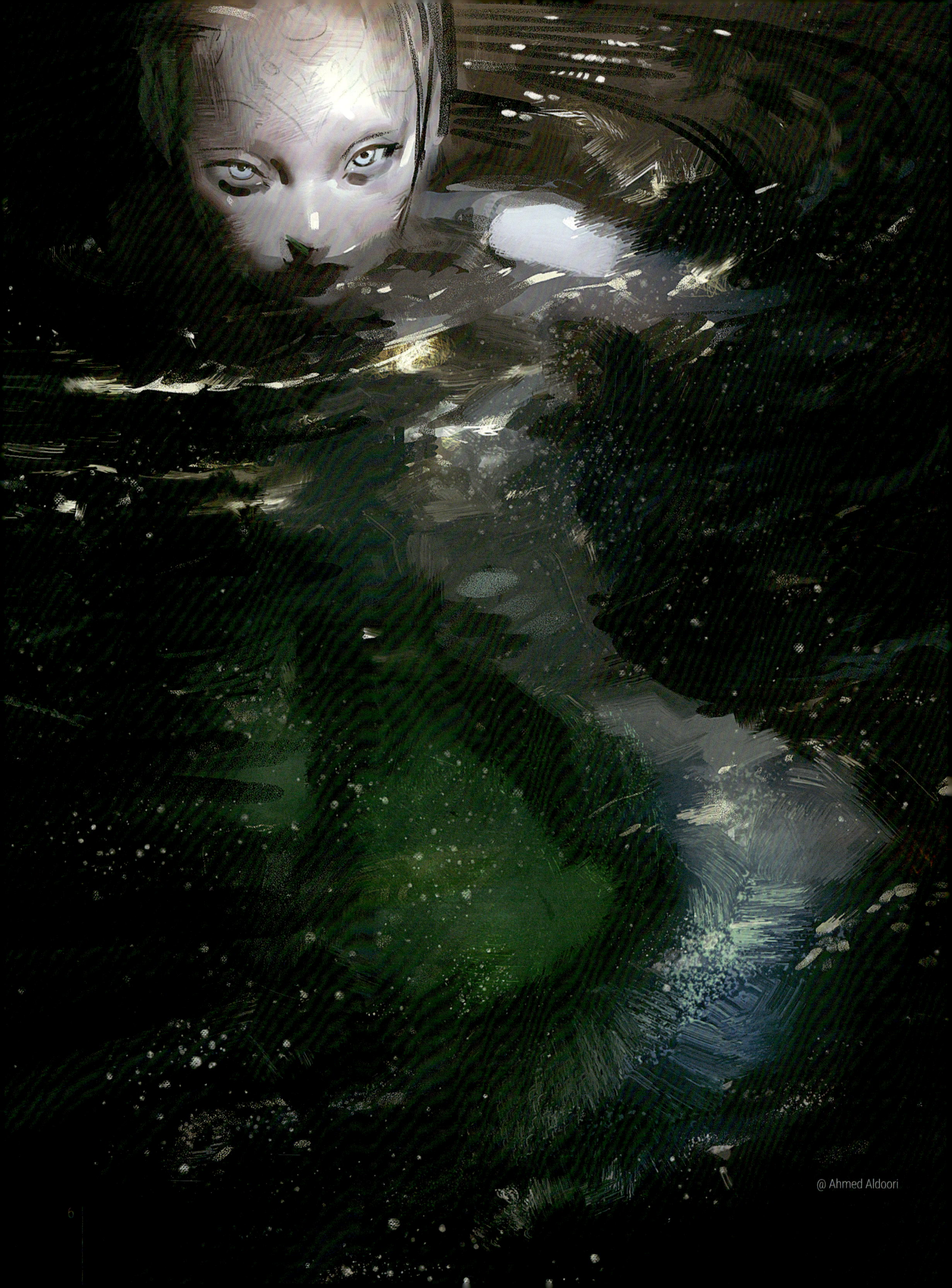

@ Ahmed Aldoori

FOREWORD BY AHMED ALDOORI

Meeting Djamila Knopf at LightBox Expo 2019 was a highlight for me, as I was already an admirer of her art. I still vividly recall discovering her beautiful work. Her paintings stand out amid the chaos of the art world, inviting us into her realms. Each piece, with its blend of light and emotion, is like slipping into a calm dream. There's almost a musical quality to it: colourful notes dancing together, forming harmonious narratives that speak volumes about her journey as an artist.

Djamila's art has a unique way of capturing subtleties of emotion. I am particularly struck by the tranquil yet powerful ambience she creates. It's not just visually stunning; it evokes a sense of peace and introspection. This deeply resonates with me, especially during times when my own art feels rushed. Emphasizing the meditative process of creation, Djamila's approach teaches the value of patience and contemplation in my work.

Her latest collection, showcased in *Luminescence*, is a testament to her evolving craft. Djamila weaves light and colour with nuance, each detail contributing to a larger narrative. It's fascinating to see how her technique has developed, allowing her to tell more intricate and profound visual stories.

Luminescence is much more than an art book; it's a journey through Djamila's creative mind. It delves into how she finds inspiration, channels emotion, and brings her ideas to life. The book offers rare insights into her creative process, from the evolution of her concepts to the intricacies of visual storytelling. For artists and enthusiasts alike, this book is a treasure chest of inspiration and guidance, illuminating the quest for anyone on their own artistic journey.

You can't help but be inspired by Djamila's artistic universe. It's a world where each element, from the subtle play of light to the thoughtful composition of shapes, invites exploration and reflection. Her willingness to share her journey makes this resource a true gem.

As I reflect on Djamila's impact on my art and the broader art community, I'm reminded of the power of sharing our creative journeys. Her work does more than just fill the eyes with wonder; it inspires the heart and mind, encouraging us to share our own creative potential.

Djamila – thank you for lighting the way with your art. It's not just a visual treat, but a source of endless inspiration, reminding us of the magic that happens when we pour our hearts into our work.

Ahmed Aldoori, Artist

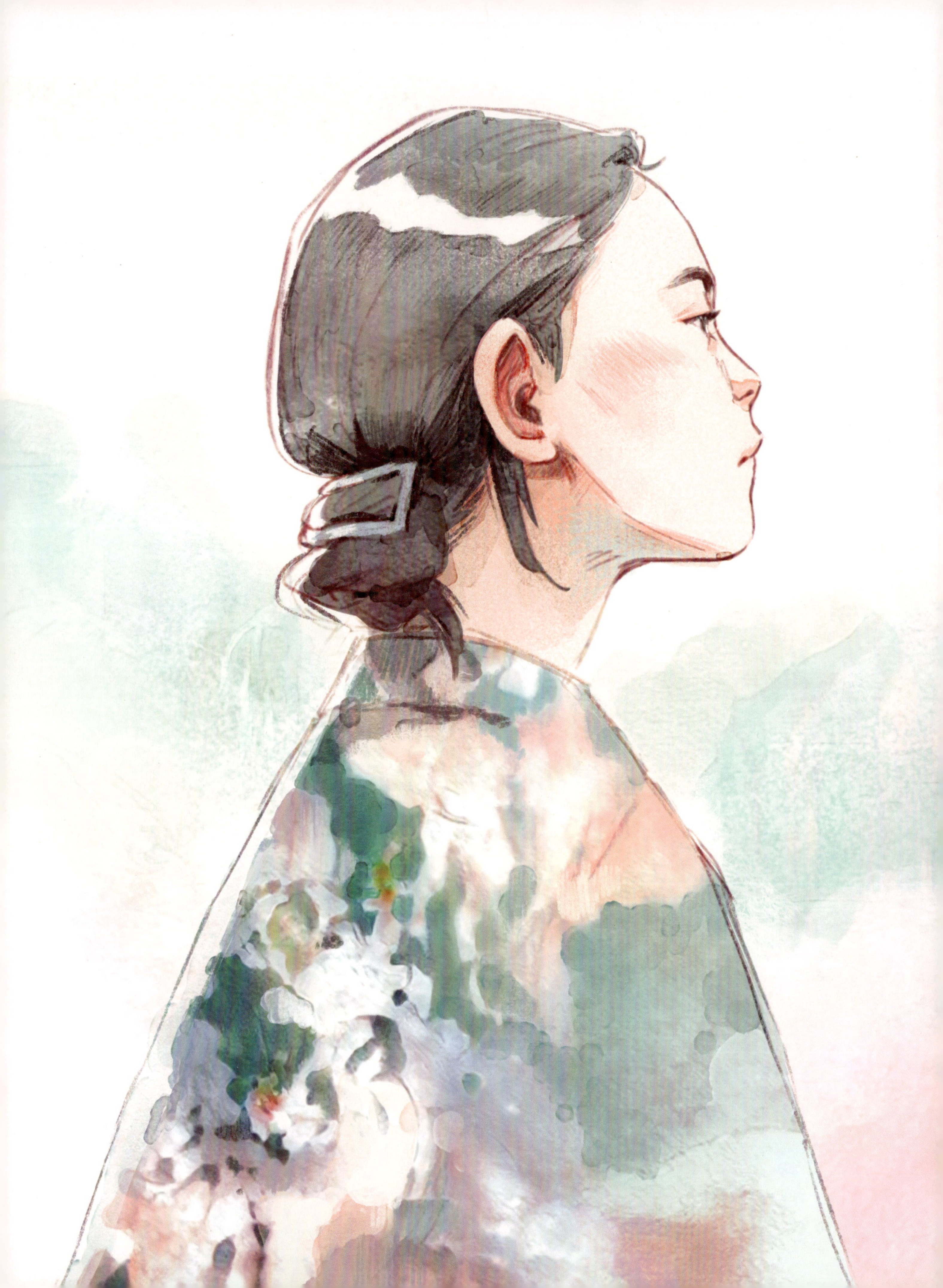

INTRODUCTION BY DJAMILA

Two of my favourite things in life are art and books, so bringing them together in this way is the most rewarding endeavour I can imagine.

I am incredibly grateful to have been given the opportunity to compile this volume as a sequel to *Komorebi: The Art of Djamila Knopf,* as it allows me to talk about the creative process, with all its ups and downs. Making art comes with its fair share of challenges and I painted many of the illustrations in this book during a difficult period in my life, when world events and other circumstances dulled my enjoyment to create and left me feeling overwhelmed – so much so, that I almost completely forgot why I started making art in the first place. It was a time when optimism gave way to cynicism, when I'd abandoned all my curiosity and sense of wonder. But now that I'm slowly leaving that phase behind, this book is a way of reclaiming everything I'd lost or forgotten. It's a reminder of why I love art.

I wanted to create a resource that my readers and I could return to time and time again to remember how miraculous it is to be an artist. I see it as a light in the dark – something that gives me orientation and hope, hence the title *Luminescence*.

My goal is to demystify the creative process, to break it down into smaller parts and make it accessible. I'm answering questions such as: *Why do I make art? Where do I find inspiration? How do I approach visual storytelling? How do I evoke emotions through artwork? How do I make art that is unique and personal?* I share experiences and anecdotes, but also pose questions to you, the reader. Through answering them, I hope you will gain a deeper understanding of who you are as an artist and how your own creative process works. I want to help you think about *what* you're making, *why* you're making it, and *how*.

Creating art is a messy business. It's not straightforward. What I believe to be true today can be different tomorrow. Just like everyone else, I am constantly changing and so is my attitude towards my work. But instead of seeing this as a bug that needs fixing, I am becoming more and more comfortable with the idea that a certain degree of disorder is simply a part of the equation. So, everything I share in this book is not only the accumulation of what I've learned over the past years, but also a momentary record of my current art and philosophy. Your own creative process may be entirely different from mine, and that's what makes this whole thing exciting. If we were all the same, and approached art the same way, there would be no point to a book like this.

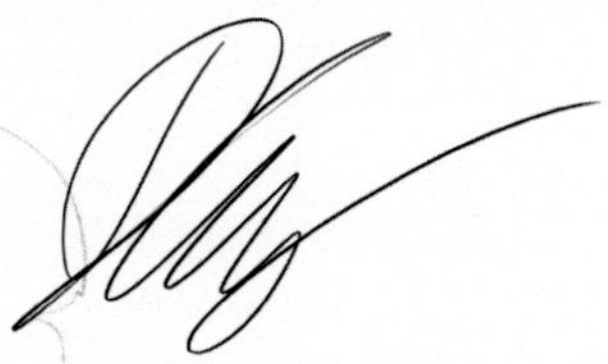

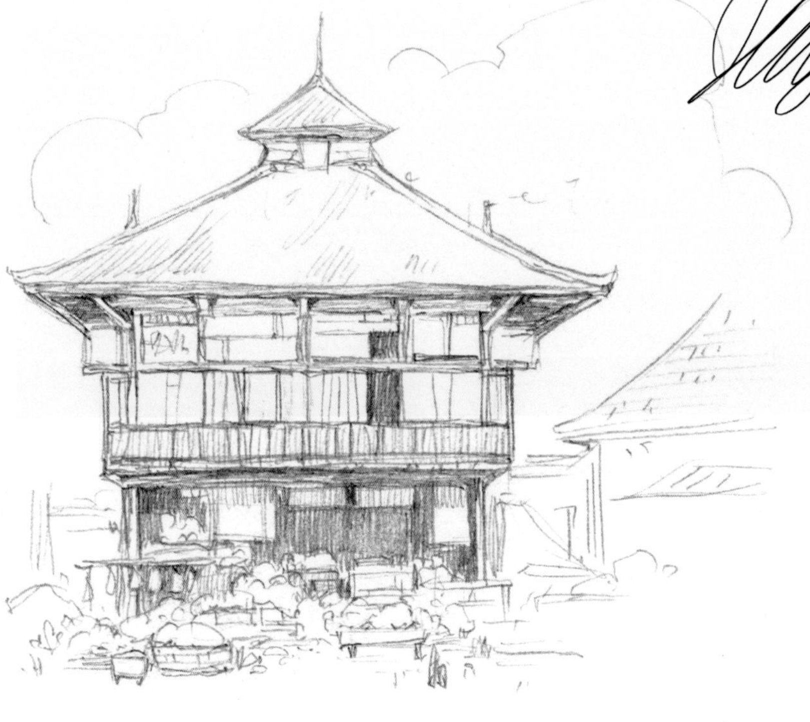

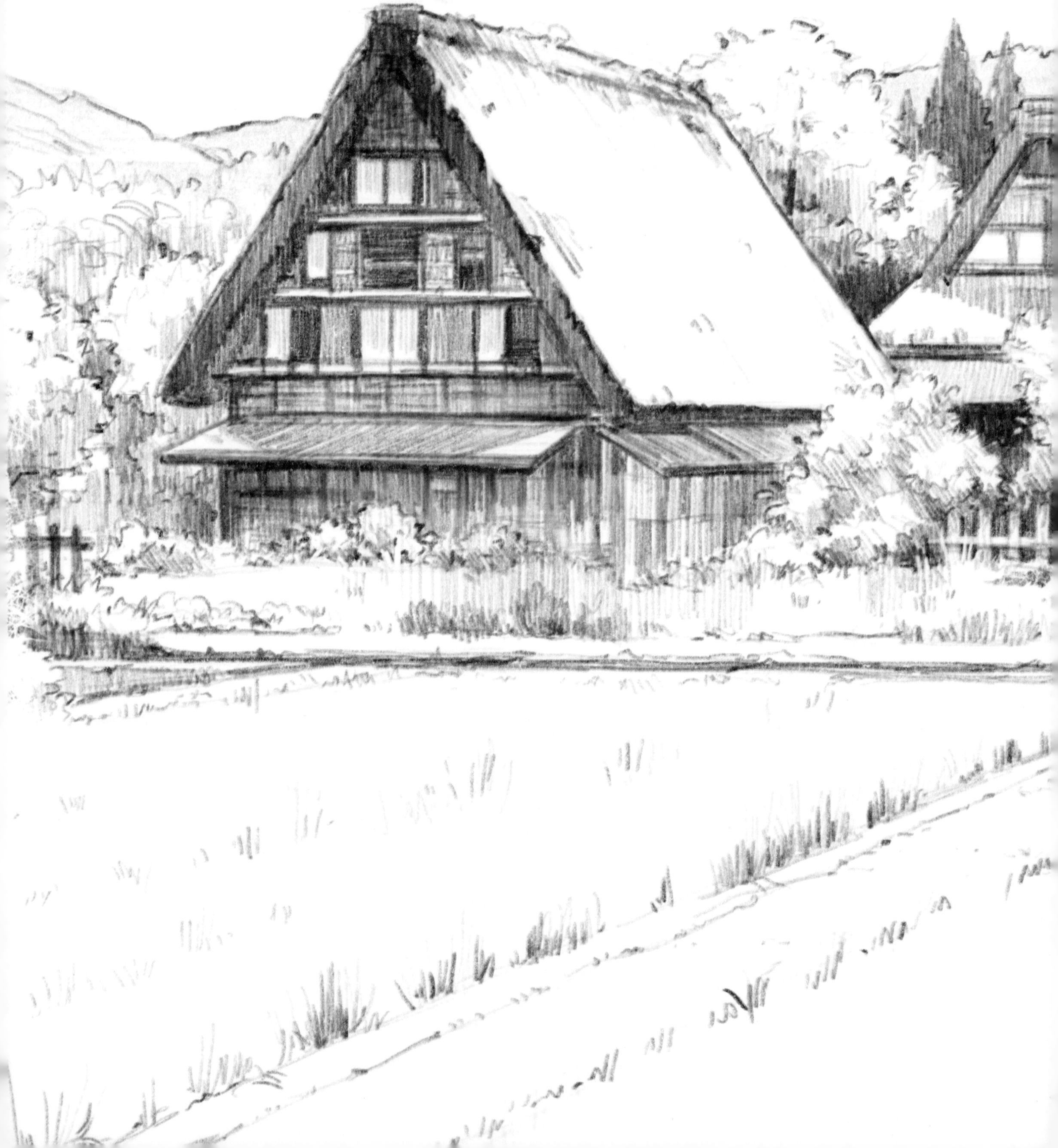

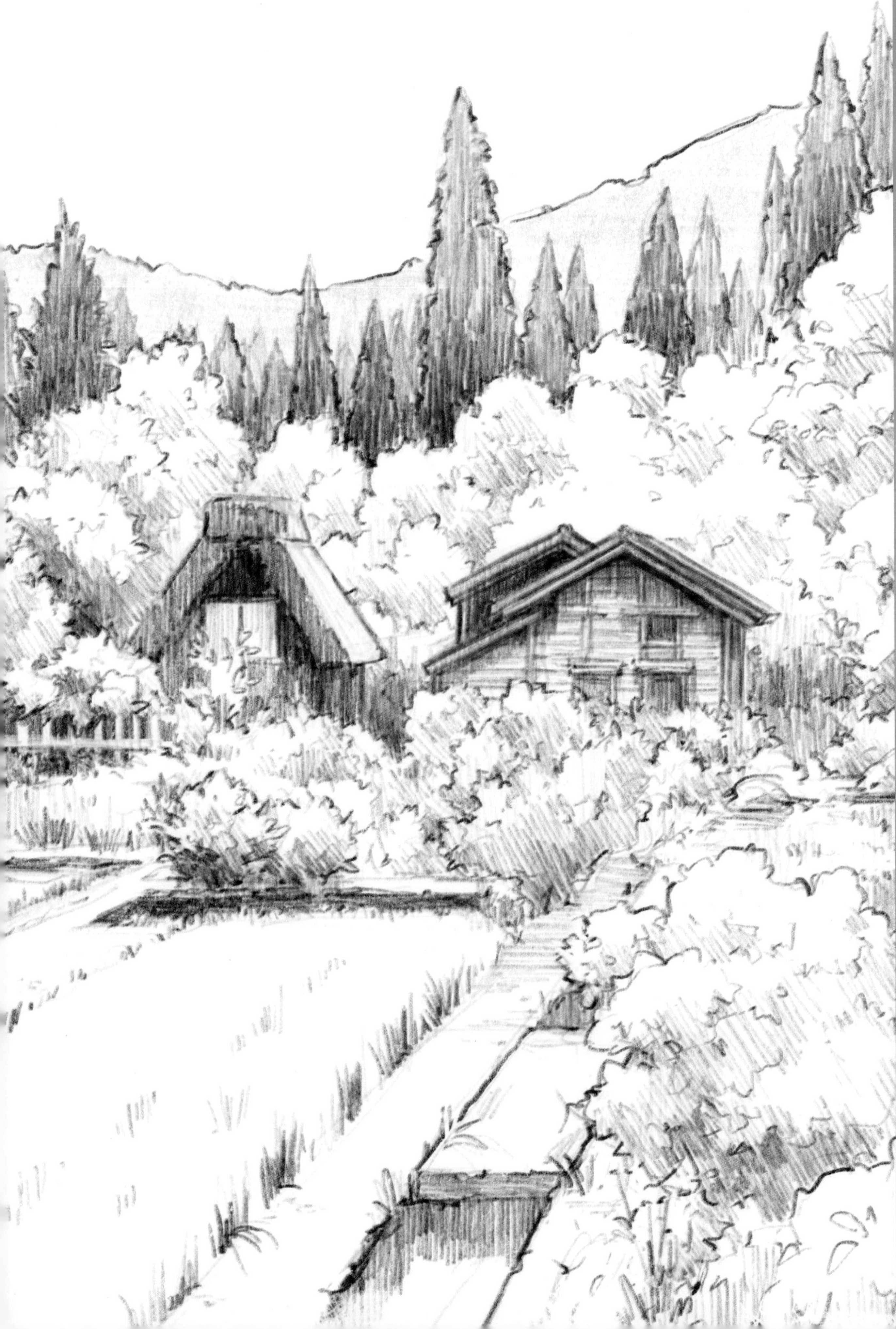

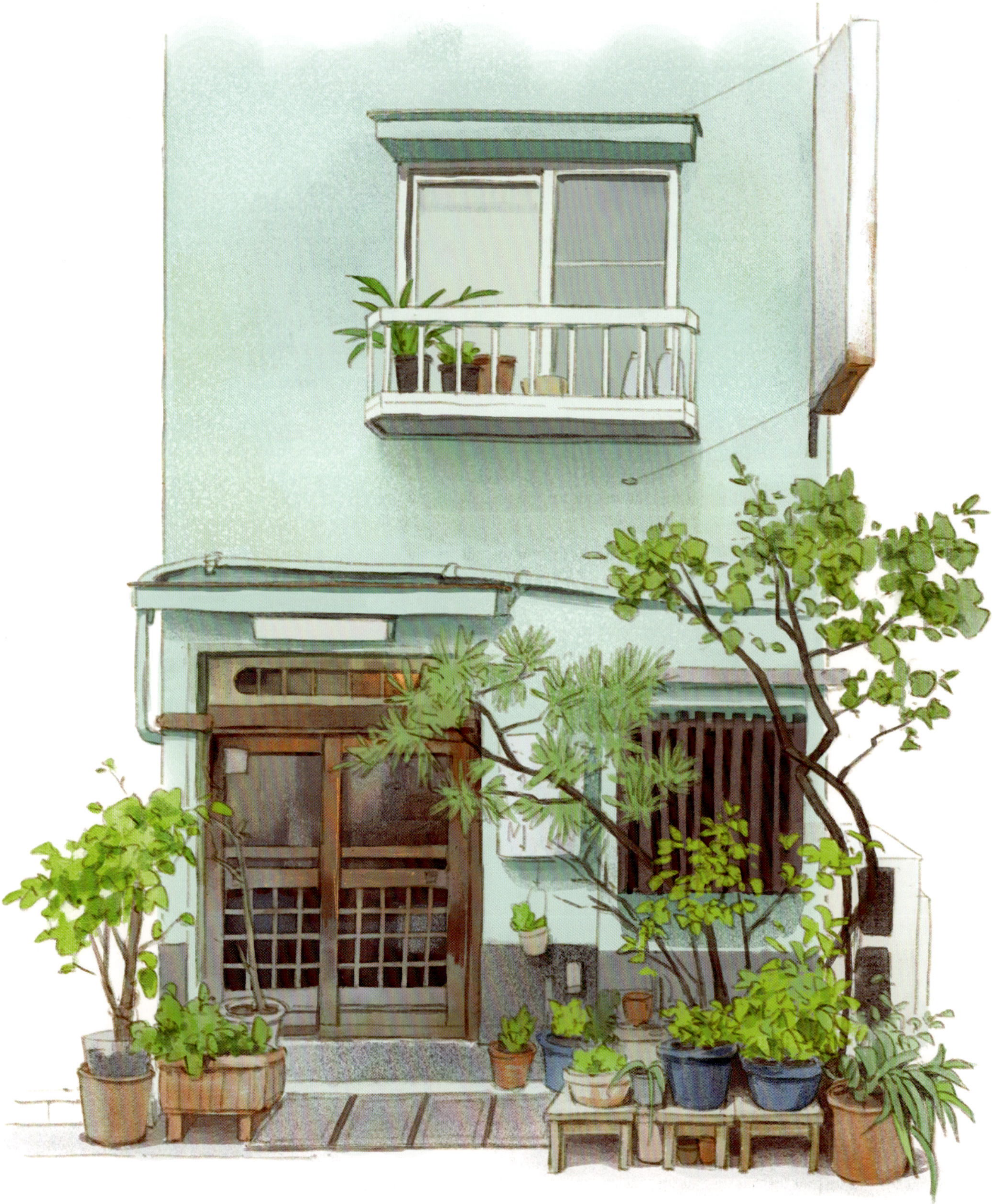

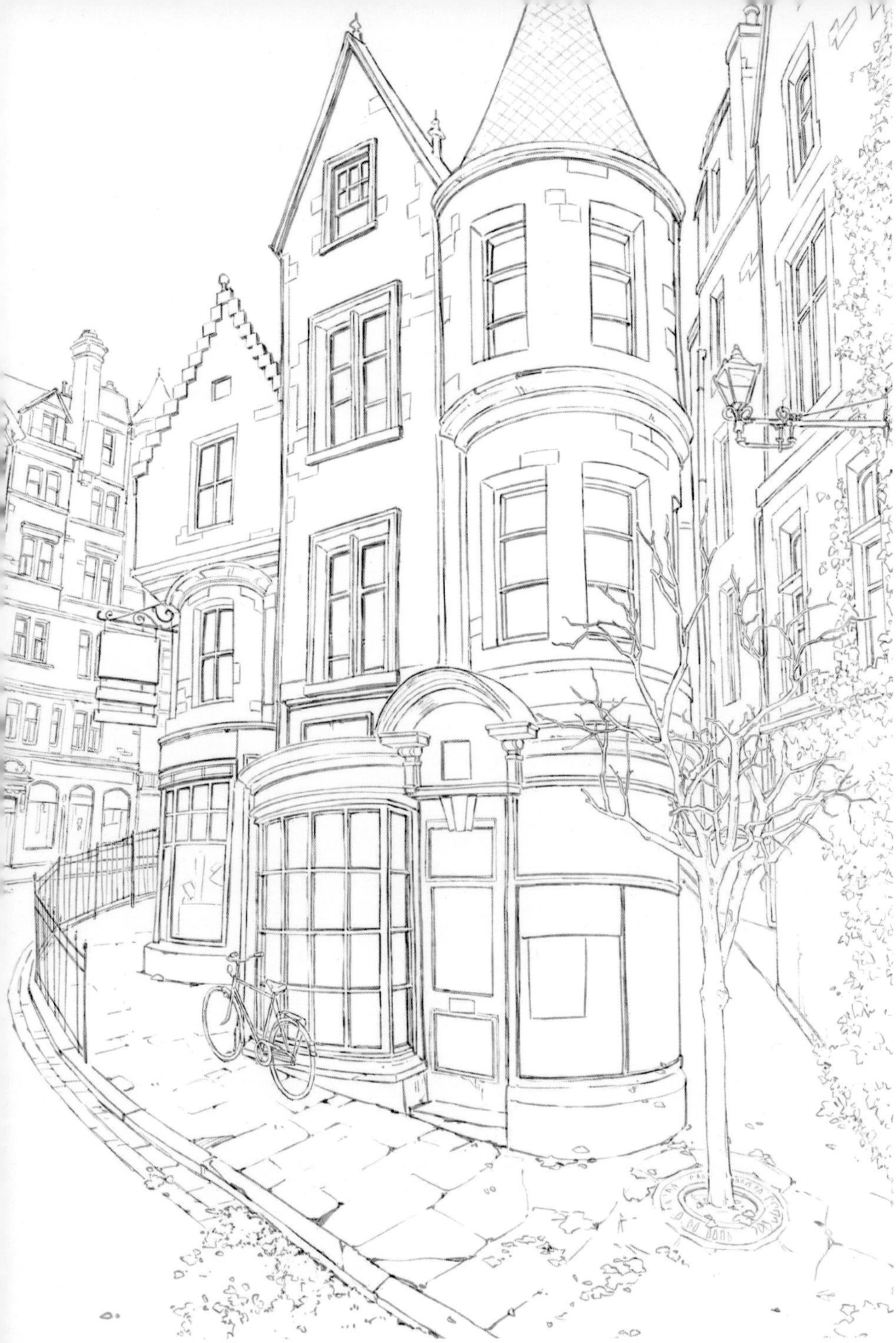

When I ask myself why I make art, the first thing that comes to mind is a quote by author Neil Gaiman: 'The world always seems brighter when you've just made something that wasn't there before.' The more I think about it, the more I believe it to be the core of what drives me. The ability to create something out of thin air – the mere act of *making* – exerts this magnetic pull that I haven't been able to escape. Through art, whether it's painting, writing, music, or any other means of creative expression, I can turn a moment into something permanent. The result is this unique mosaic of the things I see with my own eyes and the things I imagine only in my mind. Making art allows me to bring things to life that no one else is bothering to make. When I see something and find myself thinking, 'I wish there were more like this', I will get to work and create it myself. I can paint anything and everything, build whole worlds if I wanted, and all I need is a piece of paper and some paint.

This is not about leaving a legacy. I don't care about that. I won't know if anyone is looking at my paintings after I'm gone, and I'm not wondering whether my creations will outlive me or will have some relevance in the future. To me, it's about the current moment: I'm here now, and painting is a fundamental part of my existence on this earth.

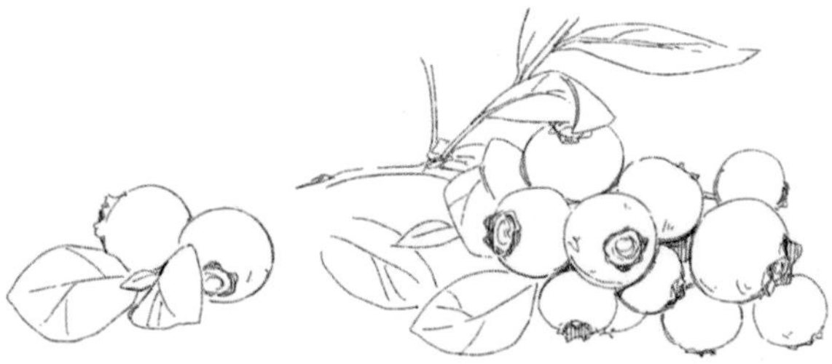

Art has always been my way to frame and reshape my own reality. It provided an escape when I was young, and now it's become a mirror. It helps me perceive things more mindfully, brings me clarity when I'm working through something I don't quite understand, and tells me a lot about myself. When I create, I forge a deeper connection to myself and to my surroundings; it helps me make sense of the world and my place within it.

'THE WORLD ALWAYS SEEMS BRIGHTER WHEN YOU'VE JUST MADE SOMETHING THAT WASN'T THERE BEFORE' – NEIL GAIMAN

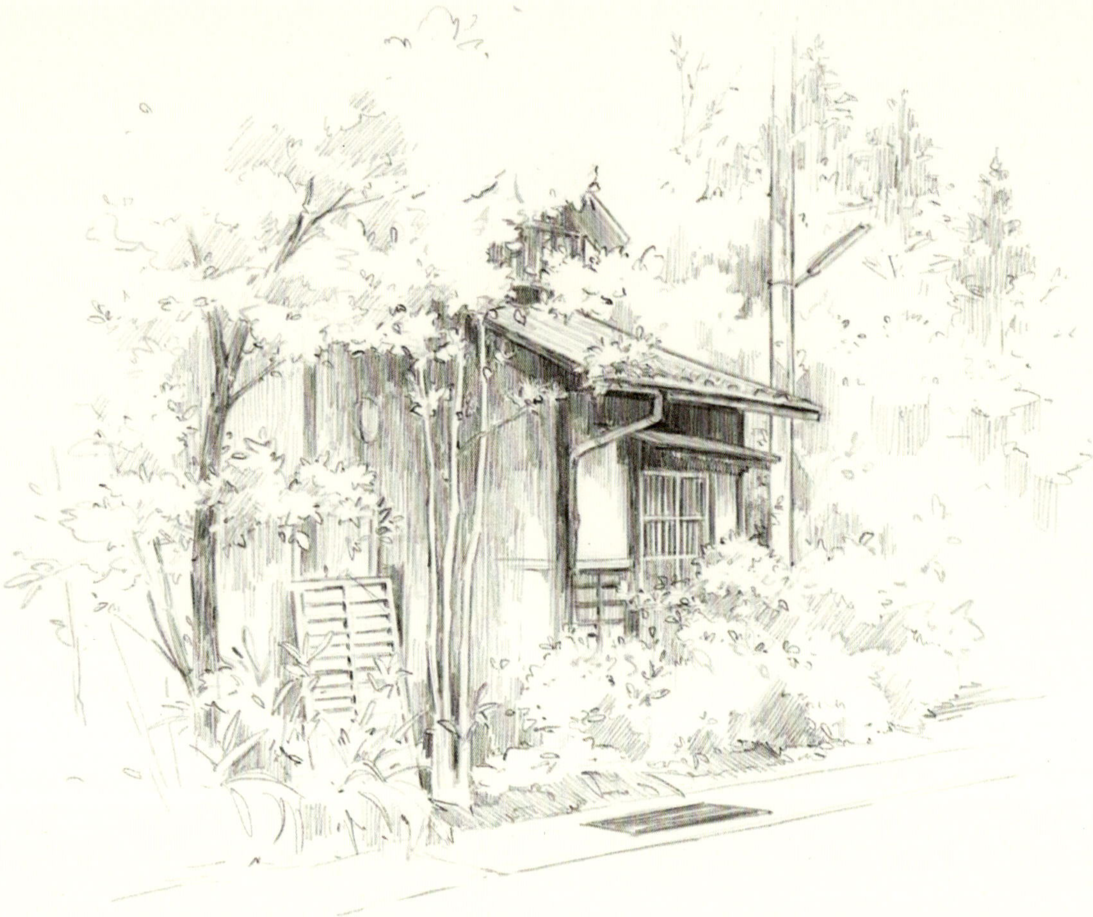

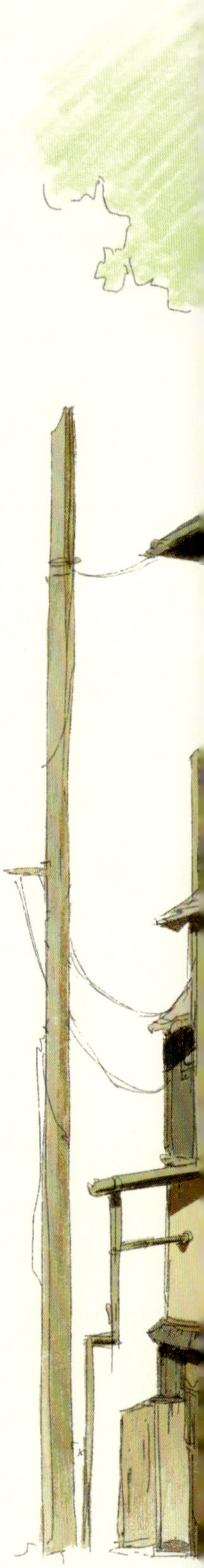

Creative expression is a natural cycle for me that is a part of everyday life: information, impressions, and inspiration go in, and art comes out. It's always been that way. It's an act of conservation, a record of me being alive. I can look back at a certain period in time, consider my paintings, and see changing themes and motifs, as well as snapshots of my state of mind and interests. From underwater scenes to upside-down cityscapes, they are all traces of my wanderings that have been given shape and substance. Each piece becomes a memento.

Art is communication. Like most of us, I learned how to draw before I learned how to write, so drawing became my first and primary means of creative expression – a language influenced by the culture and aesthetics surrounding me. By making art, I get to show those aspects to others who may or may not have been exposed to similar things throughout their lives, and it becomes a shared experience.

I have often asked myself whether I could even exist independently of my art, as it's so strongly entangled with my identity and self-worth. I have come to the conclusion that I could probably live without painting, but I would immediately immerse myself in a new endeavour: writing, carpentry, sewing… anything. Creativity is what holds me together, and to me, being alive means being creative. I need a purpose and goal to ground me. I need to know that I'm progressing in a certain direction, not standing still. Deeply immersing myself in something challenging makes me happy, and I need that little bit of discomfort and unease to keep things exciting. What I absorb needs to be redirected and simply being a recipient has never been enough. I associate art with continued learning, endless possibilities, and personal growth. It keeps changing with me, and it will stay with me my entire life if I choose to let it.

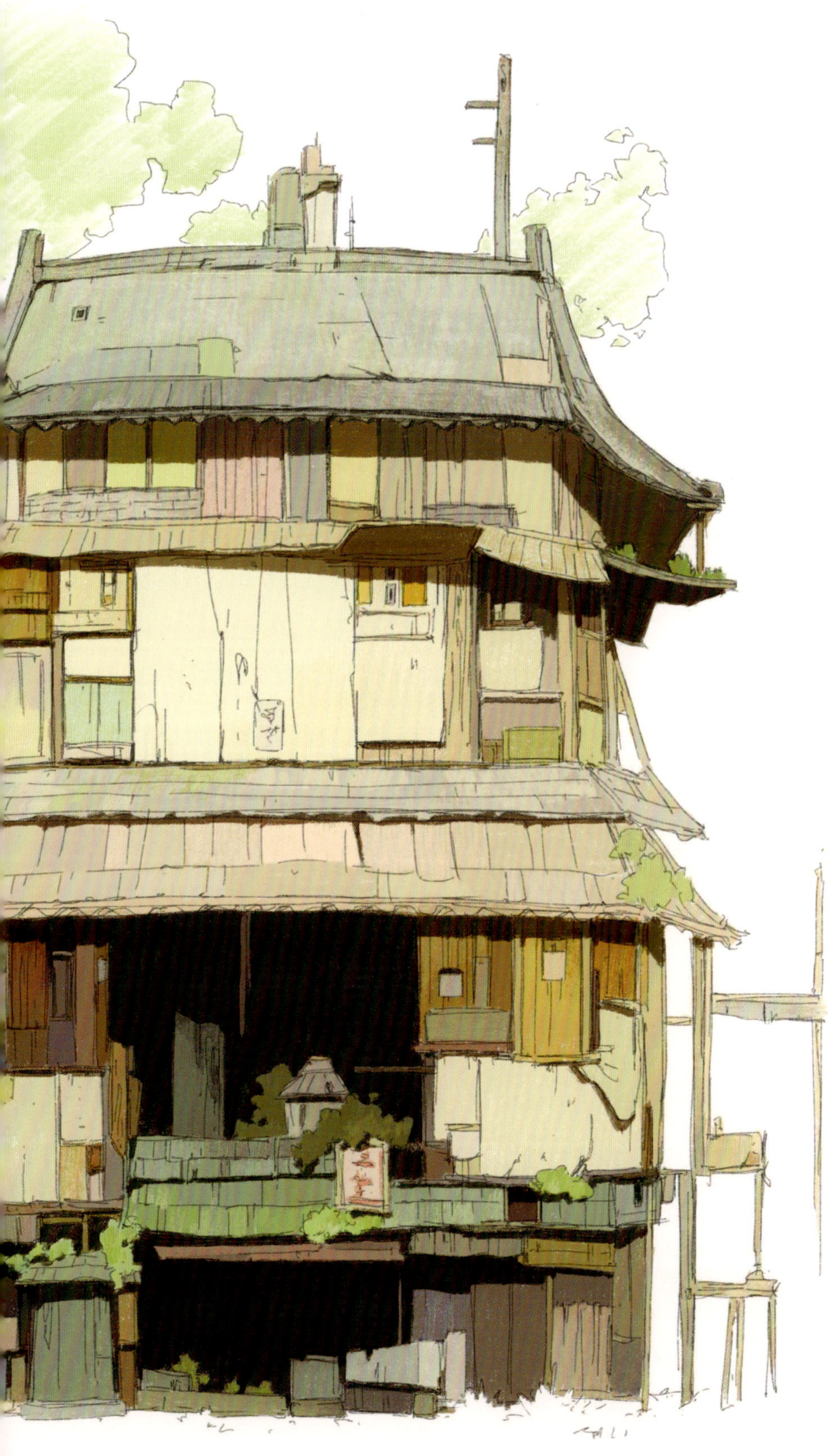

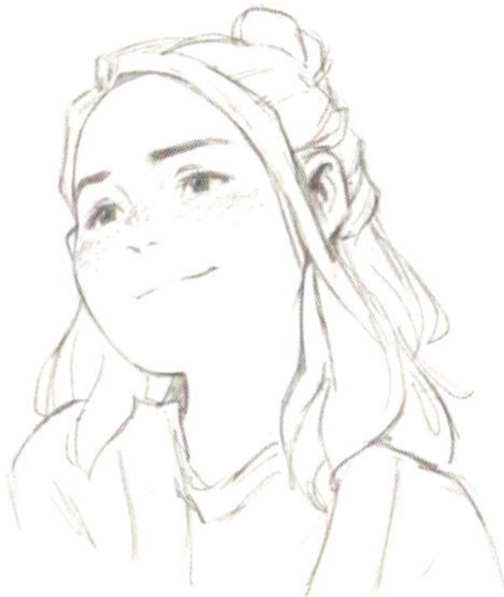

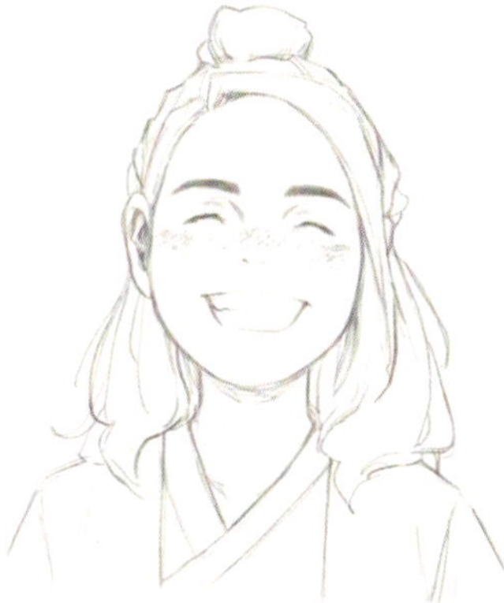

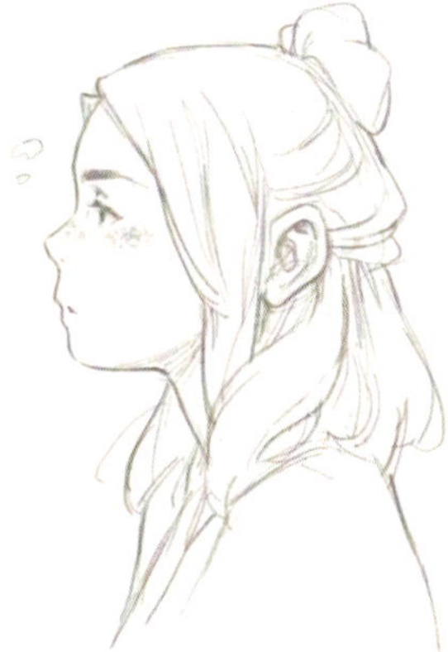

GUIDING QUESTIONS:

- Why do you make art? What motivates you to make art?
- Why did you choose drawing and painting as your means of creative expression?
- What does art mean to you?
- What needs does art-making fulfil?

If you have difficulty answering these questions, revisit them after the next chapter on Artistic Voice.

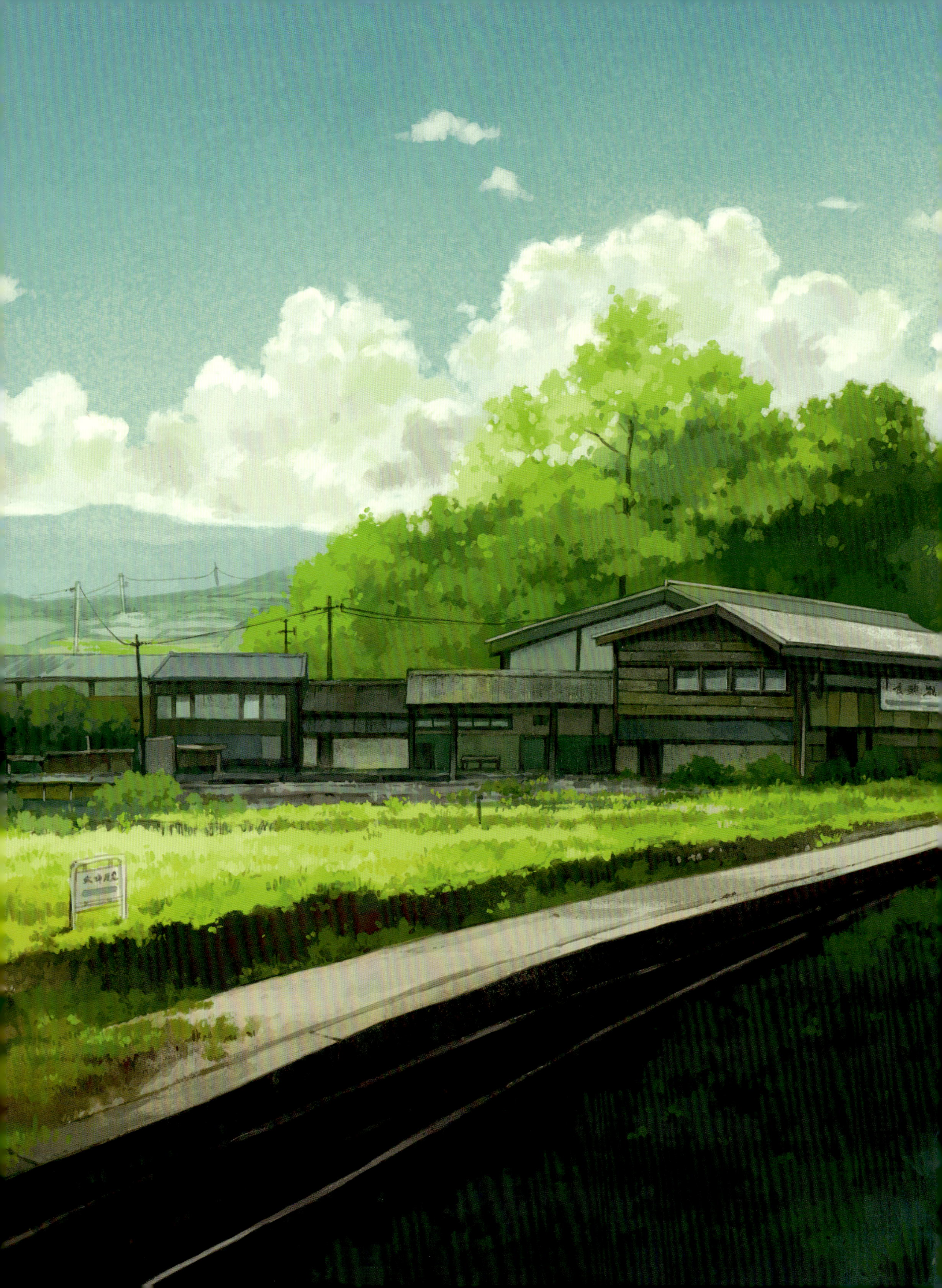

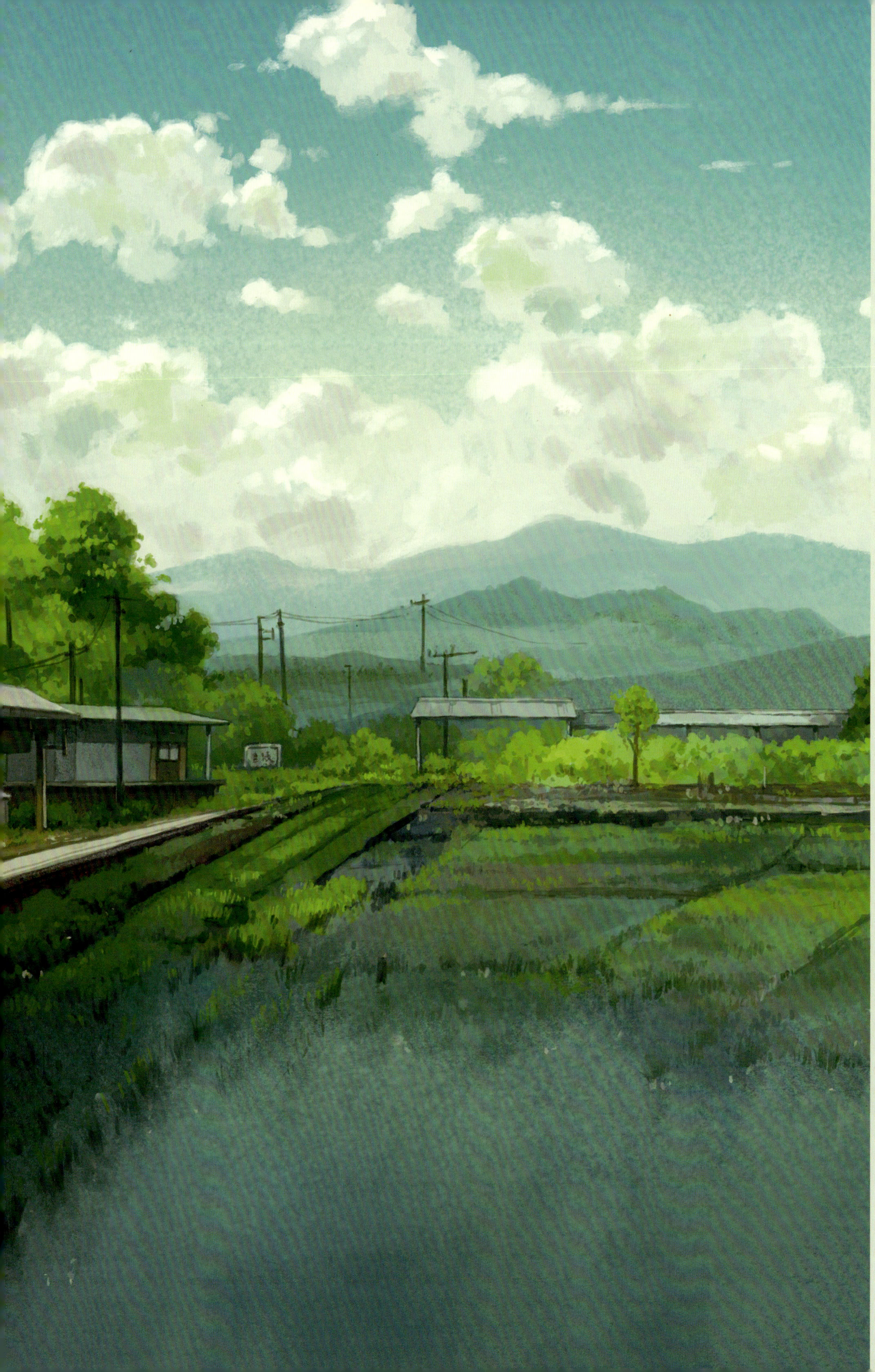

THE CONCEPT OF ARTISTIC VOICE

The term 'artistic voice' may sound elusive and mysterious, and in a way, it is, because it describes what makes you different from other artists and what distinguishes your work from theirs. It's that certain quality that's often difficult to grasp and articulate. We tend to be so immersed in our own work that we fail to recognise its unique characteristics; we are so used to being ourselves that we become blind and take our creative decisions for granted, not least because many of them occur at a subconscious level. But once we step back and examine the individual parts that make up our artistic voice, we can get a clearer picture.

It's not just about how your work looks, although that's one component. It's more about what lies beneath the surface, all those quirks that make you an individual, big and small. Artistic voice consists of three parts*:

I) Your interests and personal experiences
II) Your taste and aesthetics
III) Your techniques and materials

Putting all of these things together will inform your point of view as an artist and drive your creative decisions. Strengths and weaknesses may also play a role because they determine how precisely and purposefully you can express yourself. Though a few years in your artistic journey may revolve around building technical skills, at some point, the question arises as to what subject matters you want to portray and how. Getting to the bottom of all this may require some introspection, but it will be worth it for the clarity it provides.

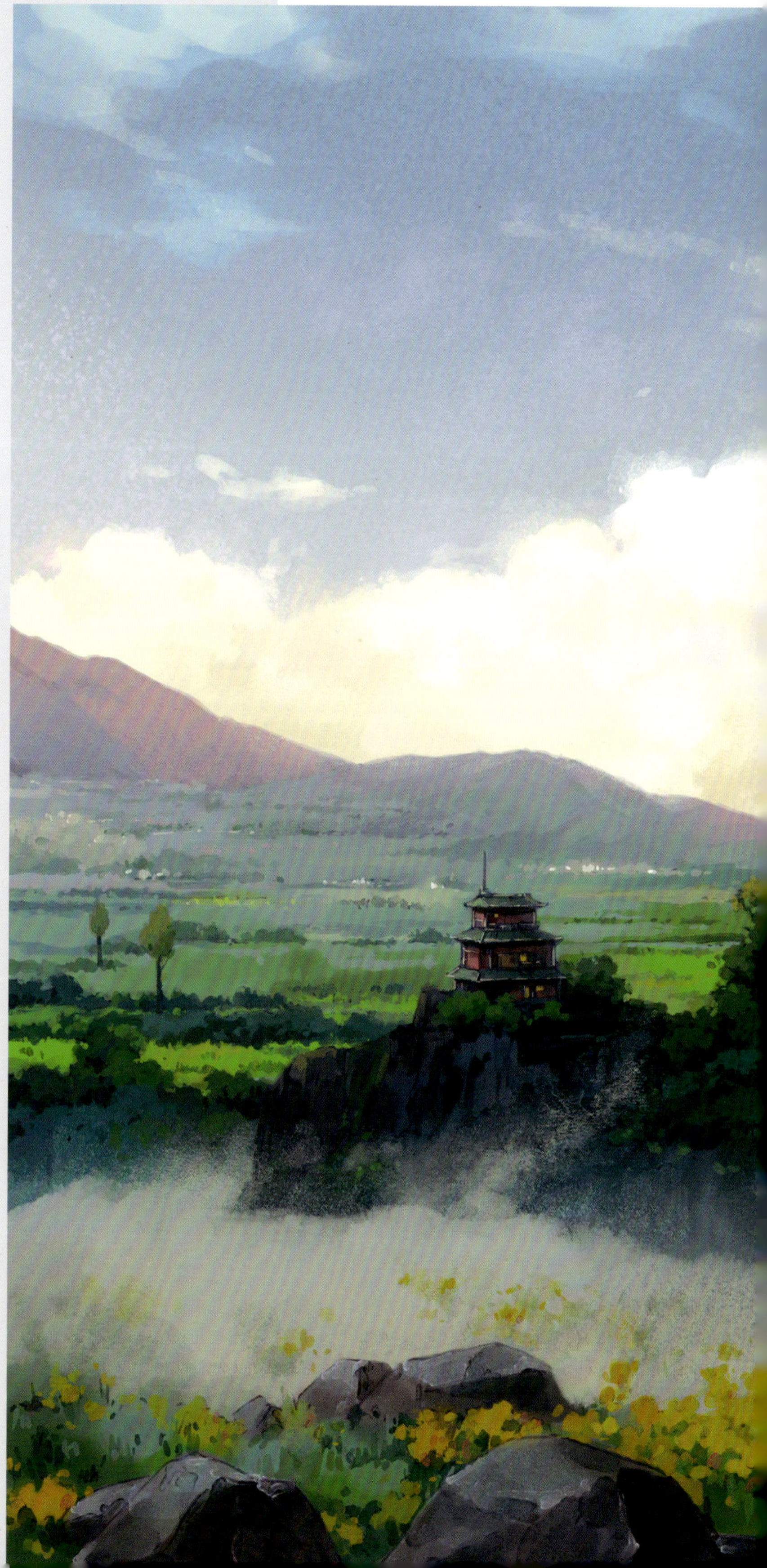

Mountain Temple

These landscapes are quite stylized in their colours and shapes. They seem more like they were taken from an animated movie

*I adapted this classification from the essay 'On Style' by Rovina Cai, as I believe it applies to the concept of artistic voice.

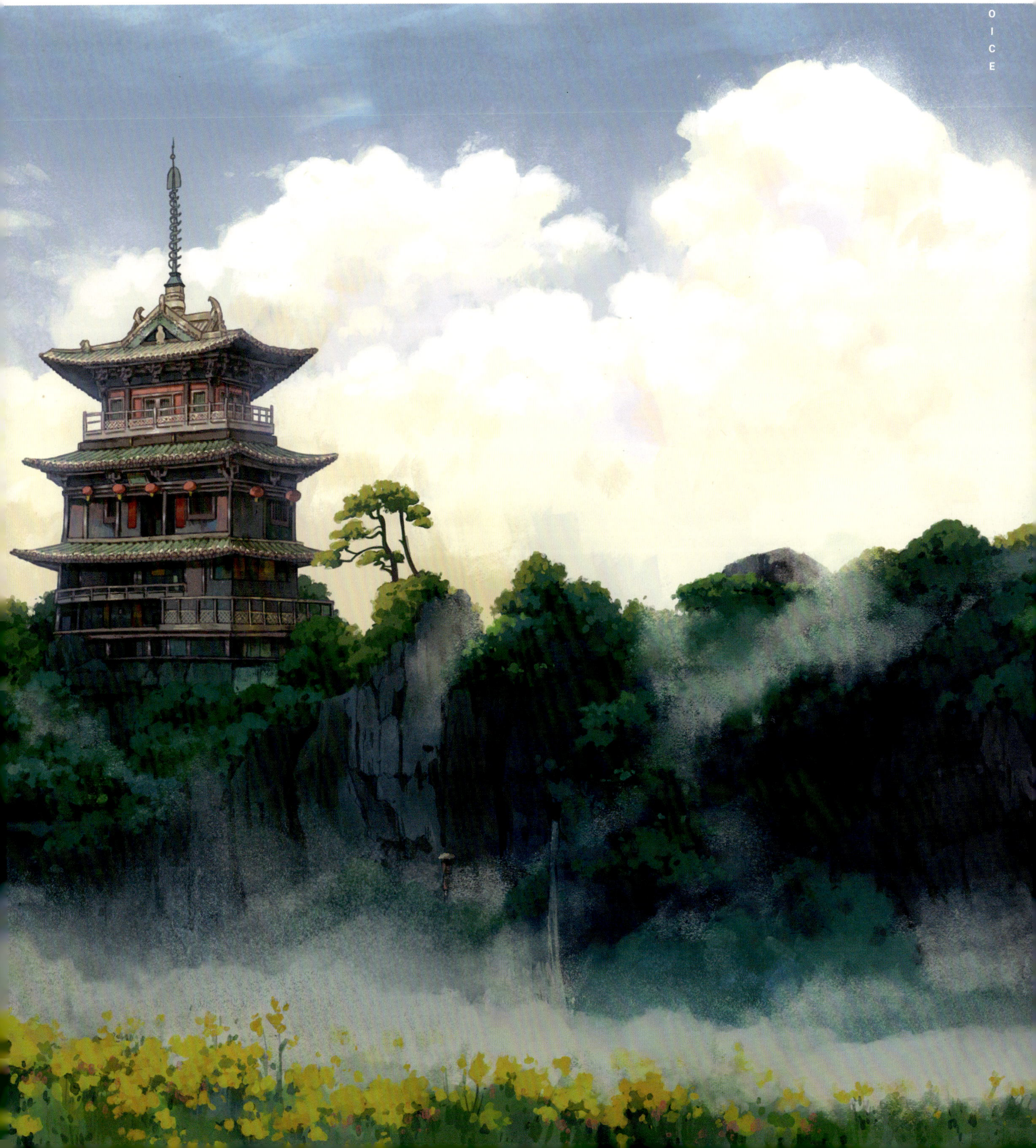

ELEMENTS & COMPONENTS OF ARTISTIC VOICE

1) INTERESTS & PERSONAL EXPERIENCES

I believe that this is the most important component of the three, as it essentially deals with *what* you paint rather than *how*, and in my opinion, the choice of subject matter says even more about the artist than their preferred medium or colour palette. It's fascinating to delve into this never-ending stream of memories, people, places, pastimes, and media – from moments of your earliest childhood memory to the book you read last week.

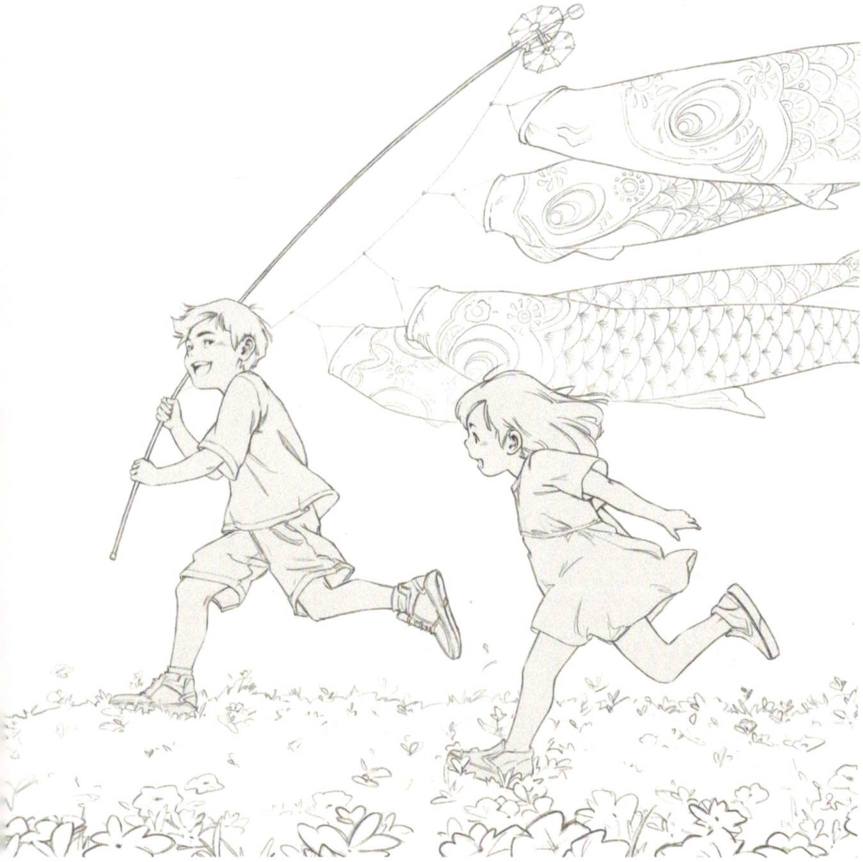

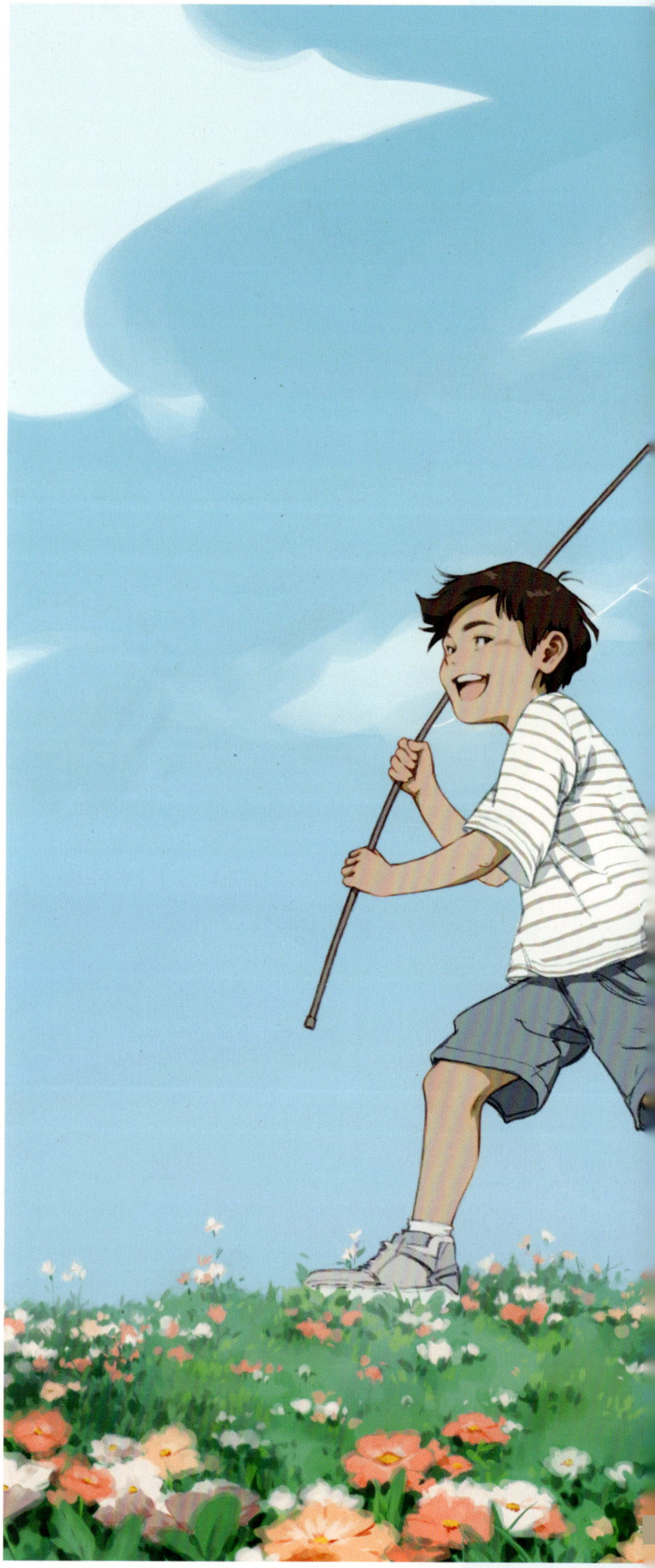

Children of the Sky

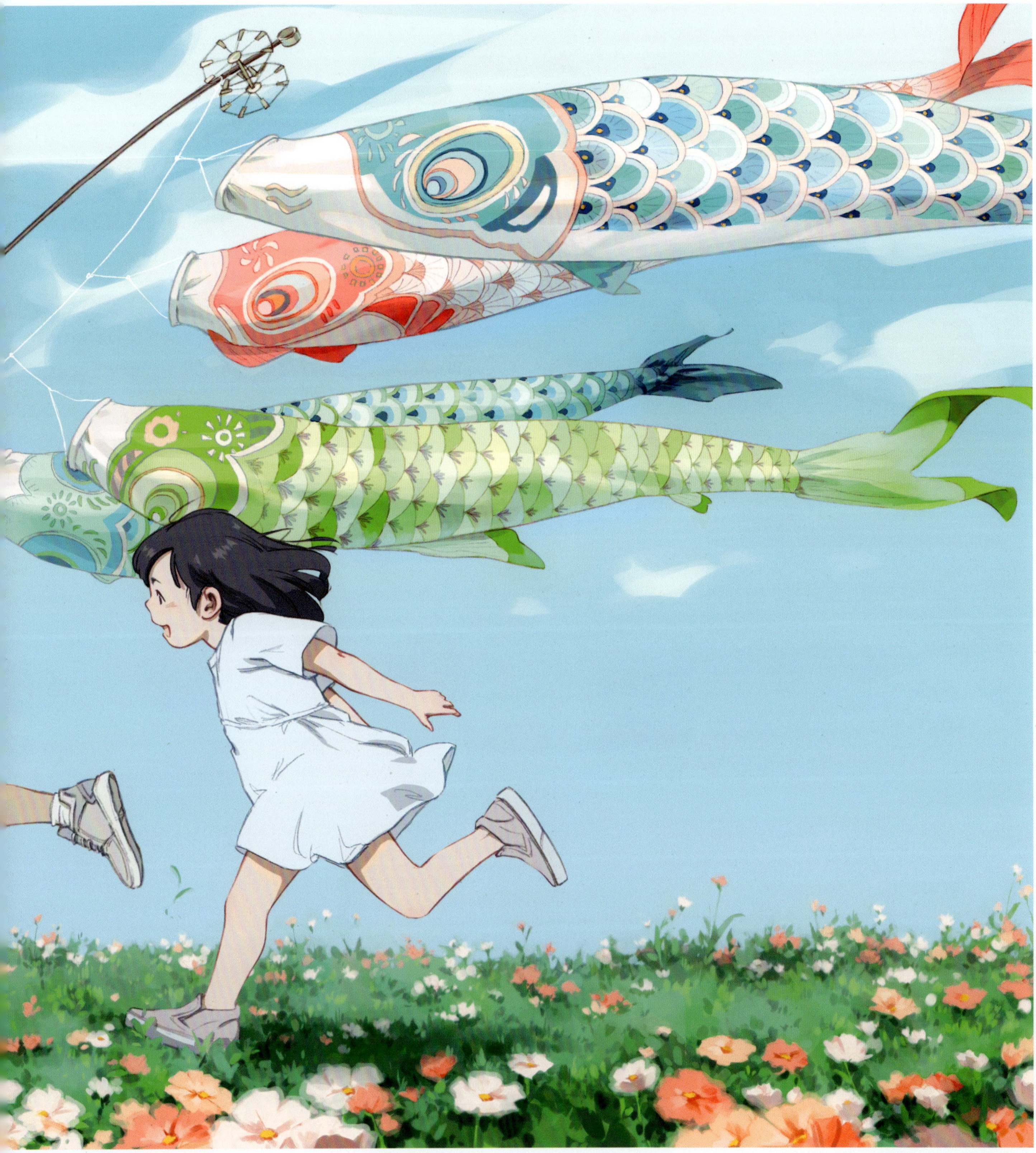

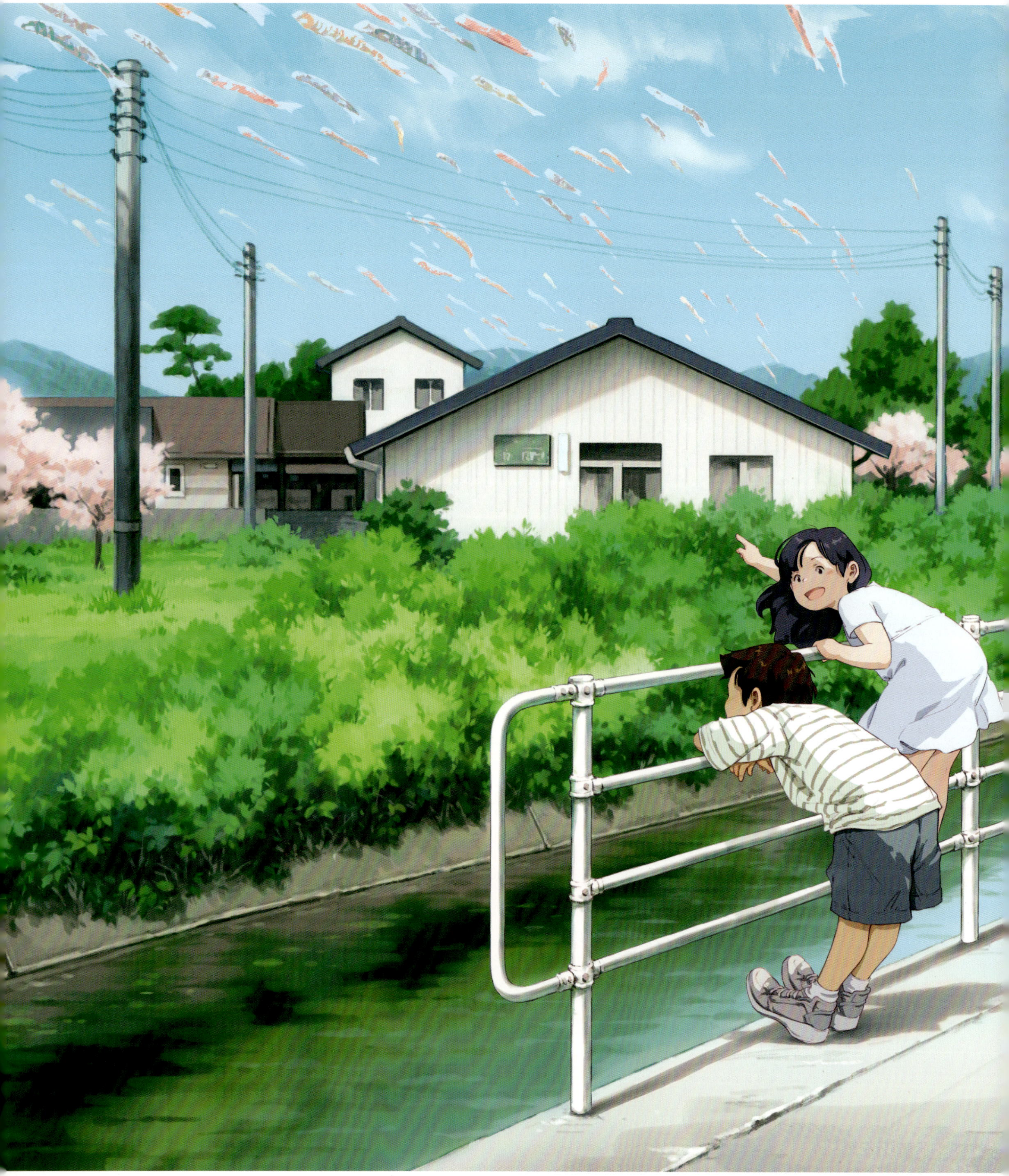

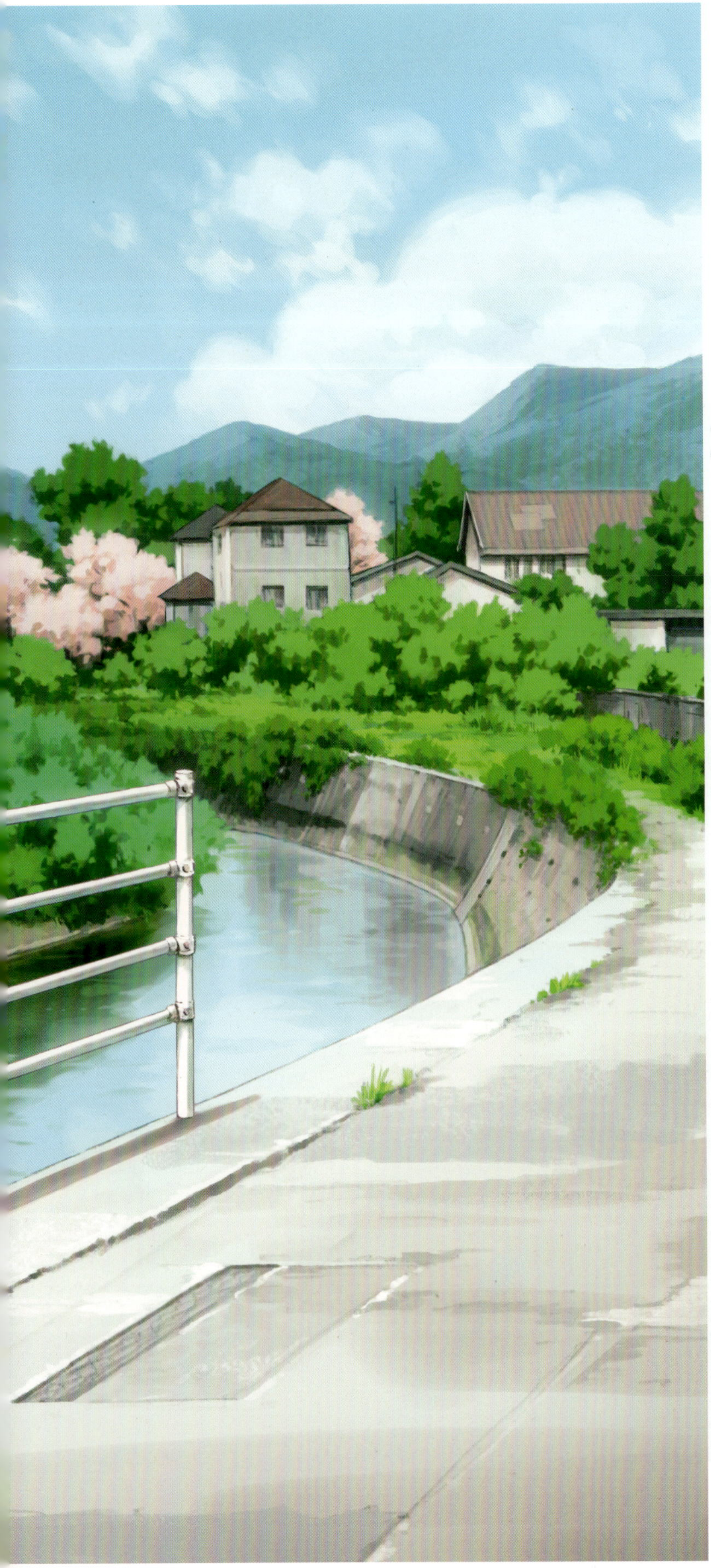

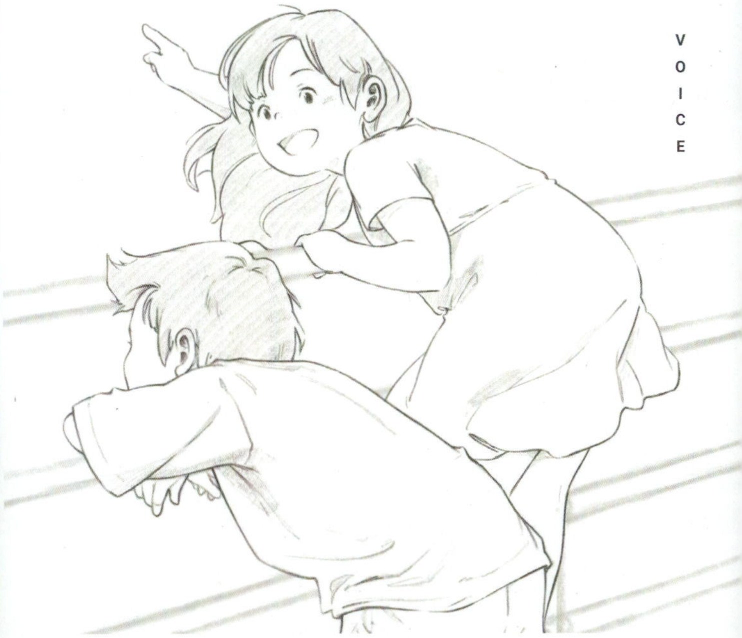

I've often talked about how formative the summers in my grandparents' garden were for me as a child, and how much they shaped my perception of nature. Add the vast amounts of anime I watched back then, and you get a pretty good idea of my main influences. But, of course, it doesn't stop there. Human development is a continuous process. New interests and experiences are added all the time, and others fade into the background. Reading has become my biggest source of inspiration, and my preferences have shifted towards literary fiction, memoirs, short stories, and essays, when it used to be 1,000-page fantasy tomes that captivated me. But I still love nothing more than good stories.

Children of the Sky II

These scenes are not necessarily autobiographical; my goal and inspiration was simply to capture the feeling of being a child

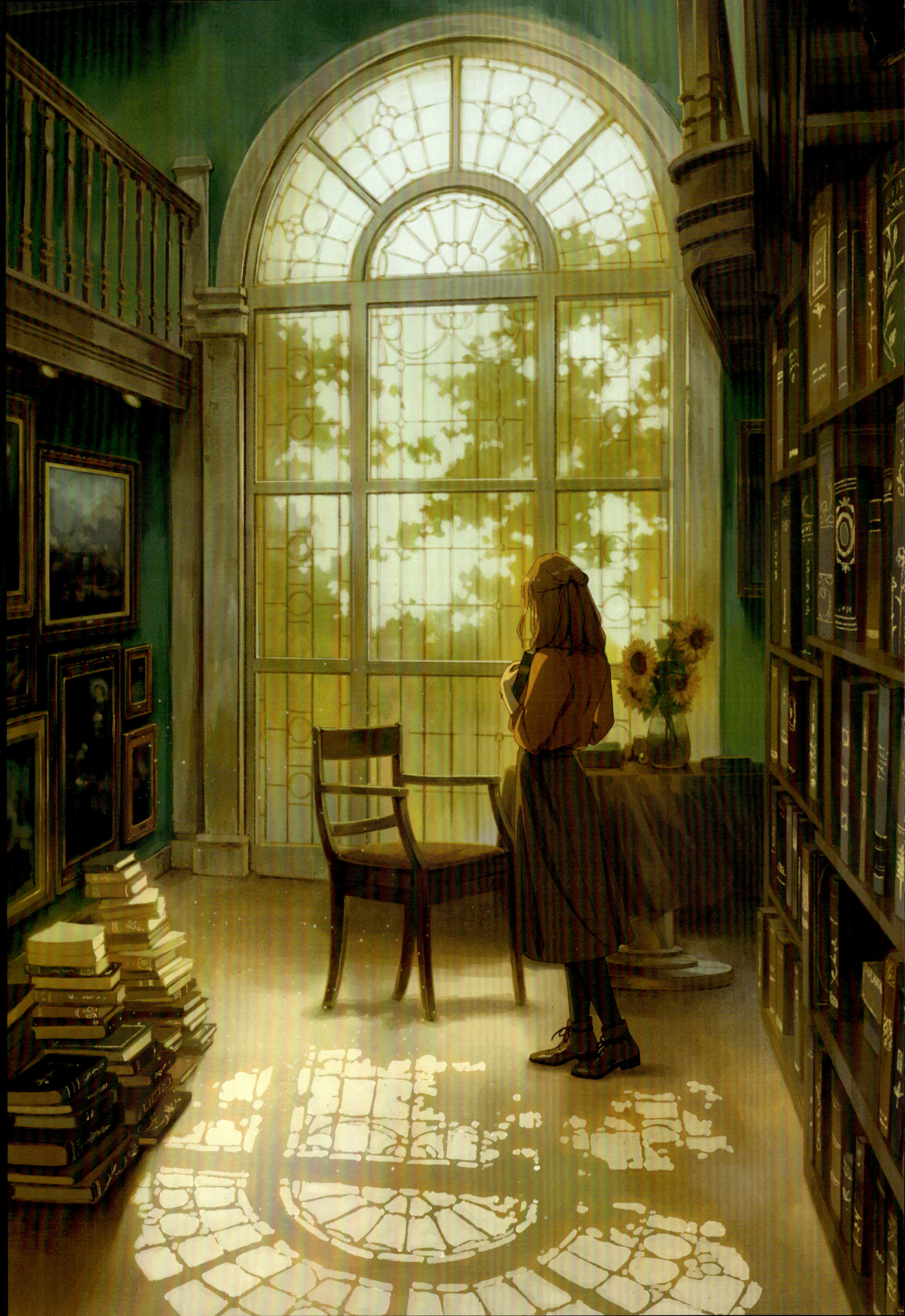

The Old Library

This is my homage to books

I am also interested in Japanese customs and rites, especially those related to natural phenomena and the transition between life and death. Besides that, I have a strange fascination with the past; I mostly listen to music from before I was born, while old photographs (of places I've never been) give me the strangest feeling because I can't bear the thought of that moment being gone forever, the environment having been changed. If you put all those things together, you get a vague impression of what provides me with work material. It's often those small, seemingly unremarkable details that make their way in.

GUIDING QUESTIONS:

- Who are your three biggest influences? This could be anyone: family members, painters, designers, musicians, and so on. What is it about them that has had a great impact on you?
- Where did you grow up and what was it like?
- What are the most vivid memories from your childhood? Are there any images or situations that stand out?
- What were you most interested in as a child?
- What are you most interested in today? What three topics could you talk about for hours? Do you have any obscure, niche specialities?
- What are your three favourite films, TV shows, books, or video games? What is it about them that you like?

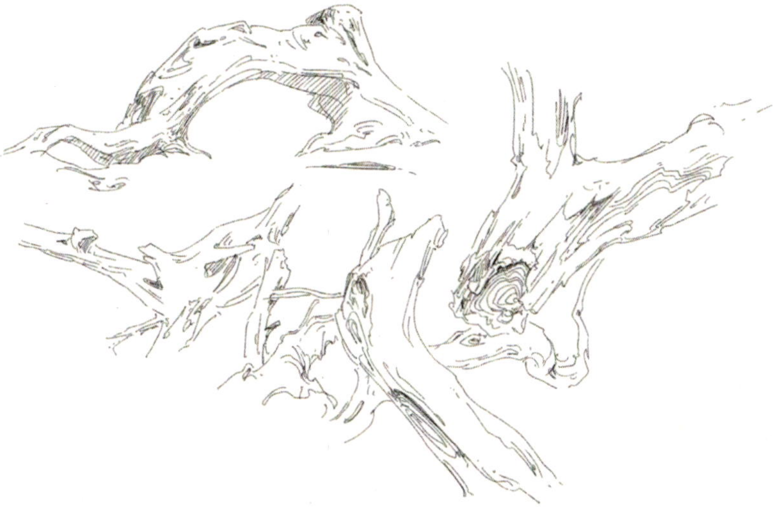

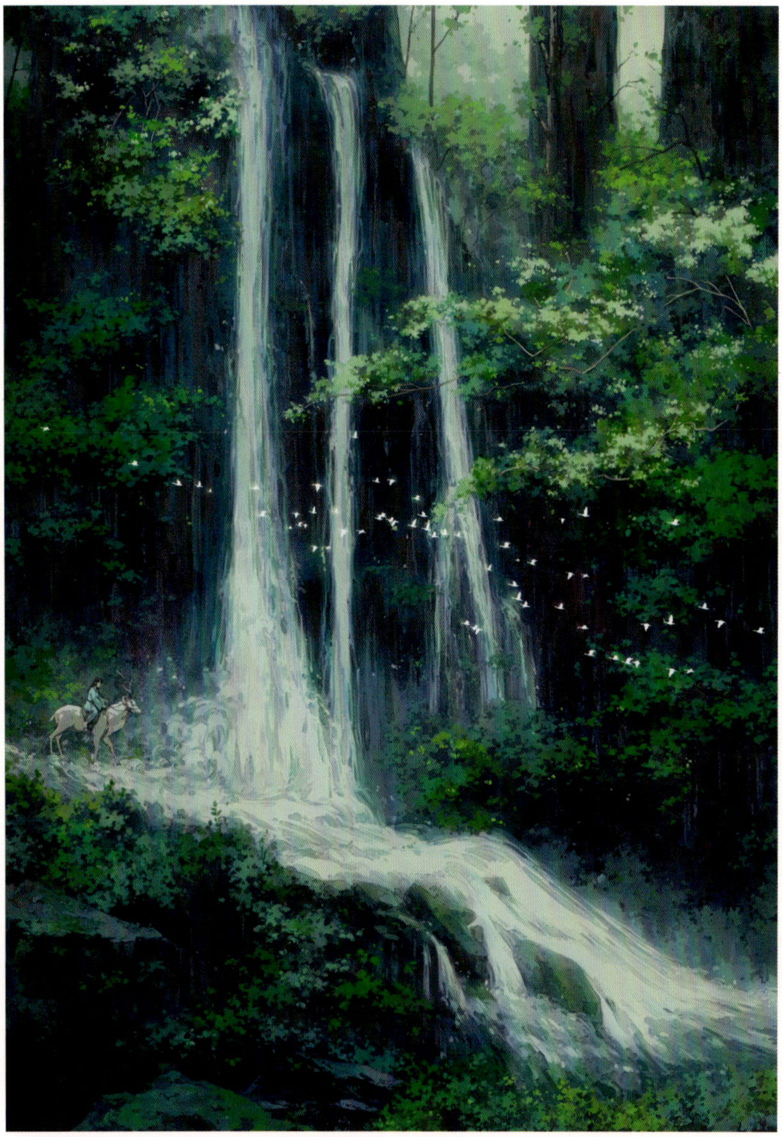

Waterfall

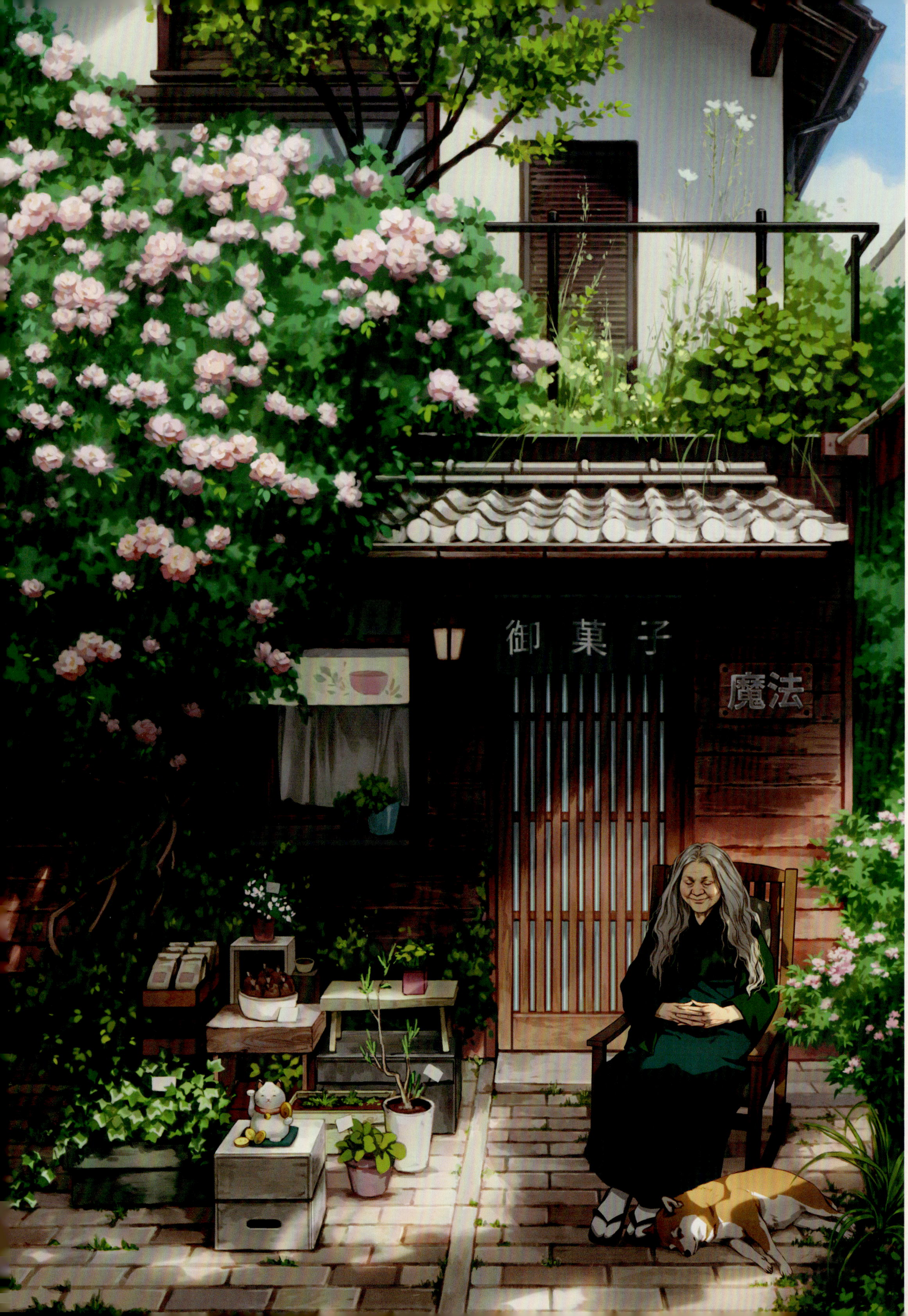
御菓子
魔法

II) TASTES & AESTHETICS

This is about the visuals and imagery you respond to – your subjective perception of beauty, the rhythms and compositions you like, the colours and shapes.

I personally like a wide range of images, all of which are very different. But the important thing to note is that not everything I enjoy looking at matches what I want to paint myself. I love the aesthetic of black-and-white Polaroids, but prefer to paint with bold colours. Realistic oil portraits are beautiful, but cause me panic attacks as soon as I think about having to make them. I think it's about finding the sweet spot between subject matter and visual appeal, as well the fun of it all (what you enjoy painting). To get an impression of what visual language moves you personally, starting a collection or an inspiration board can be helpful. Curating and compiling art in this way will inevitably reveal patterns and recurring themes that appear in your works.

When I notice new motifs creeping into my inspiration boards, it's a sign that my aesthetics or interests are shifting, and that usually leads to exciting experiments and new directions. I am firmly convinced that the images we are drawn to represent aspects of ourselves, even though we aren't the ones who created them. They reflect a part of us, and if we learn to trust our intuition and reactions towards these pieces, we will have a much easier time finding our own artistic voice. I have collected thousands of images, but if I had to summarize a general trend, it would be the following: I am generally drawn to detailed depictions of nature, greens and blues, warm sunlight, natural materials like woods and stone, and lonely figures in the scene. All these elements have already made their way into my paintings several times.

GUIDING QUESTIONS:

- In one word, what is your definition of 'beauty'? What has shaped this definition?
- What visual elements are you drawn towards, on a more abstract level (colours, shapes, compositions, and so on)?
- What subject matters are you drawn towards, on a more concrete level (faces, fruit, trees, insects, churches, aeroplanes, and so on)? What is it about them that you like?
- Among the images you're drawn towards, are there any recurring themes, motifs, or symbols (water, death, rebirth, figures with their eyes closed, liminal spaces, astronomy, and so on)?

III) TECHNIQUES & MATERIALS

Lastly, it is also about the painting and drawing tools you choose, as well as the way you apply them. When we're talking about traditional versus digital art, types of software, paints, brushes, paper, and pens, this sounds straightforward enough, but when we delve deeper into the matter and ask specific questions, we often make unexpected discoveries. For example, your mark-making or how much pressure you exert when drawing can both become recognizable features of your work. Take something as simple as a pencil: do you choose HB or 6B? Mechanical? How do you hold it? Do you draw big, chunky lines, or thin ones? Do you only draw outlines, or add shading? Cross-hatching? Do you smudge with your fingers, or a blending stump, or not at all? All these things matter and are more or less unique to you.

When I work with a pencil, my drawings are tiny, delicate, and detailed. I mostly use HB mechanical pencils and keep the shading minimal. I have tried softer pencils, as well as broad, sweeping strokes, but I just can't make that work for me. In my digital art, I will go through great lengths to make my illustrations look less digital. For instance, instead of relying on brush effects, I will paint each individual leaf by hand. Overall, my approach is very similar to that of traditional painting. When it comes to programs, I use Procreate and Adobe Photoshop. In my experience, Procreate is better for clean lines and perspective drawings, and Photoshop offers more leeway for colour exploration and adjustments.

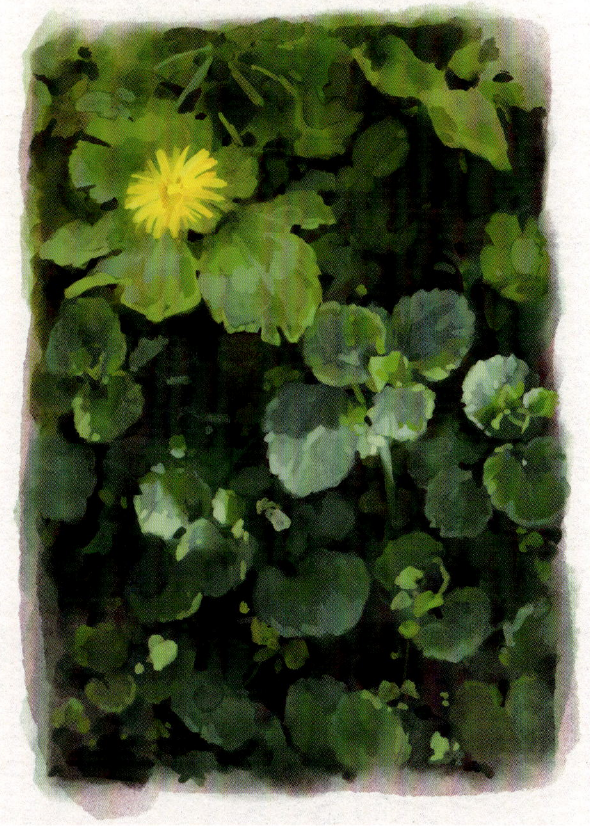

Nature
My goal with this digital painting was to mimic traditional media as best I could

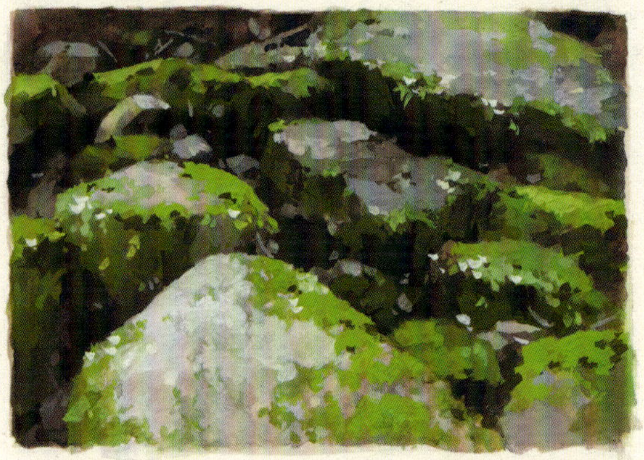

Of course, breaking old patterns and stepping out of our comfort zone can produce interesting effects, and I always recommend being open to new things. Nevertheless, each of us has a distinctive way of using our chosen media, which plays a part in the way we express ourselves artistically.

These are actual traditional paintings I made a few years later with gouache and coloured pencils

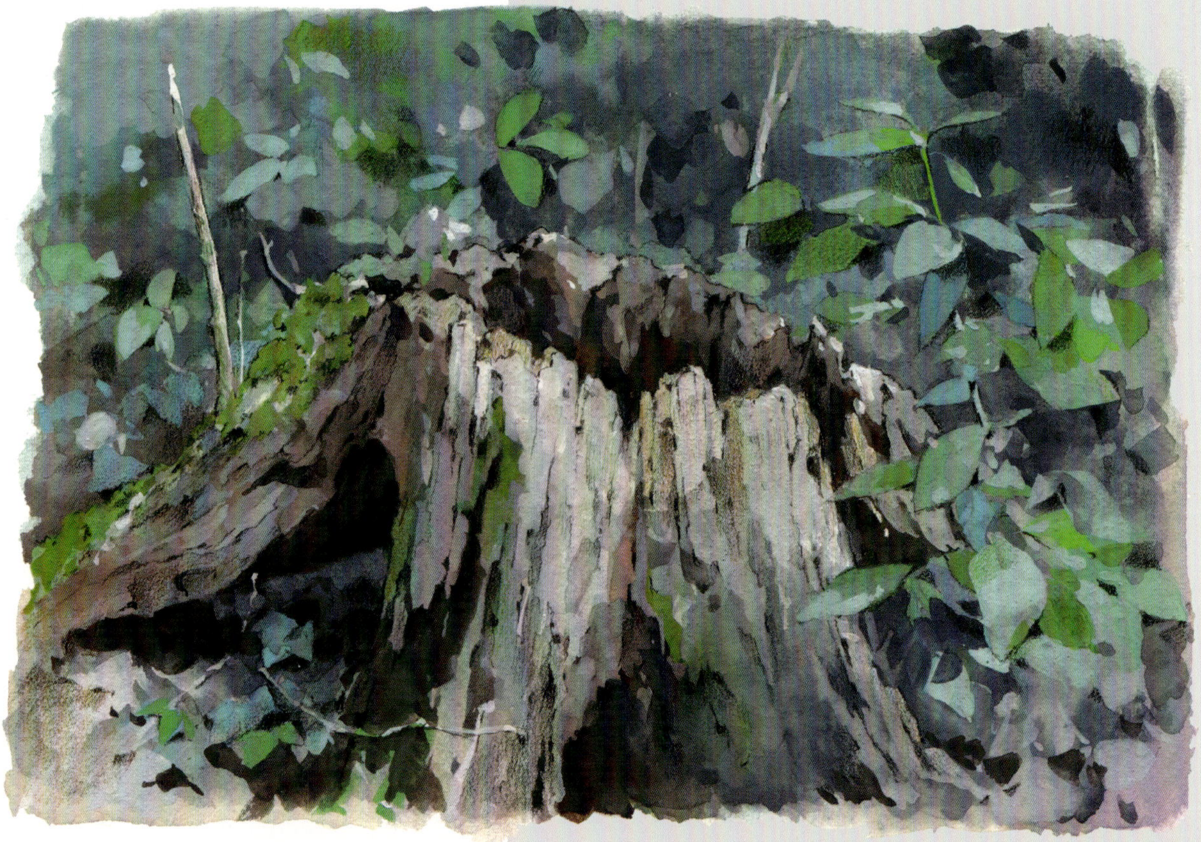

GUIDING QUESTIONS:

- What medium do you like best? What do you like about it?
- In what way are you using it and why? What kinds of brushes, papers, and pens do you like to use, and how do you apply them?
- What medium do you use for sketches, what medium for finished artwork? If they are different, why? What about each of them appeals to you?
- Why do you think you prefer these materials and the way you're using them?
- Generally, are you detail-oriented or do you think in broad strokes? How does that translate into your art?
- Do you get bored easily with the same tools?

ARTISTIC VOICE & STYLE

Artistic voice and style are closely related. All the aspects we've already discussed – especially taste, aesthetics, techniques, and materials – are going to inform your stylistic choices. I prefer to define *style* or *stylization* as 'the thing that deviates from reality'. I believe this idea becomes most obvious when you create a study from life; if you compare your artwork to the real thing in front of you, your style comes through in all the aspects that are 'wrong', all minor or major departures from the original.

A long time ago, I watched a video called *4 Artists Paint 1 Tree*, which perfectly illustrates this concept. In the clip, we follow four Disney artists as they paint the same exact subject matter – a tree – but end up with vastly different results. Each artist chooses a unique viewpoint and highlights certain tree features using their medium of choice. One painter focuses on structure and geometric shapes, another strives to capture the tree's vitality and movement, and another makes a detailed study of the trunk. We see a great variety of styles and approaches: simplicity versus detail, black and white versus colour, three-dimensionality versus flat shapes, thick versus watery paint – it's all represented in this small group of artists. It's all about how each of them interprets reality and how they alter it in their paintings, consciously or subconsciously. Any act of stylization is a very personal response to your subject matter; it shows how you interpret it and what you have to say about it. Your style gives a little glimpse into how you perceive the world. What you choose to enhance, exaggerate, simplify, or leave out altogether says something about you.

There are a million ways to stylize. You can simplify things, change shapes, make things more angular or rounded, exaggerate colours, add colours that aren't there, work with textures, add outlines, add ornaments and patterns... the possibilities are endless.

Many artists have realism as their ultimate goal, but I often find unique styles much more interesting. When I think of my own art, I certainly don't aim for realism, but for 'believability' or 'truth'. I want to find a representation of reality that is true to how I see things, what stands out to me, and what I want to highlight. It reminds me of an anecdote I once heard about Hayao Miyazaki: he made an employee repaint a background illustration because it looked too perfect, too much like a photo.

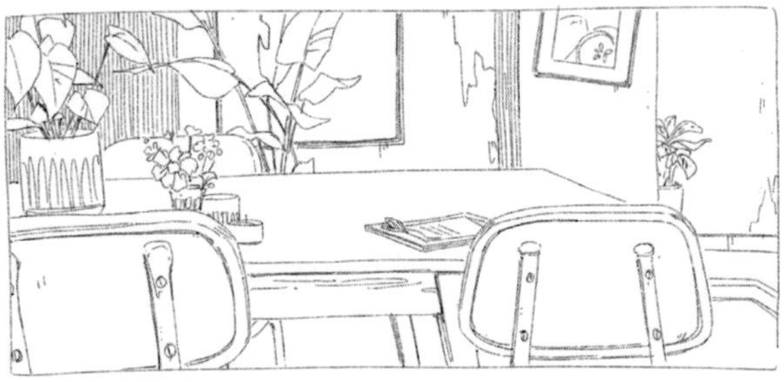

For many, style is something that comes naturally, but for some, it takes a little more experimentation and effort to extract. One way to carve out a personal style can be to first study and imitate other artists until your own natural tendencies start taking over. This process of imitation can happen consciously or subconsciously. As artists (and as humans in general), we constantly absorb stimuli and influences from our environment and process them on a subconscious level. All the artistic works that have impressed us throughout our lives may sneak into our own creations. This is a good thing and it's also inevitable, since we don't exist in a vacuum.

In the case of conscious imitation, this often takes the form of master studies, in which we copy the works of our role models in order to learn from them. The focus of these studies can be anything: anatomy, colour application, light and shadow, stylization – whatever we want to learn. This can be very helpful in accelerating our artistic progress. For example, when I started looking more into landscape painting, the backgrounds of the Studio Ghibli films (especially those painted by Kazuo Oga) were immensely helpful to me. I learned how to emphasize colours, create harmonies, and simplify complex scenes.

However useful a practice, at some point we may want to break away from the comfort of these exercises and develop our own interpretation of reality. If we don't break away and instead desperately cling to imitating a single artist, our work might never be more than a mere shadow. That being said, my work is often compared to Studio Ghibli, or anime backgrounds in general, and I don't mind – I take it as a compliment. For me, the whole anime aesthetic embodies a certain emotion – an attitude towards life that emphasizes and condenses the beautiful aspects of our surroundings. It's not about mimicking a certain artist's style, but about applying this particular camera lens.

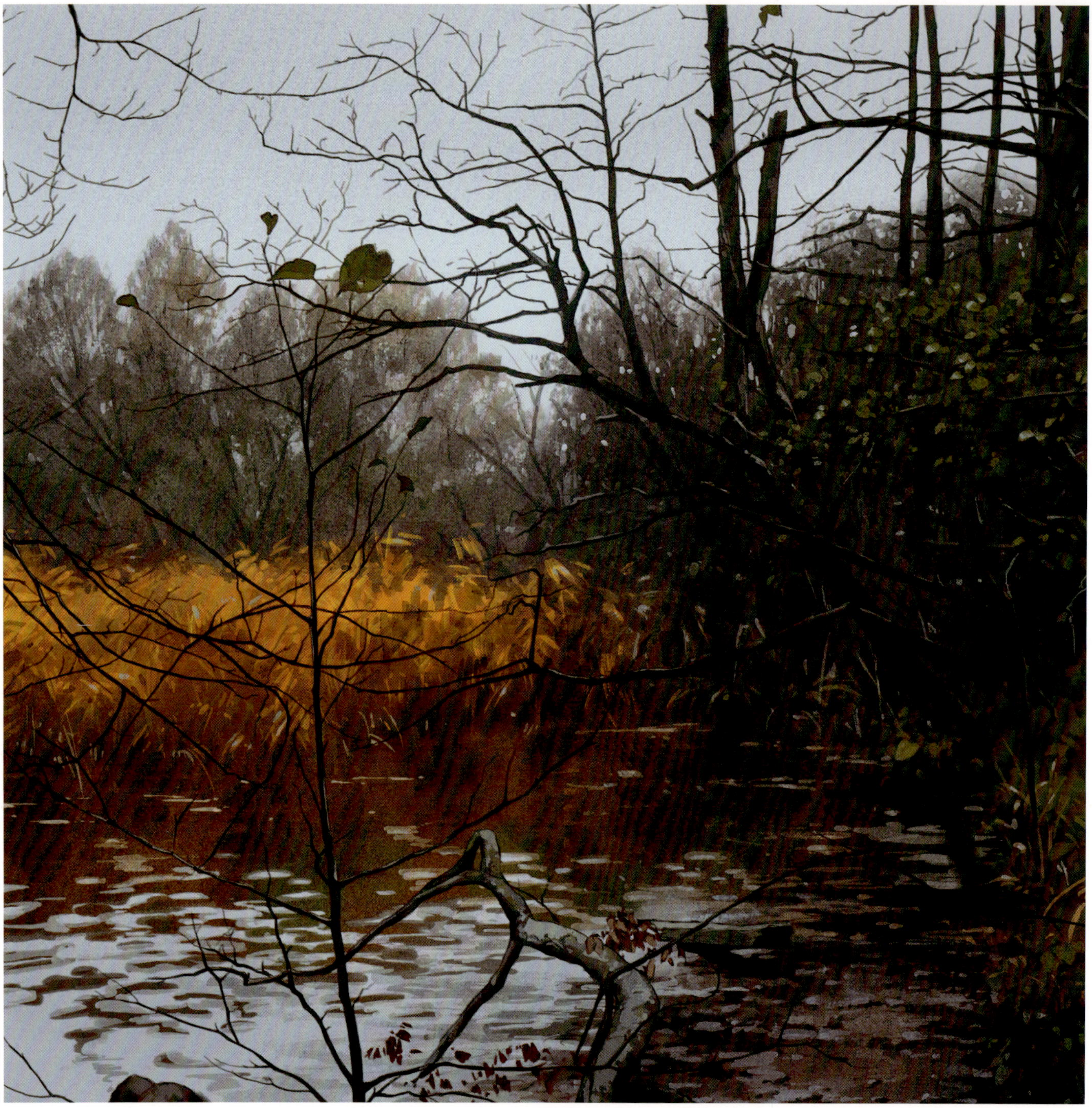

Autumn

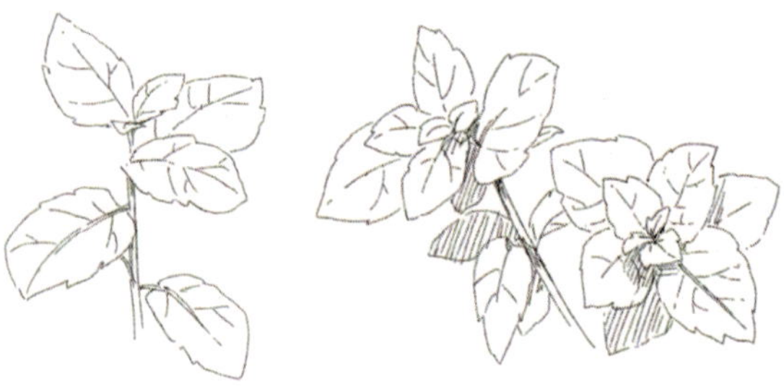

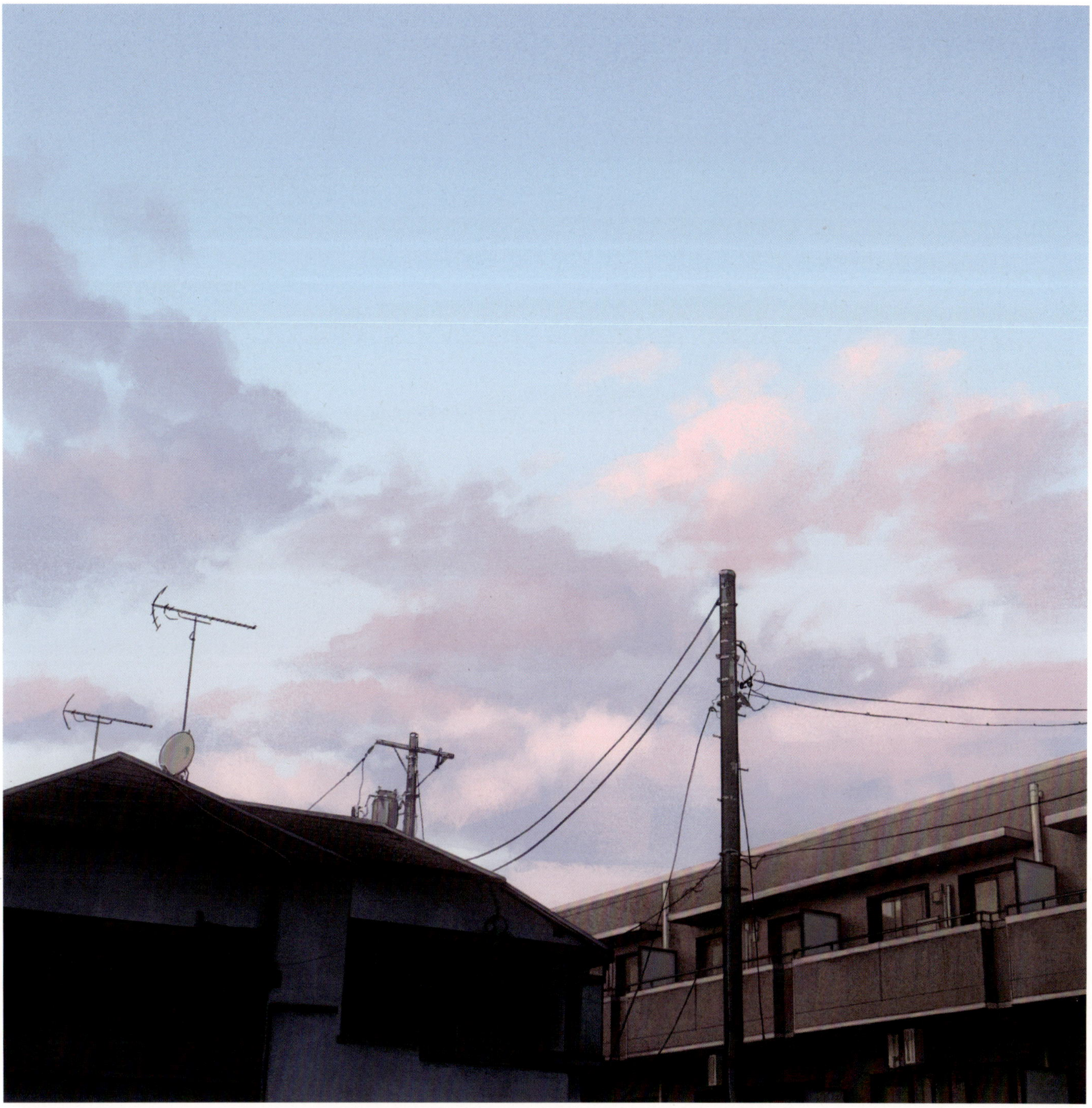

Purple Sky

These studies are more photorealistic than most of my other work

GUIDING QUESTIONS:

- What stylistic tendencies can you discover in your own art?
- In what way do you stylize certain things, compared to other artists? What makes your faces, trees, houses, and so on, unique?
- Can you detect direct influences of your favourite artists in your work? If so, which artists and what aspects of their work?
- What are some visuals that have left a great impression on you throughout your life (scenes from movies, paintings, real places, and moments from your life)?

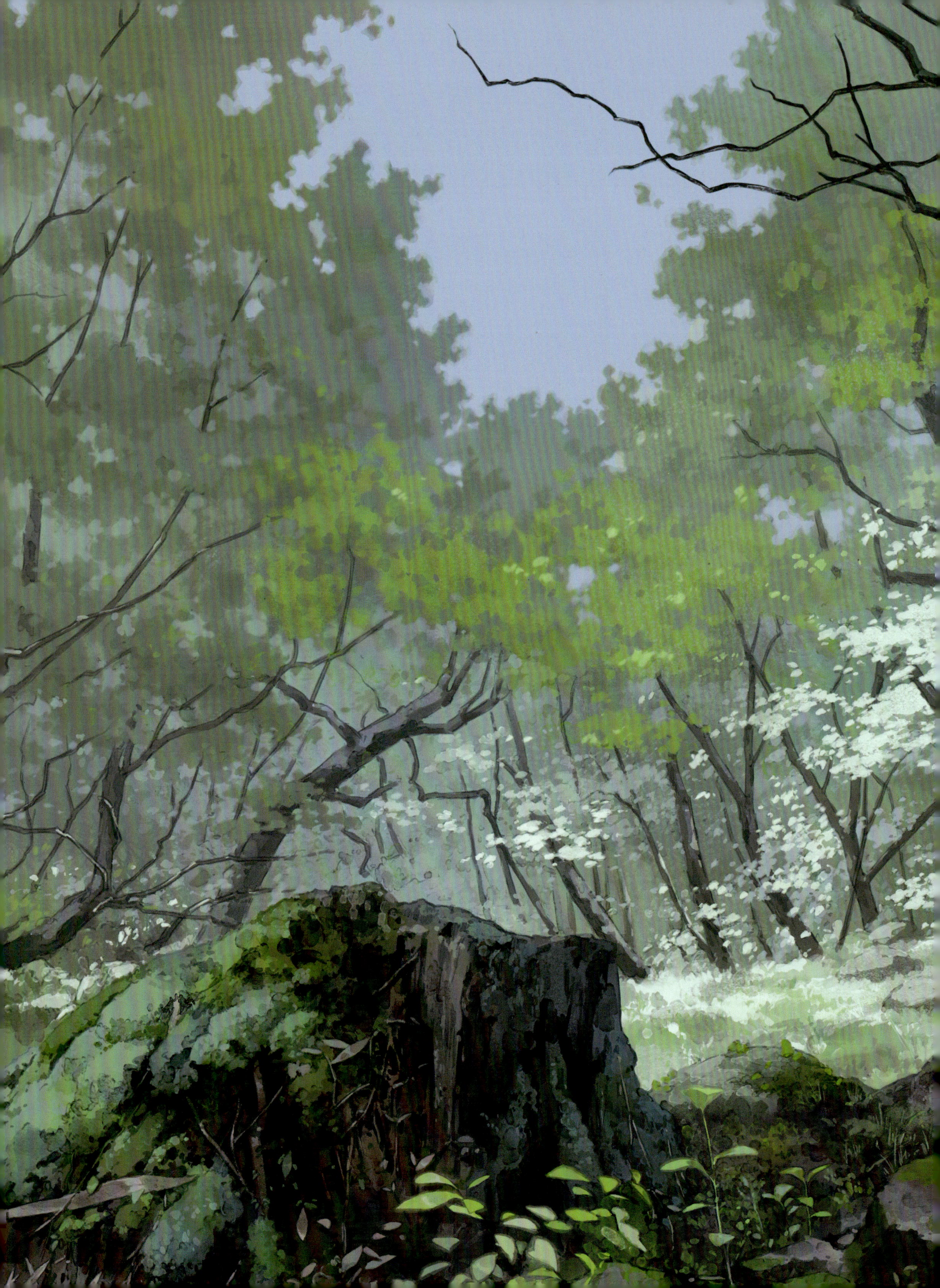

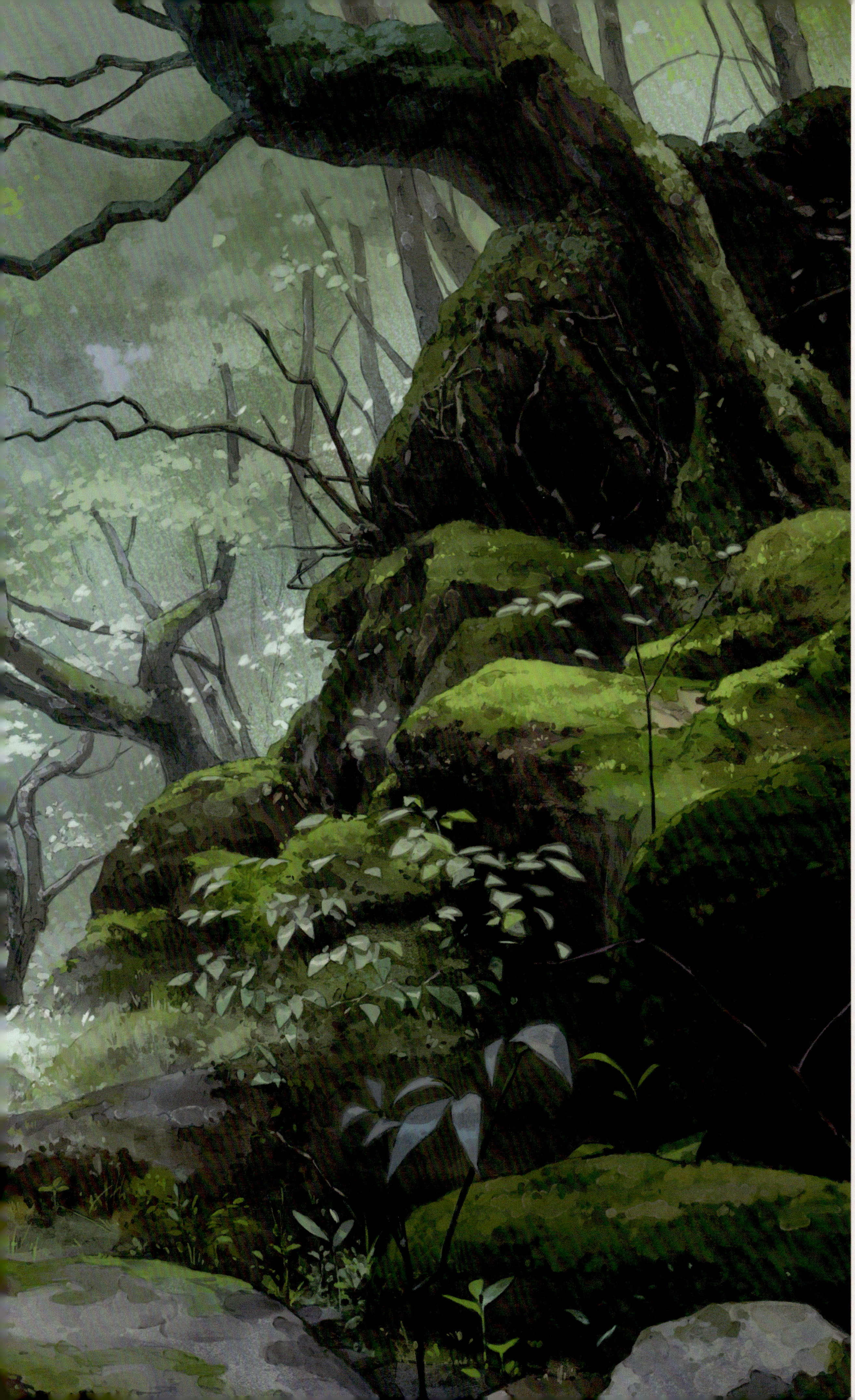

Ancient Forest

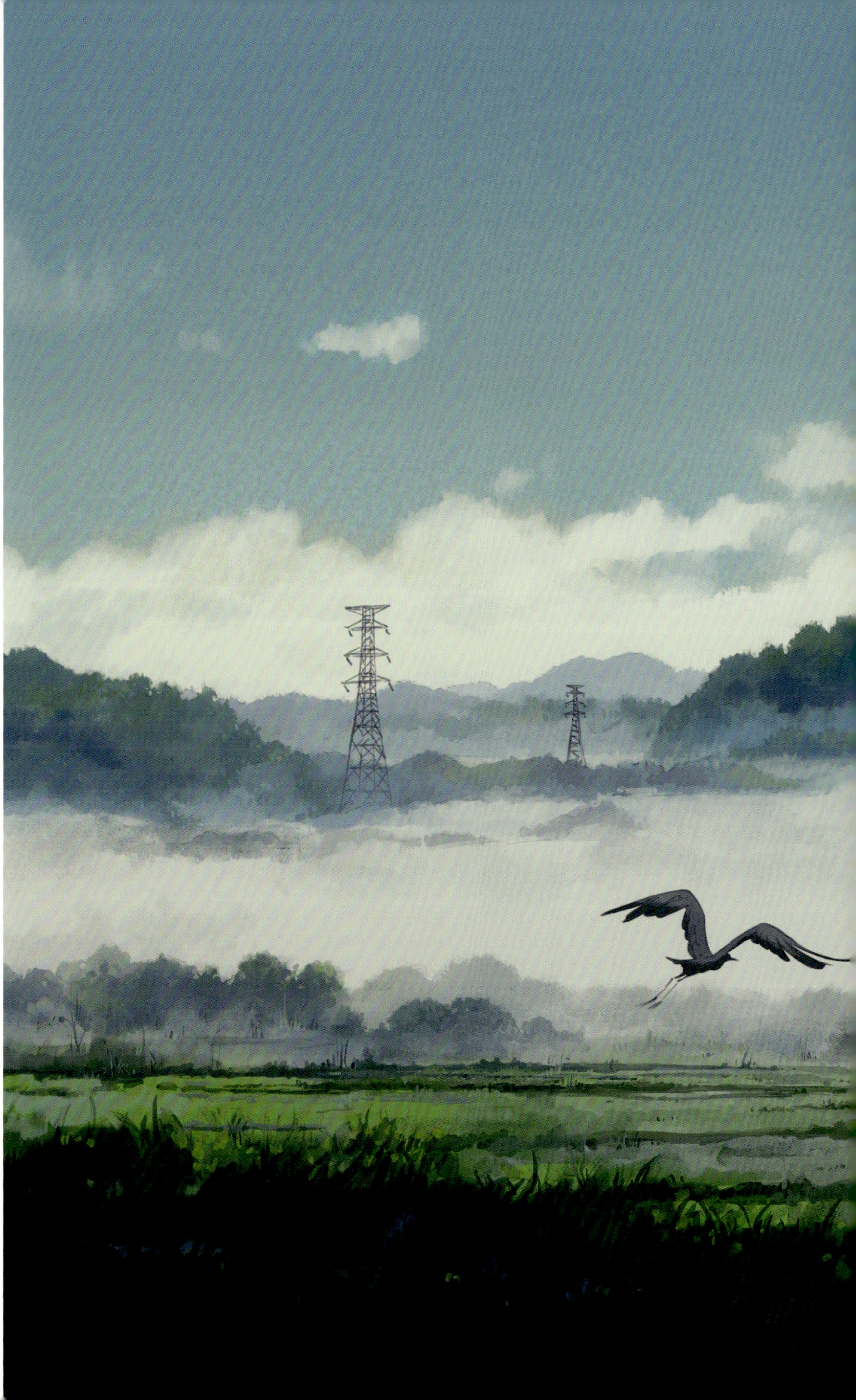

Misty Lake

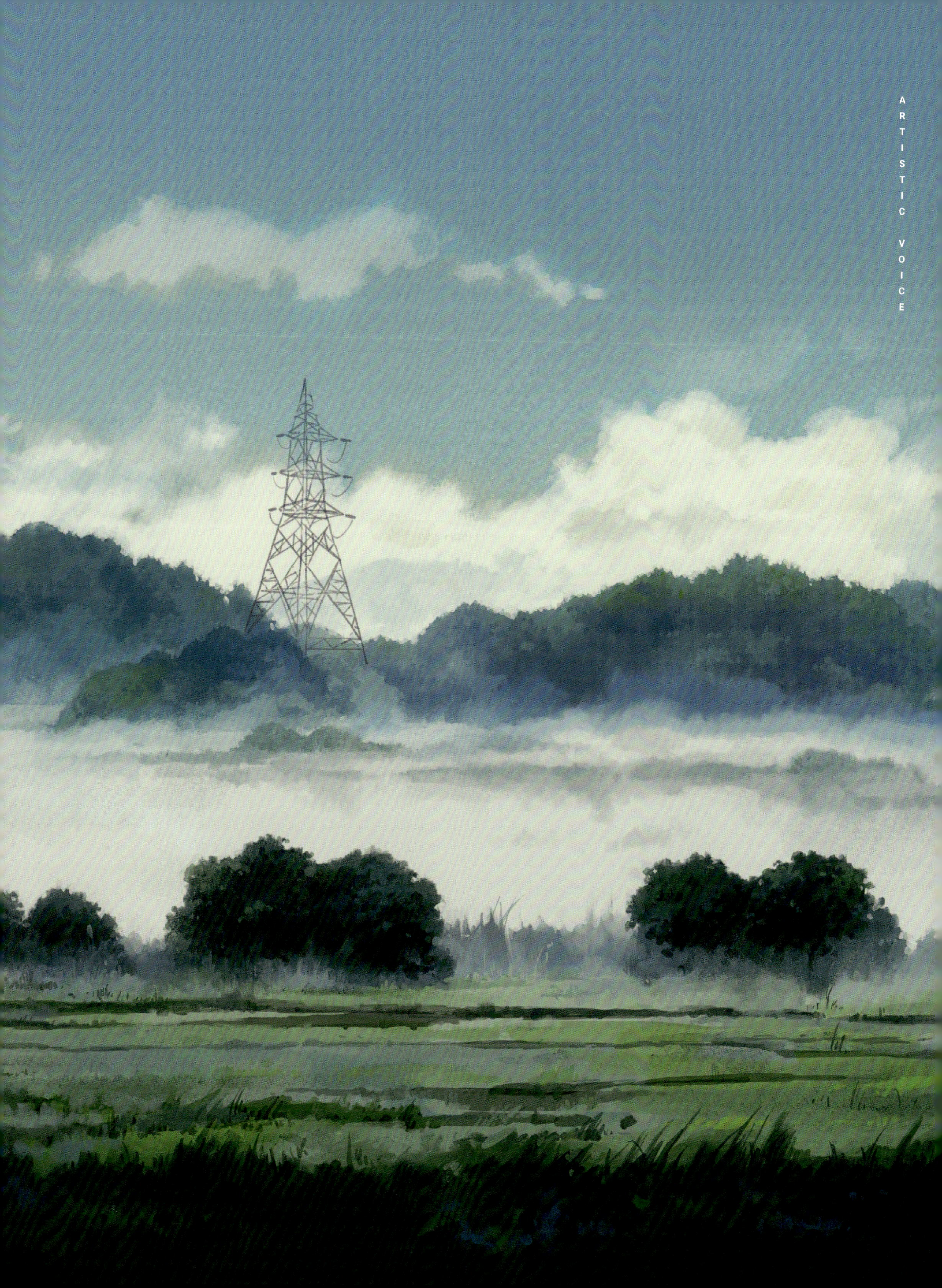
ARTISTIC VOICE

THE EMOTIONAL UNDERTONE

Another essential aspect is the emotional undertone of our work. Of course, an artist will not always evoke the same feeling in all of their paintings, but certain tendencies are often recognizable, similar to the recurring motifs I mentioned earlier. In my opinion, analysing the emotional impact of our artwork, or naming the emotions we *want* to capture, can provide guidance in the search for our unique artistic voice. It can help us to consolidate the understanding of our own work.

The easiest way to do this is to find a handful of adjectives that describe the feelings we want to evoke in our art. How do we want our paintings to be perceived? What reactions should they elicit from the viewer – how should they make them feel? As far as I'm concerned, I want my artwork to be *nostalgic*, *calm*, *quiet*, *contemplative*, *colourful*, *lush*, *magical*, and *cosy* – these are the adjectives I have chosen and they often guide my creative decisions. I was able to identify them through the visual language that has emerged from my inspiration boards. If I go one step further in exploring the emotional undertones of my work, I want my art to come across as an idealized version of the world in which people appreciate the earth and work to preserve it. But by presenting this version of reality, I am also reminding the viewer that the environment, as we once knew it, is no longer the same and never will be again. It's an odd combination of hope for the future and nostalgia for the past. But it's exactly this complicated relationship that interests me.

I find it incredibly fascinating how other people perceive and describe my work. I've received comments from followers that more accurately express my intentions than I ever could myself. These are some of my favourite quotes:

'YOU MAKE US TRAVEL TO WONDERFUL PLACES WHERE WE WILL NEVER GO, OR SCENERIES WE WILL NEVER SEE. IT ALL SEEMS SO REAL, BUT UNTOUCHABLE'

'IT FEELS LIKE AN ENTRANCE TO AN ENCHANTED WORLD, A PLACE WE ONCE KNEW FROM OUR CHILDHOODS – ONE WE COULD ONLY VISIT IN OUR DREAMS'

'YOUR ART GIVES ME THIS URGE TO GO BACK TO THE PLACE I DON'T REMEMBER, BUT I HAVE THOSE LINGERING FEELINGS THAT I WAS SO HAPPY AND SAFE THERE. THERE'S AN ODD FAMILIARITY'

'IT IS LIKE A MAGICAL VEIL YOU UNCOVER WITH YOUR ART, REMINDING US TO LOOK BEHIND THE CURTAIN OF THE DAY-TO-DAY PERCEPTION'

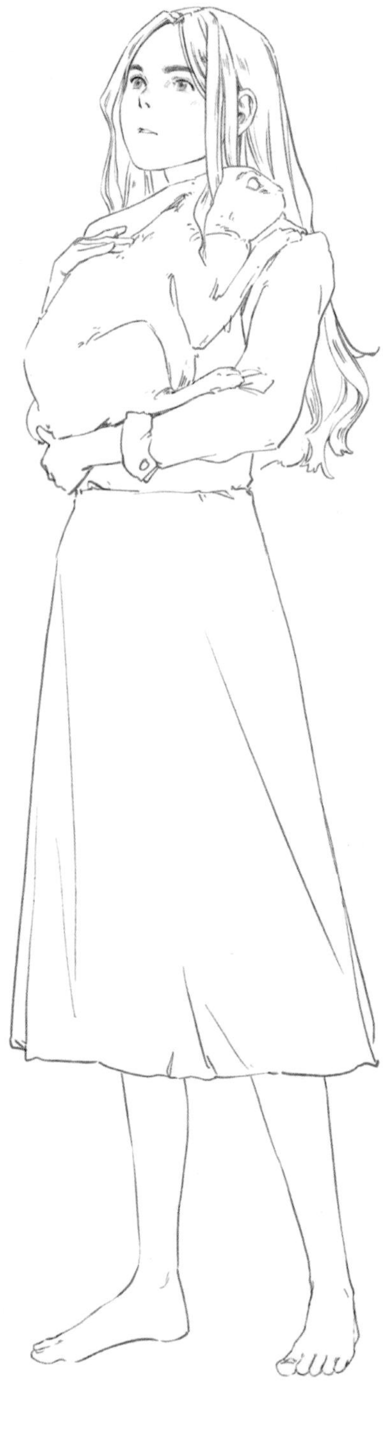

'A MYSTICAL REALM IN THE REAL WORLD'

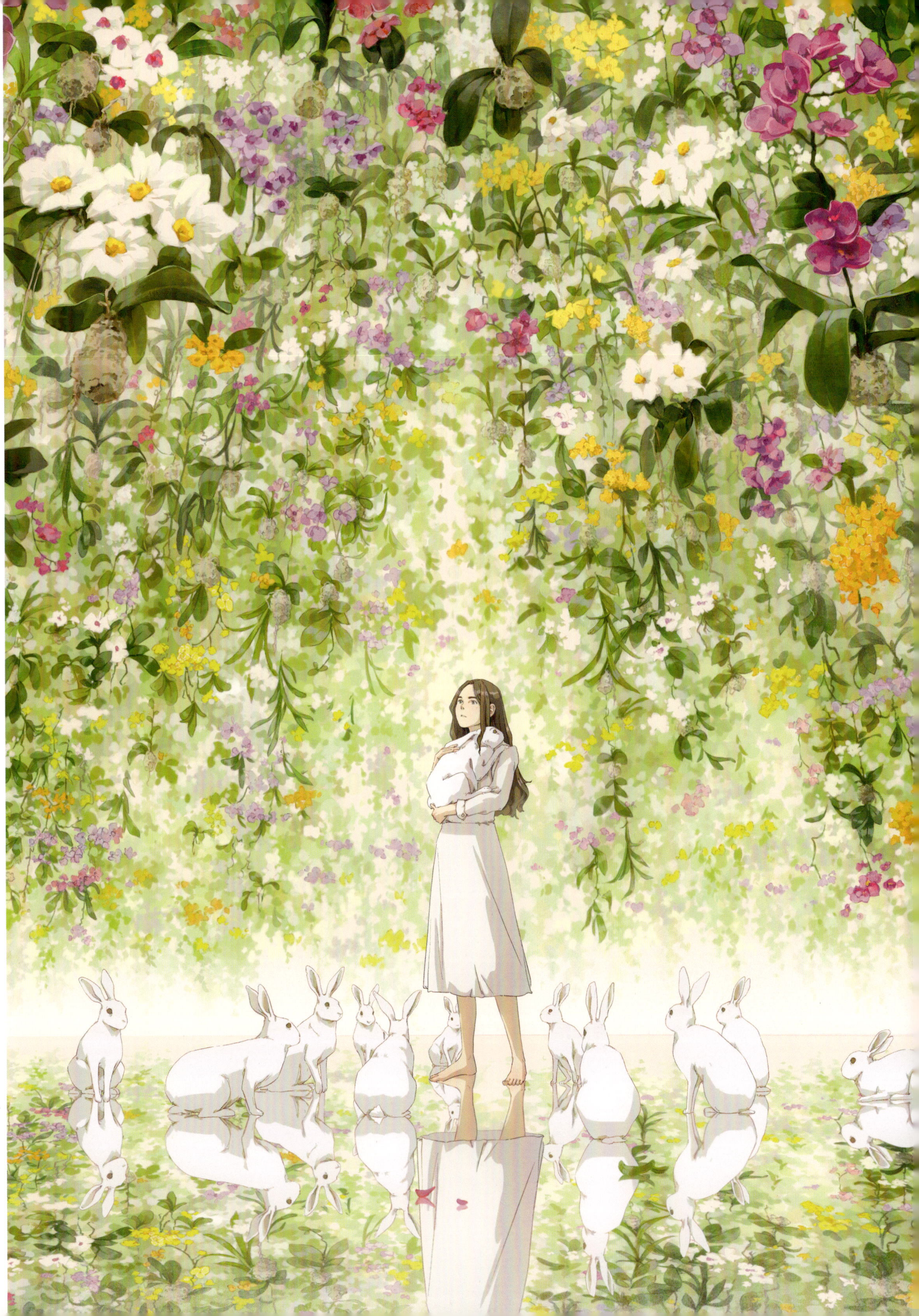

When I read comments like those, I always get a bit emotional because I feel so honoured and impressed by their precise observations and beautiful choice of words. I'm often surprised that so many of us seem to share this 'phantom nostalgia', the longing for places we've never visited. Generally, most people tell me that my work gives them a calming and nostalgic feeling, and that makes me happy because that's exactly what I set out to do.

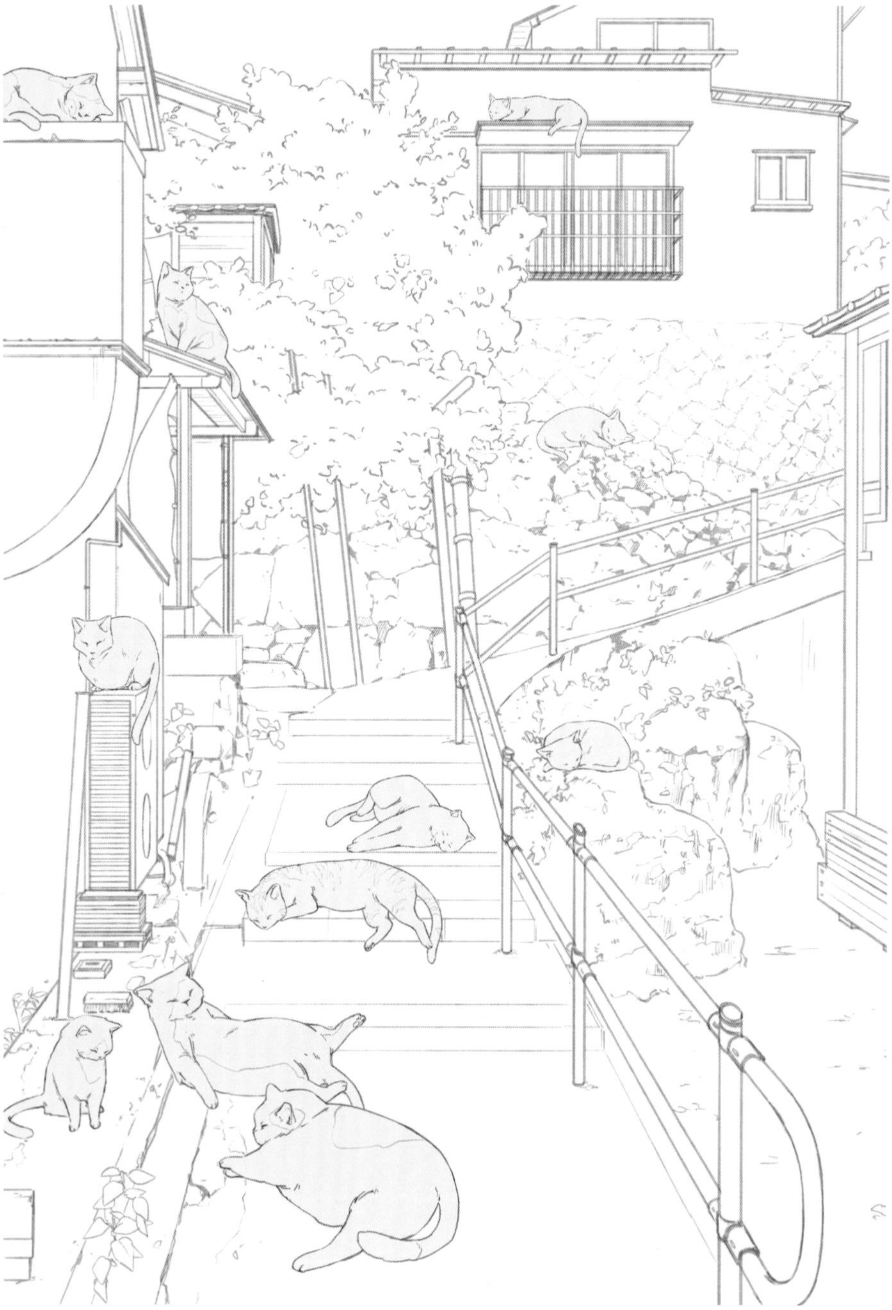

Our art is a mirror that reflects aspects of our lives, and at times, it may feel like we're revealing a little too much of ourselves. If we use our honest, authentic voice, it can feel uncomfortable and vulnerable, but I believe it is the only way we can actually create personal works of art that carry emotional resonance. Our artistic voice is a complex system of individual memories, preferences, and tendencies, and the more we harness it, the more effortless the creative process becomes. As it's so individual, paintings will emerge from it that are unlike those of any other person because each of us sees things from their own point of view.

Our perspective may change over time, but it will always remain unique.

GUIDING QUESTIONS:

- What are five adjectives that describe your current work? Don't go into value judgements like 'pretty' or 'messy'; instead, focus on the emotional undertone. If you have trouble coming up with adjectives on your own, ask your audience, or your friends and family. What adjectives do they associate with your work? How does it make them feel?
- What kind of music or sounds do you/they associate with your art?
- What would your art taste or smell like?
- What are some emotions you would like to evoke in future works? What emotional qualities are you striving for?

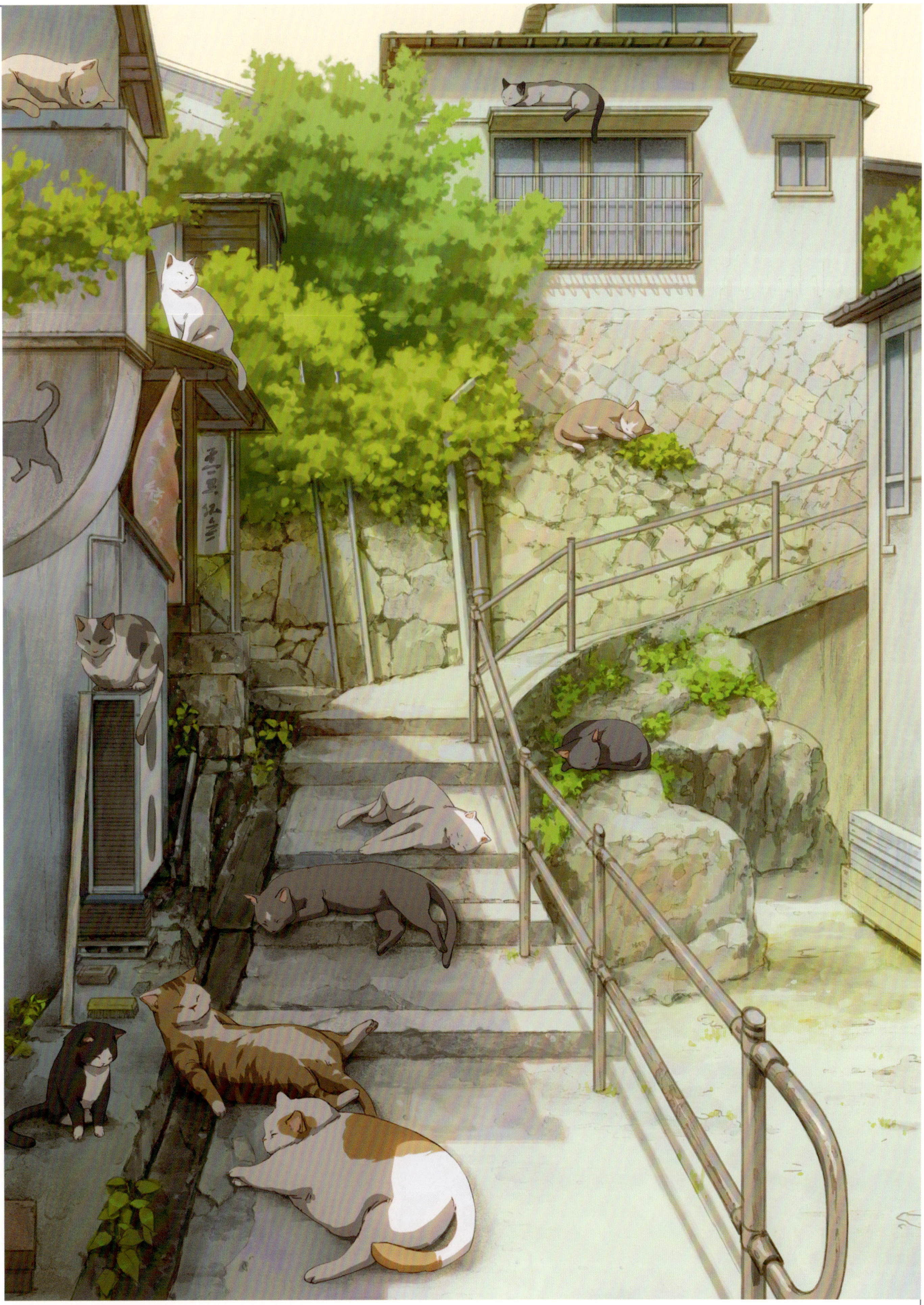

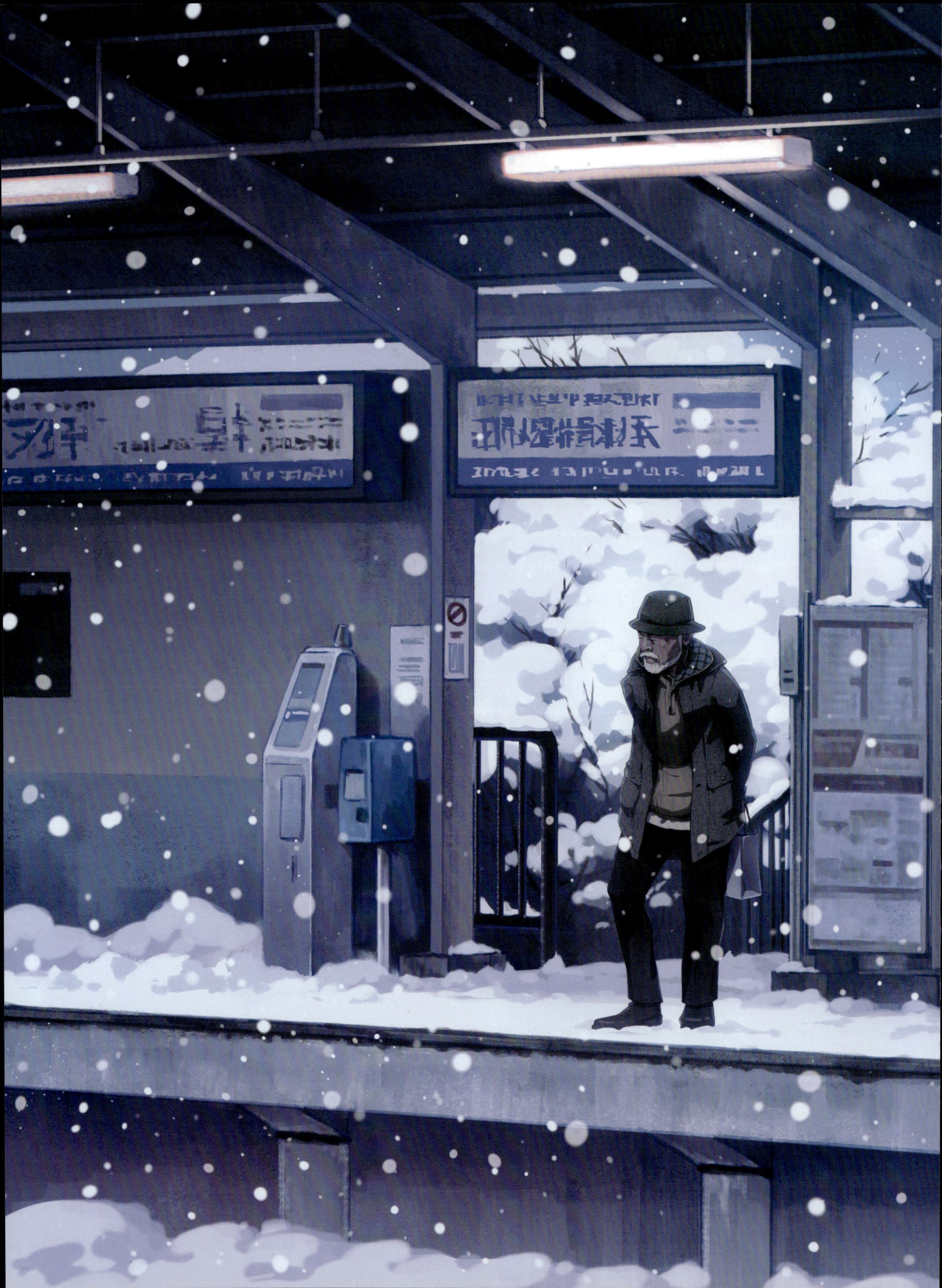

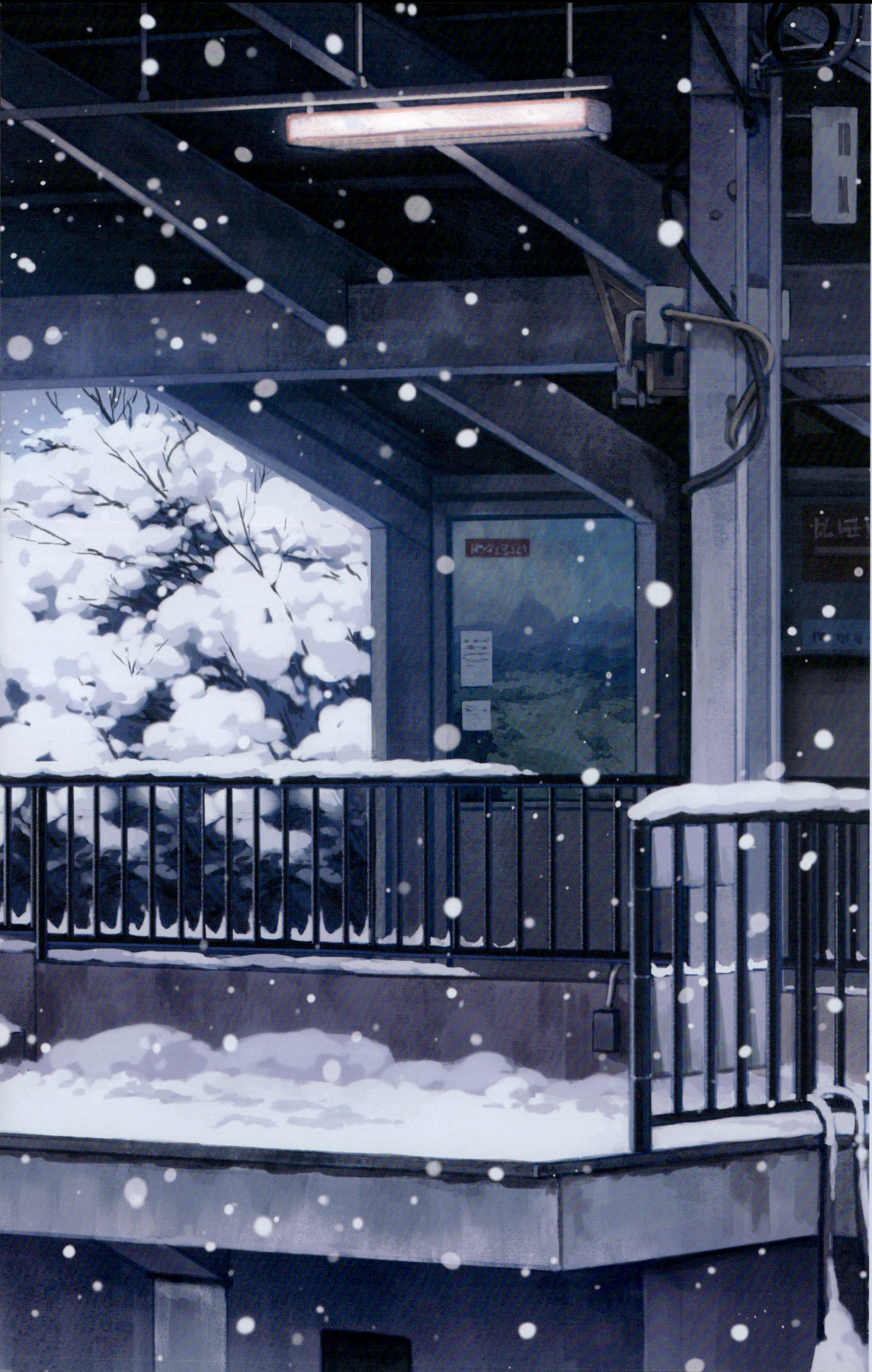

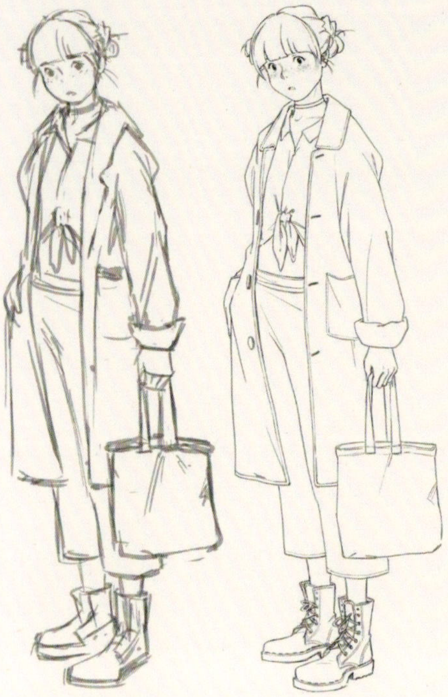

Memory Lane

This is a real place I visited in Shinjuku, Tokyo

BEING PERCEPTIVE & FINDING INSPIRATION

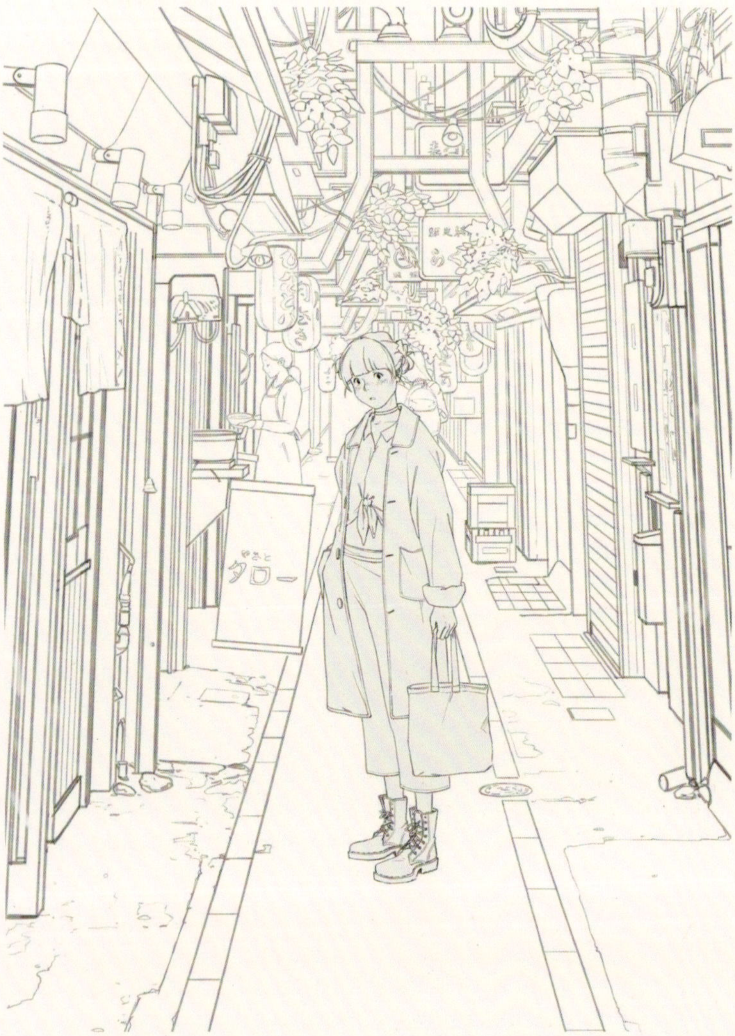

We need inspiration to be creative. But where do we find that inspiration, and how does it become art? I think too many people get stressed and intimidated by this process, and they're afraid that they're not creative enough. However, if we break it down, creativity is nothing more than the process of taking different things that already exist and combining them so that something new emerges. This 'new' thing doesn't have to be groundbreaking; it is simply something that didn't exist before.

You can find inspiration in anything, as long as you keep your eyes open. Personally, the most important thing is being present in the moment and being curious about my surroundings. I go through life collecting fragments that may or may not eventually become something, such as images of unusual characters on the train, skies after a storm, dogs with funny expressions, oddly shaped plants, conversations I overhear – anything I find in some way remarkable and worth remembering. I will store these influences inside my head, or on my phone, in the form of photos and written notes. I read that the writer Haruki Murakami follows a similar process: he observes everyday life very closely, creates a kind of inner archive, and then carefully threads a novel out of these individual elements. I love this approach, and it feels a little like collecting souvenirs. It also lends authenticity to the work. We have infinite raw material around us, and when we become aware of this and cultivate our sense of wonder, we naturally lay the foundation for creative work.

I'm not good at making things up, and I'm certainly not an inventor. For me, it's more about curating and capturing what I discover, as well as what impresses me. I often just want to paint what I see in front of me, but to do that, I need to make sure that I actually see things, and get out enough.

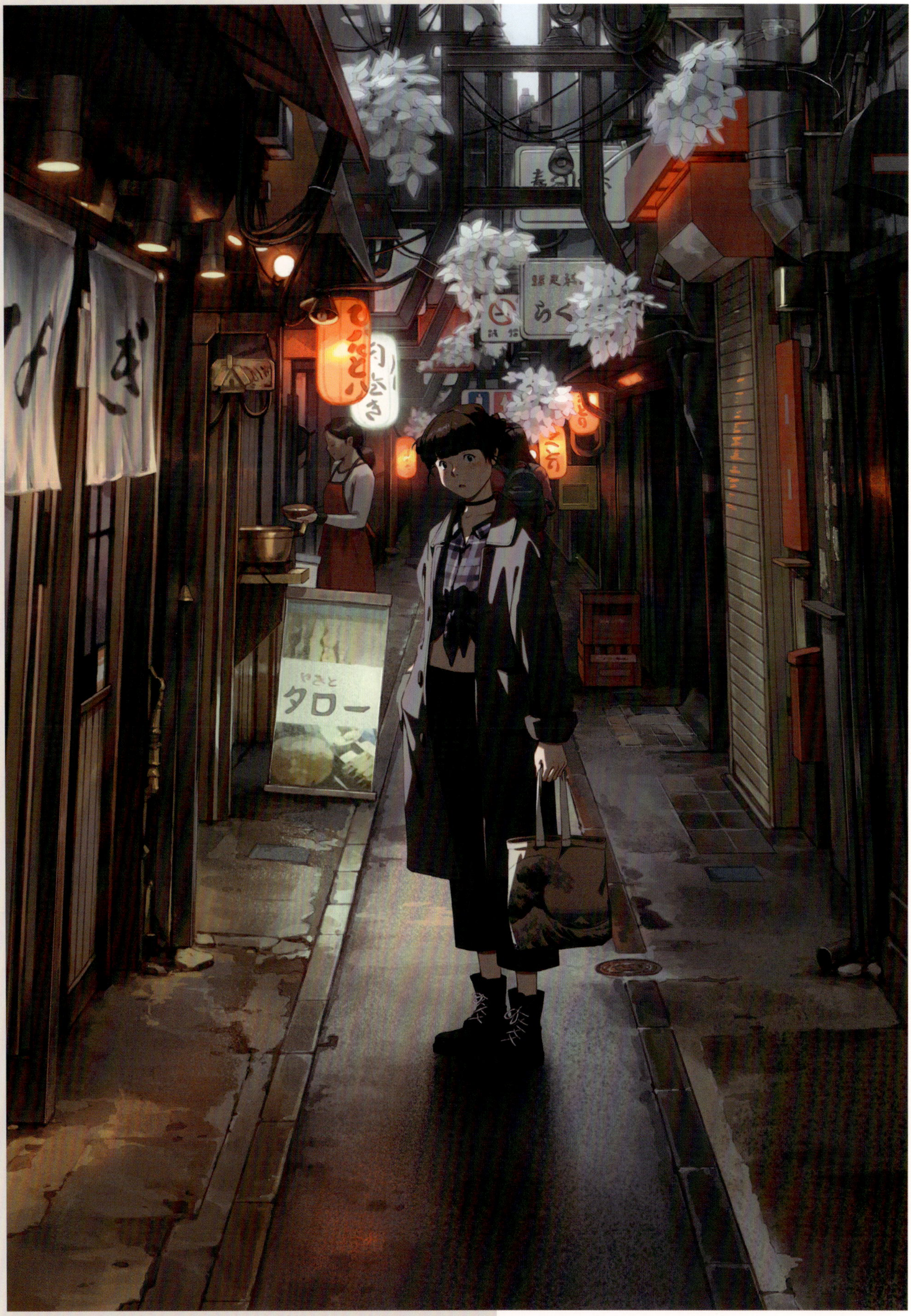
タロー

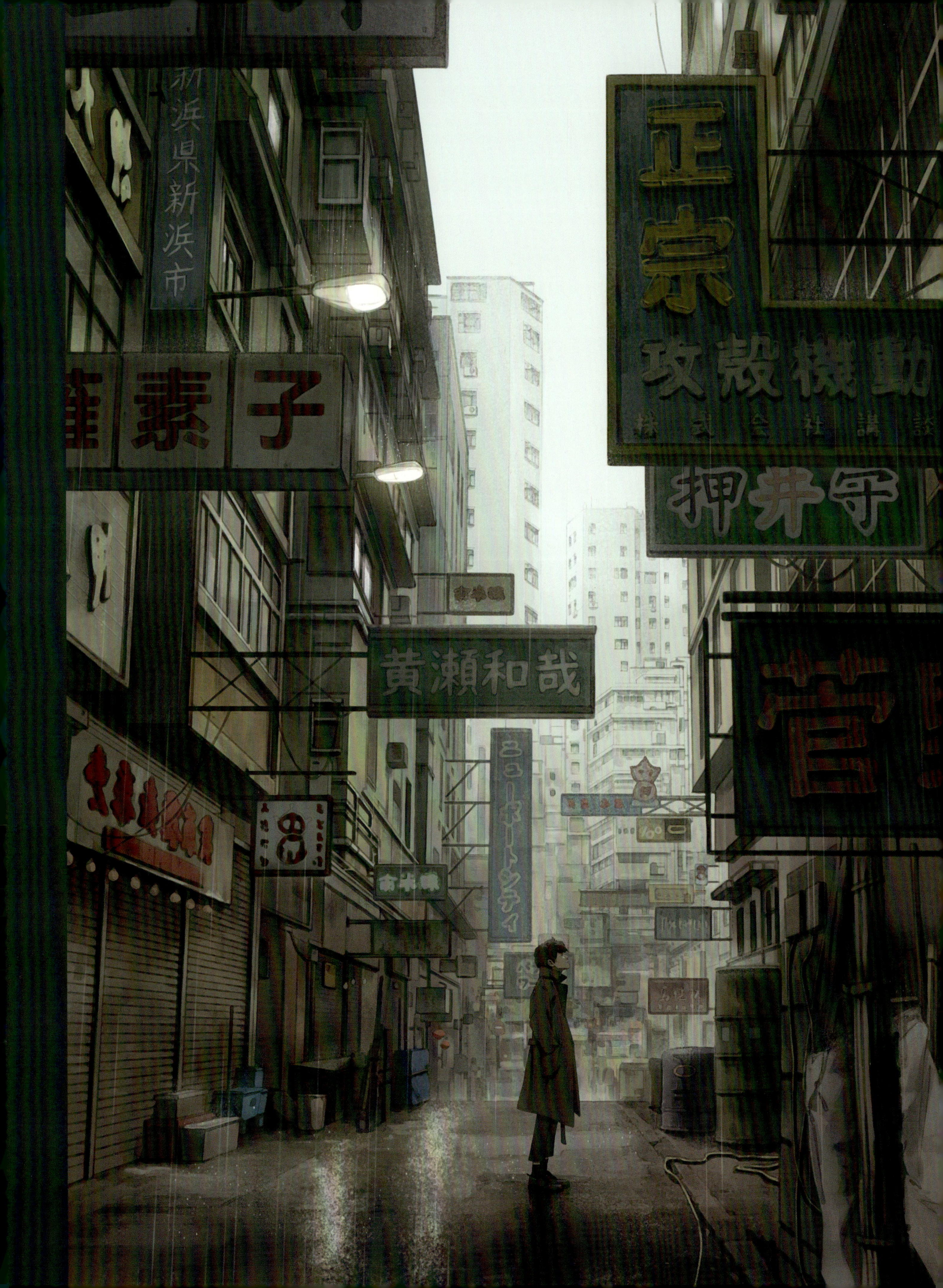

新浜県新浜市
正宗
攻殻機動
株式会社講談
押井守
黄瀬和哉

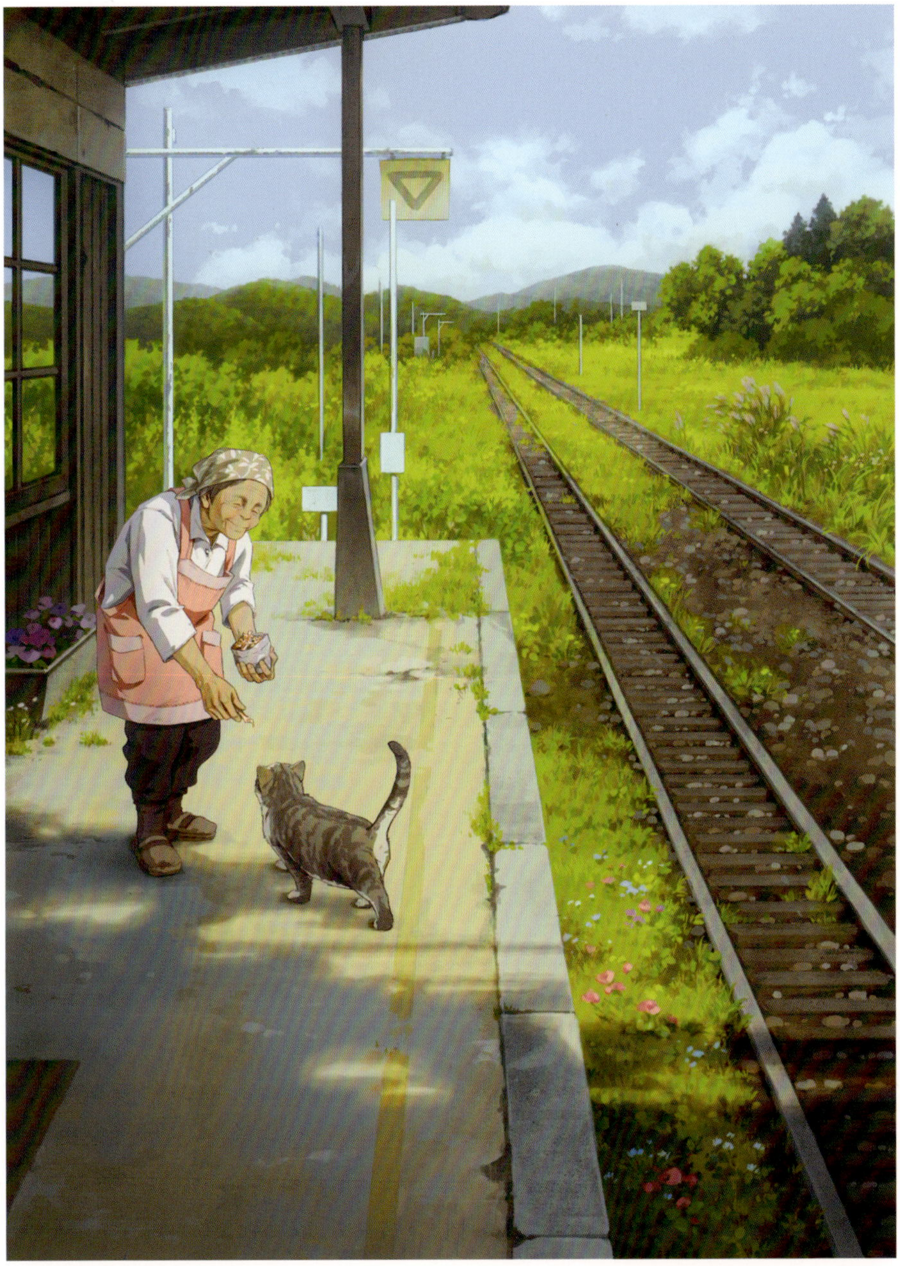

It's absolutely essential that I leave the house regularly (which can sometimes be difficult as a self-employed person), and go out into nature whenever possible. But also just taking my work to a café or a library every once in a while offers so many more new impressions than my desk at home. Whatever the environment, I try to perceive it with all my senses; I want to get a feel for the place. For example, take a forest after a summer rain pour: a heavy, slightly musty smell hangs around you, the air feels thick enough to drink, muted greens surround you, mud clings to the soles of your rubber boots, water drips from leaves, you hear rustling and chirping – there is so much going on. Wherever I am, I try to pay attention to what things attract me the most, both visually and emotionally, and try to recognize patterns. It is often the small, unremarkable things that catch my attention – I ignore the imposing architecture of a cathedral because I am more fascinated by the birds that find shelter in its nooks and crannies. I think, for me, it's more about the little details that bring places to life, not what's generally most impressive. If you look closely, there is so much beauty in the mundane.

Apart from everyday life, I also find inspiration in words. I find that losing myself in books or songs stimulates my imagination because if there are no images, I inevitably conjure up my own. But words are not only meaningful to me as a recipient; I regularly write down my thoughts, observations, questions, and ideas in the form of journal entries. This is a habit I developed after reading an autobiography by Patti Smith, who is a multifaceted creative – a singer, songwriter, poet, painter, and author. I'm deeply impressed by her ability to recall events in her life so vividly and accurately. She makes the mere act of living appear to be something creative in itself. Through her books, I get to experience the *spaces between* her art: her everyday life and thoughts, and how she will linger on certain topics to turn them over and over in her mind. I also use my journal to record the everyday observations I spoke of earlier, and to explore and better understand topics that are on my mind at that moment. It helps me make sense of things, recognize patterns, and draw conclusions. Writing is a way for me to refocus my scattered attention, capture ideas, and to think them through thoroughly. In fact, the text in this very book is the result of many journal entries filled with my armchair philosophies, opinions, and research on art.

Colourless Streets **(Left)**
I was inspired by the movie *Ghost in the Shell*, which is visually based on the cityscape of Hong Kong. Even though I have never been there myself, I tried to recreate the atmosphere through close observation and research

Obaasan **(Above)**
This illustration is based on a video by YouTuber *Dogen*, who is an excellent storyteller. The video is about an old woman who lives in the Japanese countryside and regularly comes to the local train station to feed a cat

GUIDING QUESTIONS:

- Where do you find inspiration?
- When you come to a place, familiar or new, try to perceive it with all your senses. What do you see? What do you hear? What do you smell or taste? What does it feel like?
- Where do you direct your attention? What things do you notice in particular?

HOW IDEAS ARE CONCEIVED

'YOU GET IDEAS FROM DAYDREAMING. YOU GET IDEAS FROM BEING BORED. YOU GET IDEAS ALL THE TIME. THE ONLY DIFFERENCE BETWEEN WRITERS AND OTHER PEOPLE IS WE NOTICE WHEN WE'RE DOING IT' – NEIL GAIMAN

We are all capable of creative thinking. It's just that artists, in whatever field, are the ones who perceive the initial sparks and fragments, and process them into something. Conceiving ideas often takes the form of *listening*, rather than an active search. The difficult thing is to become aware of emerging ideas so we can record them. If we bring enough mindfulness and curiosity into our daily lives, it soon becomes an automatic process that drives our creative work. However, the question then arises as to how we can develop a concrete piece of art from our initial fragile seed of an idea. Visual Storytelling will deal specifically with techniques for doing this, but for now, we'll focus on how we can create the right conditions in which ideas can grow and evolve.

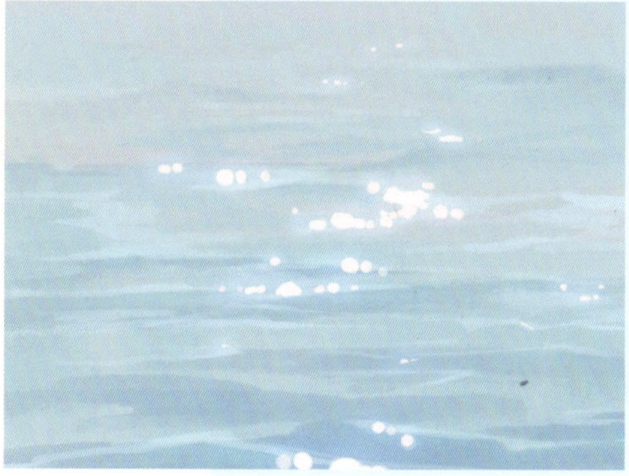

Up to this point, I have talked at length about how important inspiration and external influences are for our artistic work. Nevertheless, I firmly believe that it is equally important to take regular breaks from these external stimuli in order to let ideas sink in. Inspiration needs to take effect. As with everything, it's about finding a healthy balance. We live in a time when we are prone to fill every spare minute with the consumption of content, and we tend to be overstimulated with images and information; we do not allow ourselves to be bored even for a minute. I get the impression that my own thoughts are smothered when I permanently expose myself to too much input, so I make it a priority to regularly withdraw from all the noise. My brain needs time to process what I have seen in order to interact with it – to finally make new connections. Instead of forcing ideas, the better approach is often to first think deeply, and then let go of the subject for a while. We all know the famous shower epiphanies, and I generally find that the missing pieces for something I'm working on most often arise in moments of meditation and solitude.

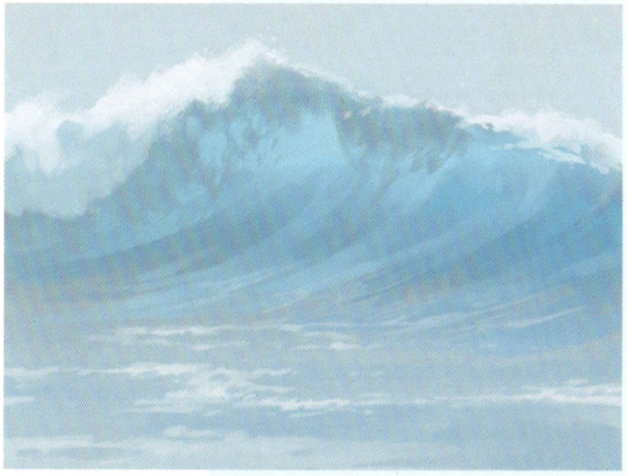

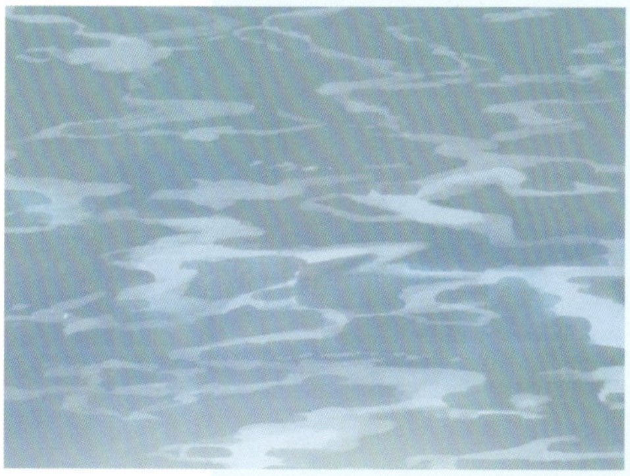

And by 'solitude' I don't necessarily mean being physically alone. Instead, I rely on an interpretation of the word as proposed by the author Cal Newport: 'A subjective state in which you're isolated from input from other minds.' Somehow, I find this view quite poetic and beautiful, and I try to let my mind wander whenever I can. It can be as simple as looking out the window while sitting on the train instead of looking at my phone, or taking a walk without a podcast playing in my ear – essentially just allowing myself a little boredom every now and then. Author Neil Gaiman's writing routine is effectively built on enforcing boredom, which is an unusual approach: he allows himself only two activities during his allotted writing time – doing absolutely nothing, or writing. He says: 'What I love about that is I'm giving myself permission to write or not write, but writing is actually more interesting than doing nothing after a while.' I haven't tried this method myself, but I could see it working well, if you can bear the discomfort of sitting with only your own thoughts.

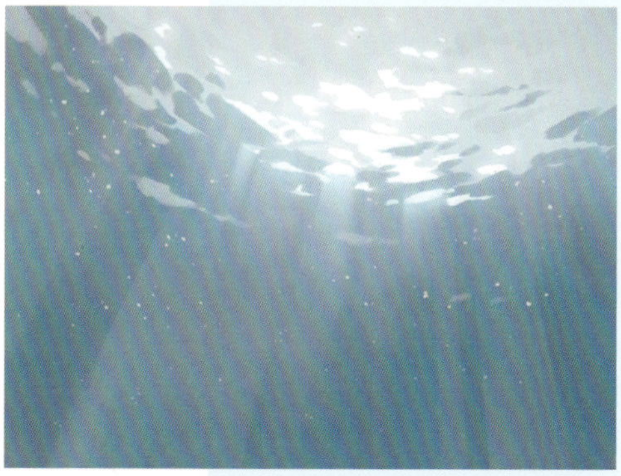

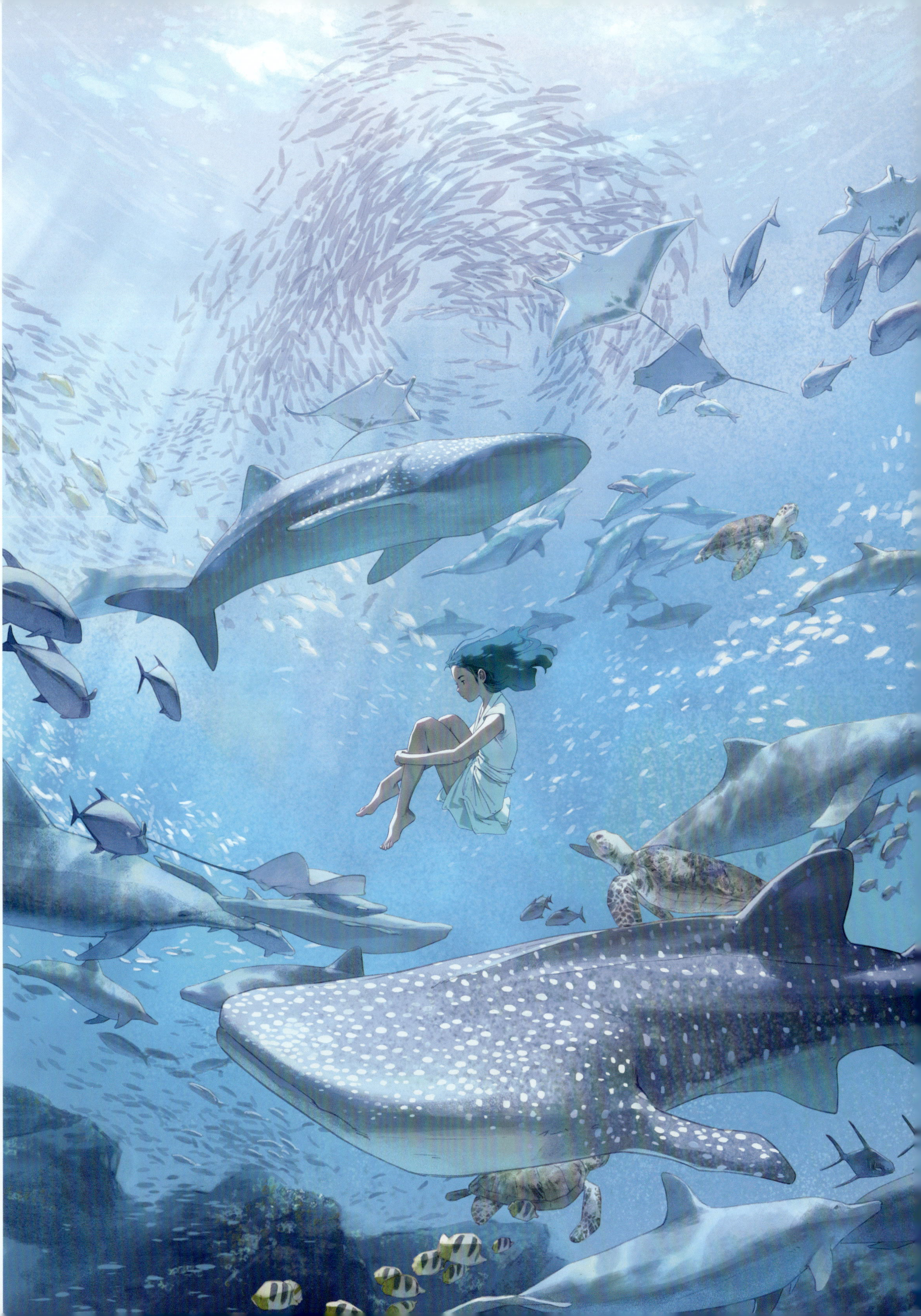

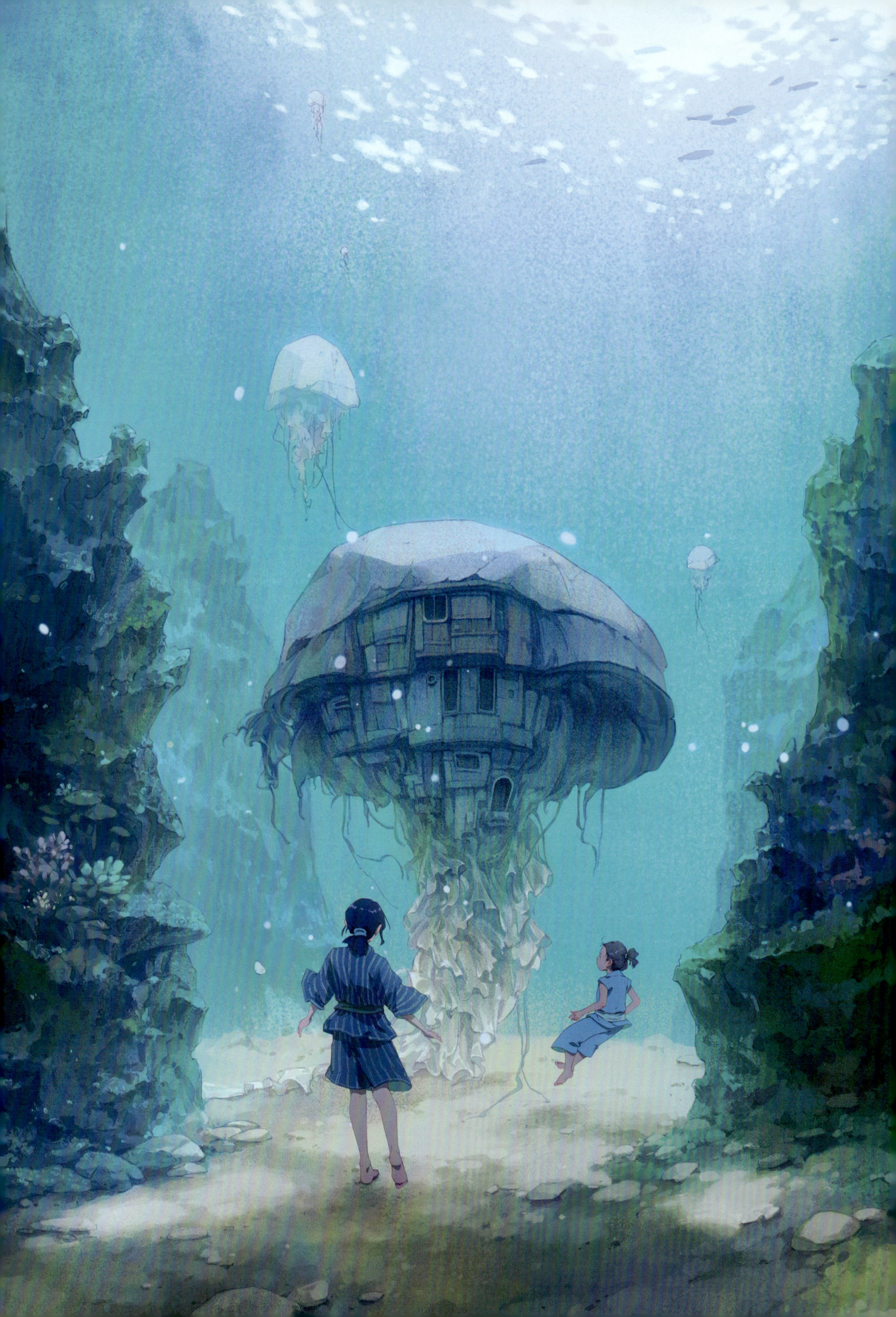

HOW IDEAS EVOLVE

Anything can spark an idea: the way a shadow falls, a facial expression, or the entrance to a dilapidated building. These observations then settle in my mind, and eventually take on a life of their own. As I create associations and ask questions, more images appear in front of my inner eye. It's fun to fill the gaps and invent little stories. In my imagination, the ordinary door I saw may hide a botanical garden inside with a pond in the middle of the house, circled by dragonflies. As I write this, I can vividly see the scene before me, and I have a clear sense of the atmosphere, prevalent sounds, and smells. It is often surprising what paths the mind takes when we give it free rein.

When my mind is blank and I can't think of anything at all – no ideas whatsoever – I often start with a question to spark my imagination. I deliberately choose questions that are emotionally charged and evocative, as these produce the more interesting results. For example, 'What is it like to walk around alone at night in a strange city?' or 'What's it like waiting for your train to leave for summer vacation?' Both of these evoke very different images that each have strong emotional connotations. They conjure up people, colours, times of day, weather conditions, certain styles of architecture, specific time periods, sounds, and different moods that slowly form a complete picture. And of course, these pictures are highly individual and strongly tinted by my personal experiences.

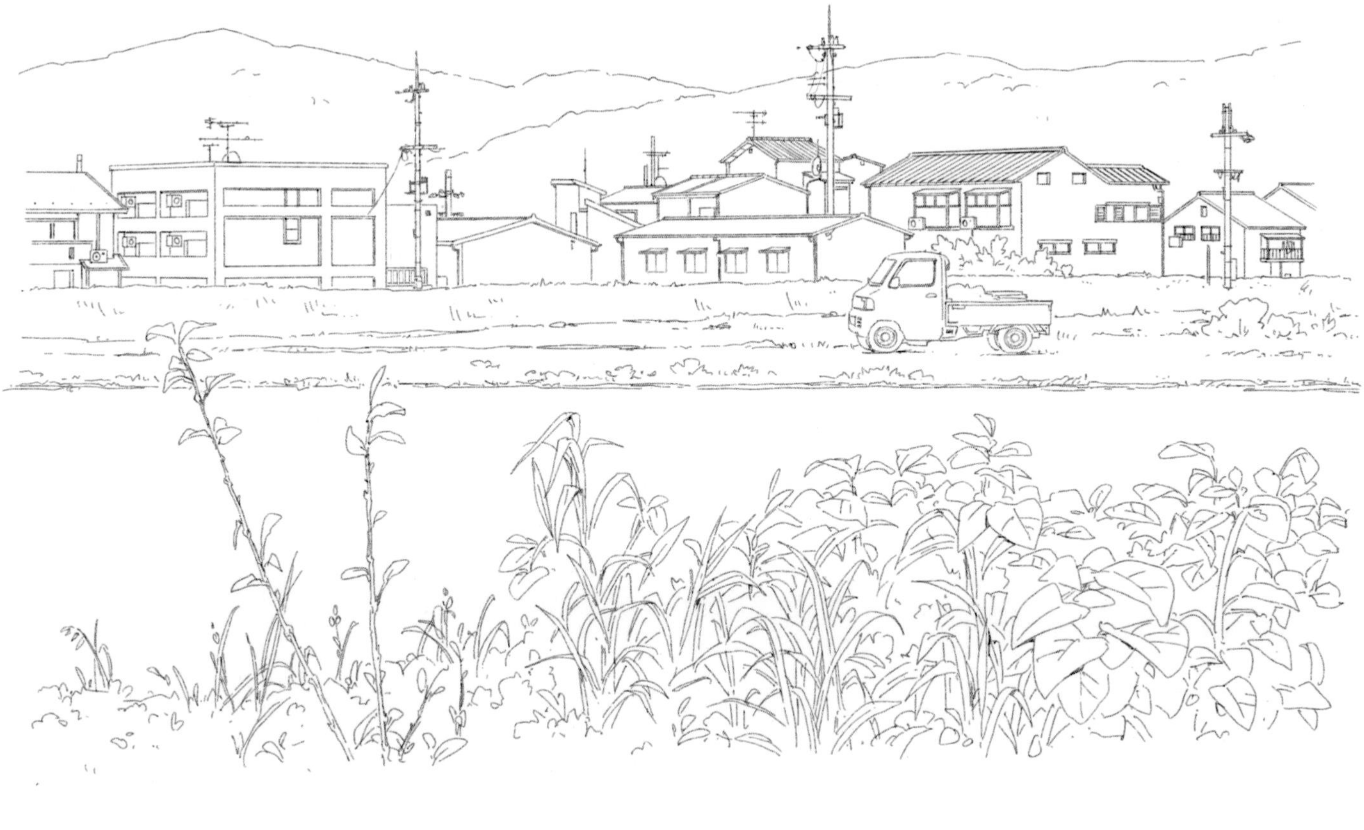

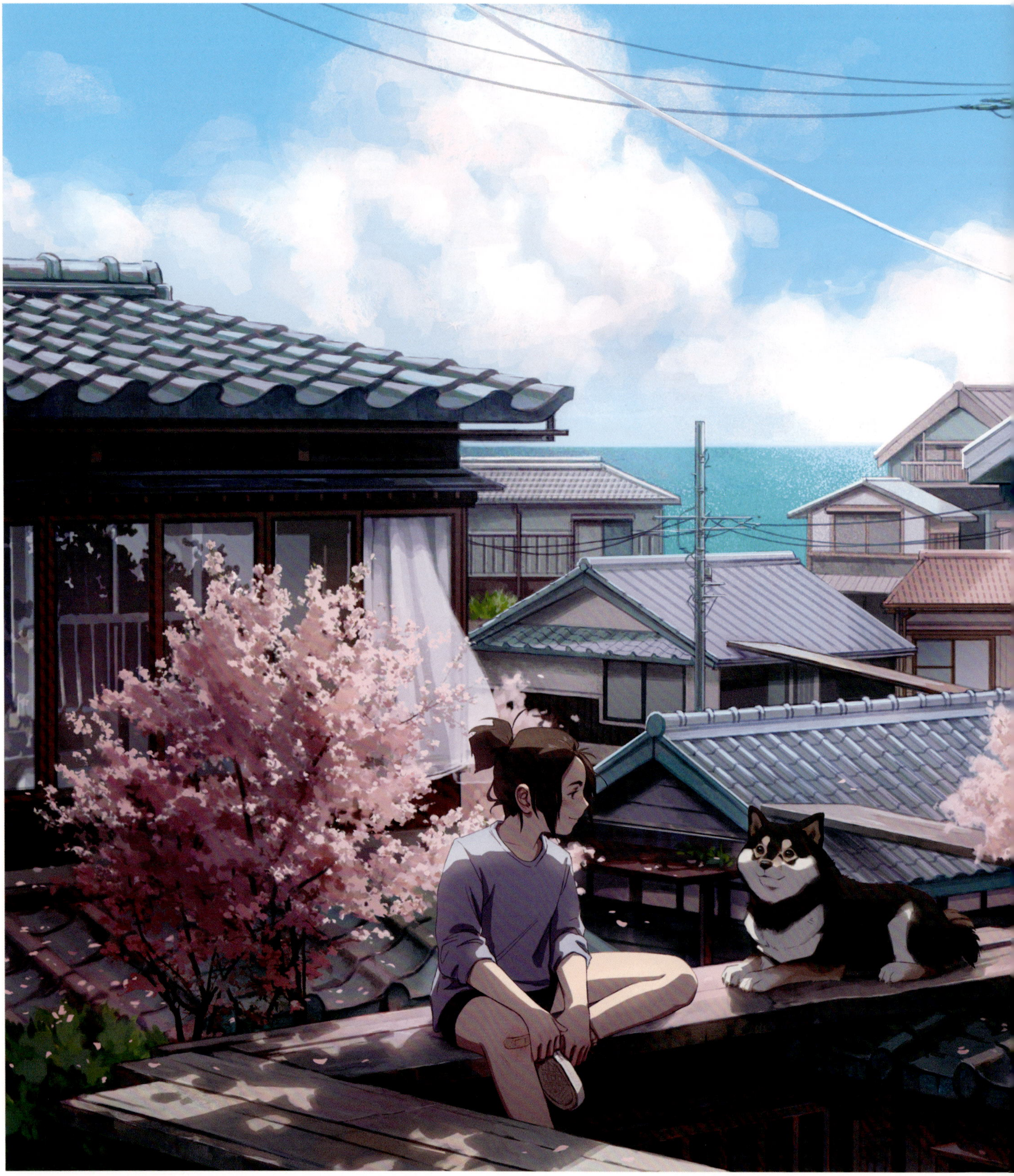

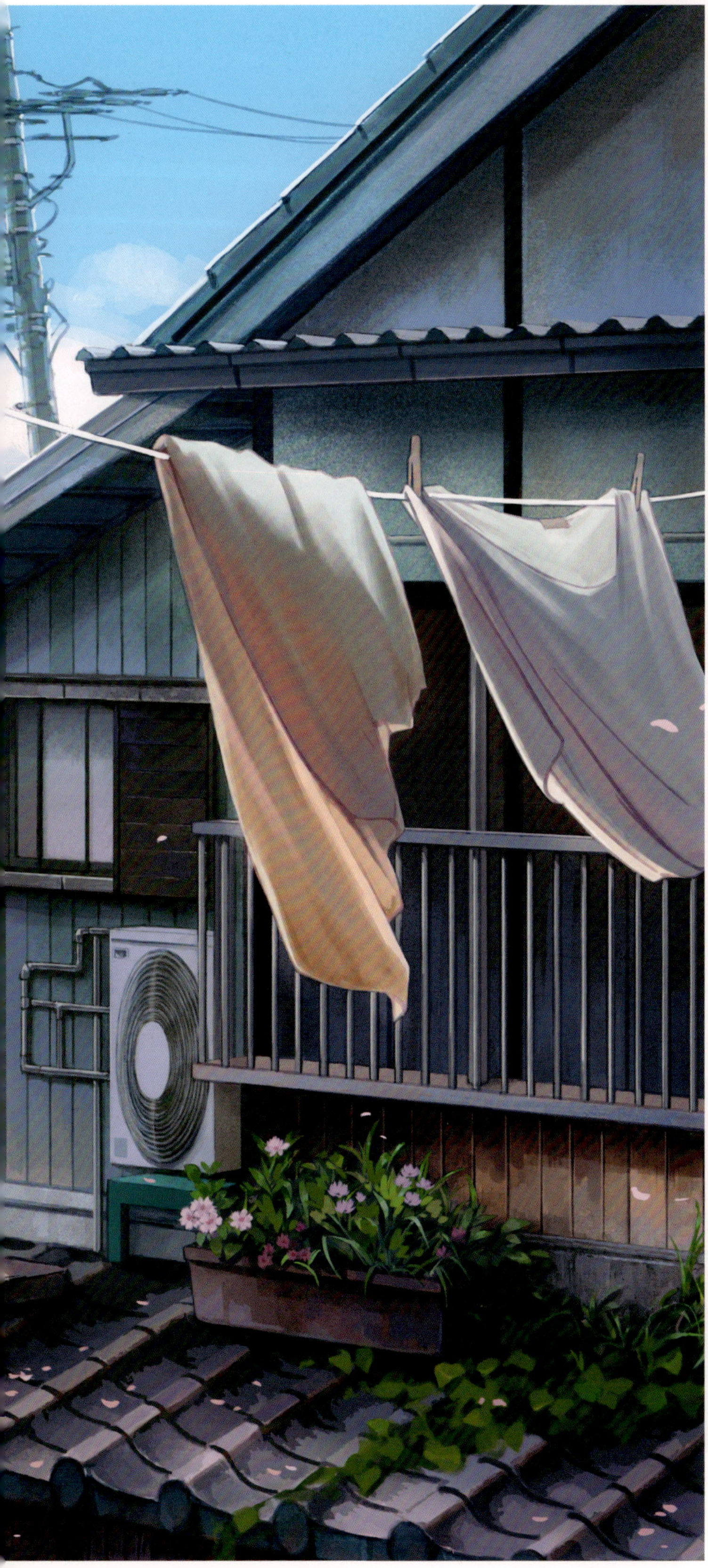

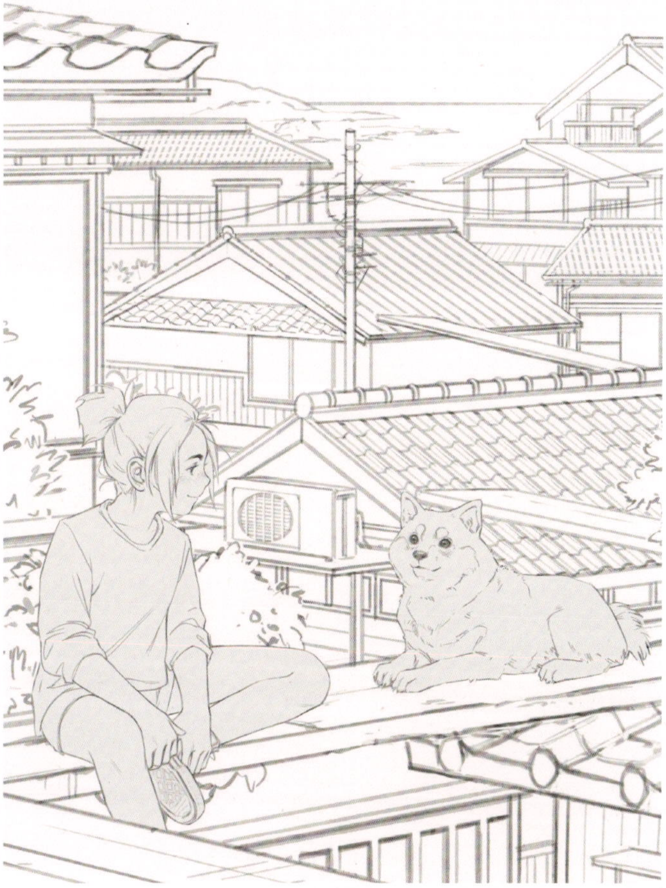

I think at the very early stages, it's important not to judge or censor thoughts and ideas. I just leave them be and let them change and evolve for a little while. Nonetheless, at some point, I'll need to decide which of them I want to pursue further and develop into a painting. That decision largely depends on how much visual potential I see in it, and how persistent the idea seems. If it won't leave me alone for weeks, I will eventually commit to it. And what I mean by 'visual potential' is how many things I can bring to the scene that I enjoy painting and find aesthetically pleasing, because if I'm dreading the painting process, I'm not doing myself any favours. After all, I just have to *care*, because if I don't even care about my idea, no one else will either.

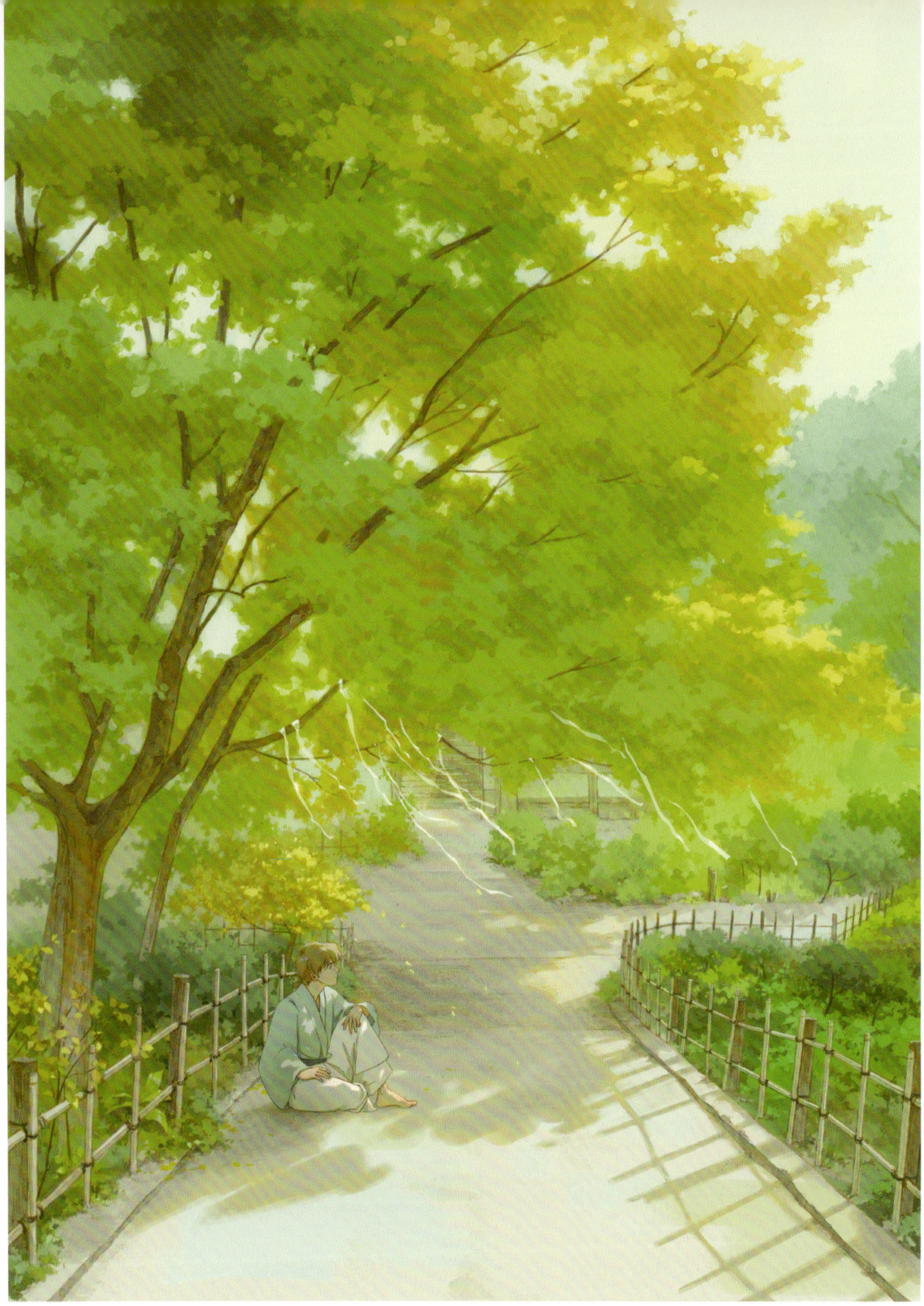

EXERCISE:

- Choose an ordinary observation, and use it as a starting point to let your imagination take over. Follow your train of thought, and see what background stories and images emerge from it.
- Come up with three questions starting with 'What is it like to…?' What comes to mind when you imagine these scenes?

I usually don't attempt to interpret my inner images or try to understand their meaning. Most of the time, they just flash across my mind without me being able to tell exactly why – all I know is that I find the visual intriguing. Generally, the meaning or message of a work of art doesn't matter much to me, as I'm more interested in emotions. My goal is to reproduce the feeling that comes with the image in my head as accurately as possible in a painting. I find it much more compelling to simply experience art instead of dissecting it with a scalpel. I'm often surprised when people who see my work deliver these incredibly profound interpretations that I never would have thought of myself, or I think, speaking, I don't want to force my message or agenda on anyone. I love this quote by musician Nick Cave, which captures my attitude towards this topic pretty well: 'I'm not in the business of telling people what to do. I'm much more in the business of describing things, situations and stuff like that and leaving them out there, and you can make up your minds about them.' I often prefer open endings and just leaving things up for interpretation. At the end of the day, life is complicated and doesn't always provide clear answers. Things aren't always good or bad, black or white, and I've grown comfortable with that ambiguity.

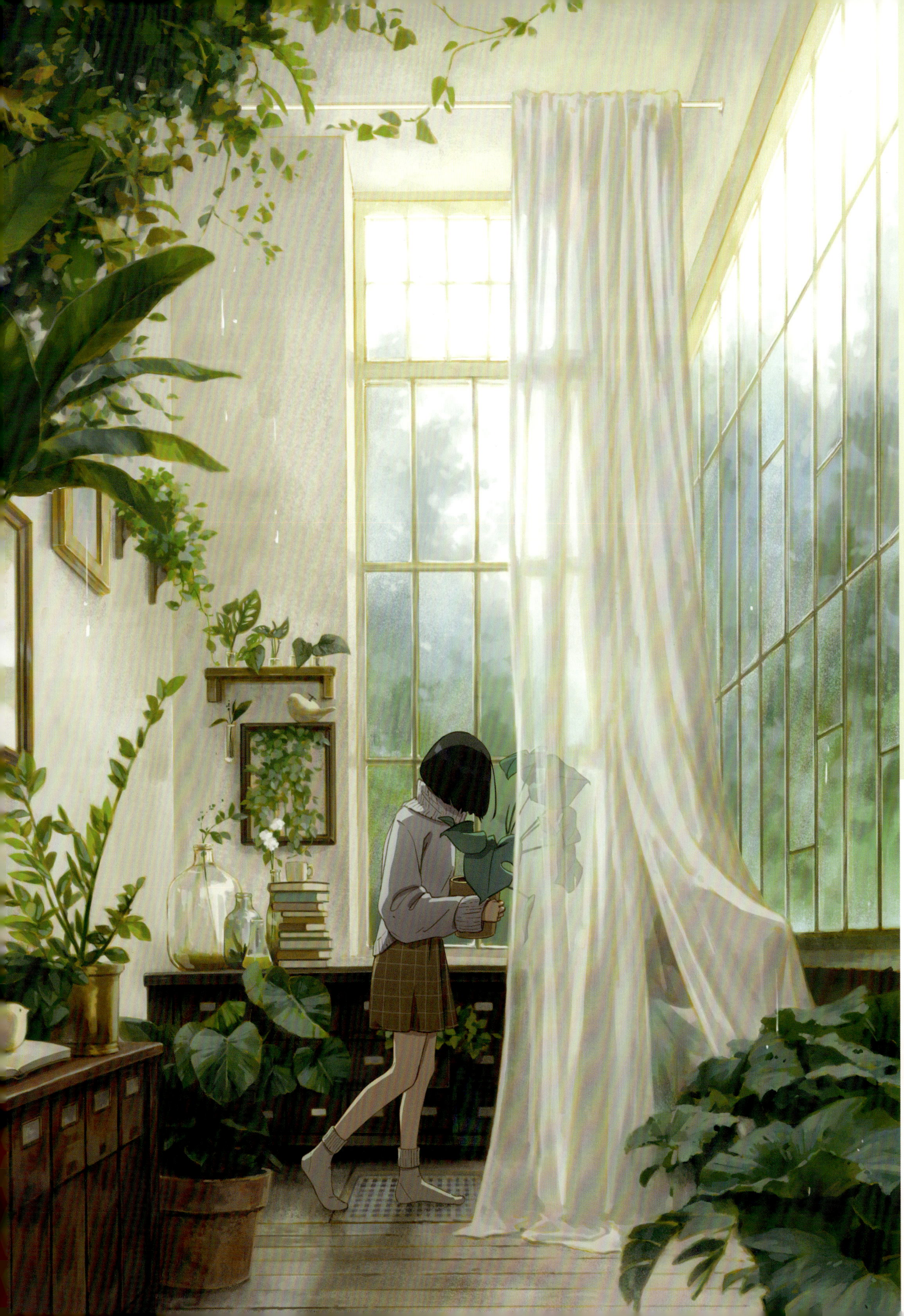

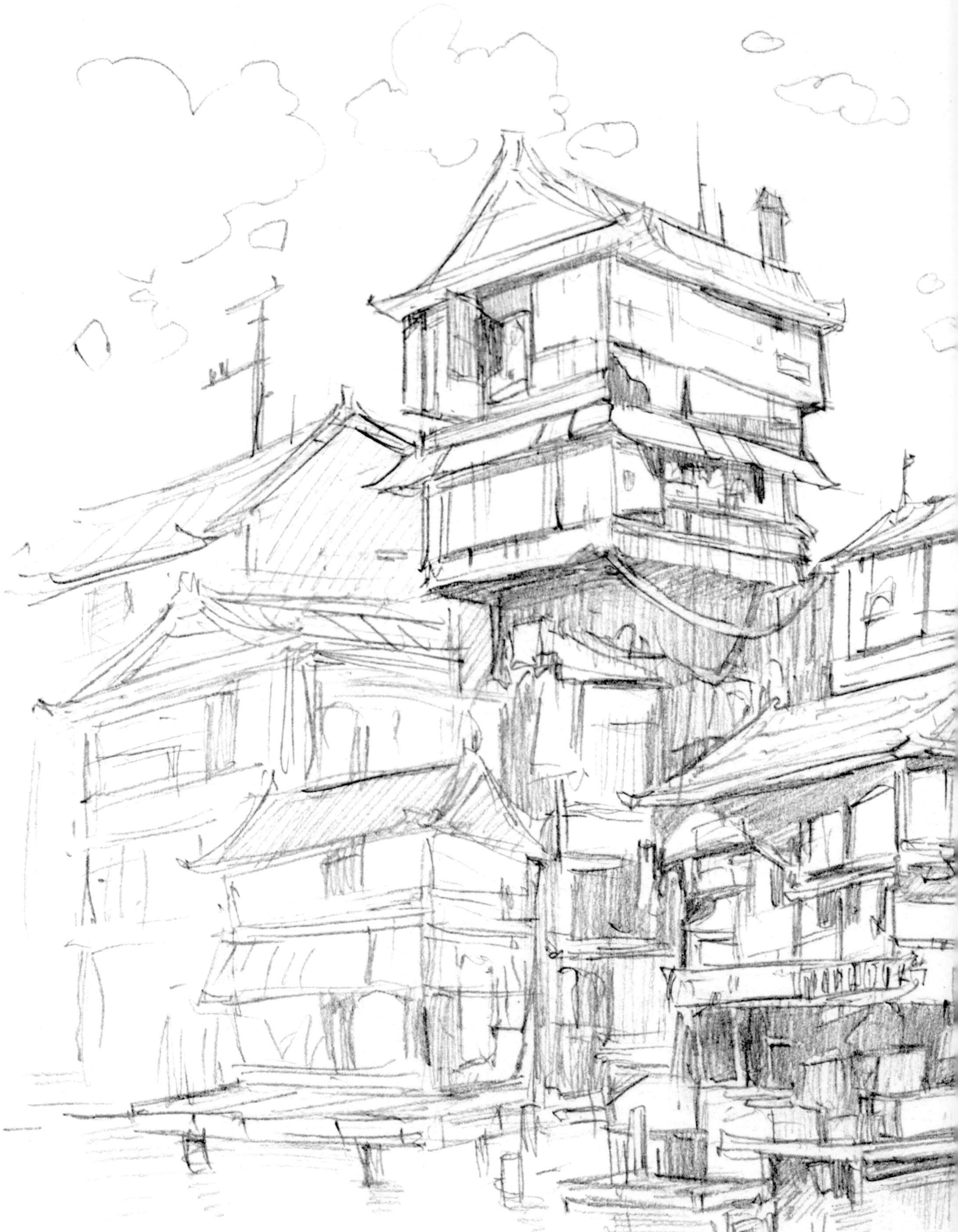

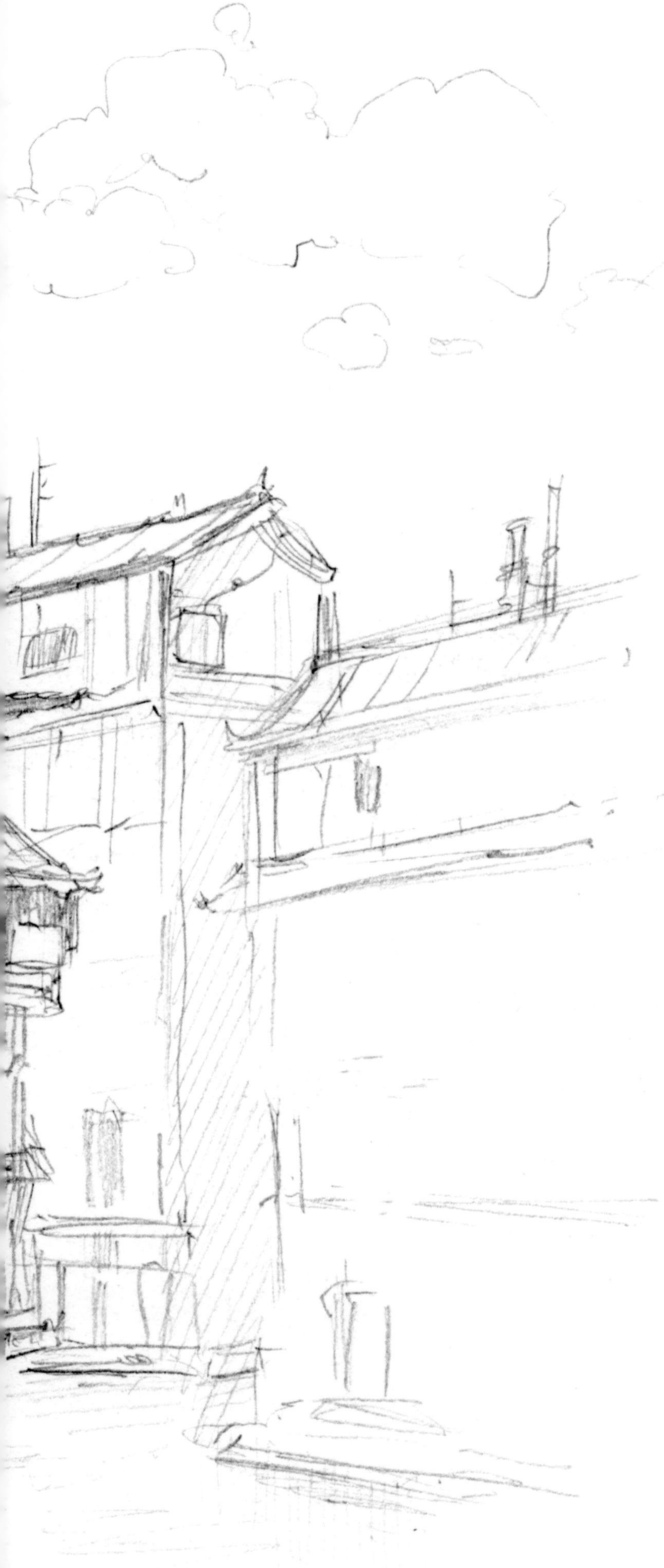

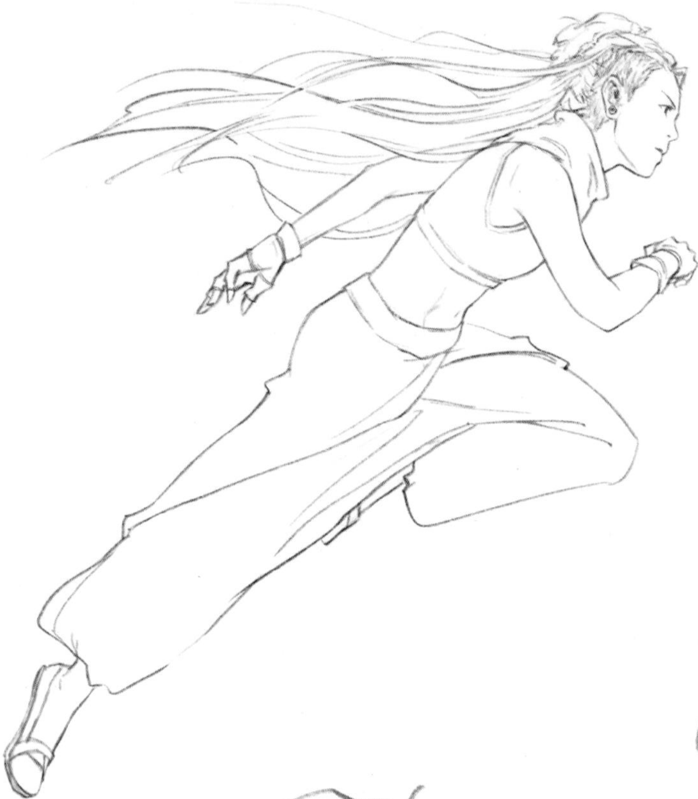

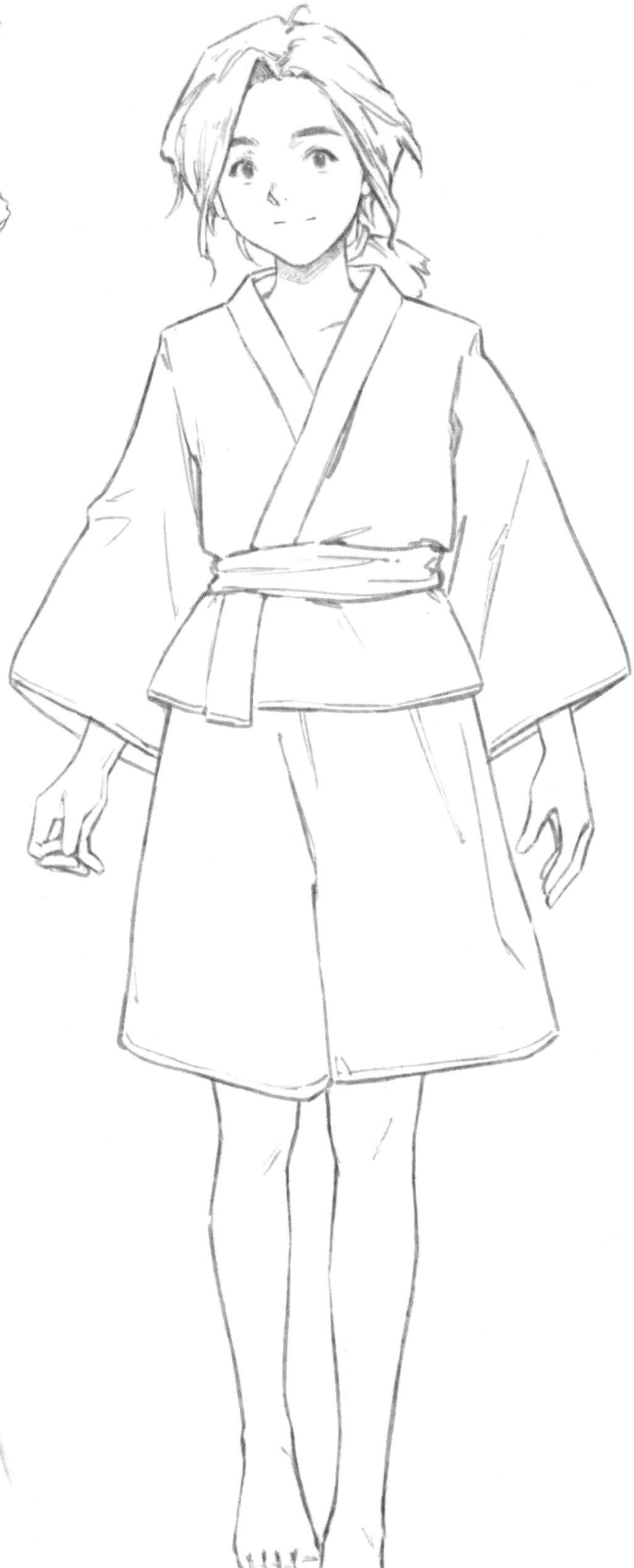

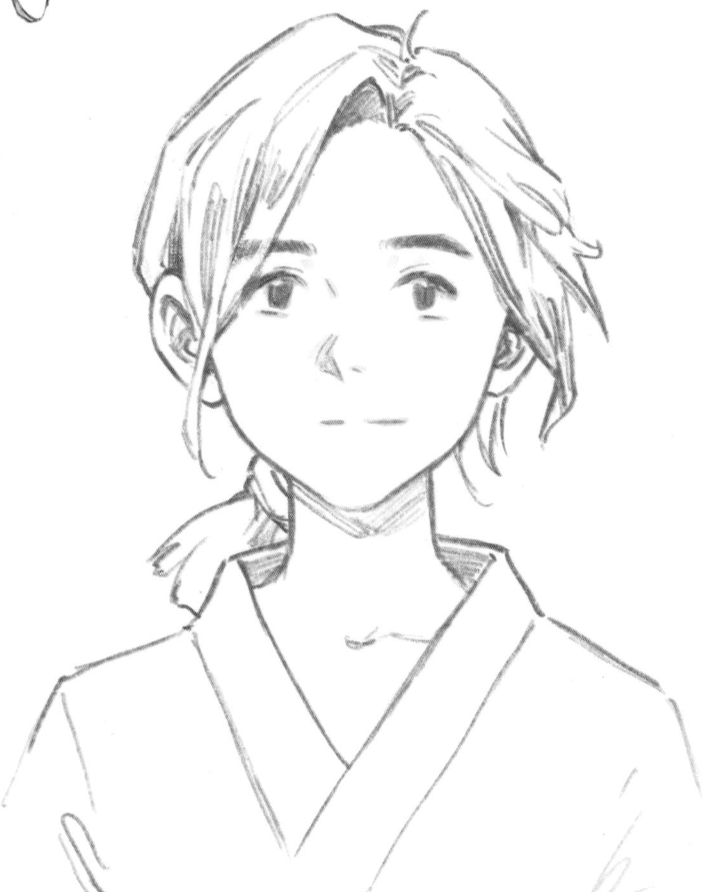

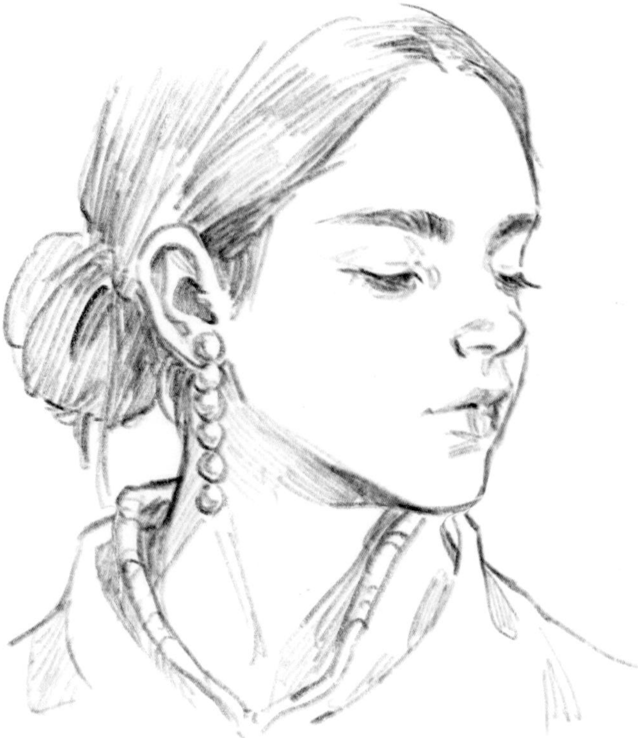

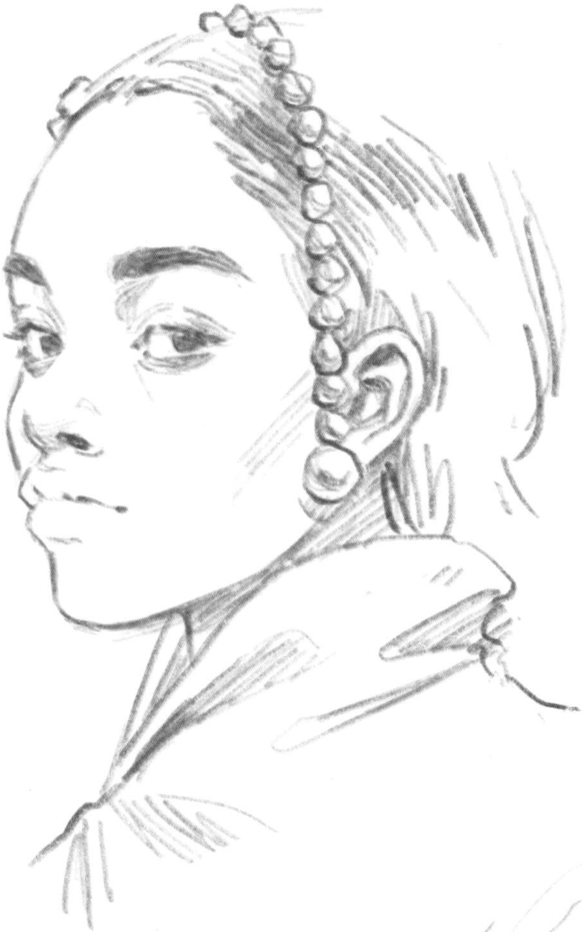

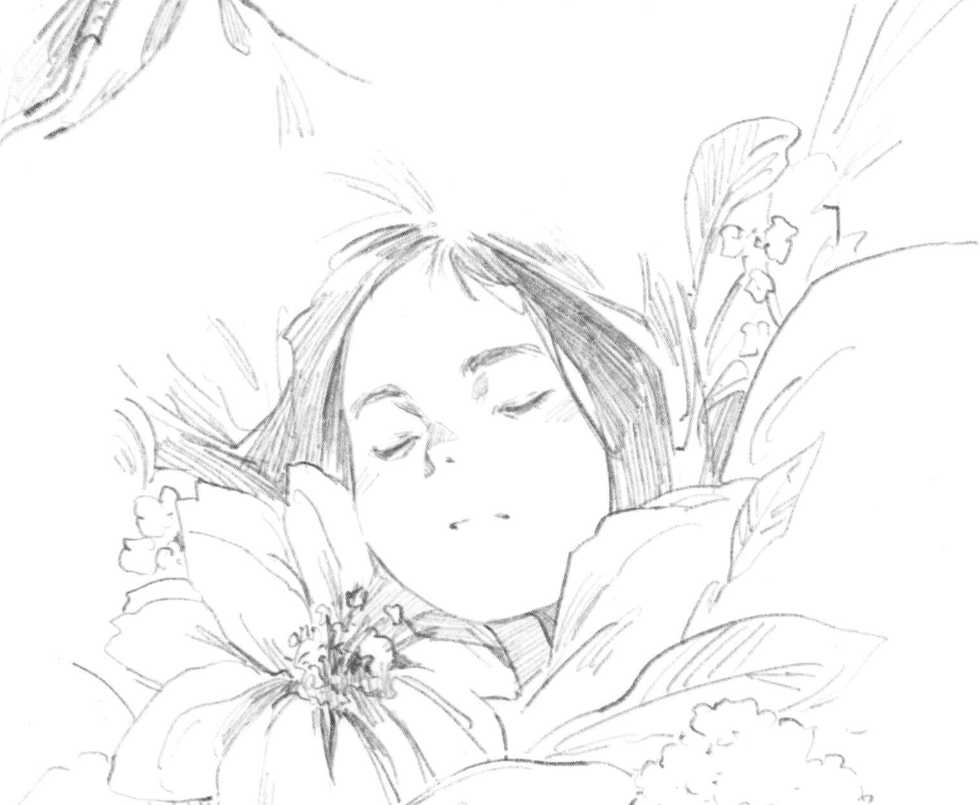

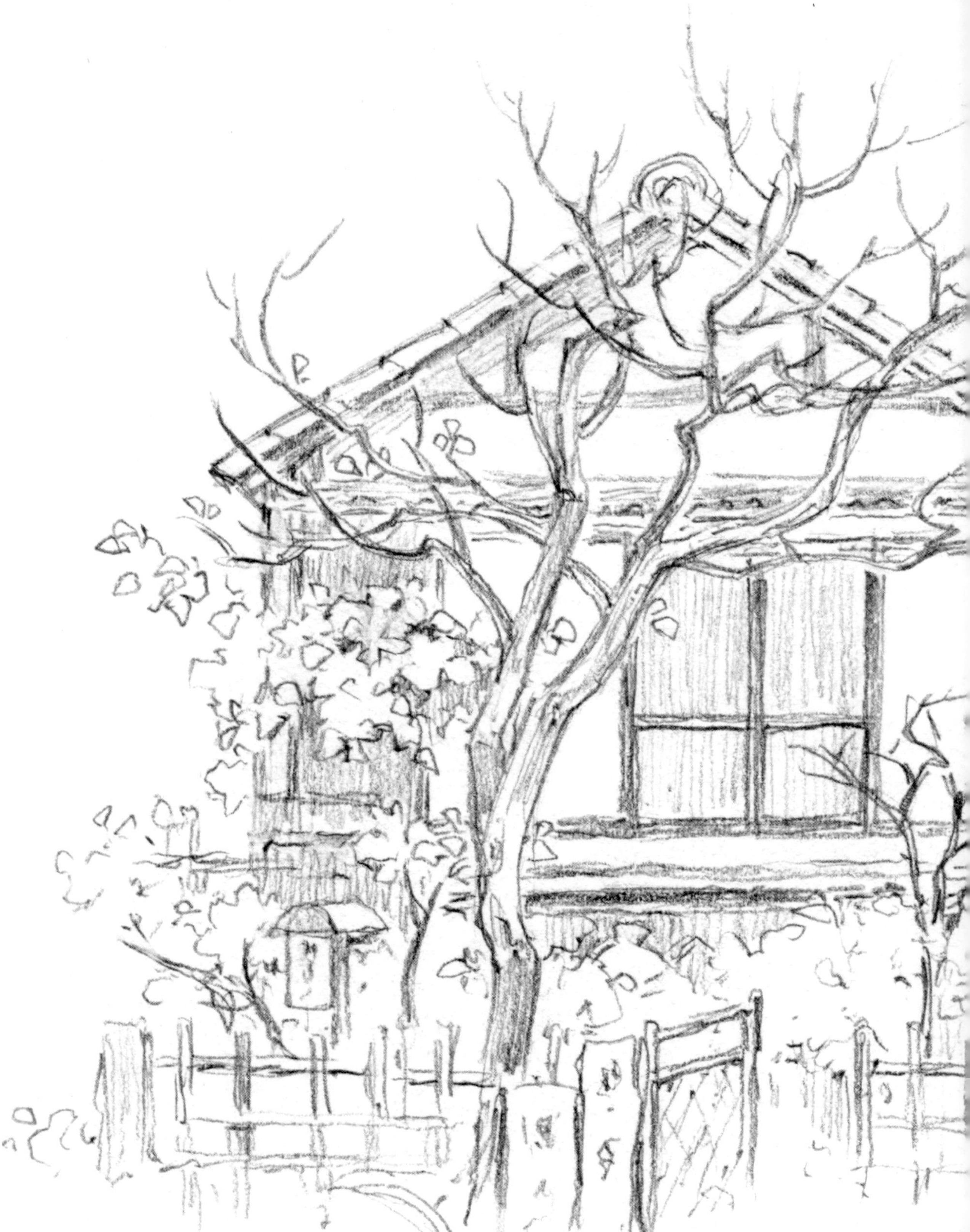

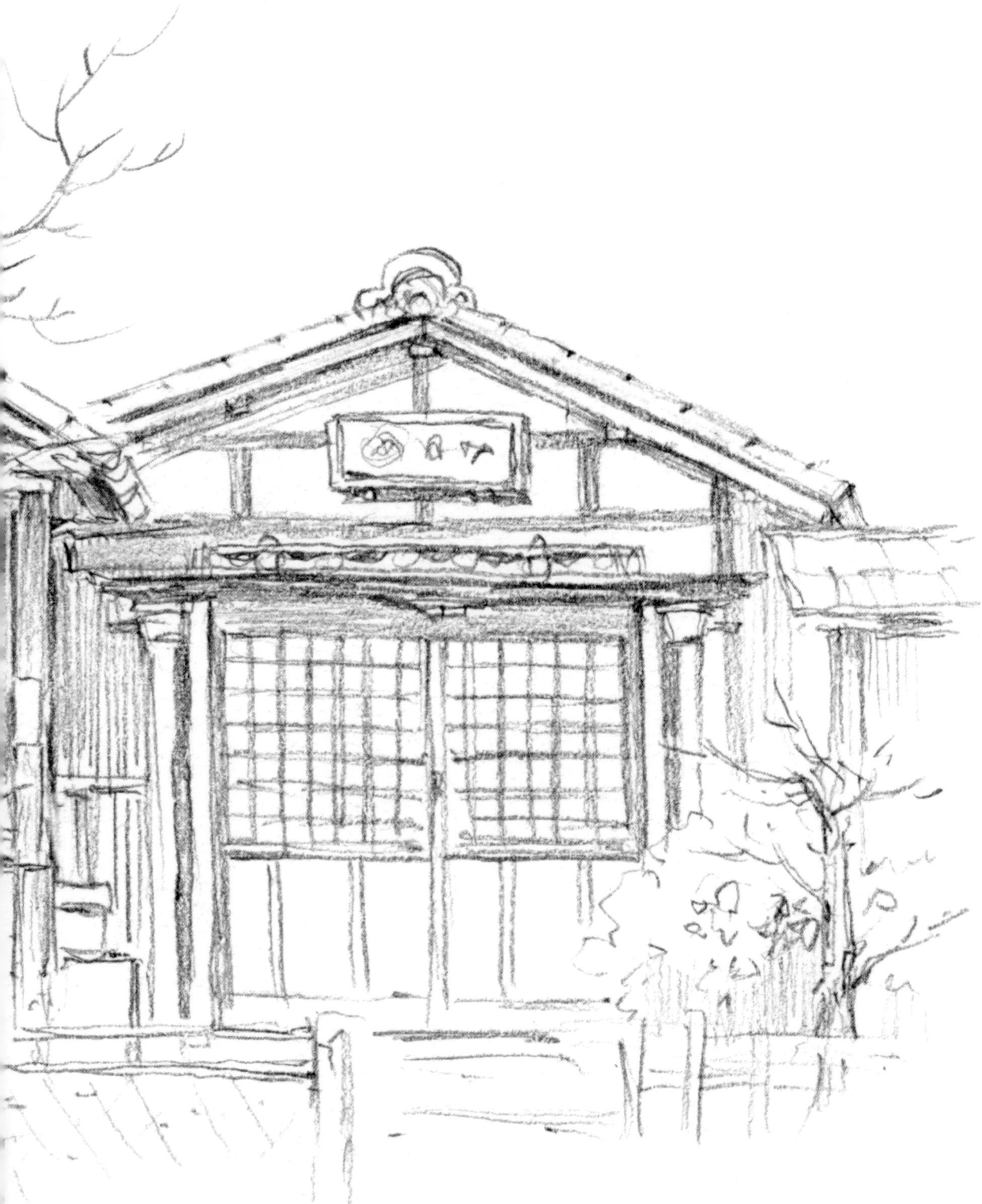

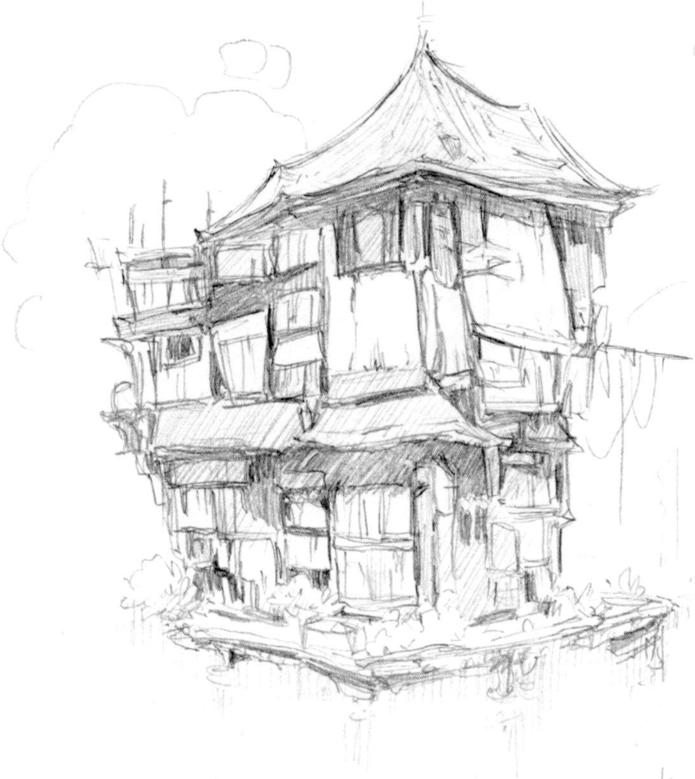

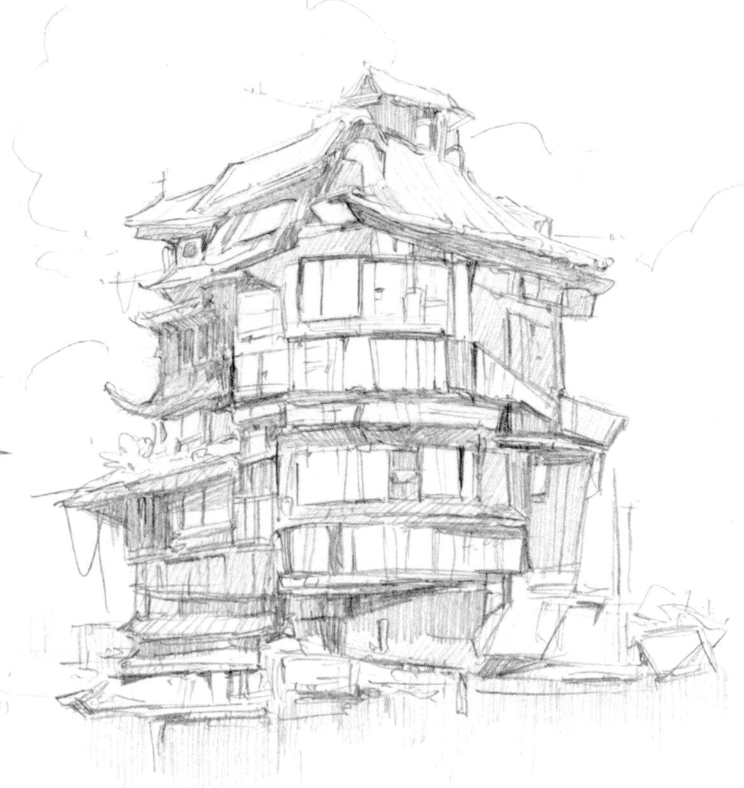

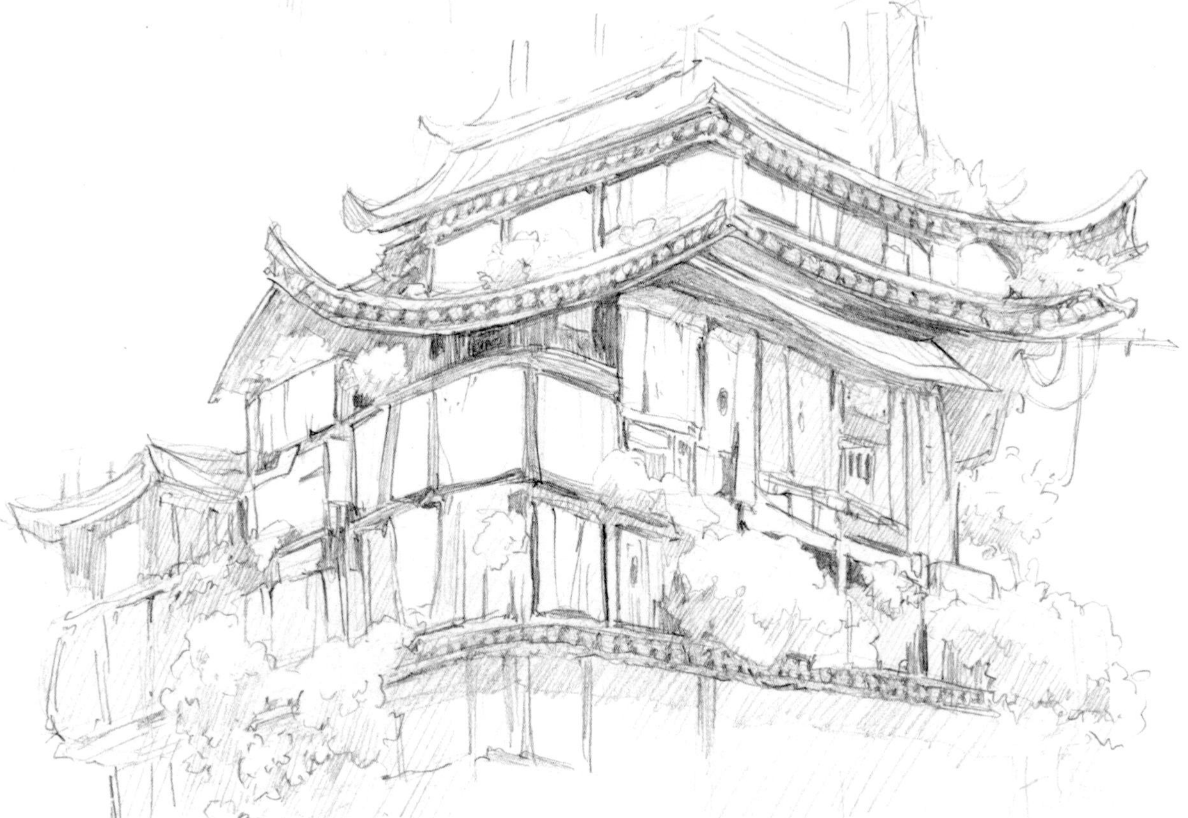

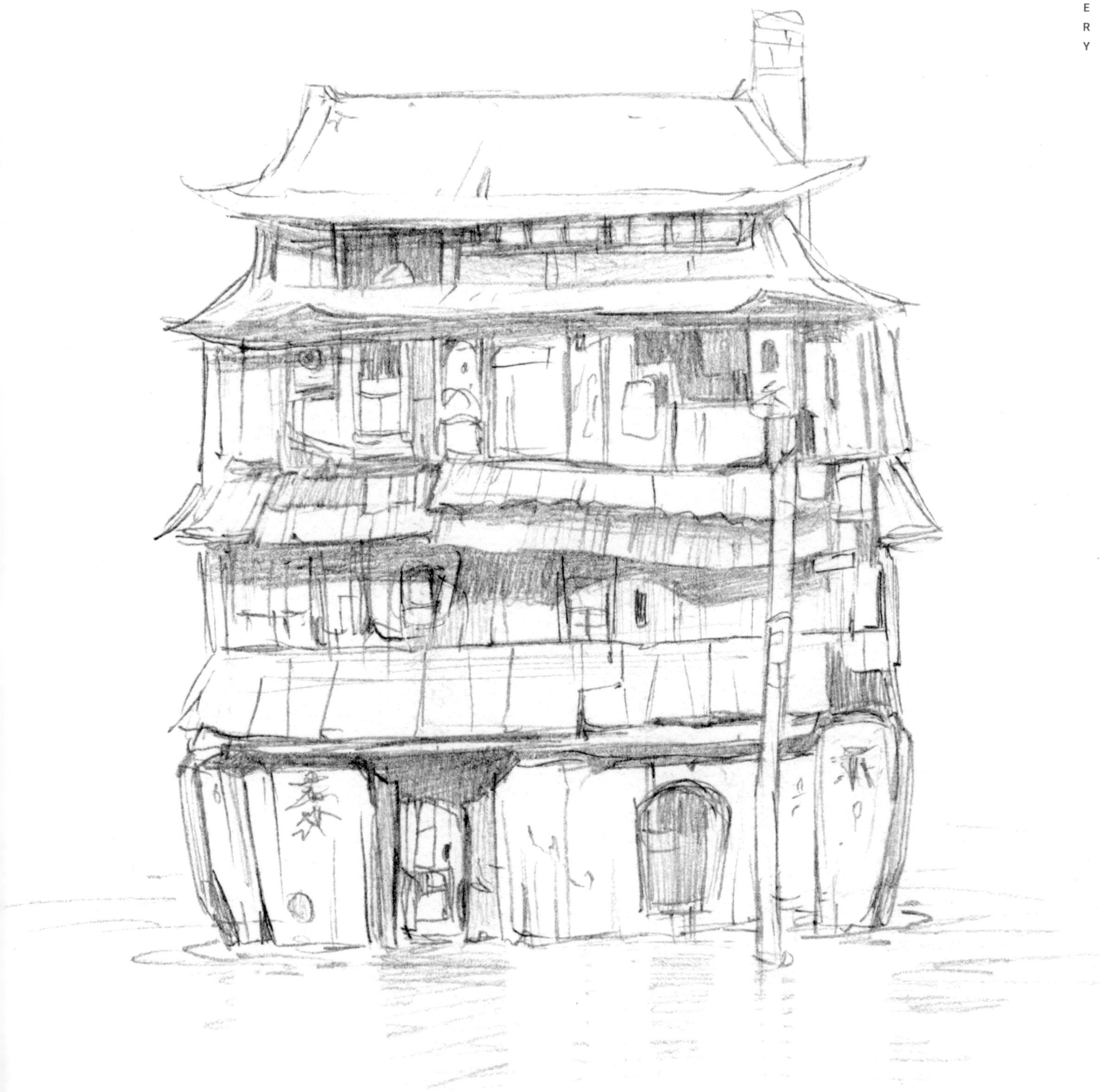

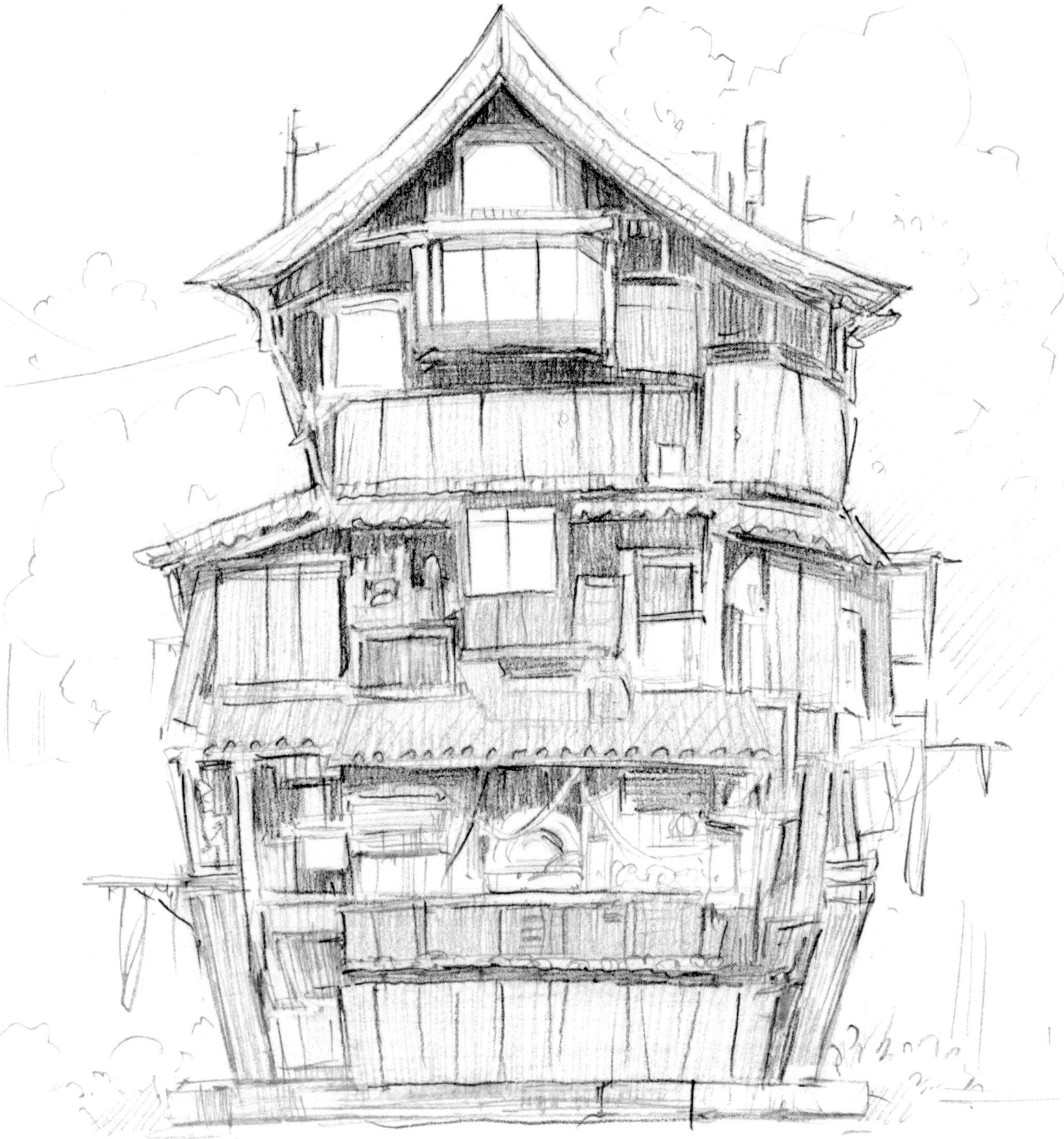

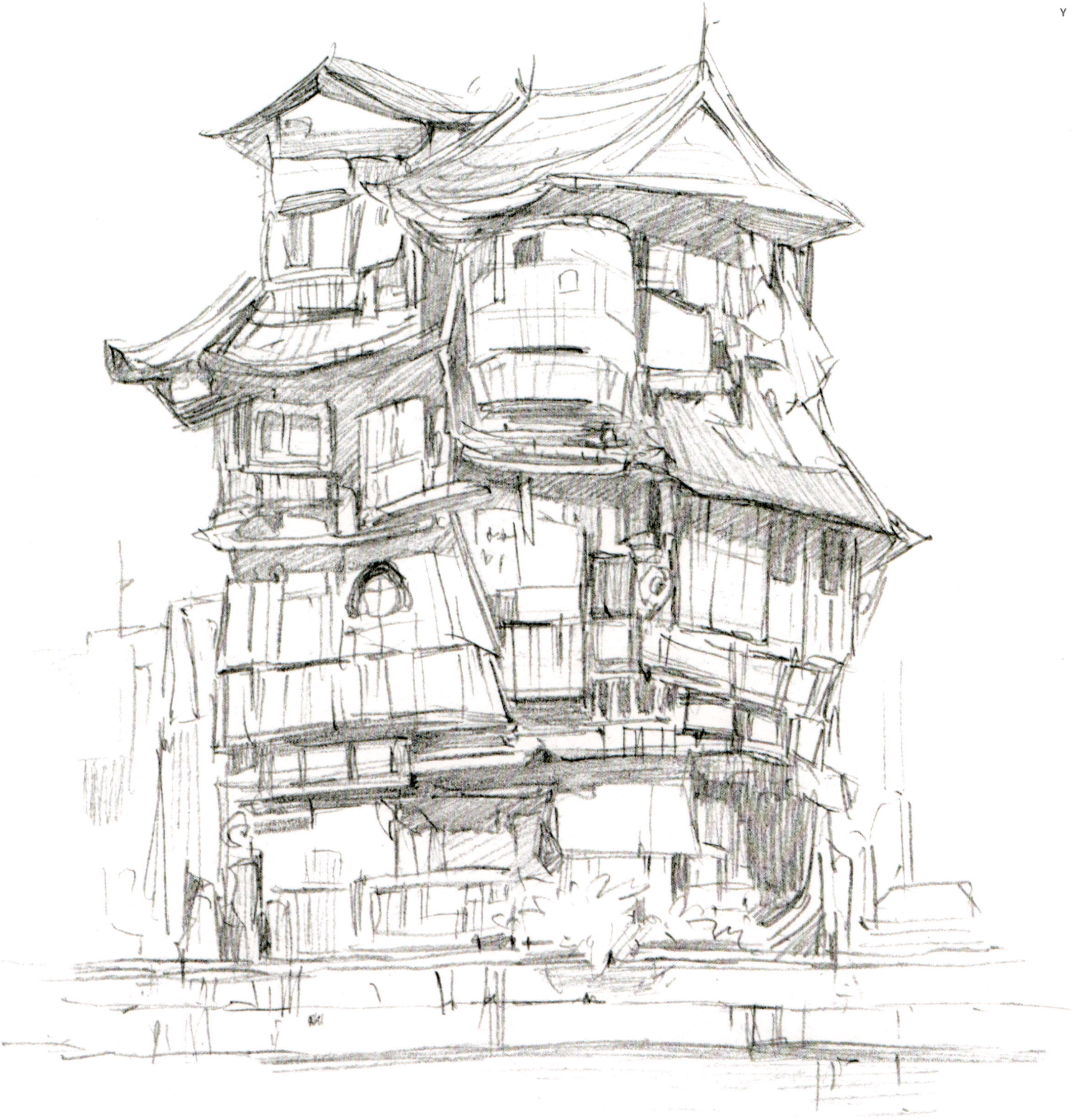

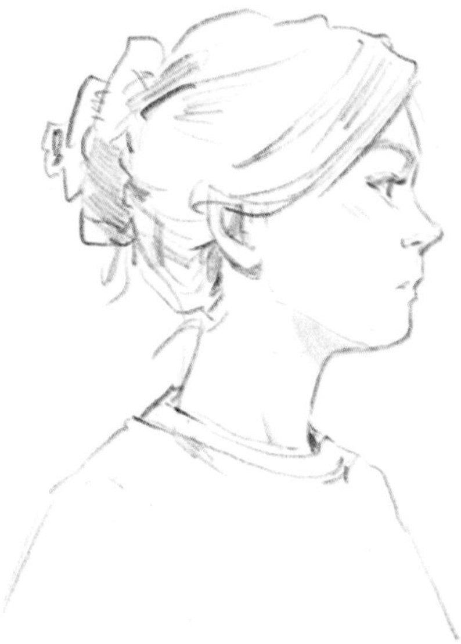

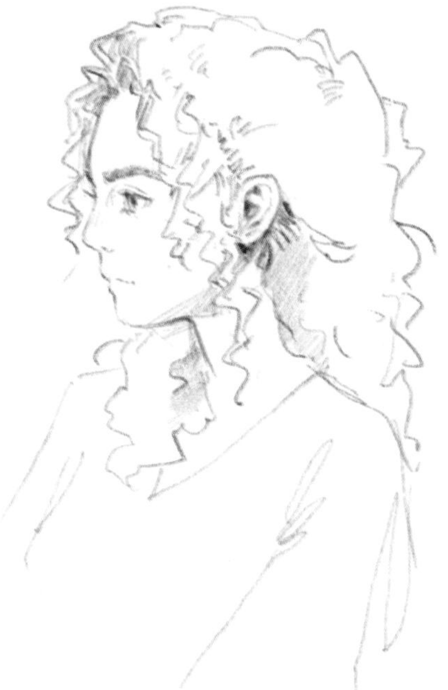

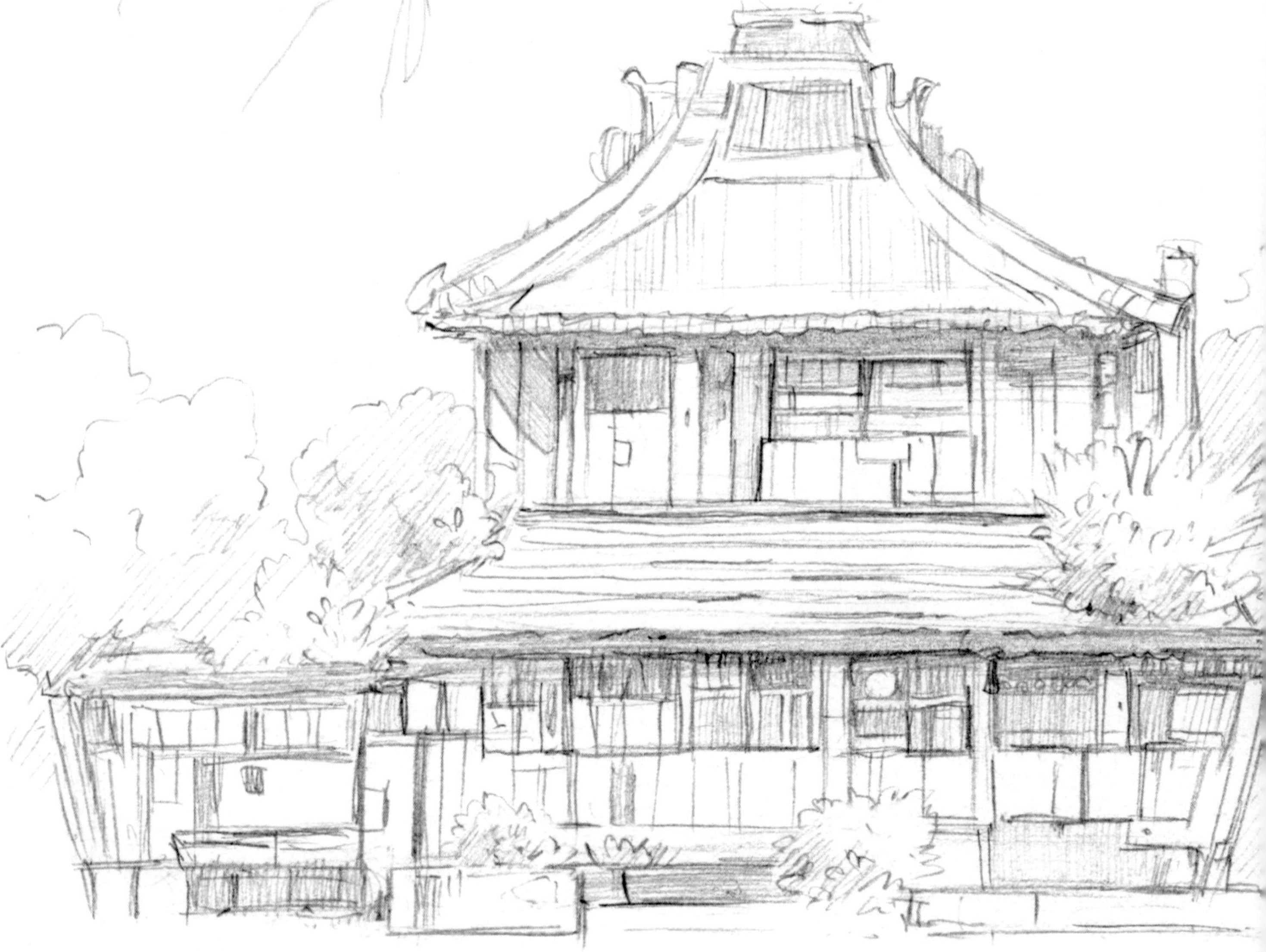

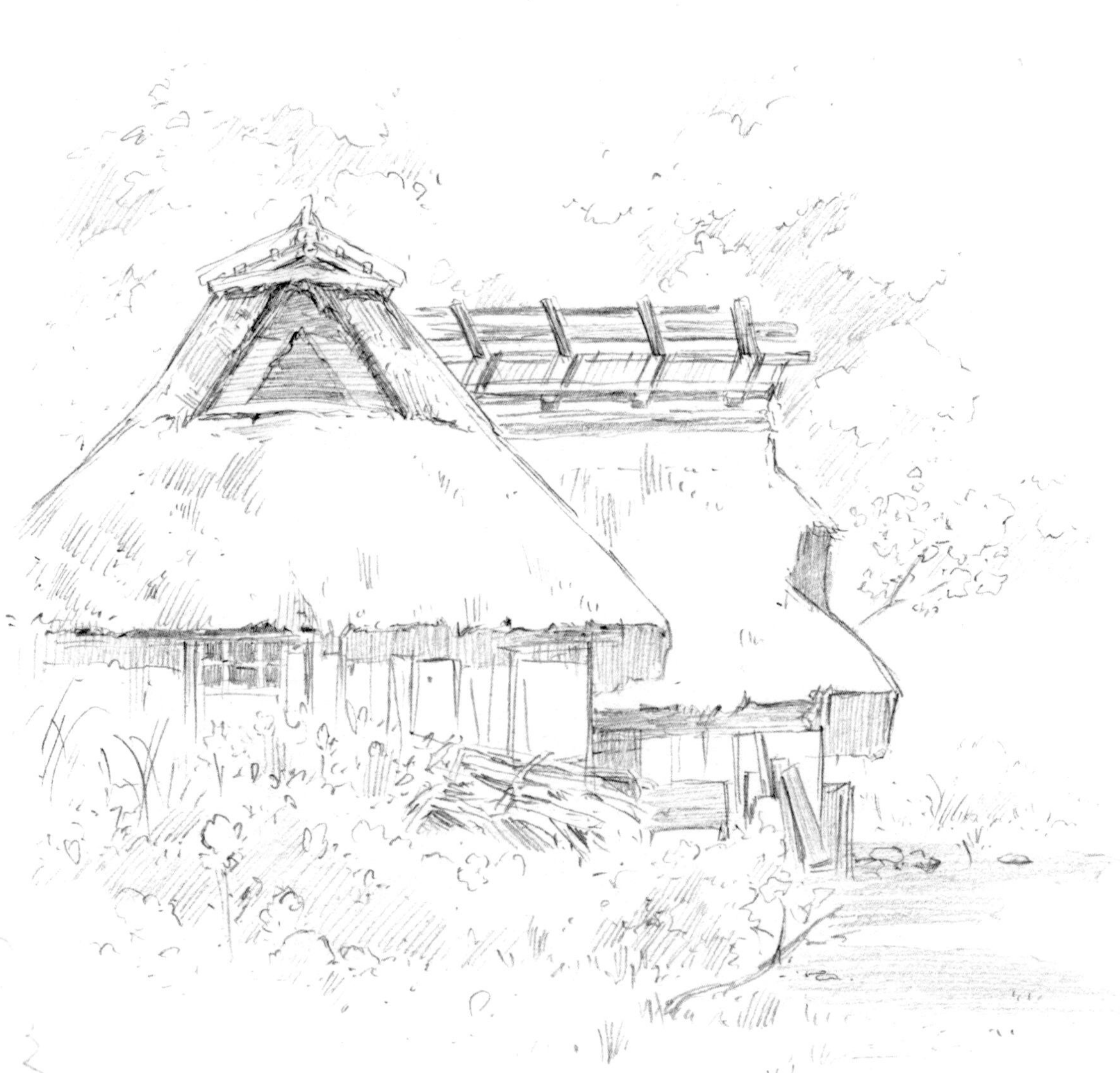

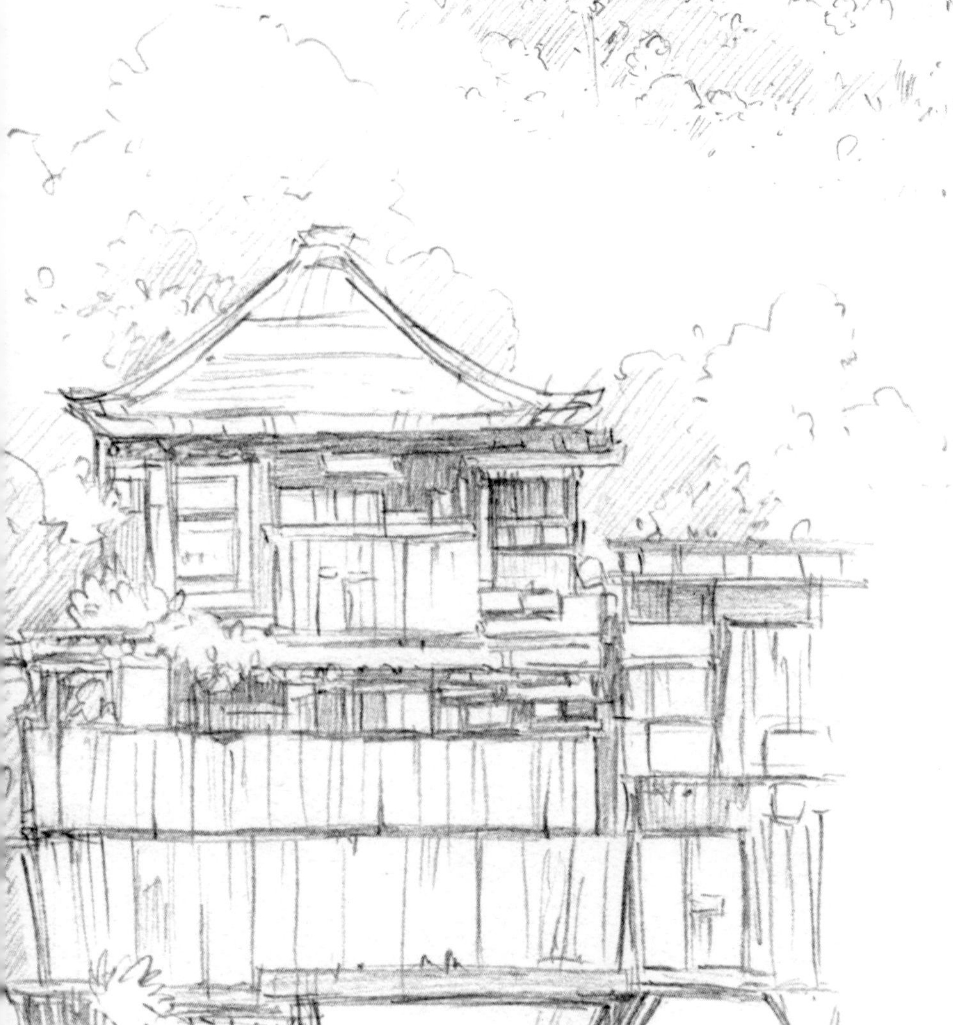

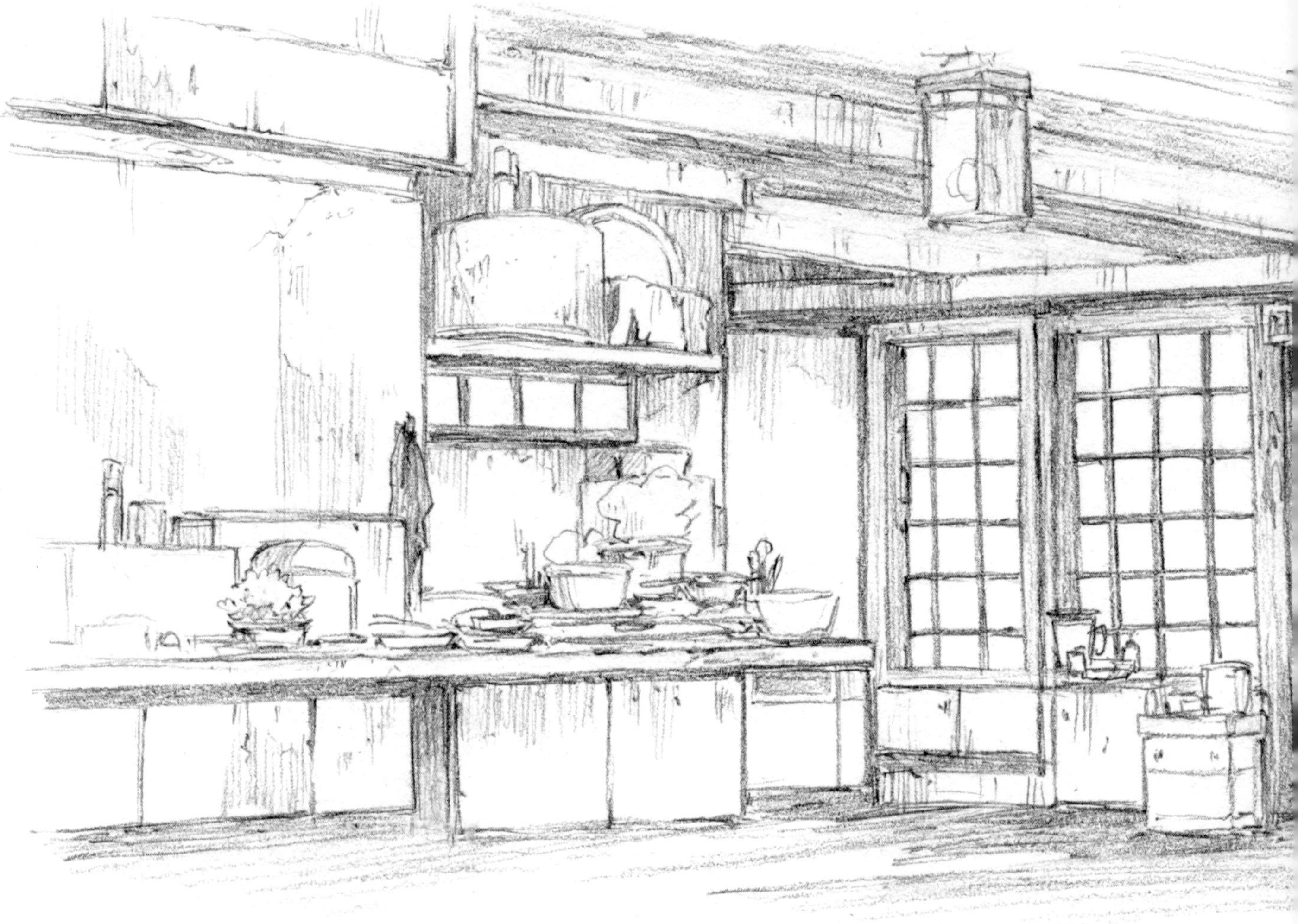

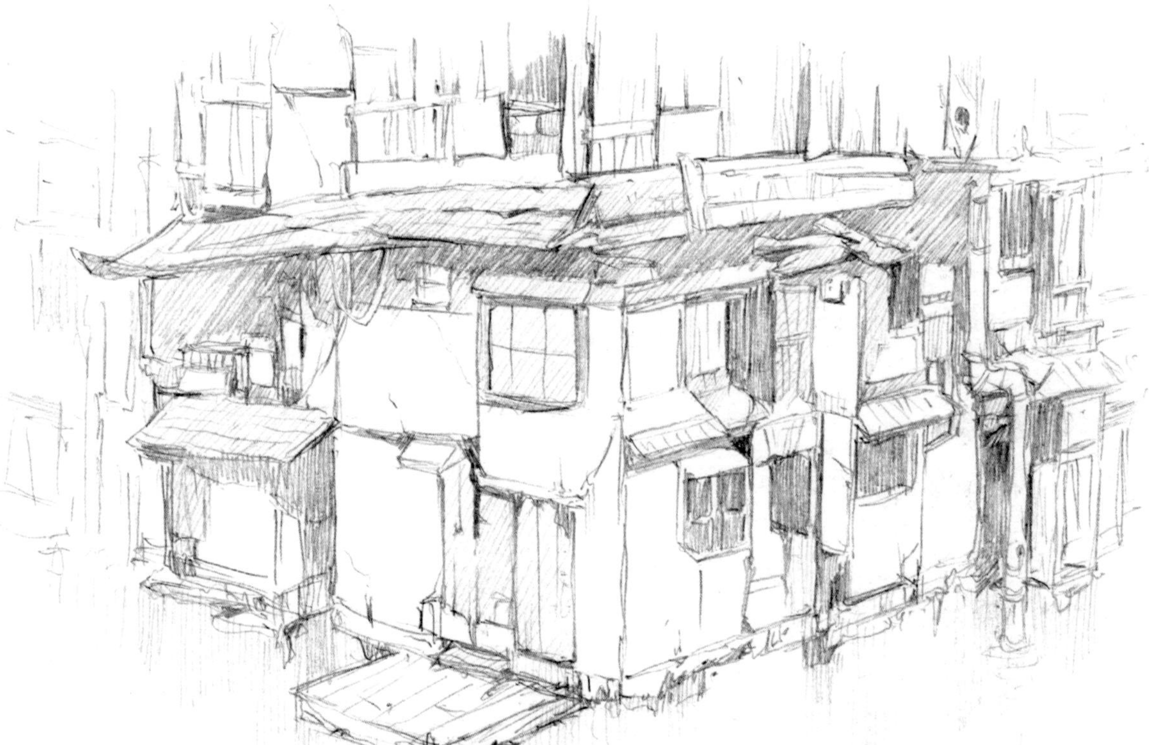

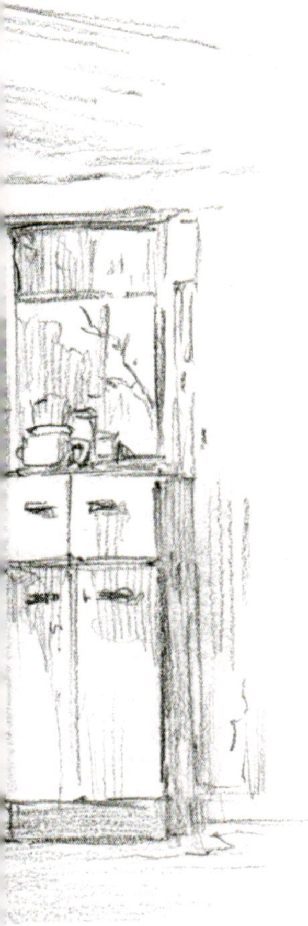

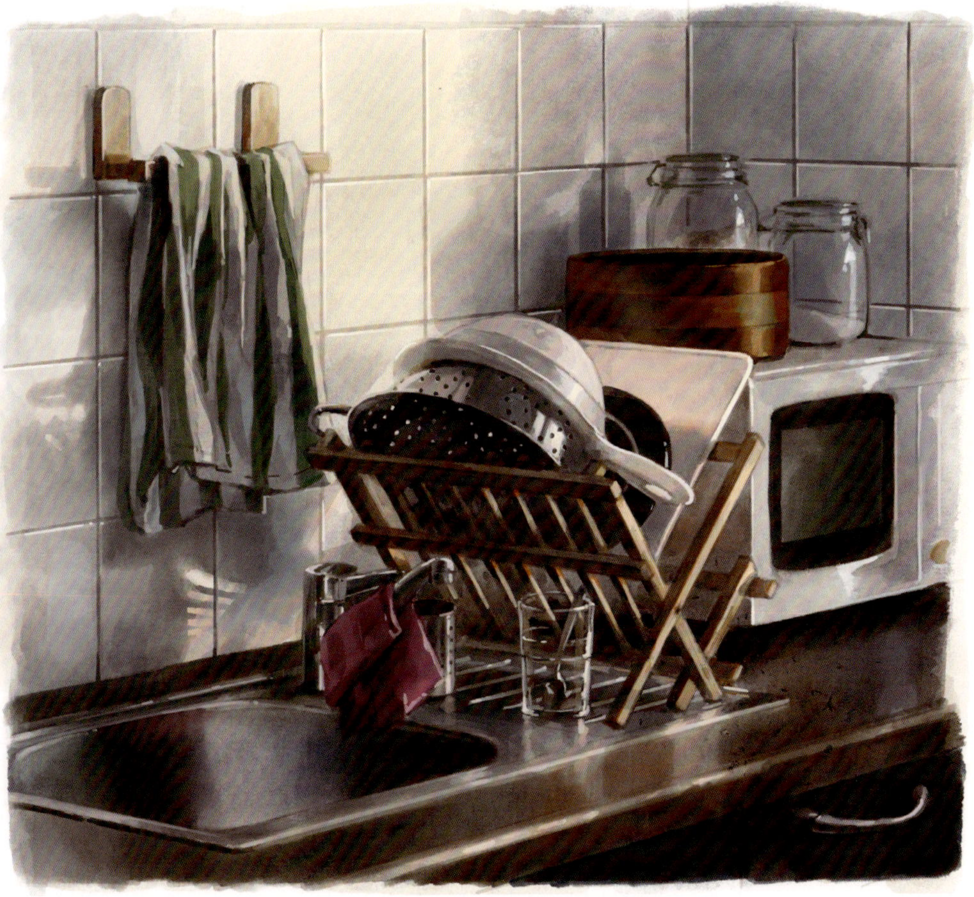

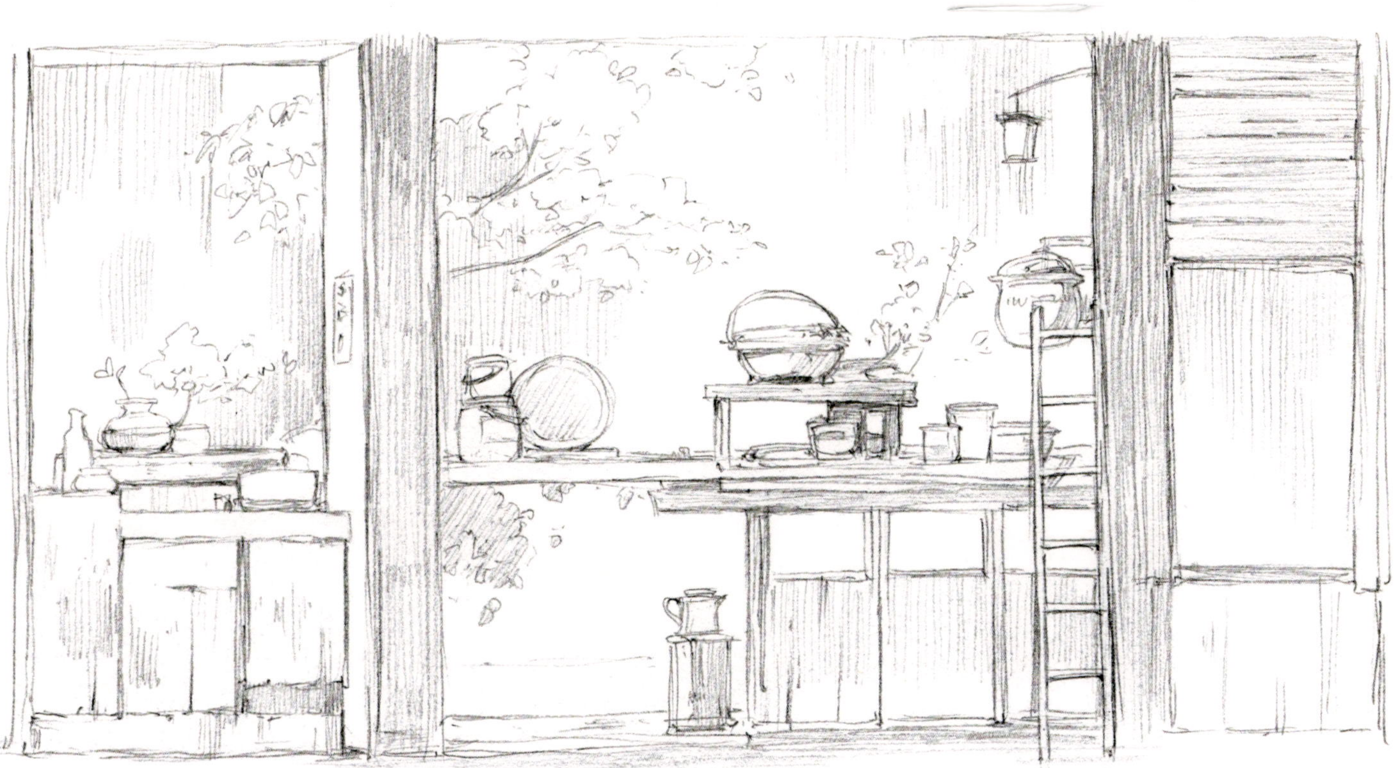

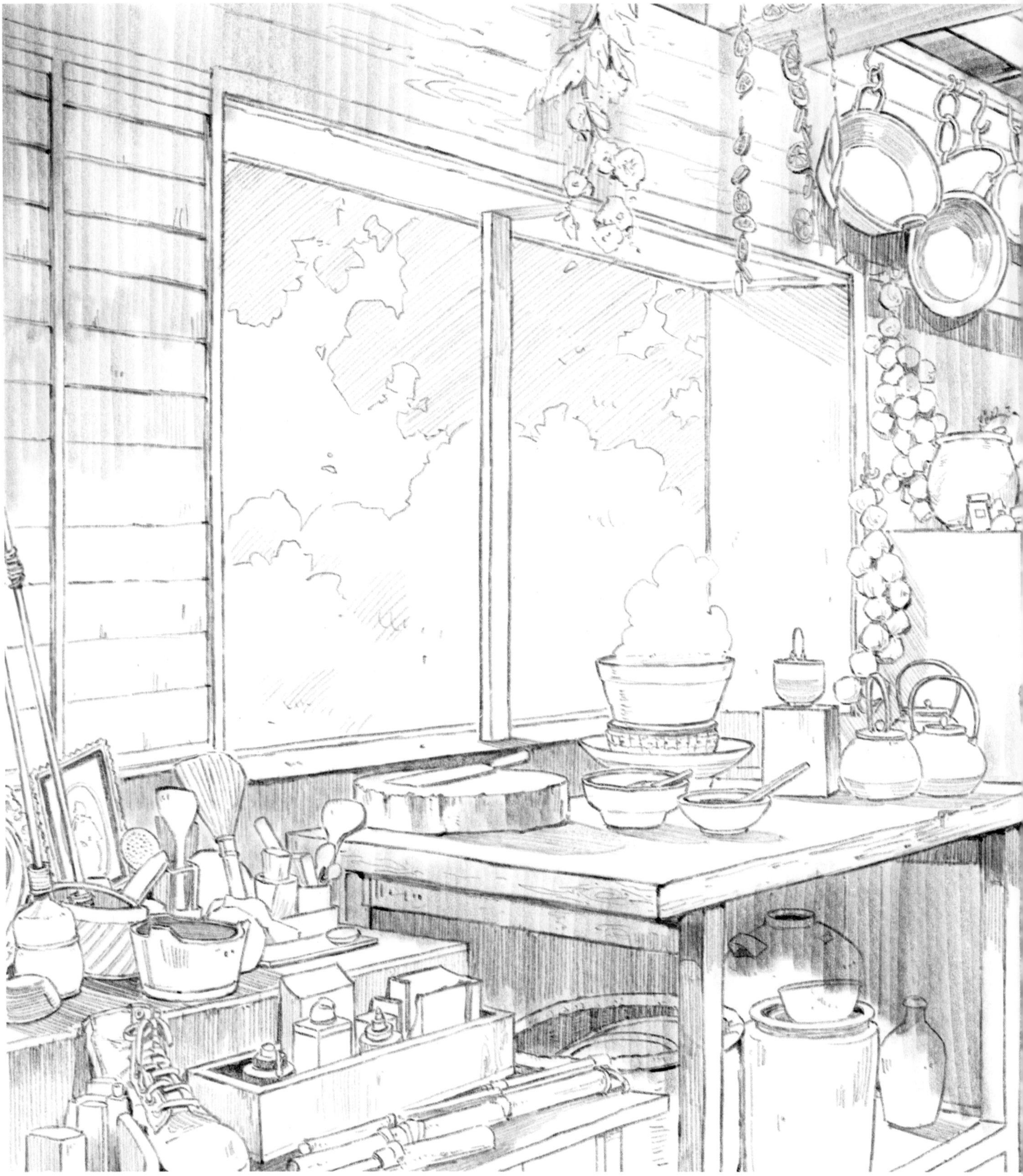

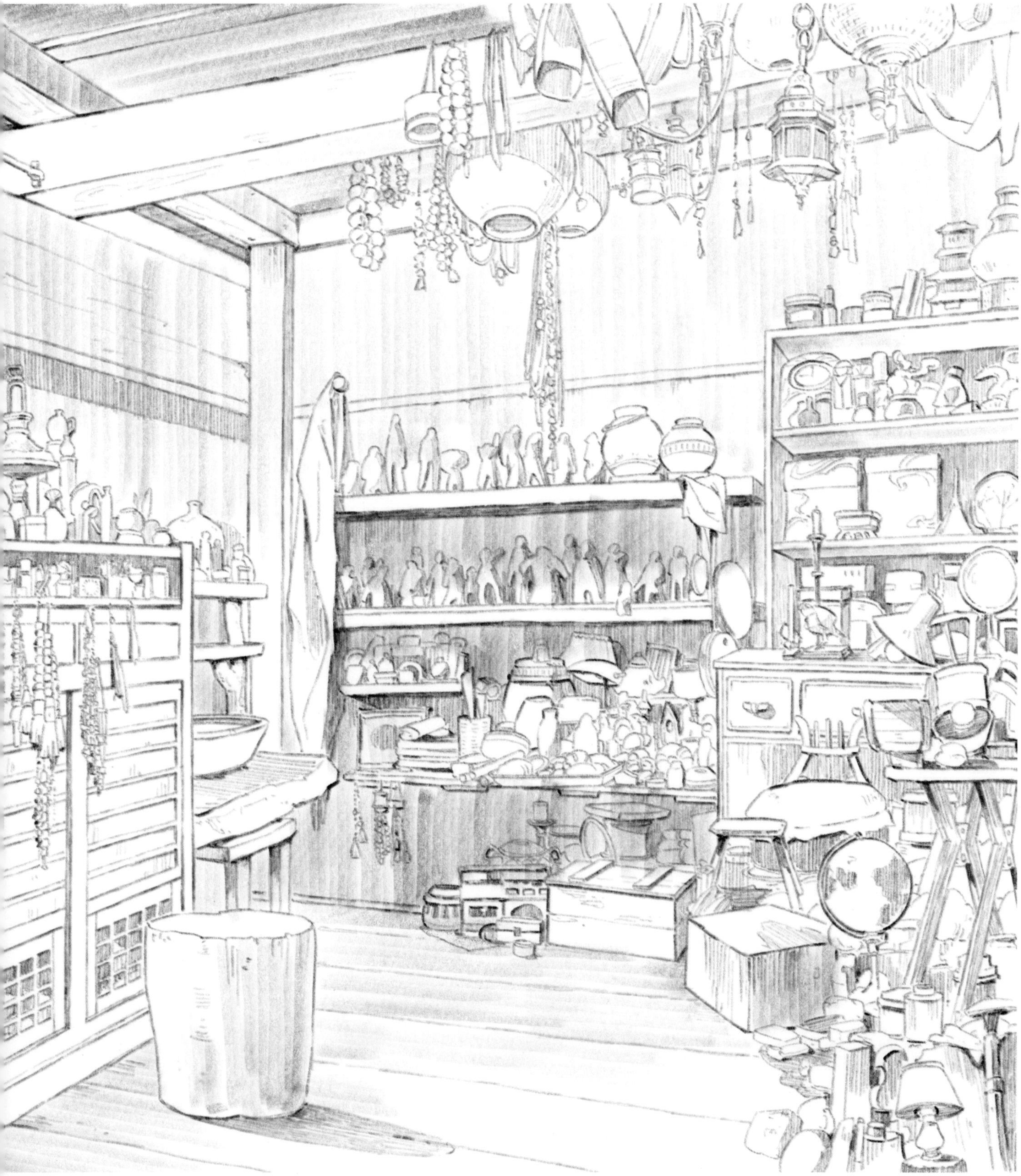

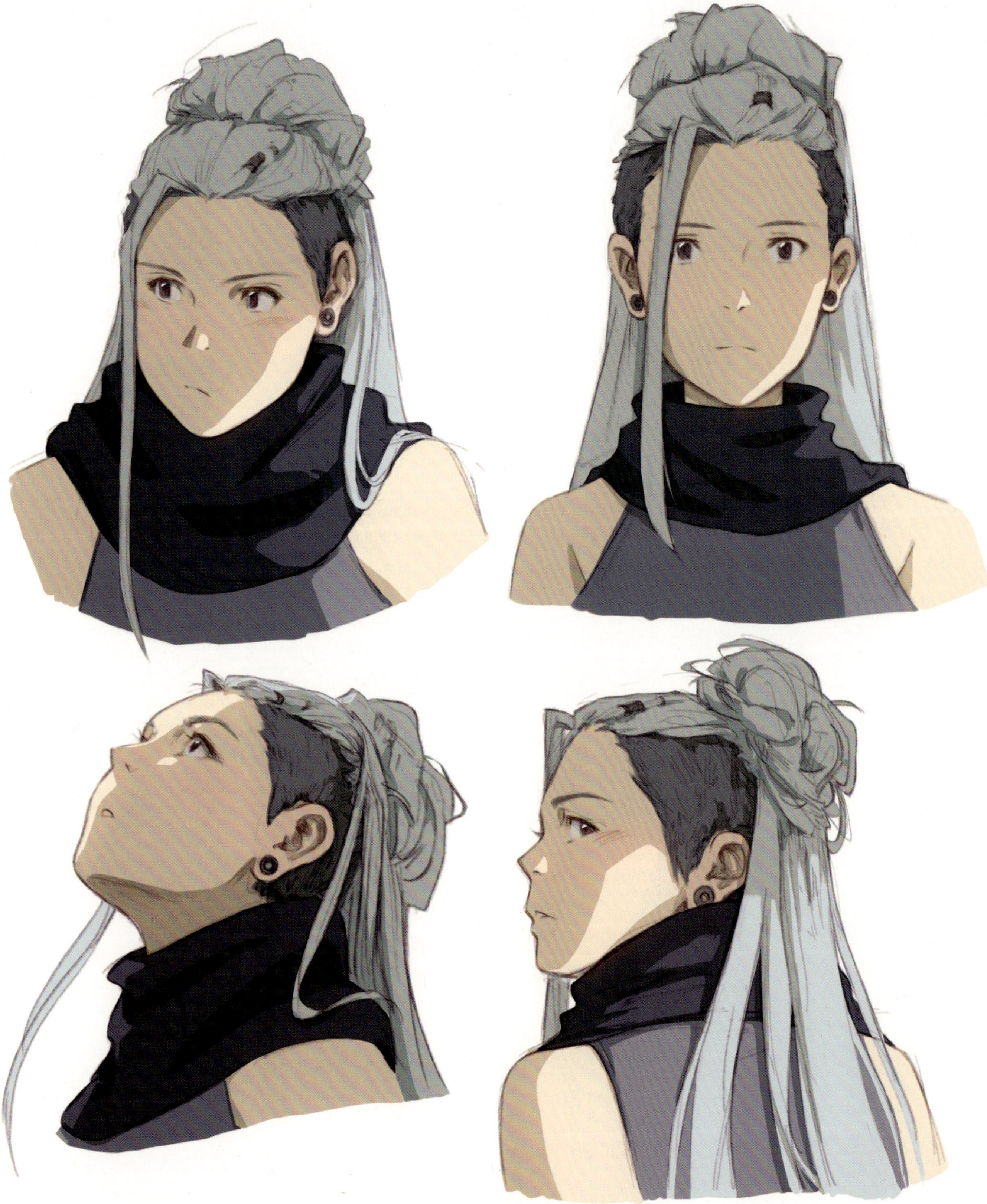

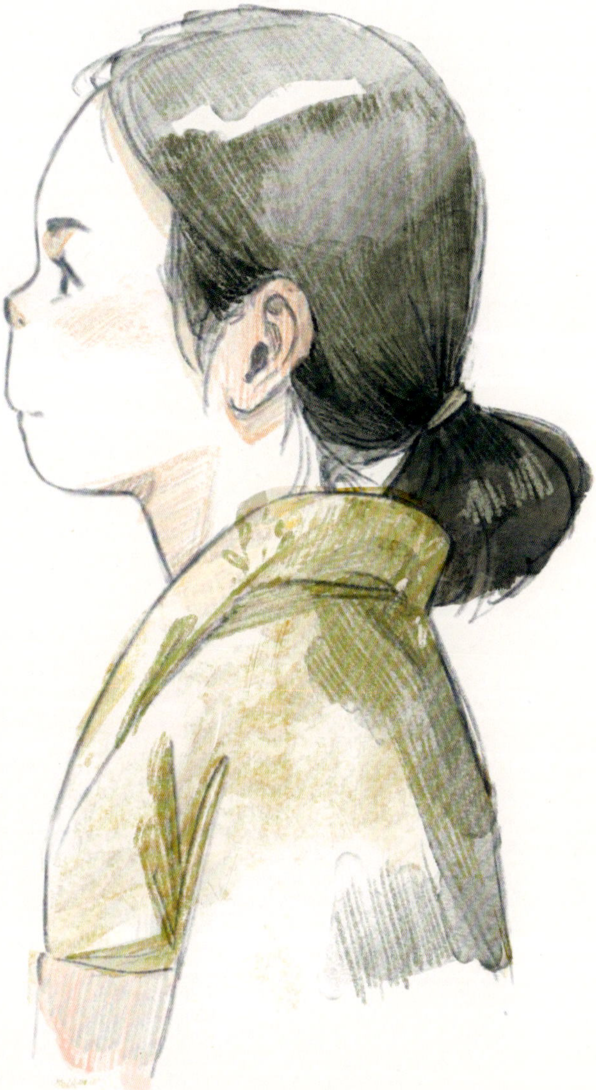

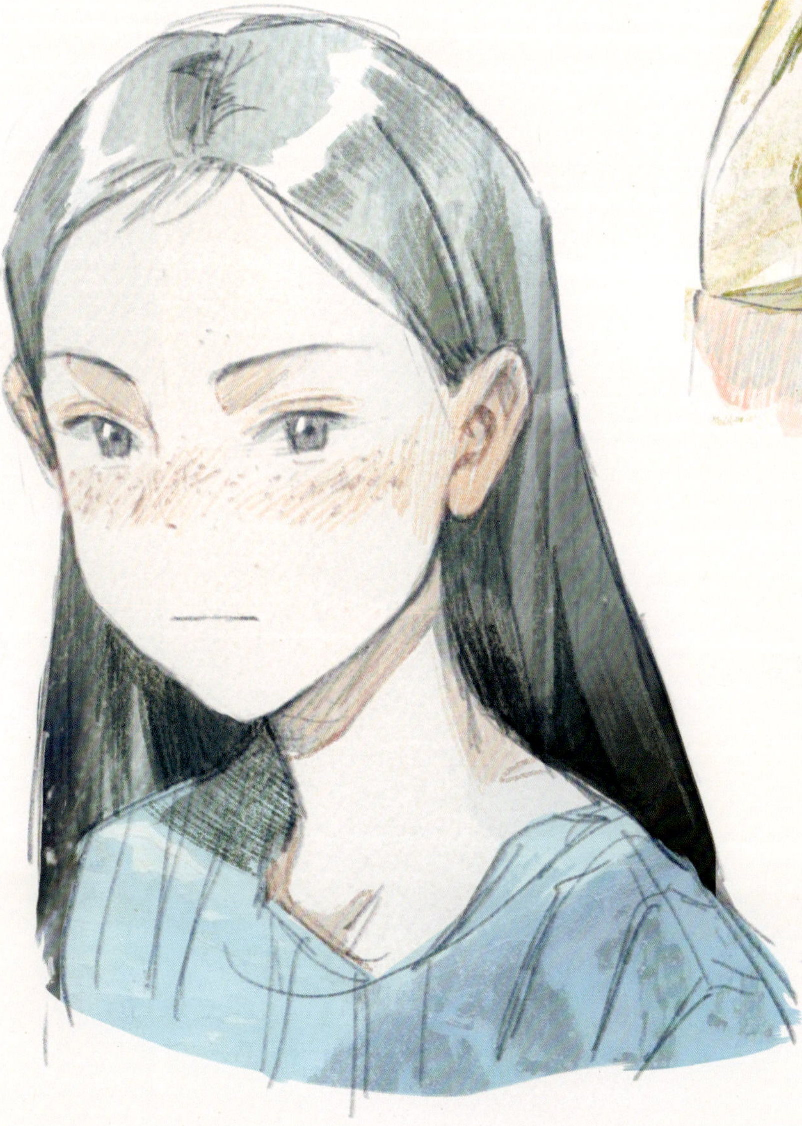

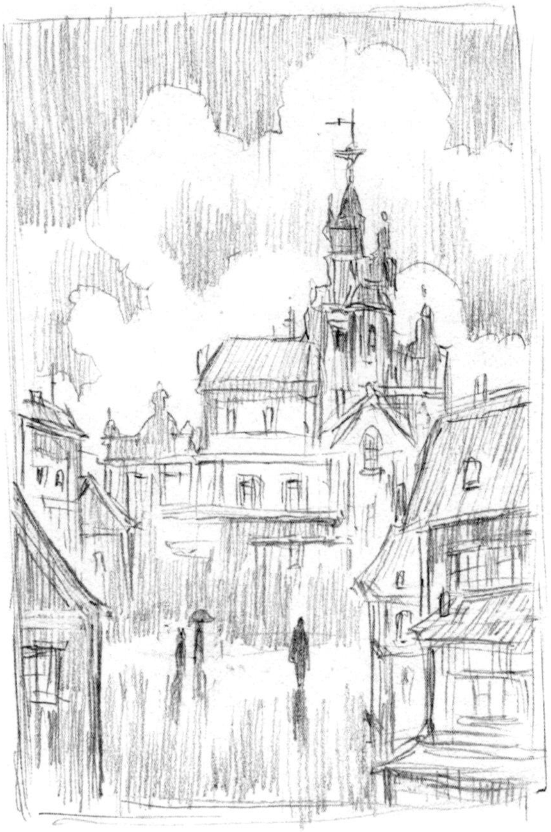

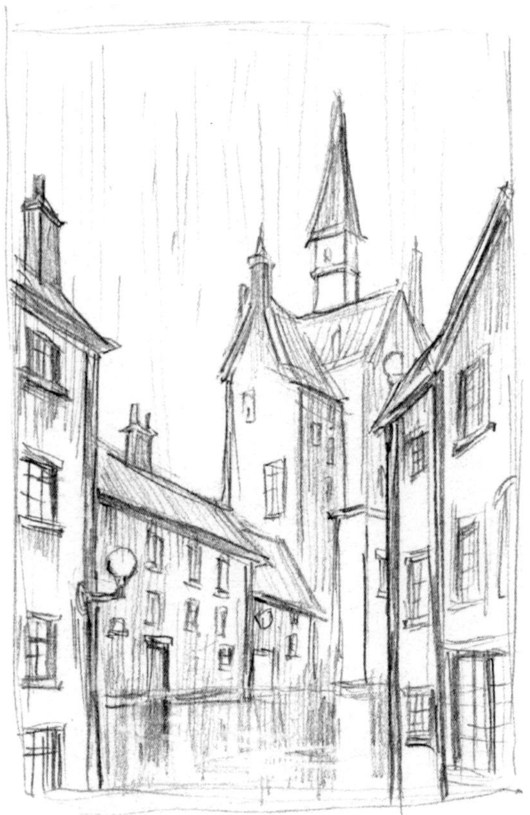

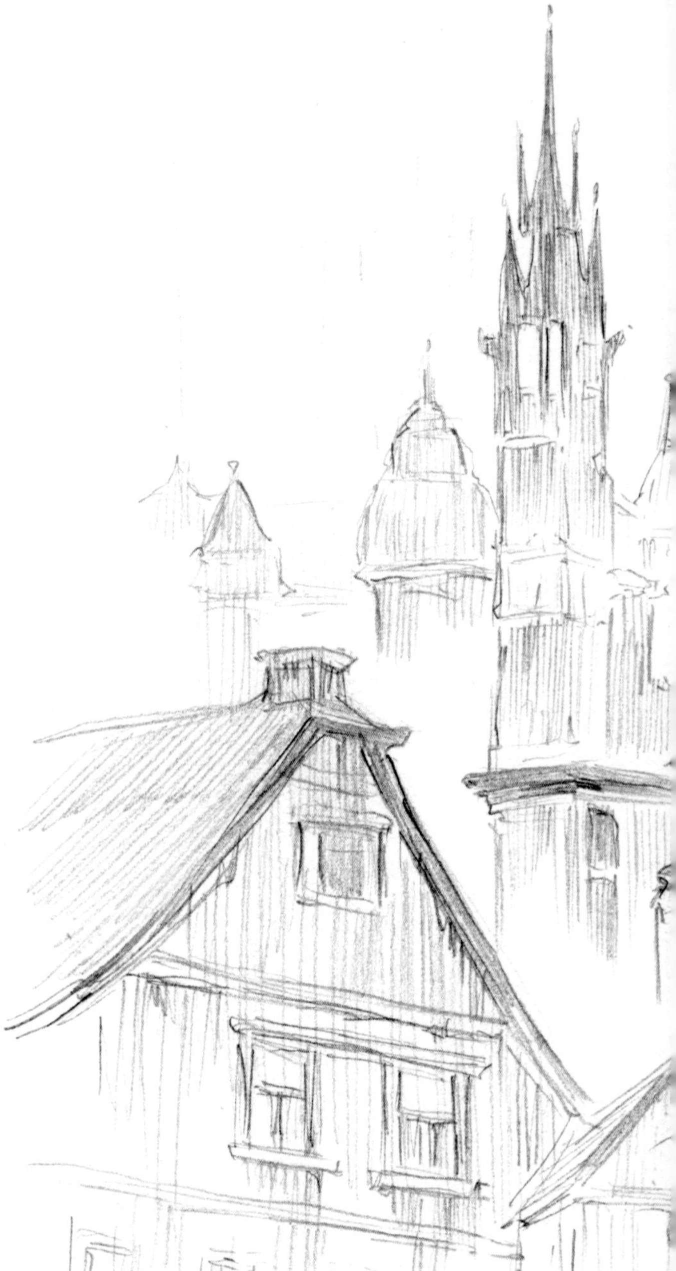

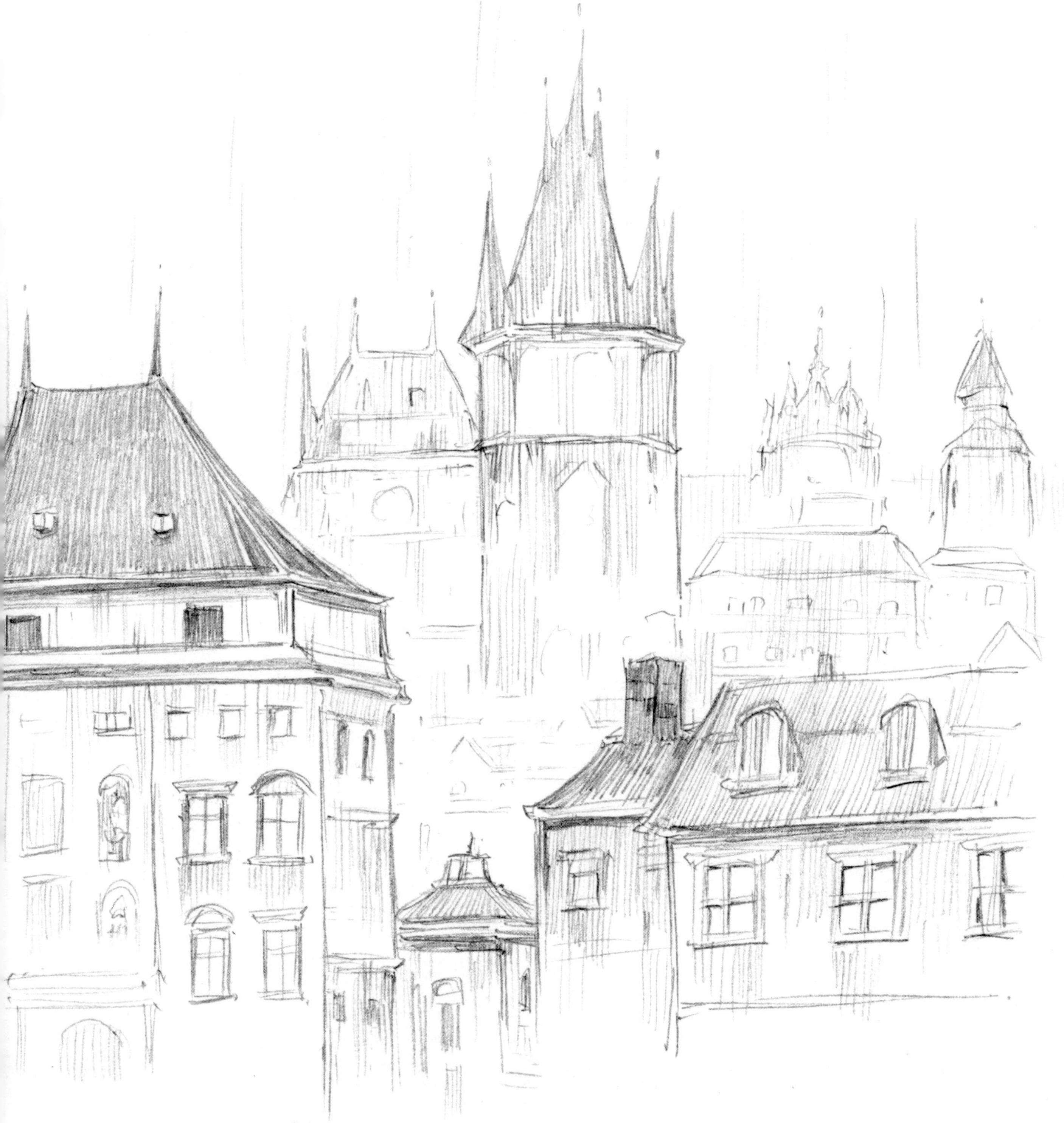

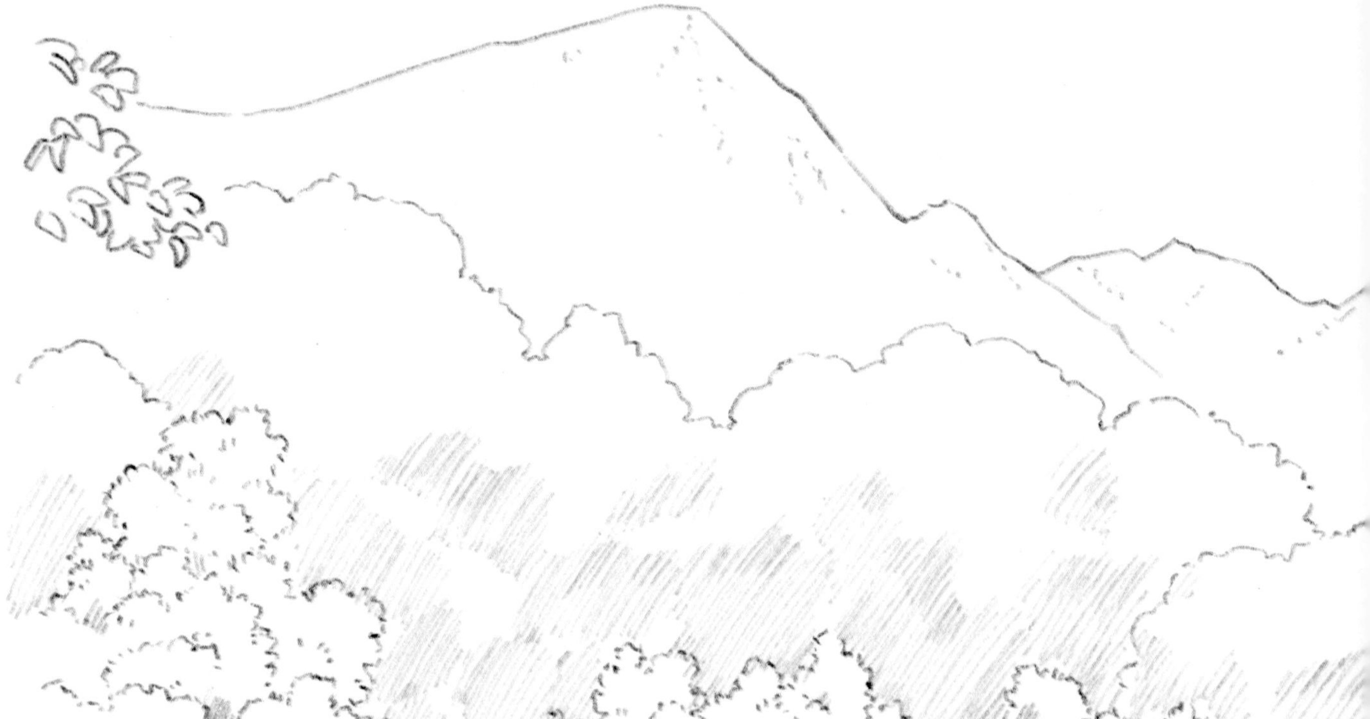

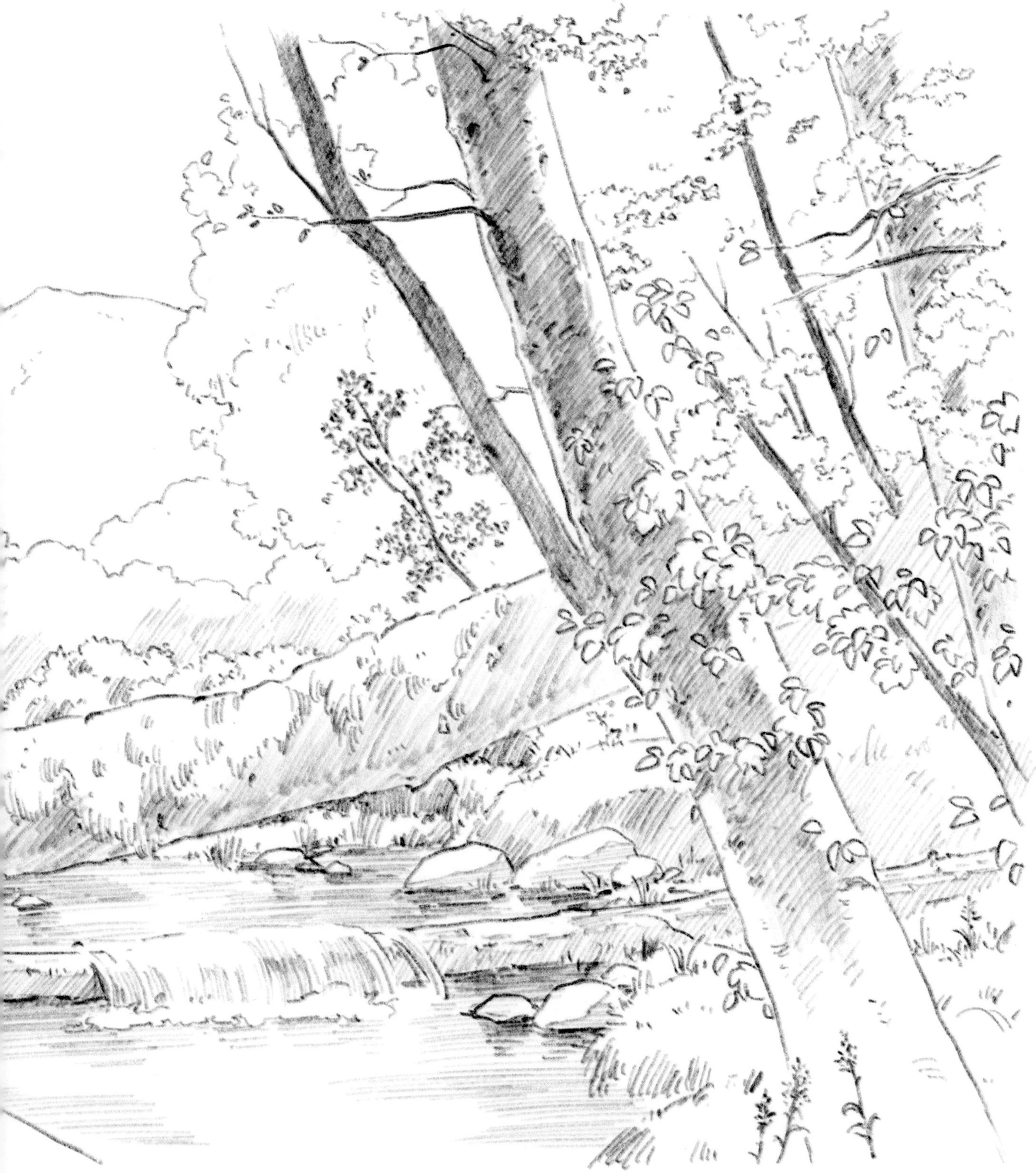

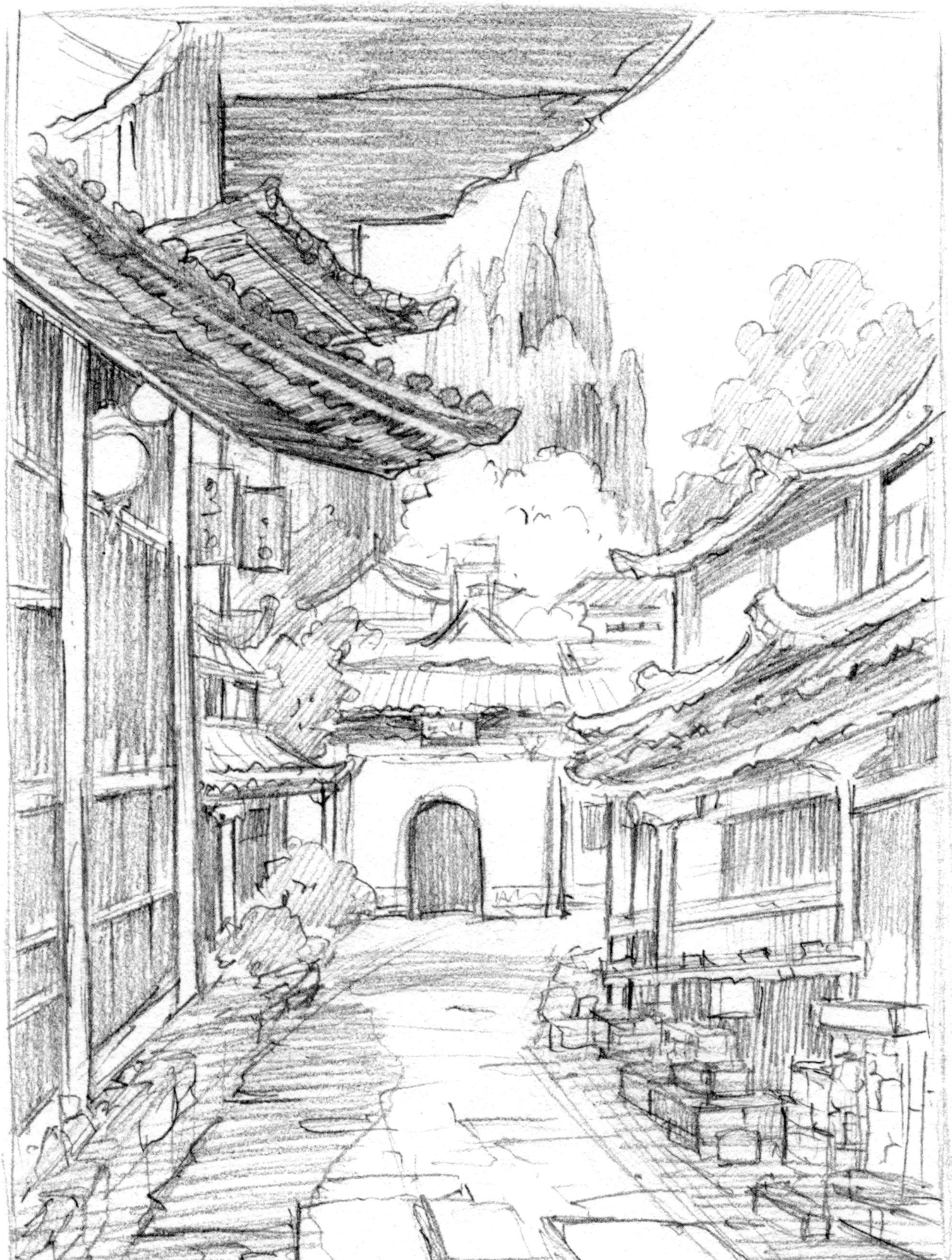

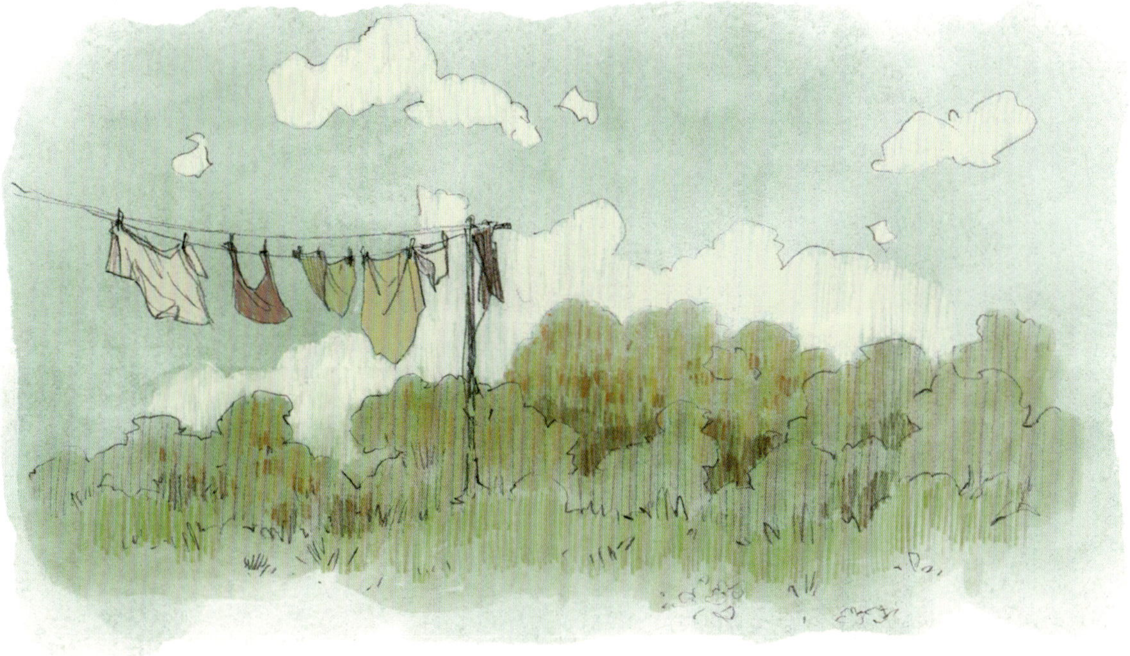

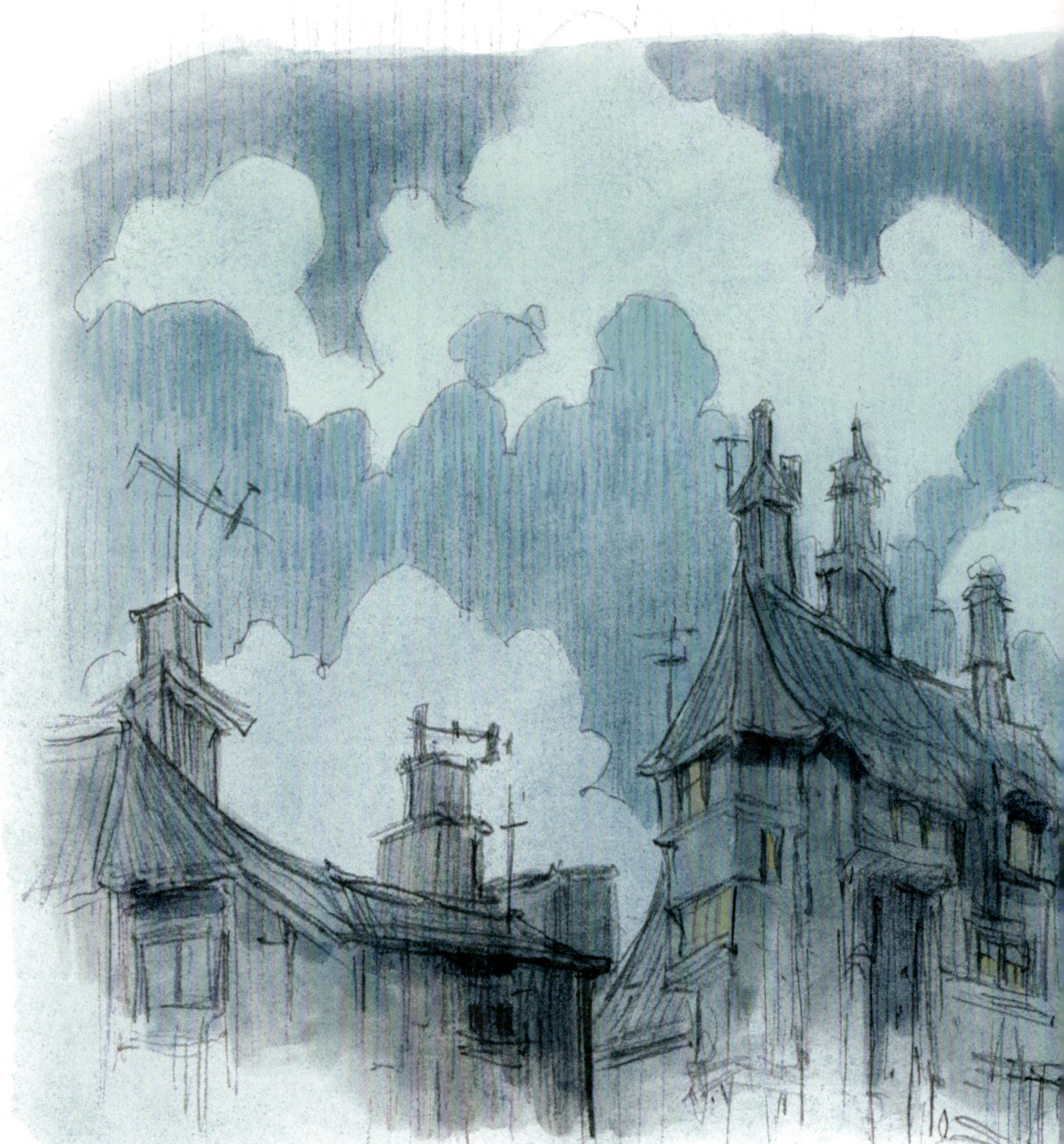

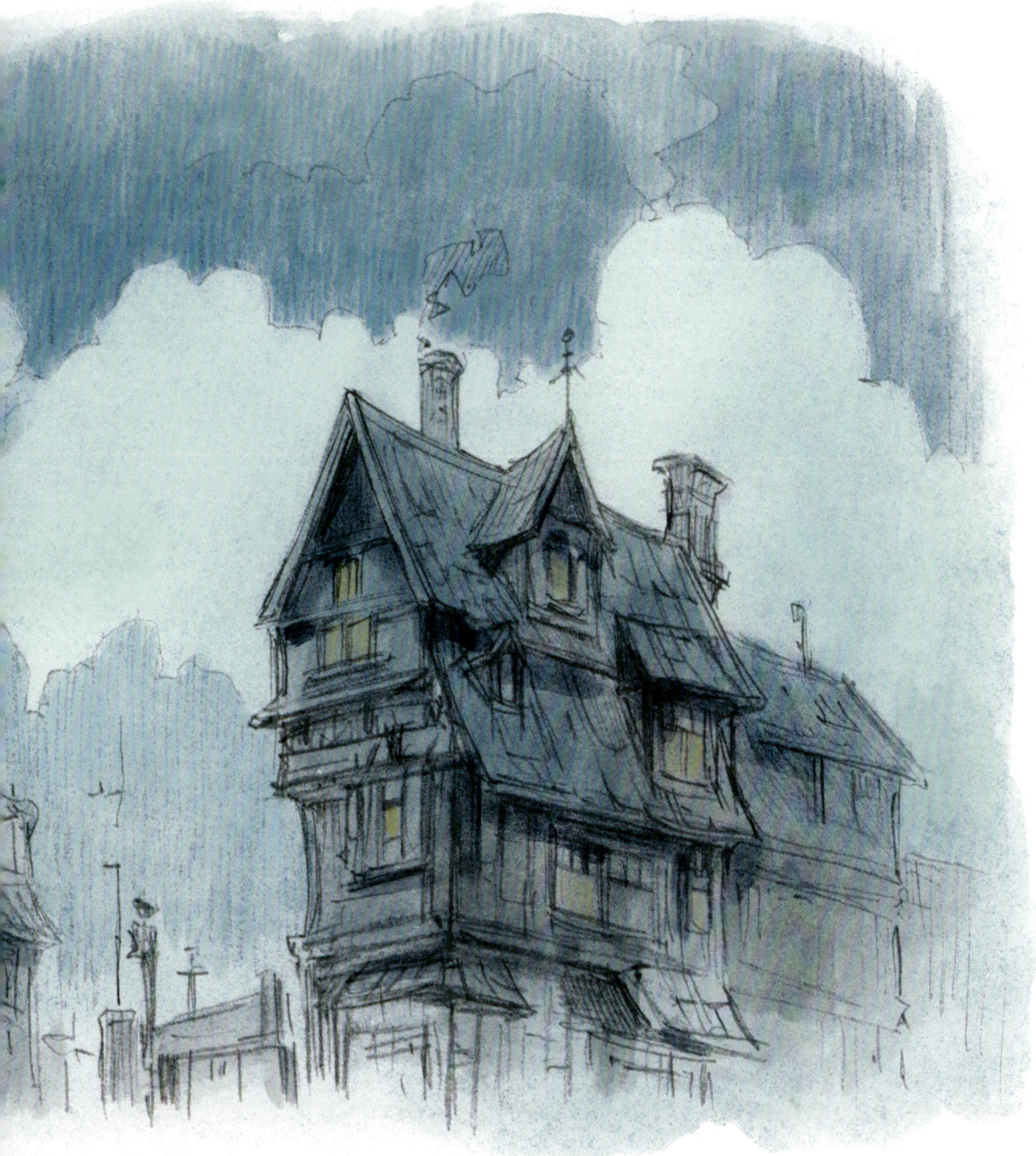

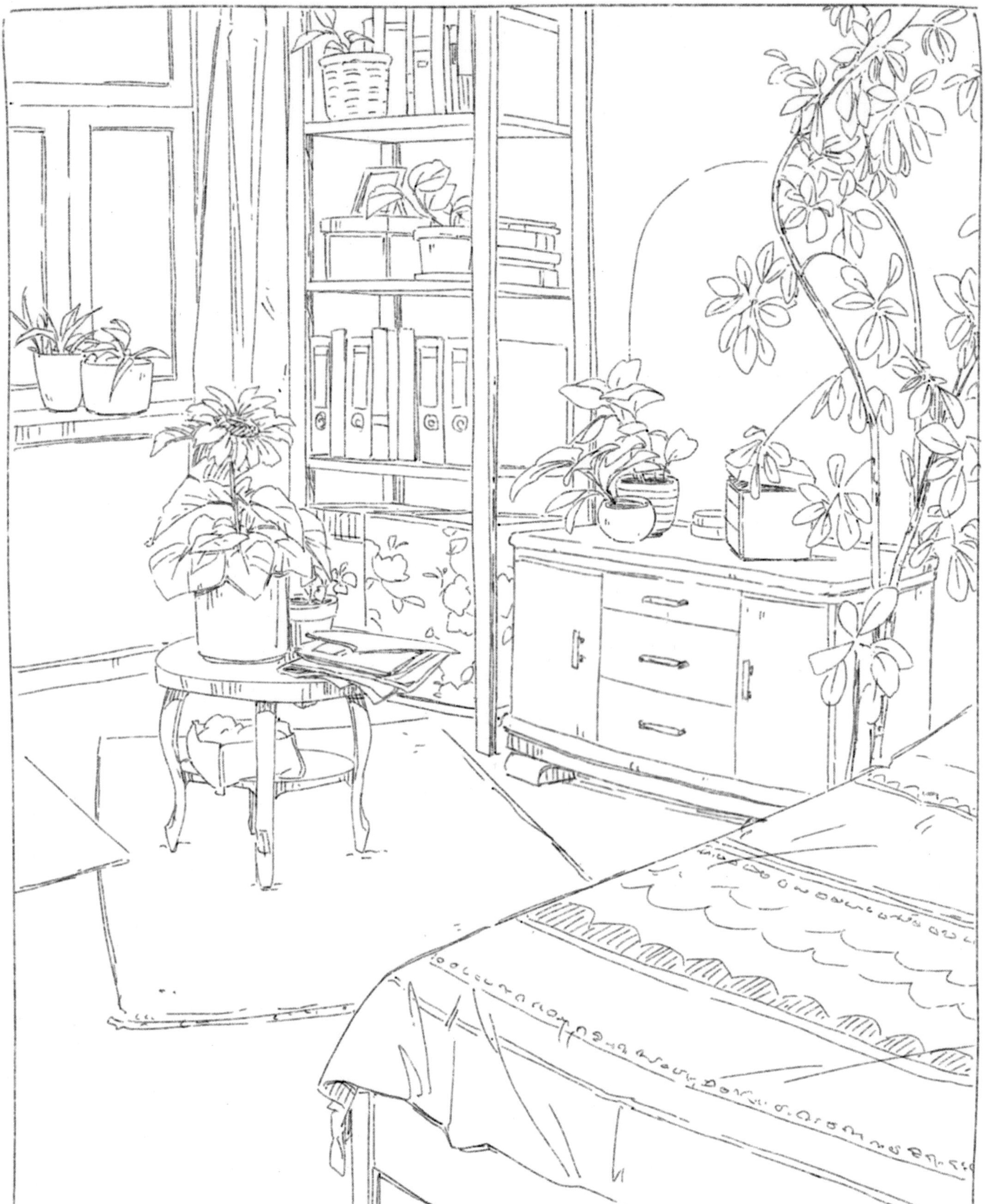

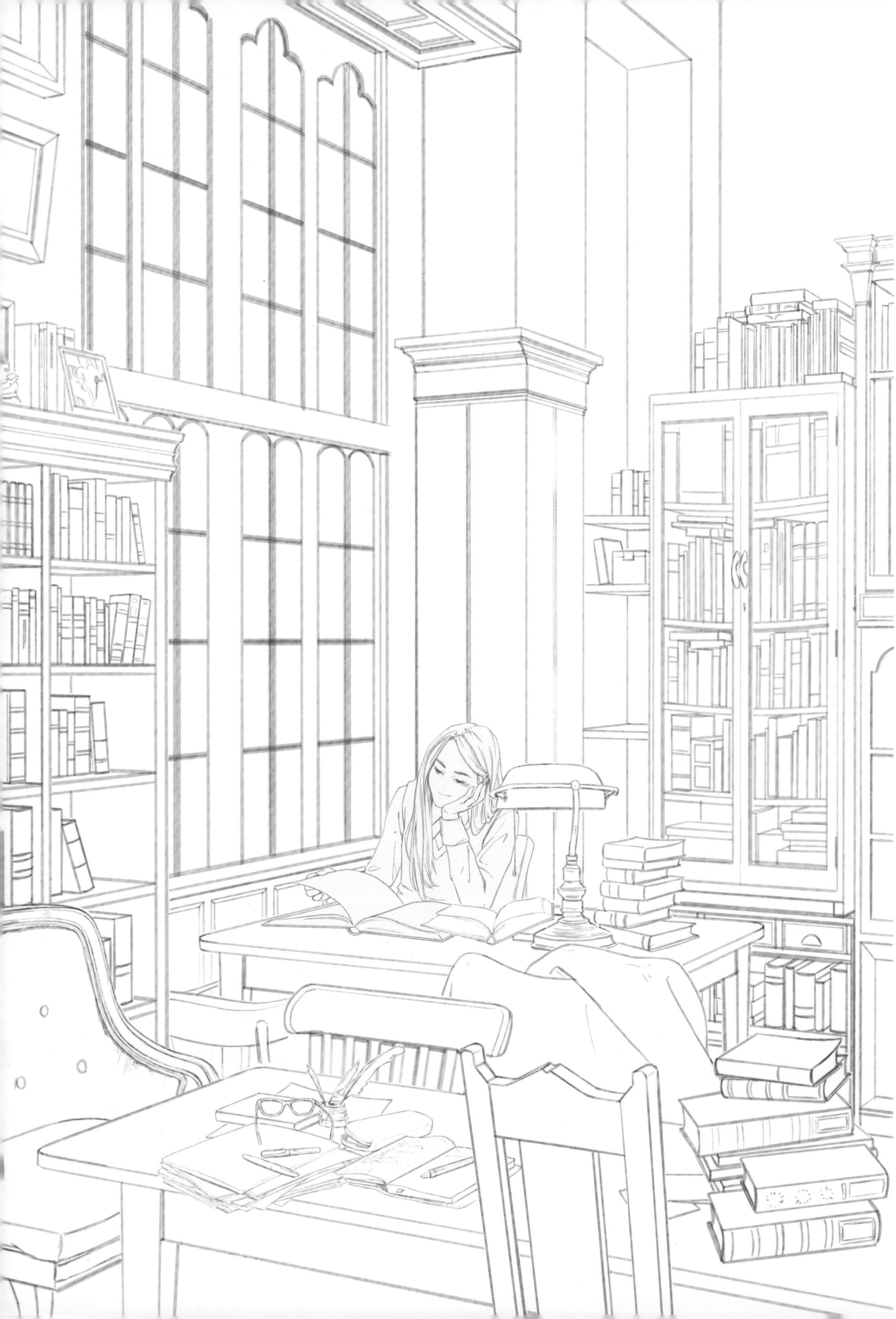

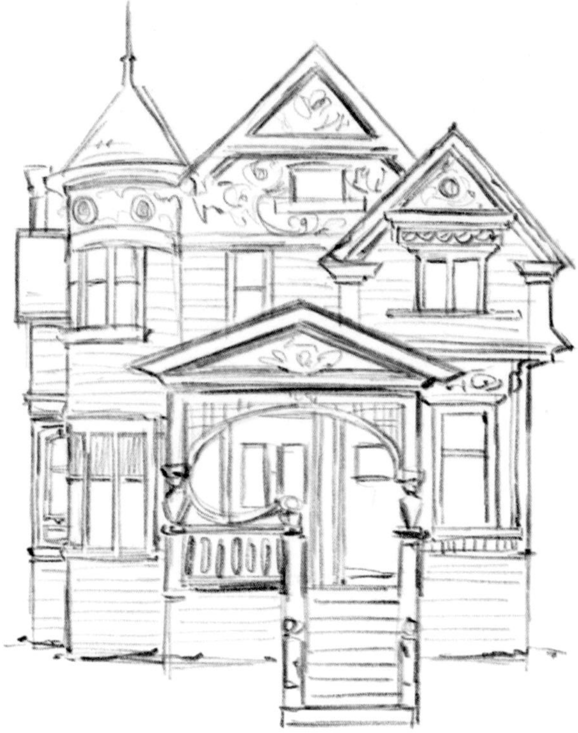

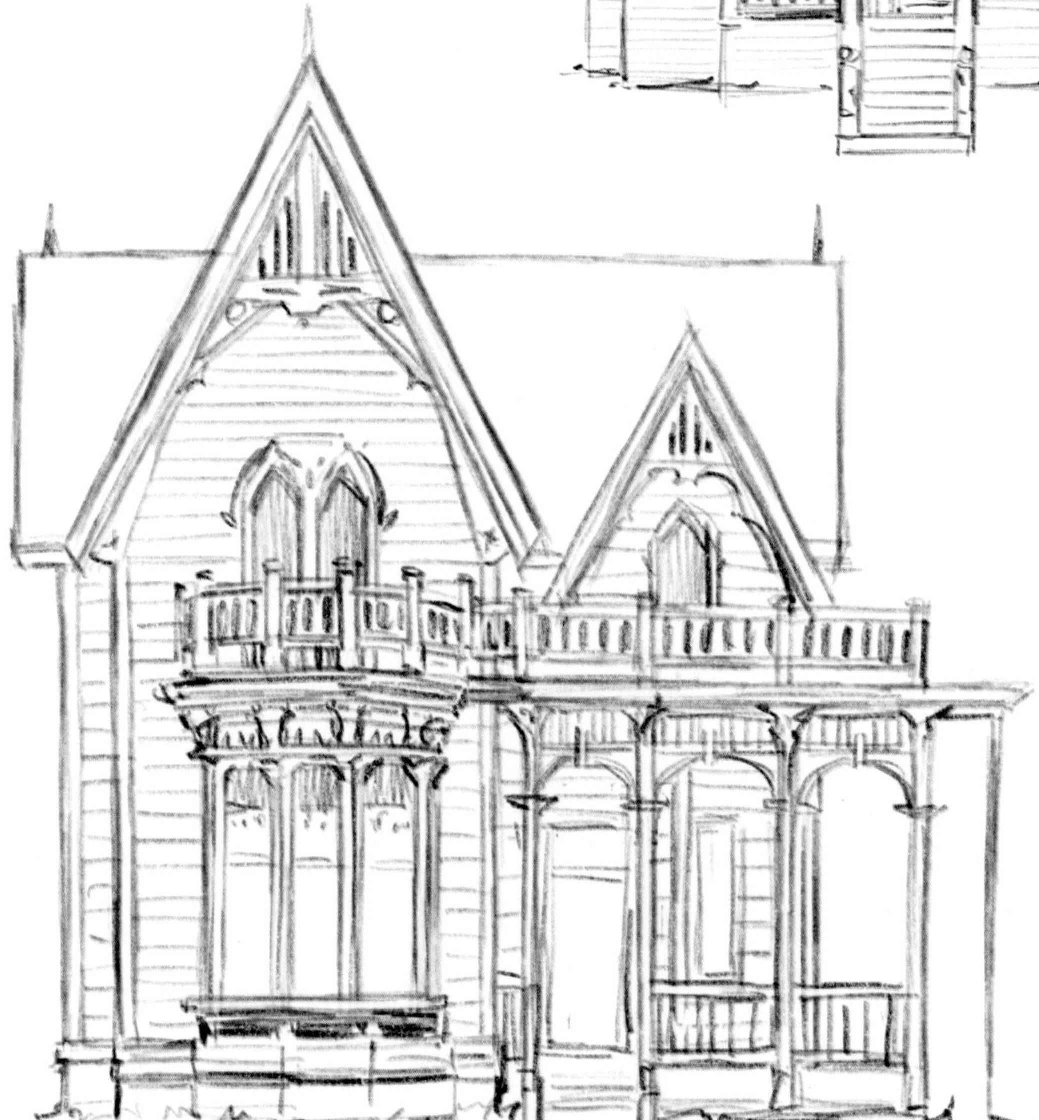

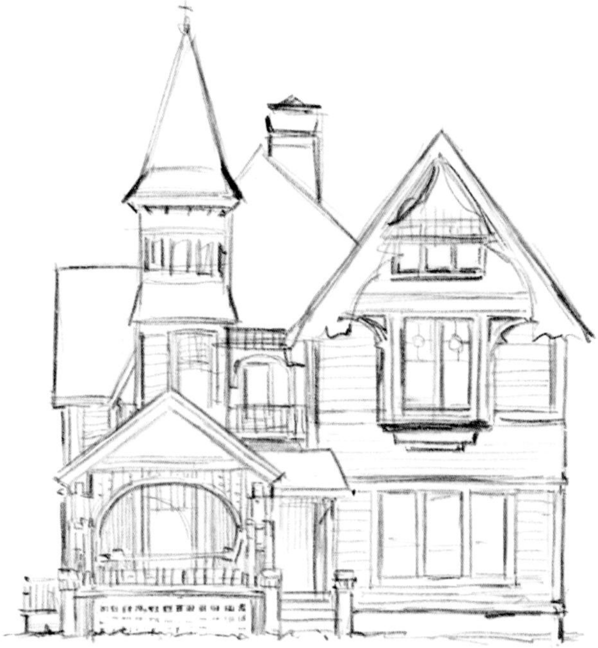

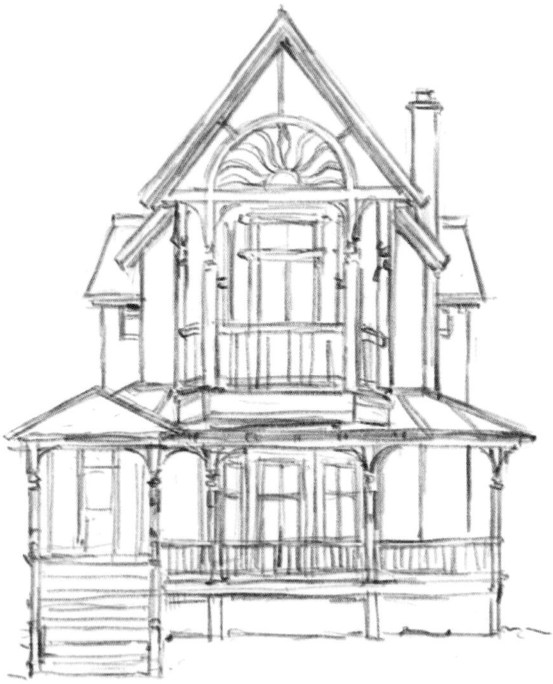

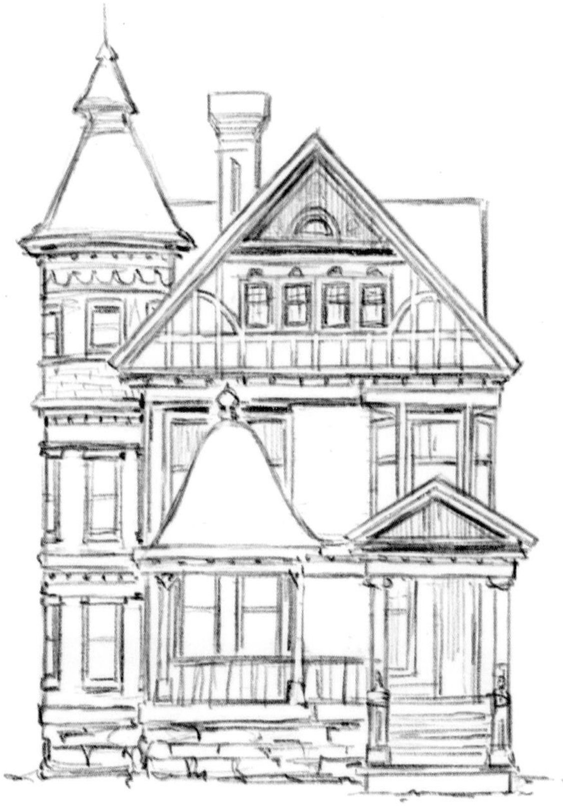

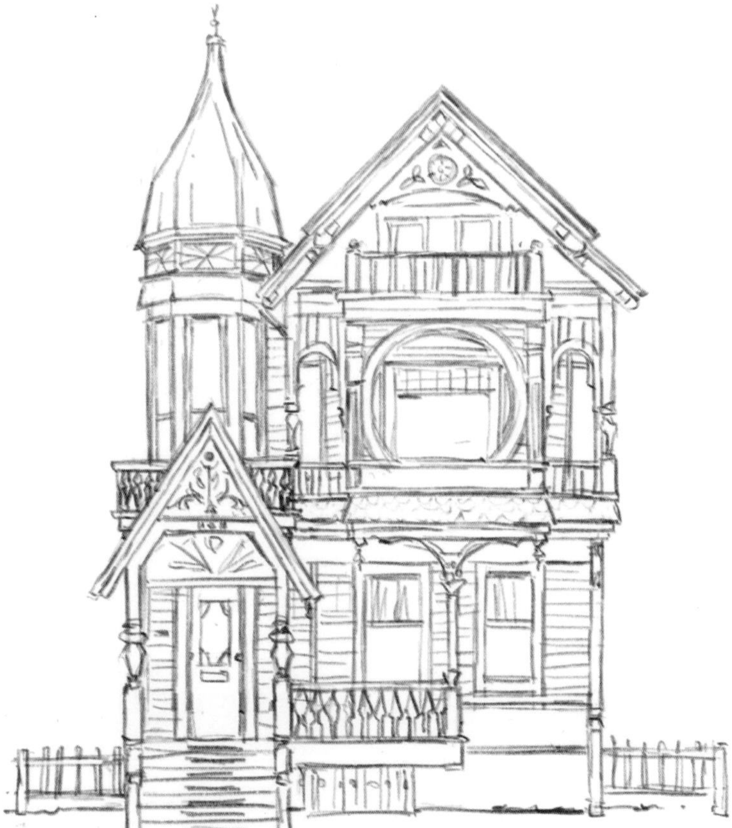

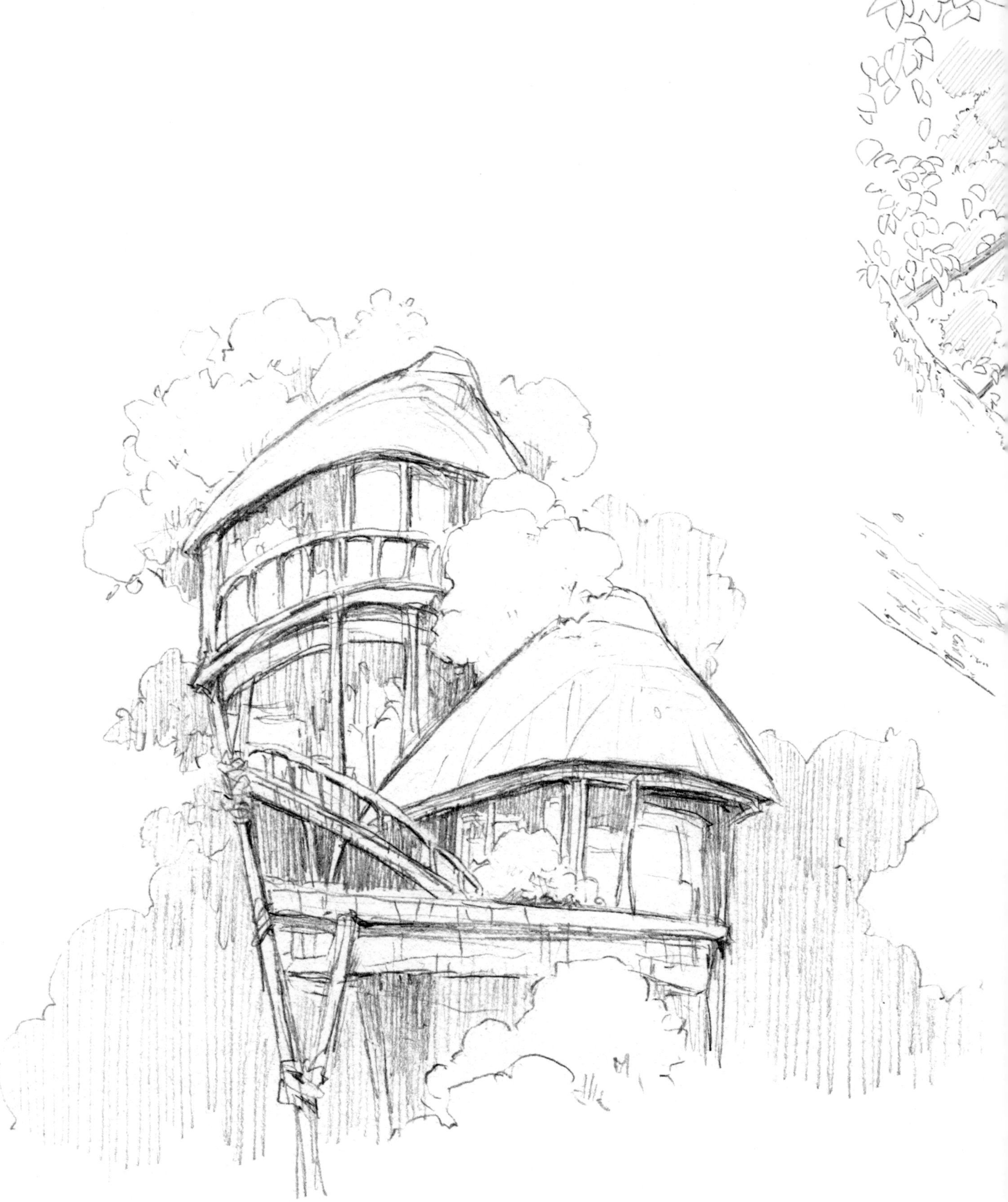

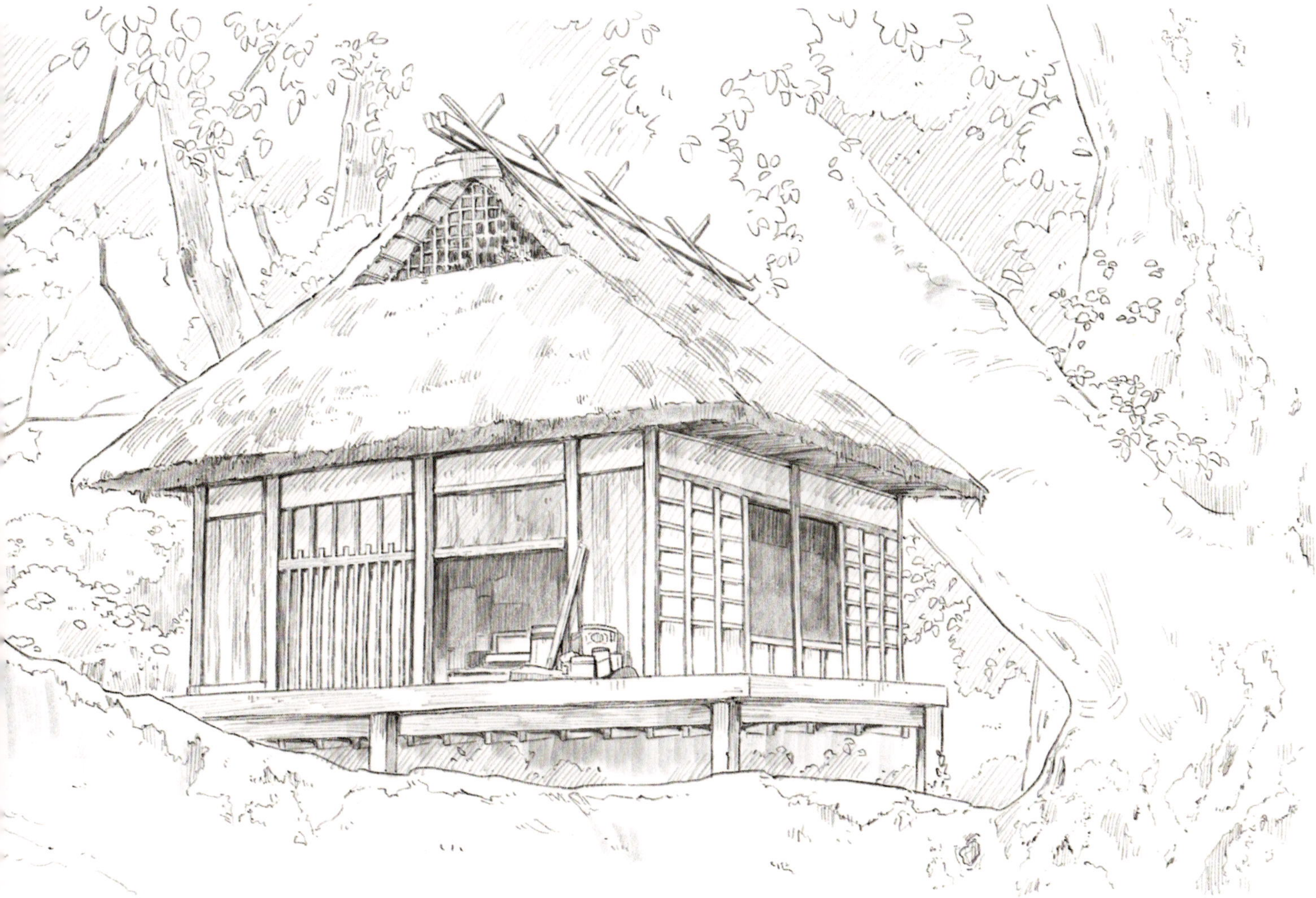

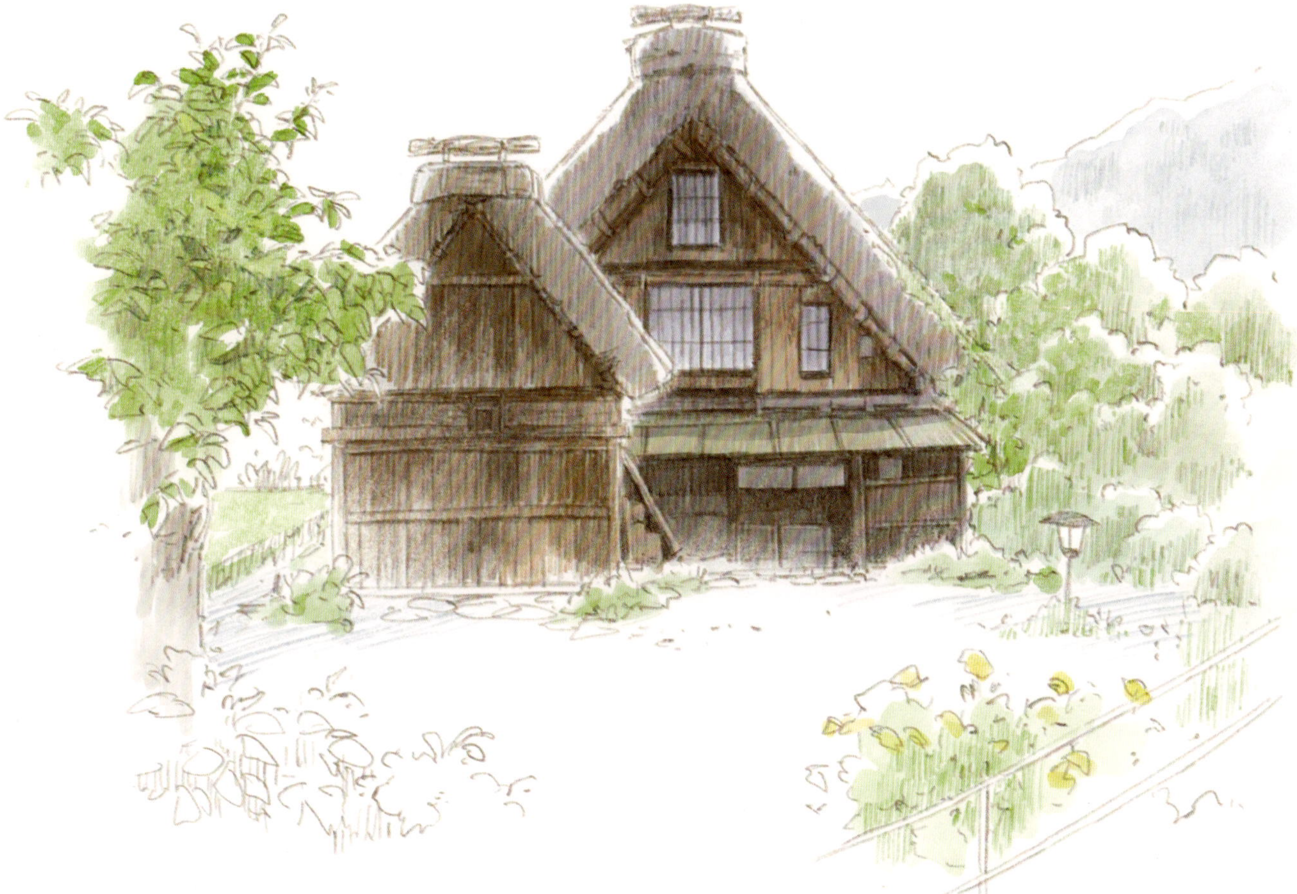

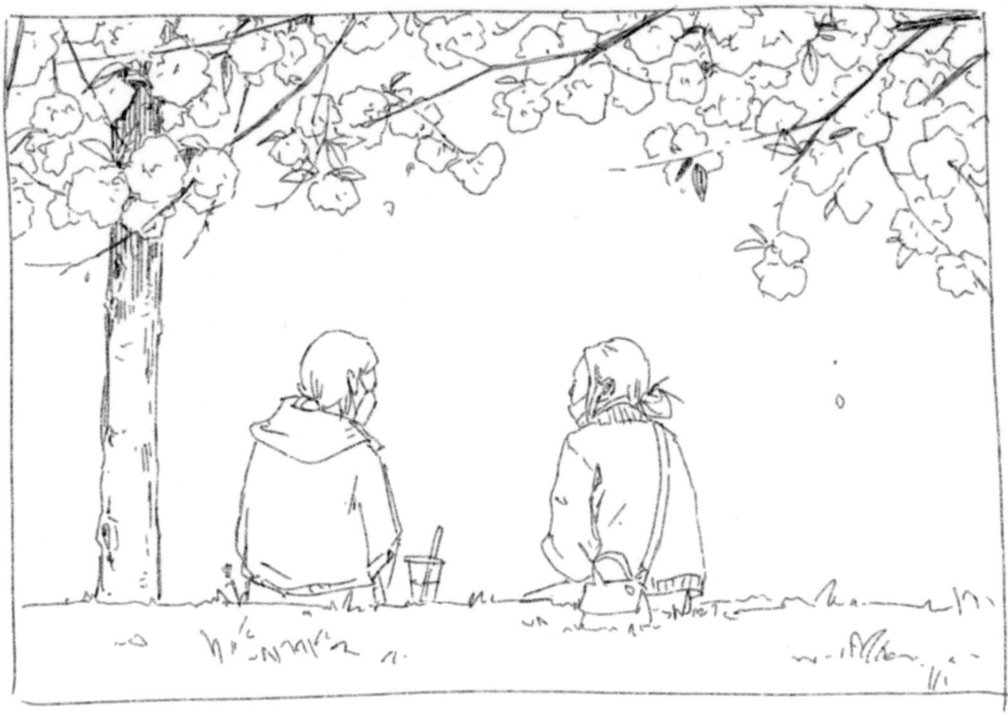

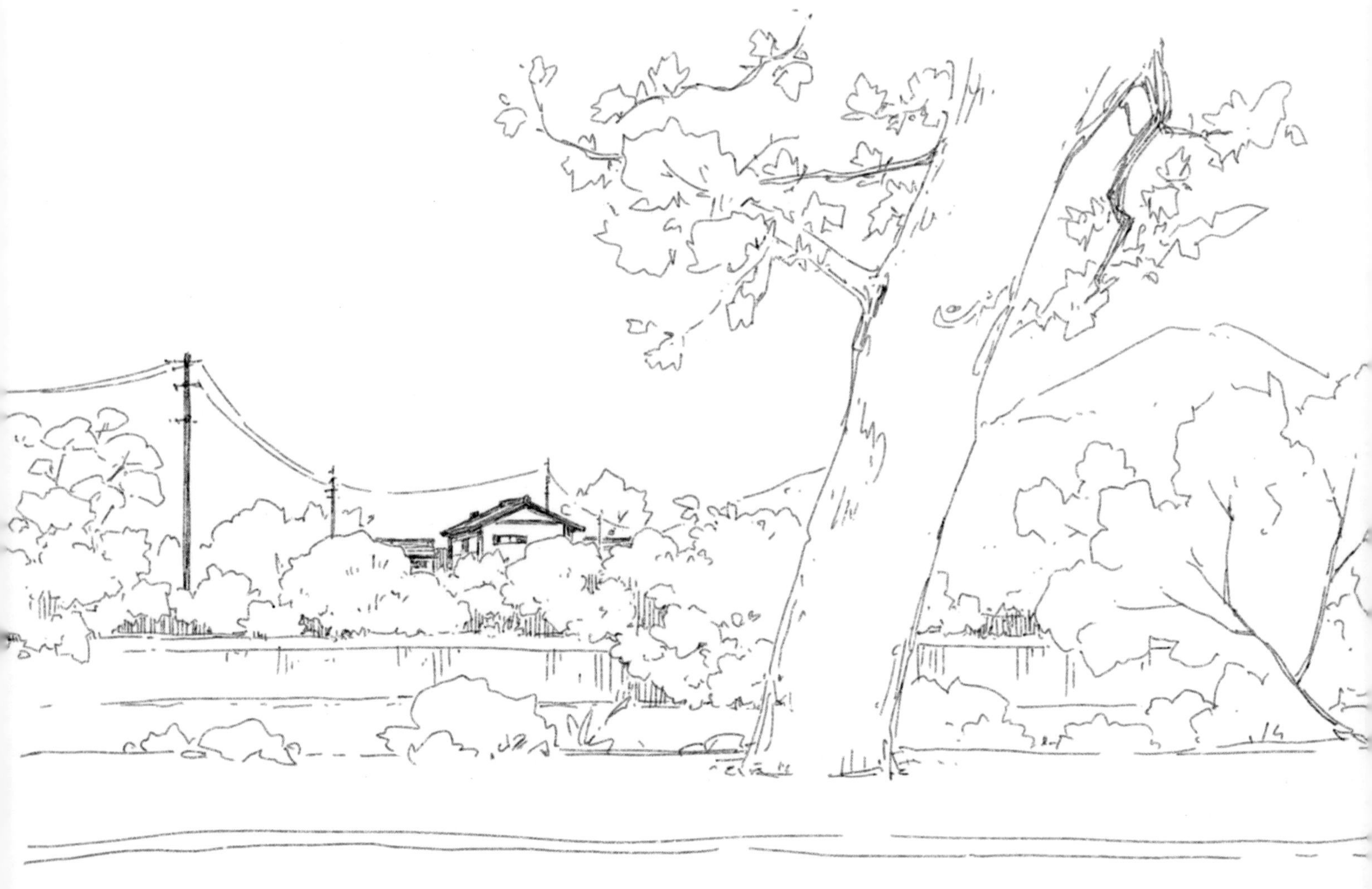

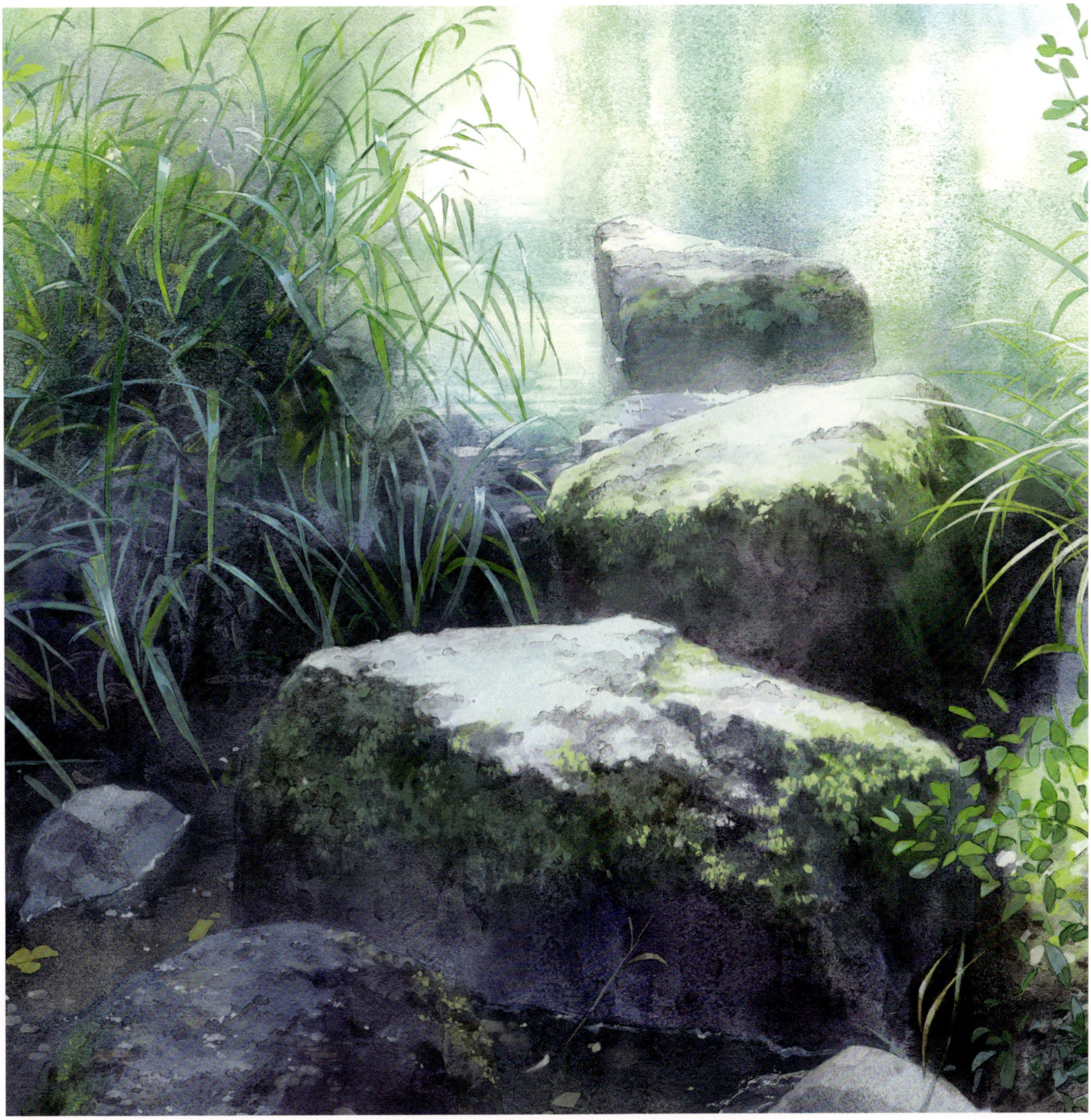

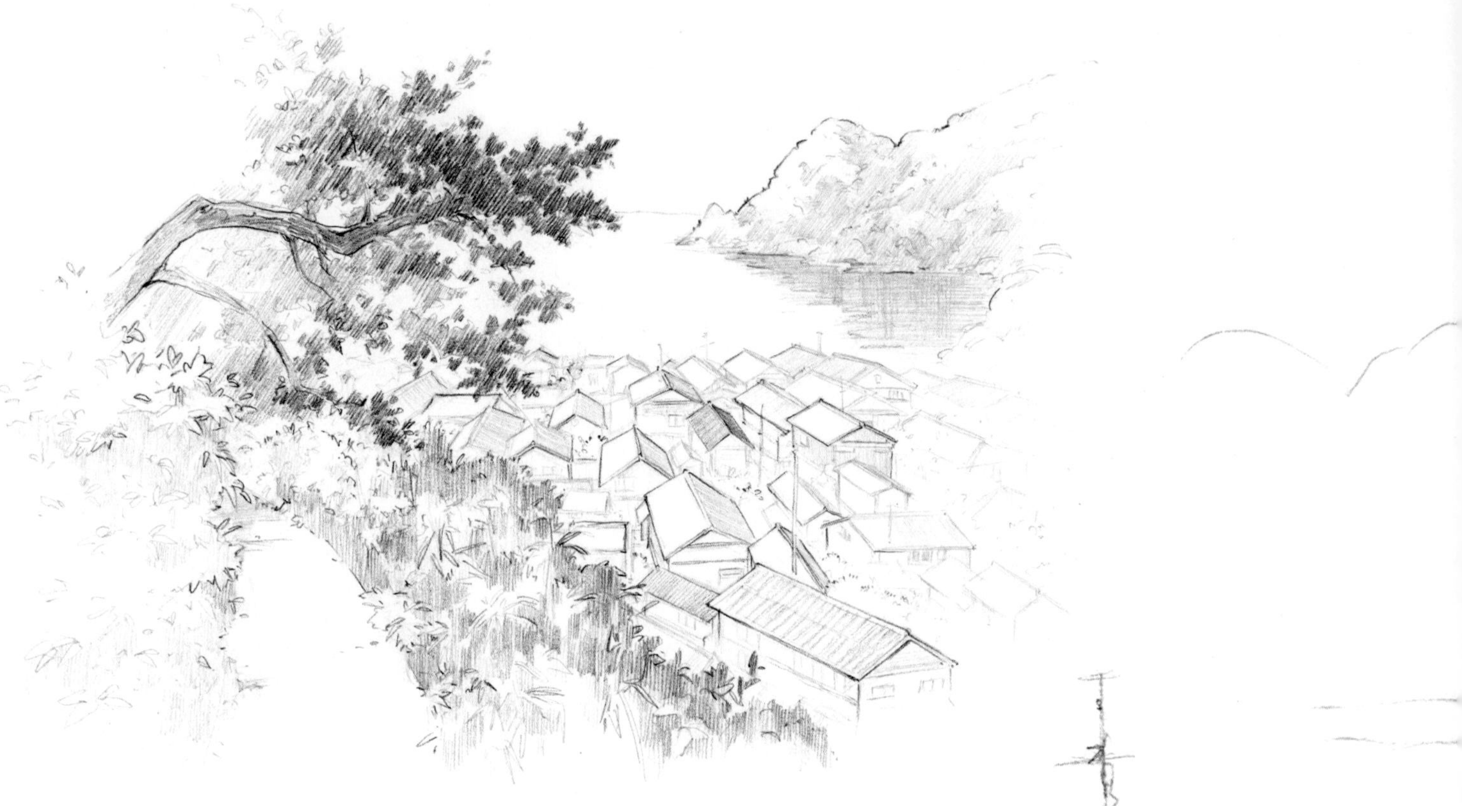

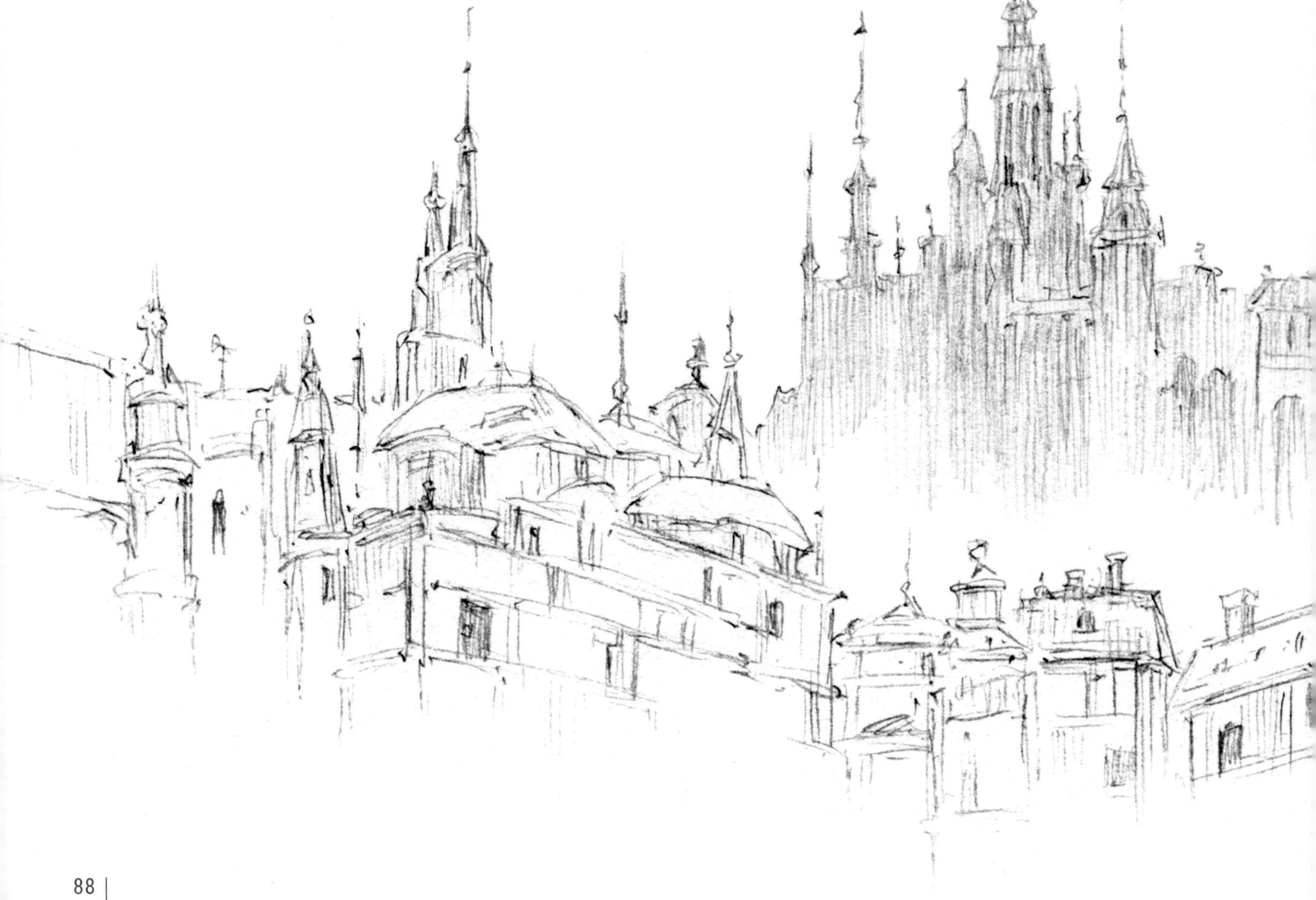

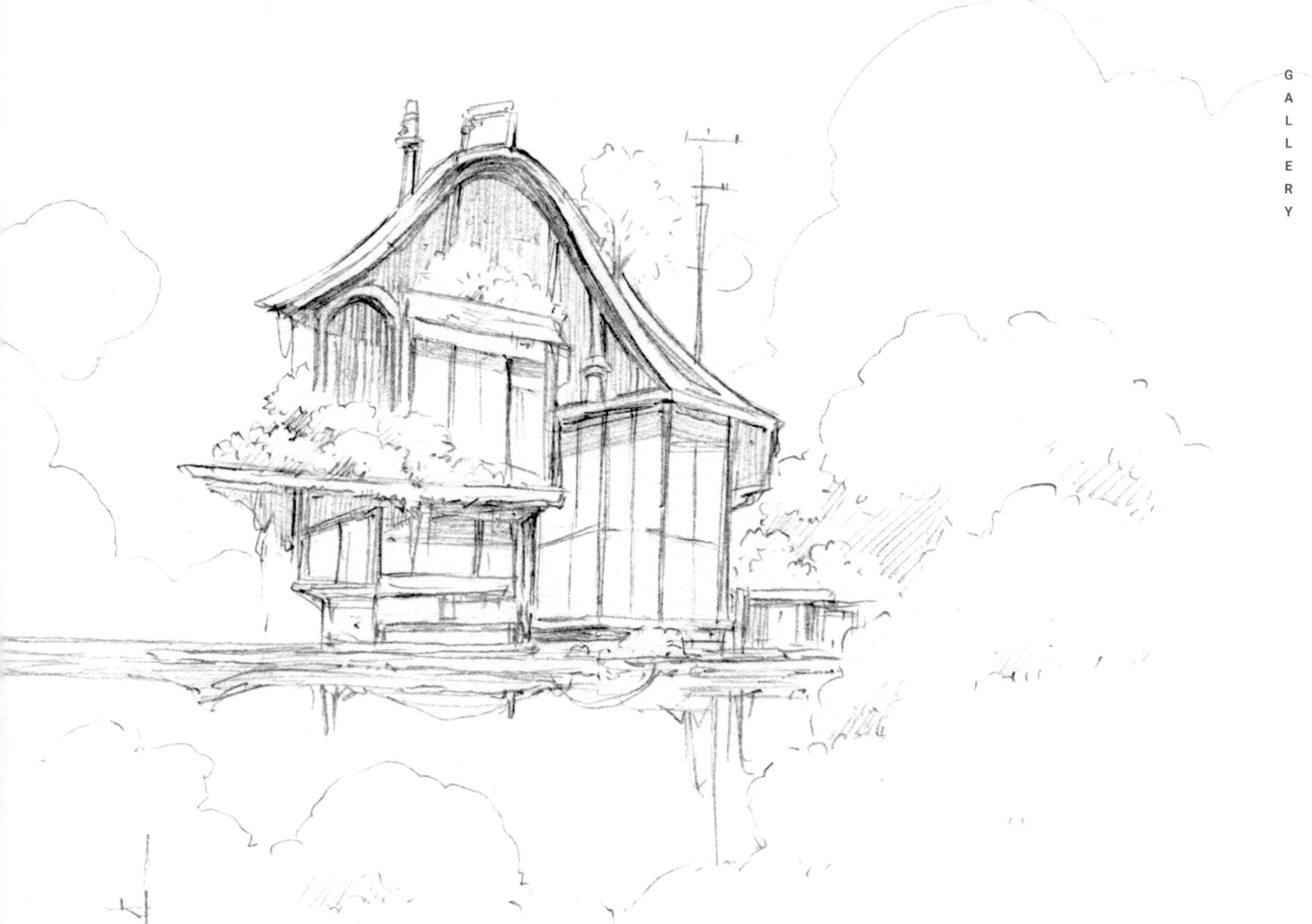

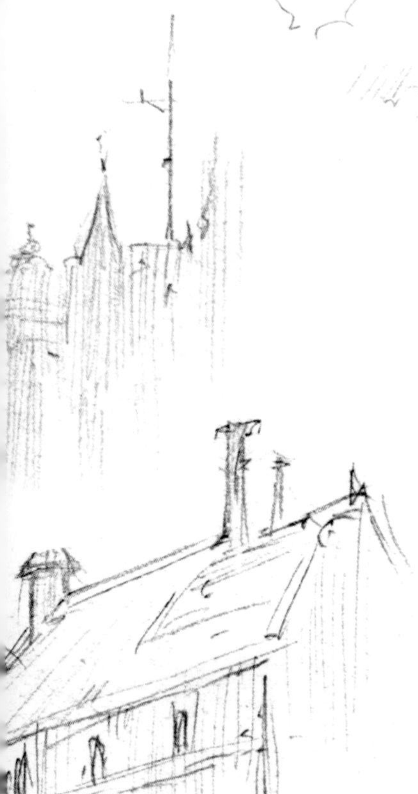

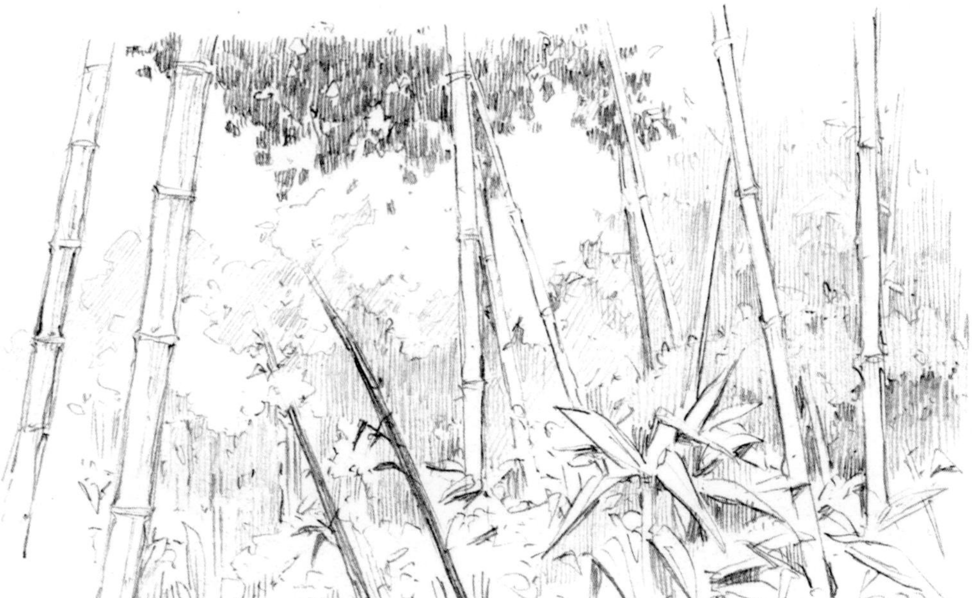

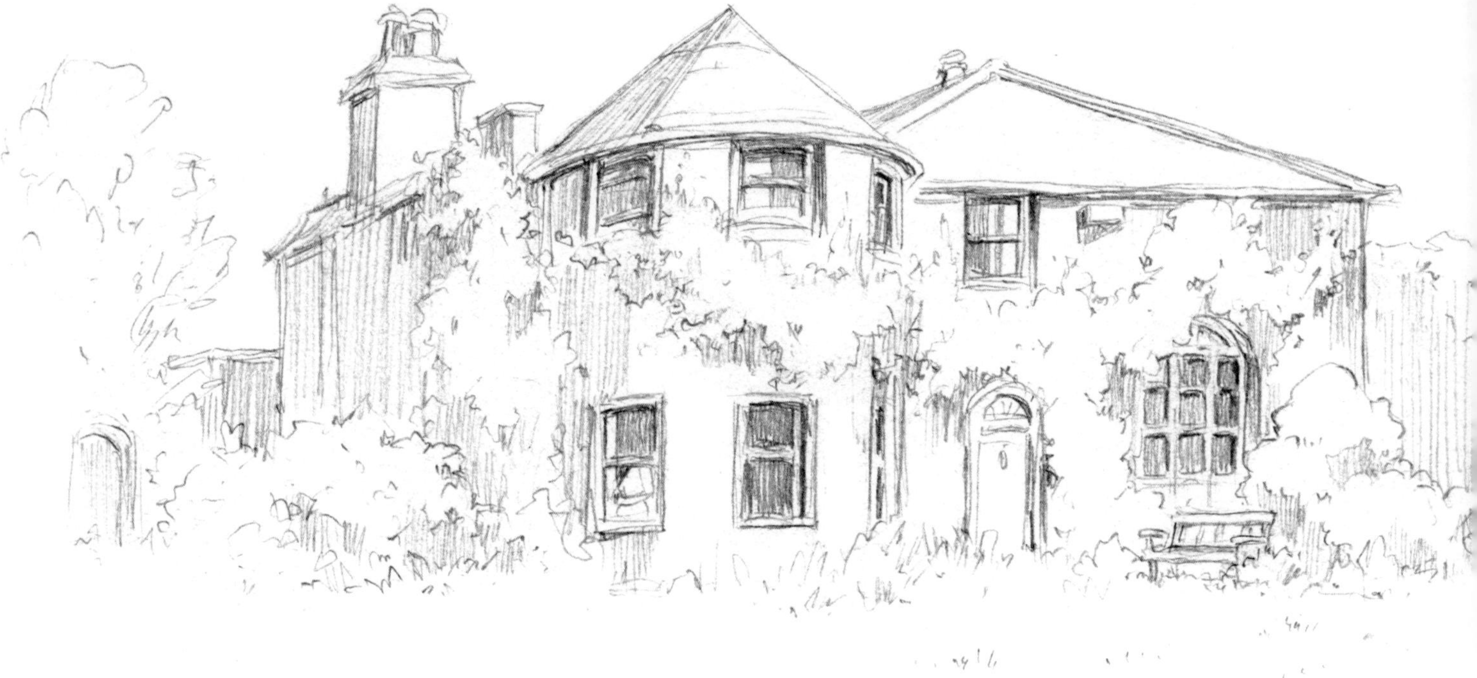

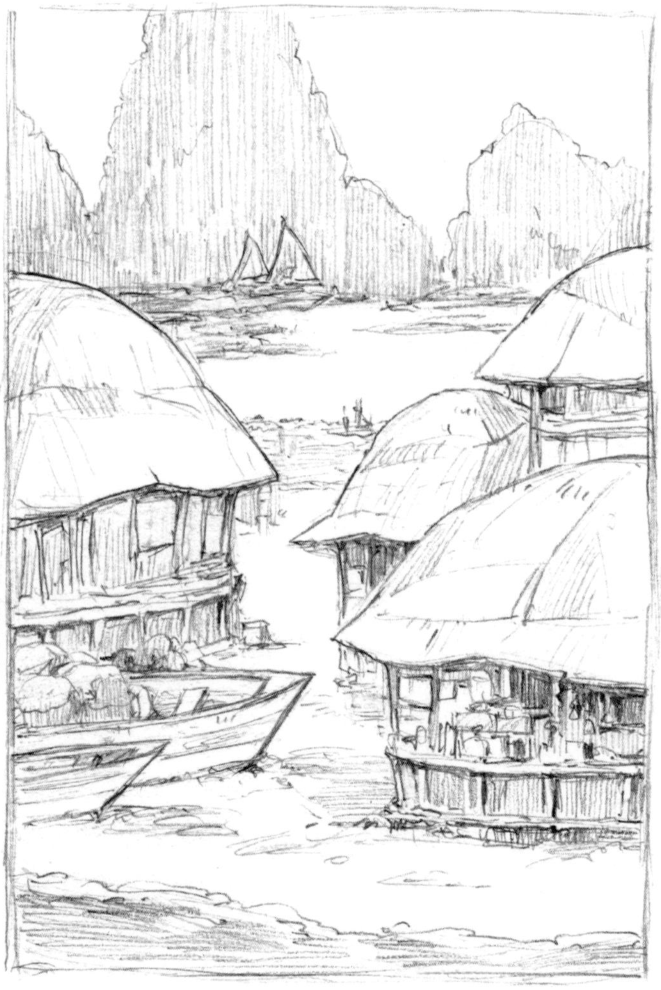

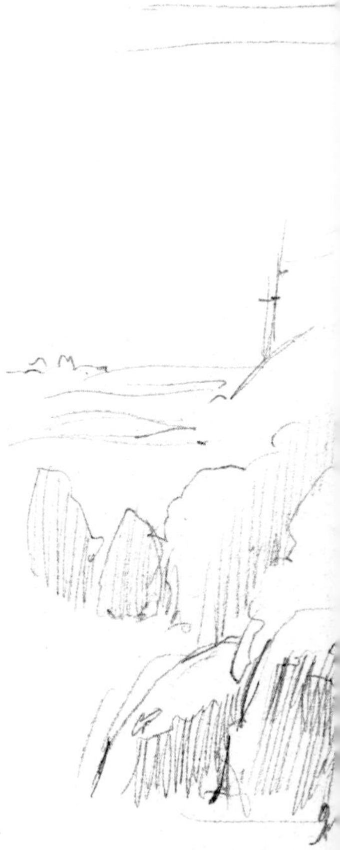

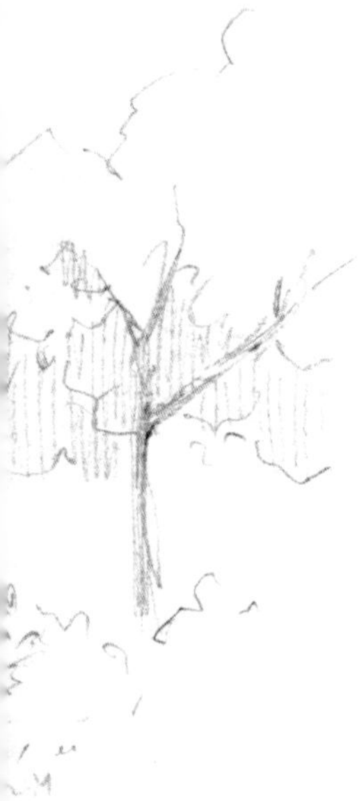

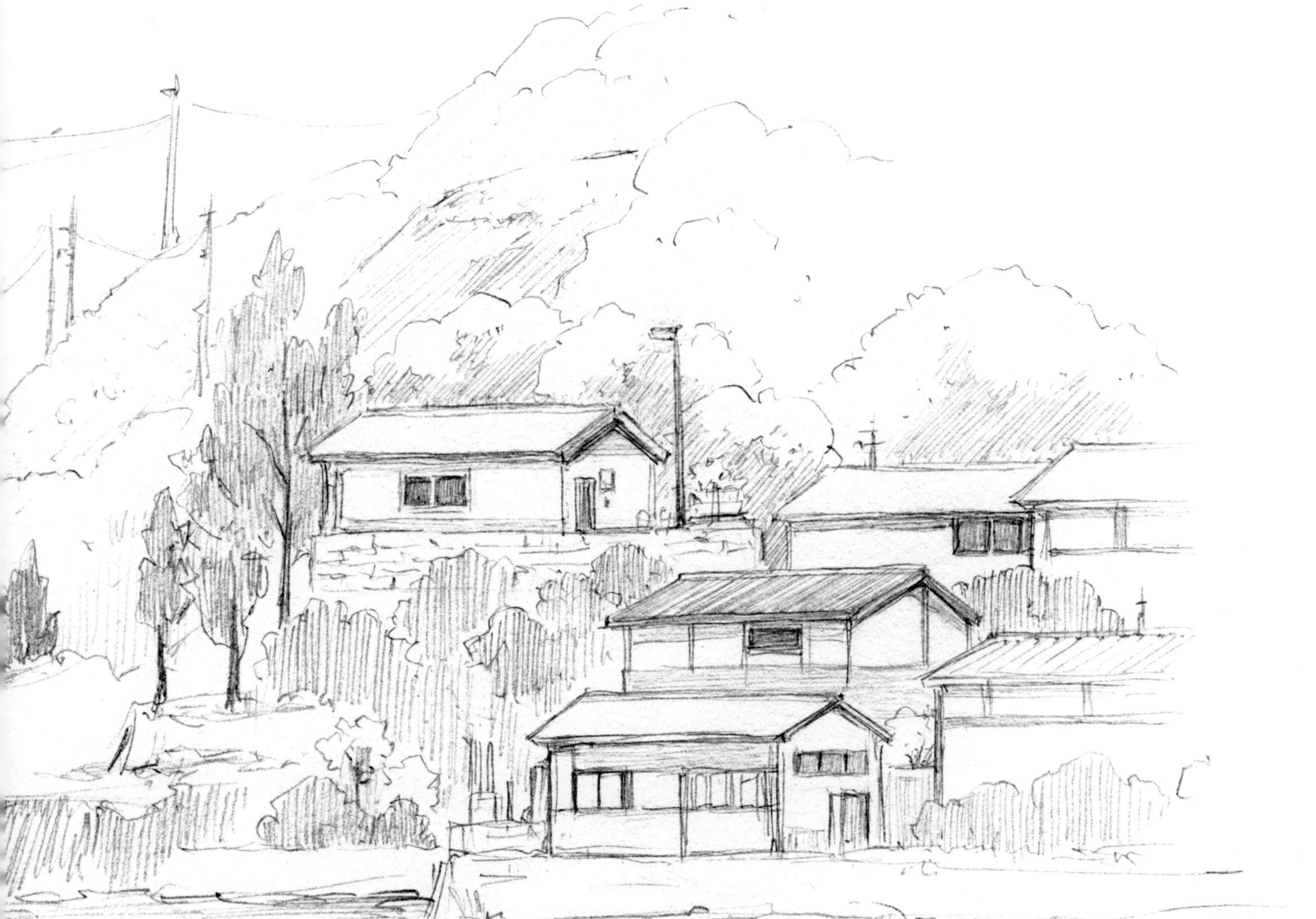

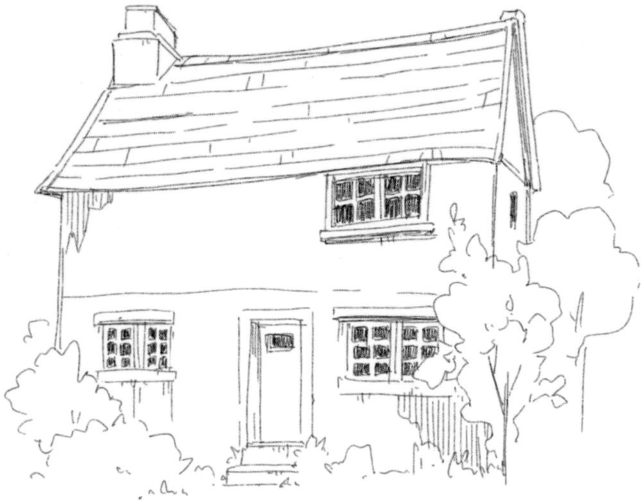

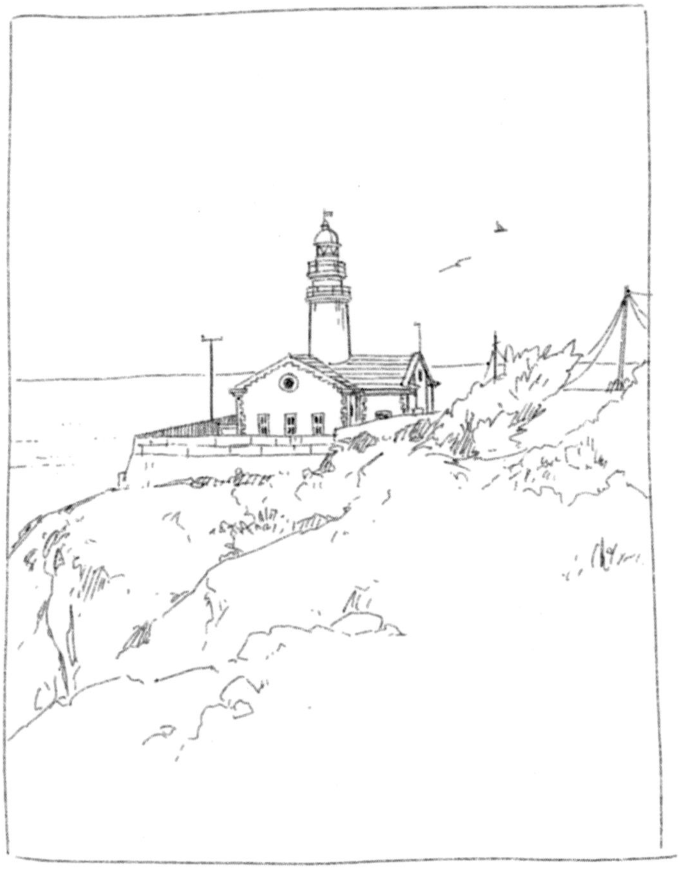

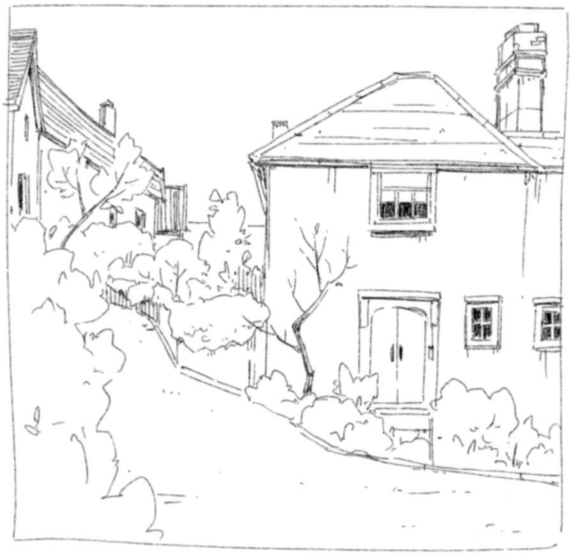

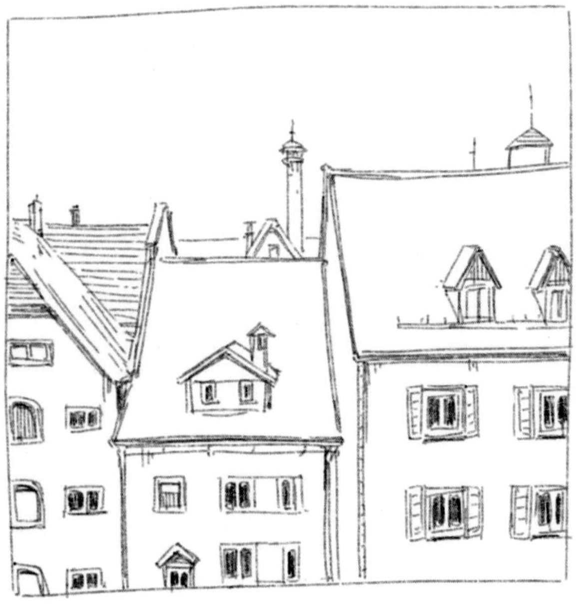

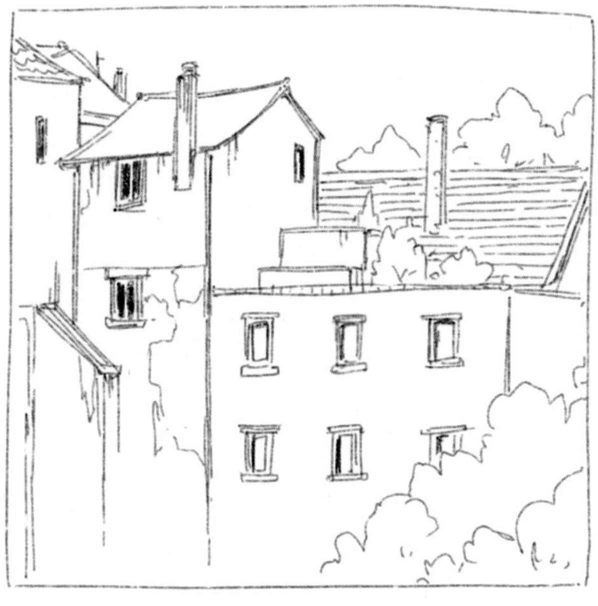

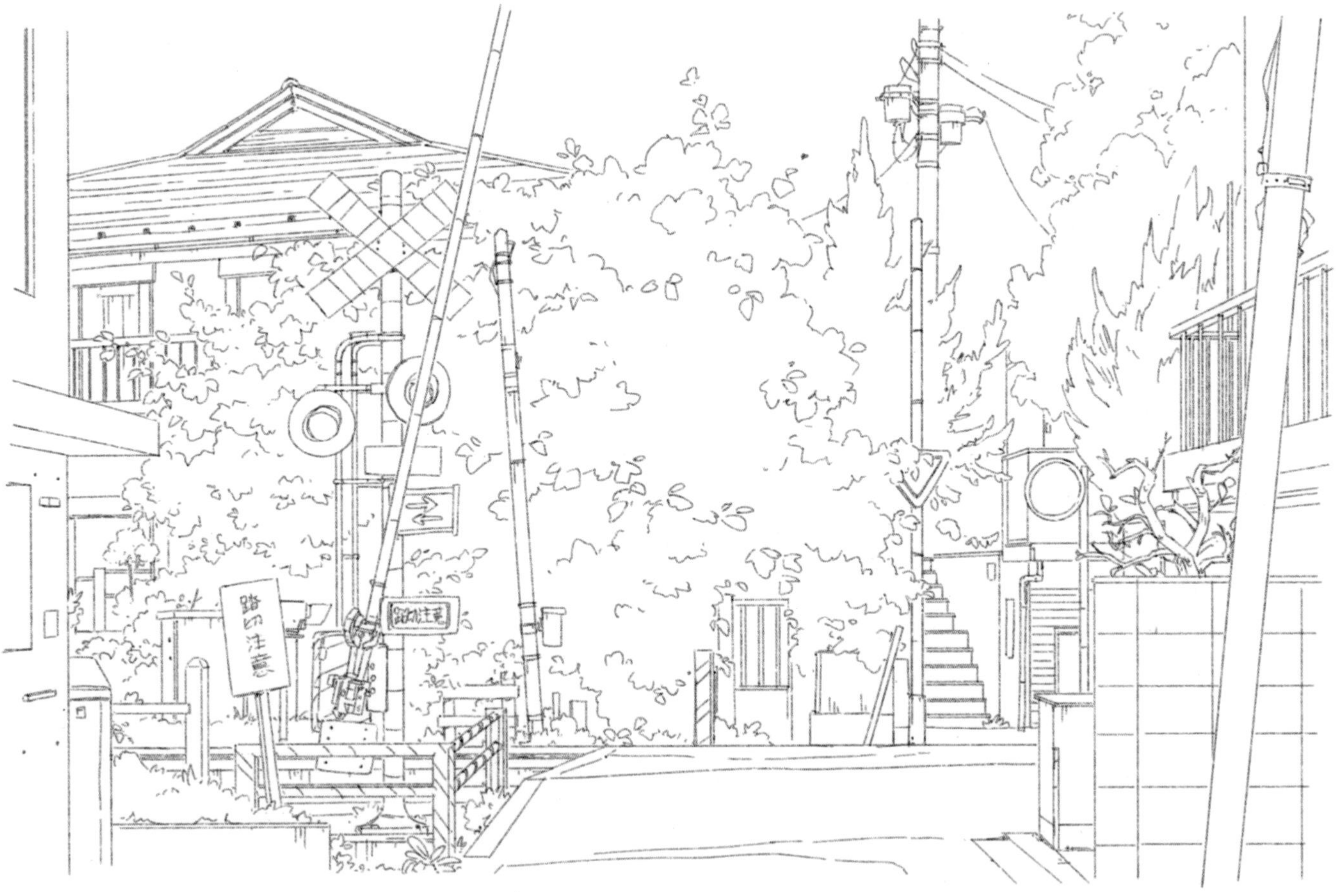

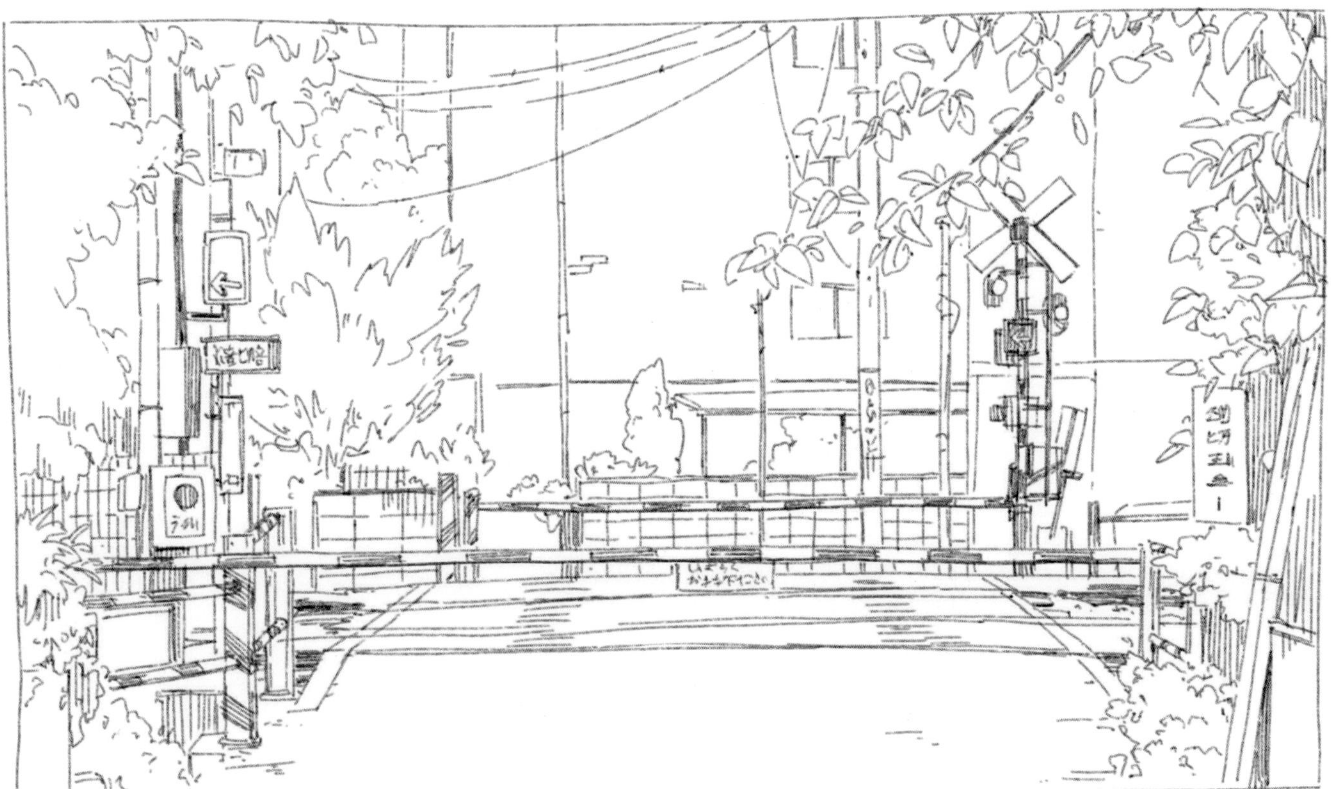

YOYOGI CROSSING

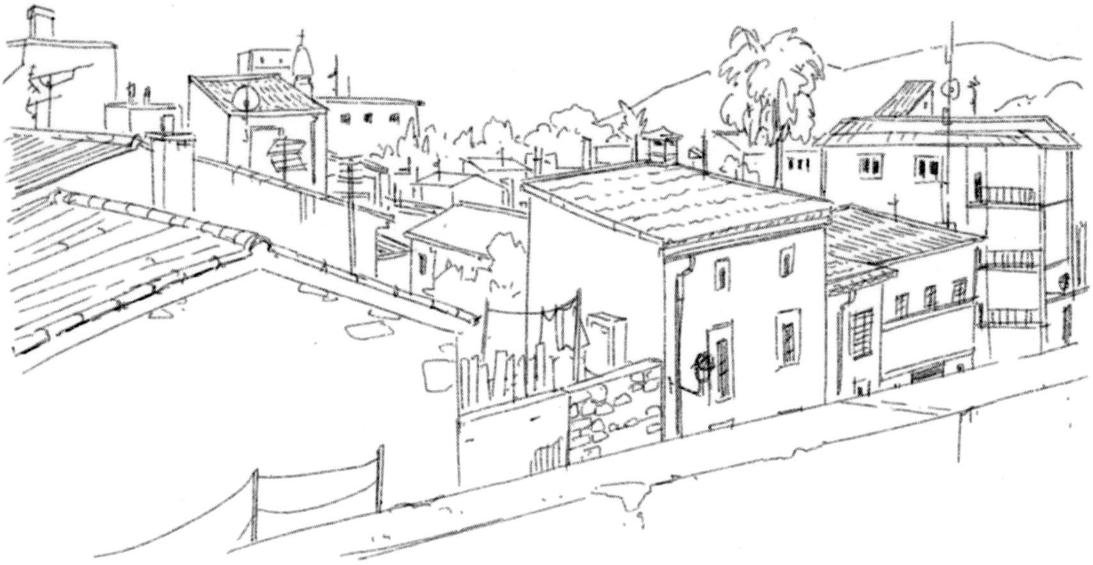

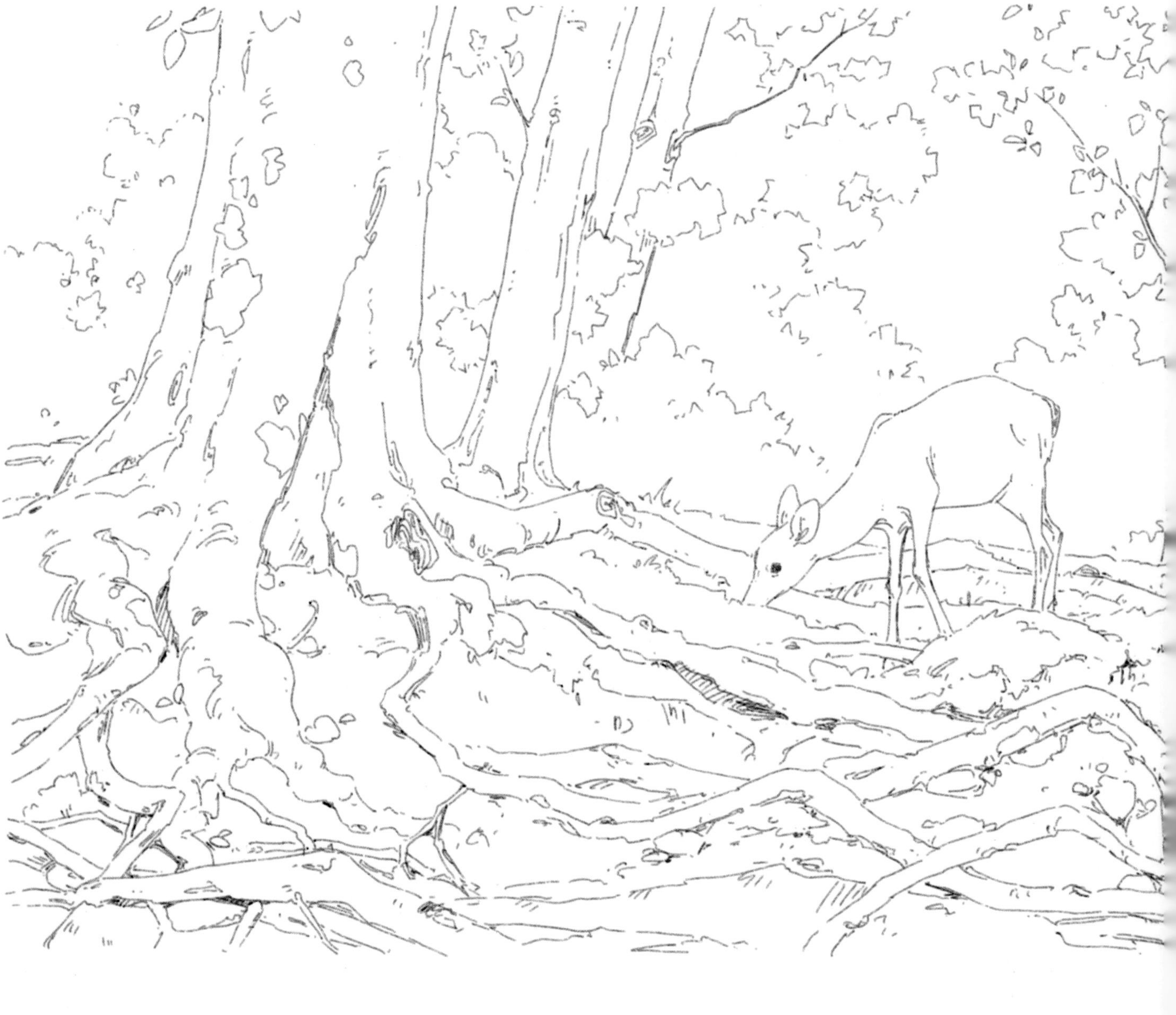

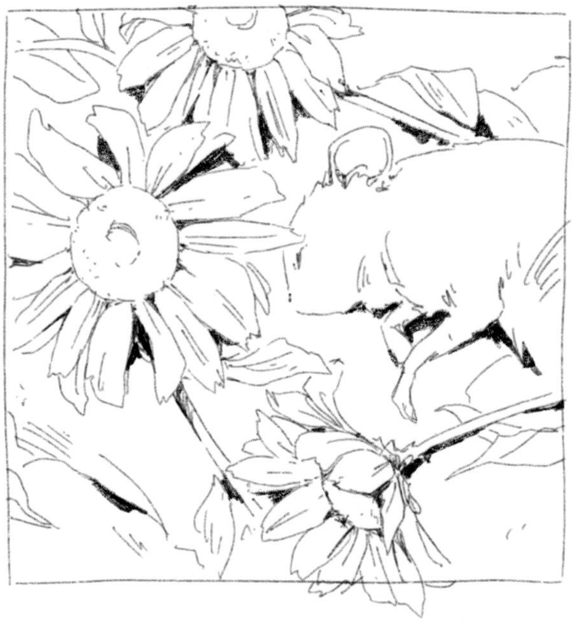

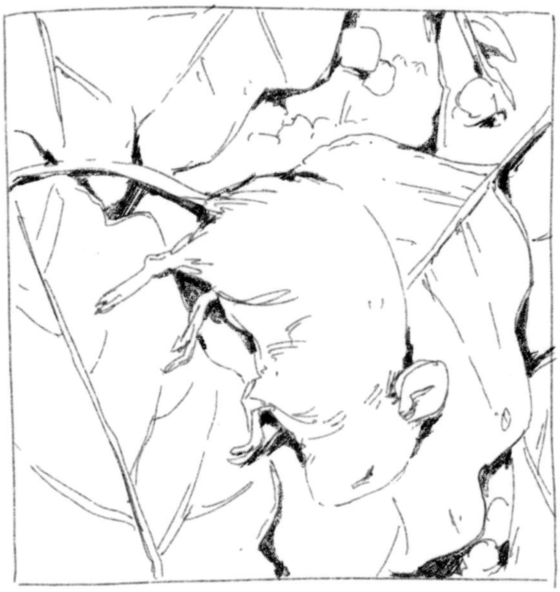

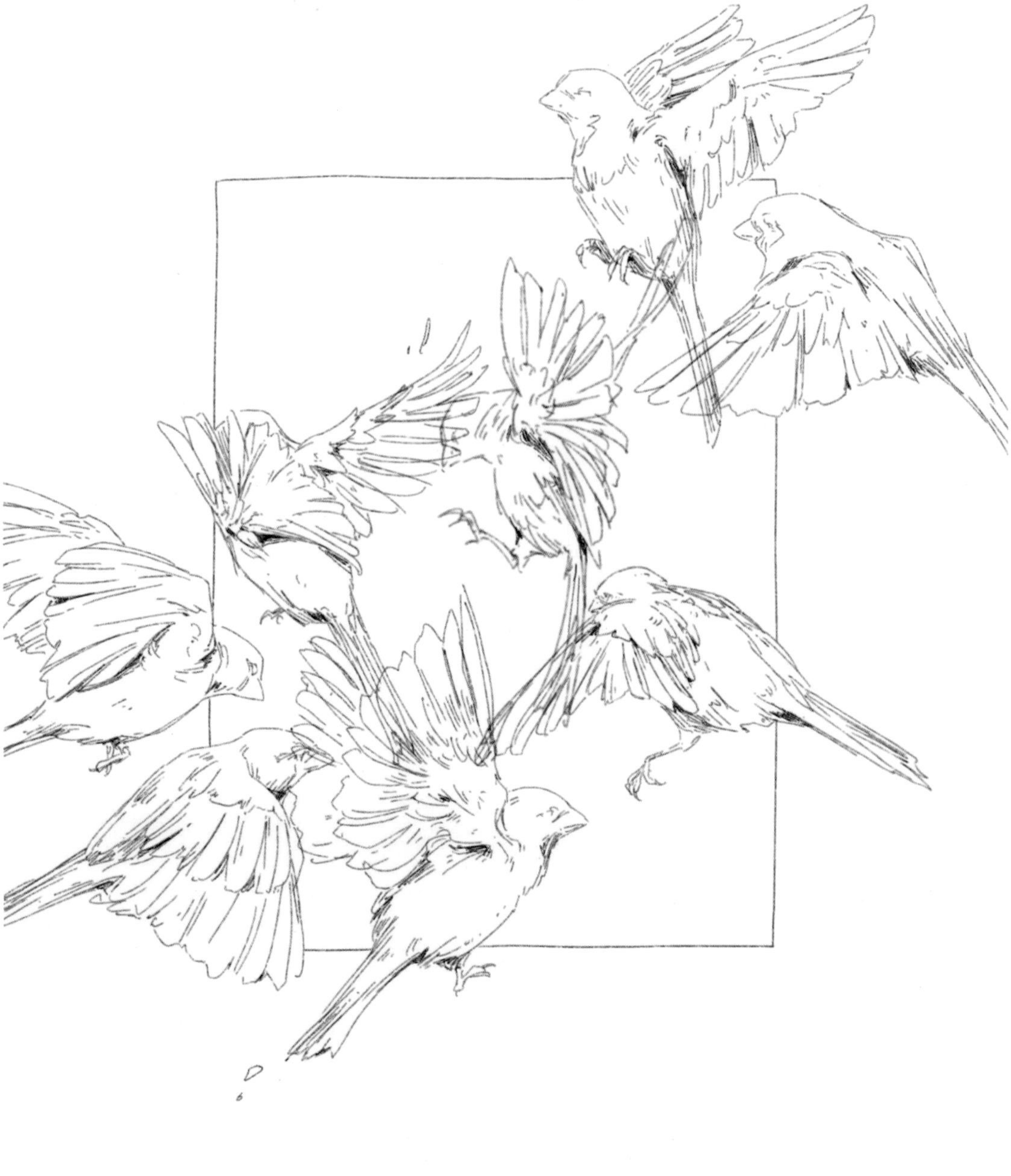

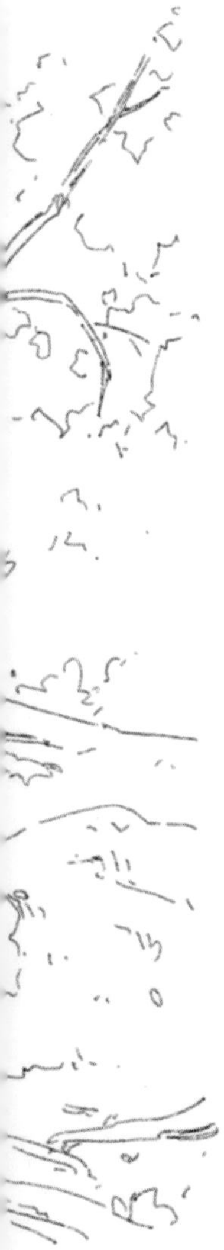

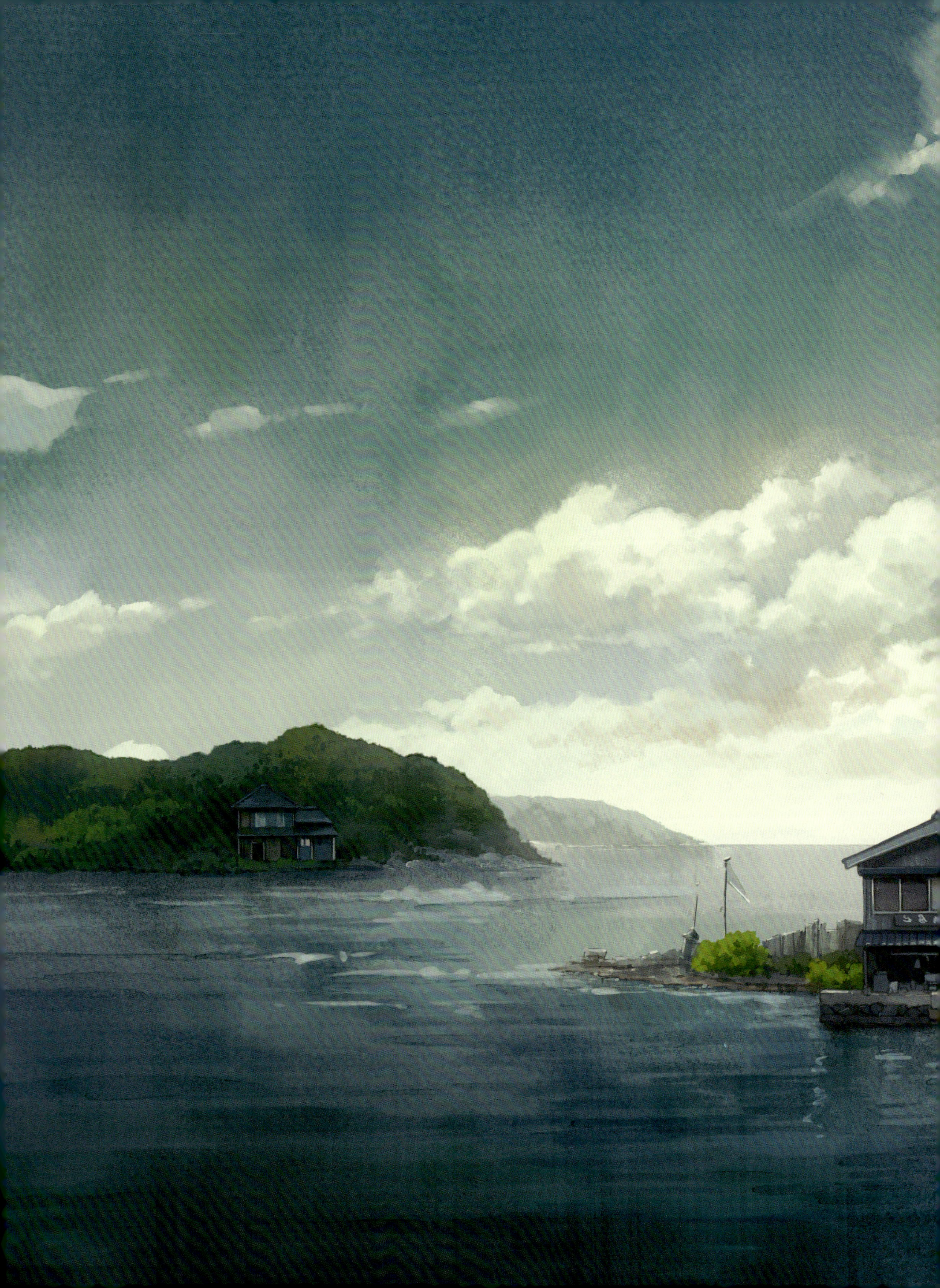

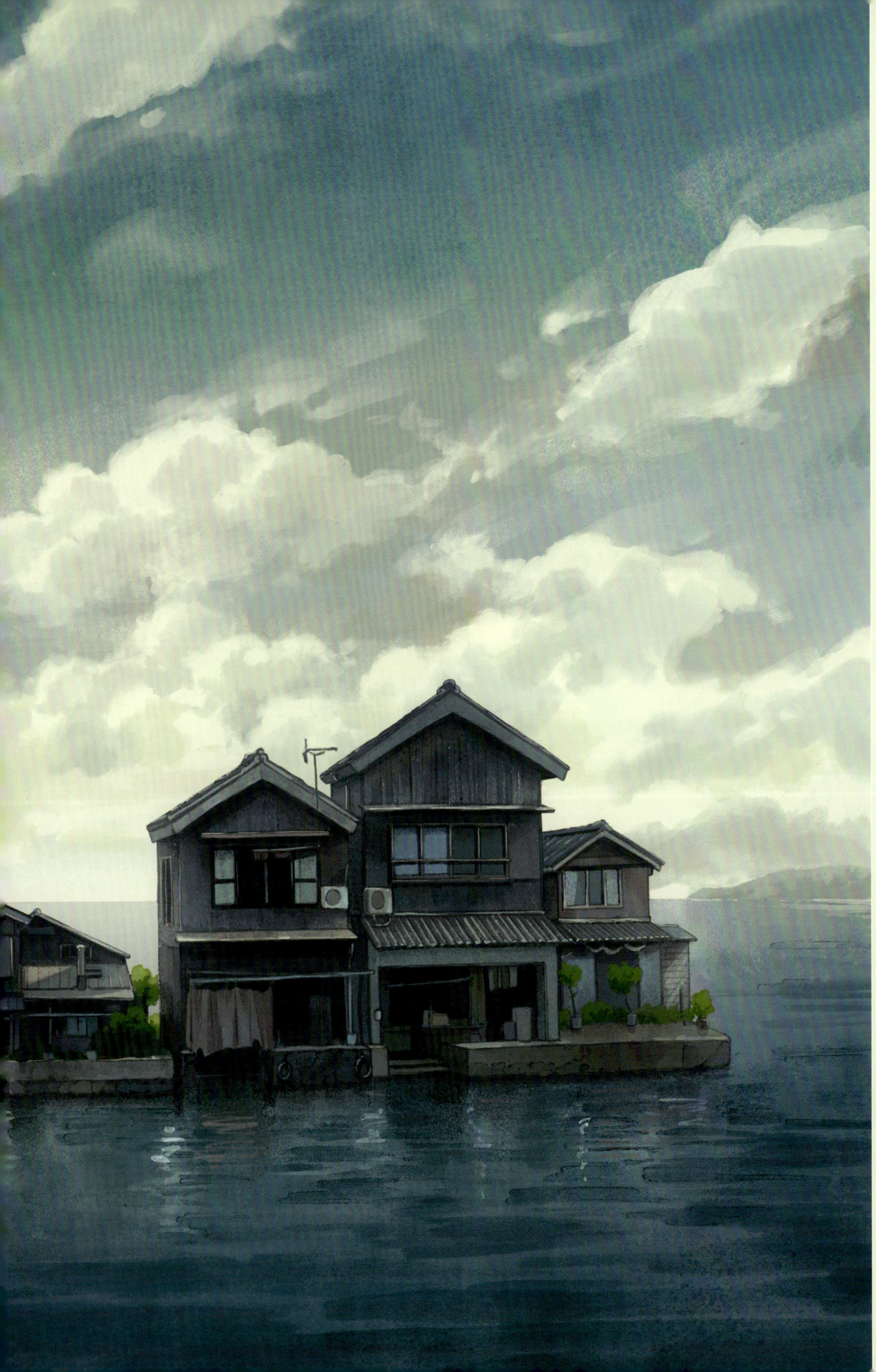

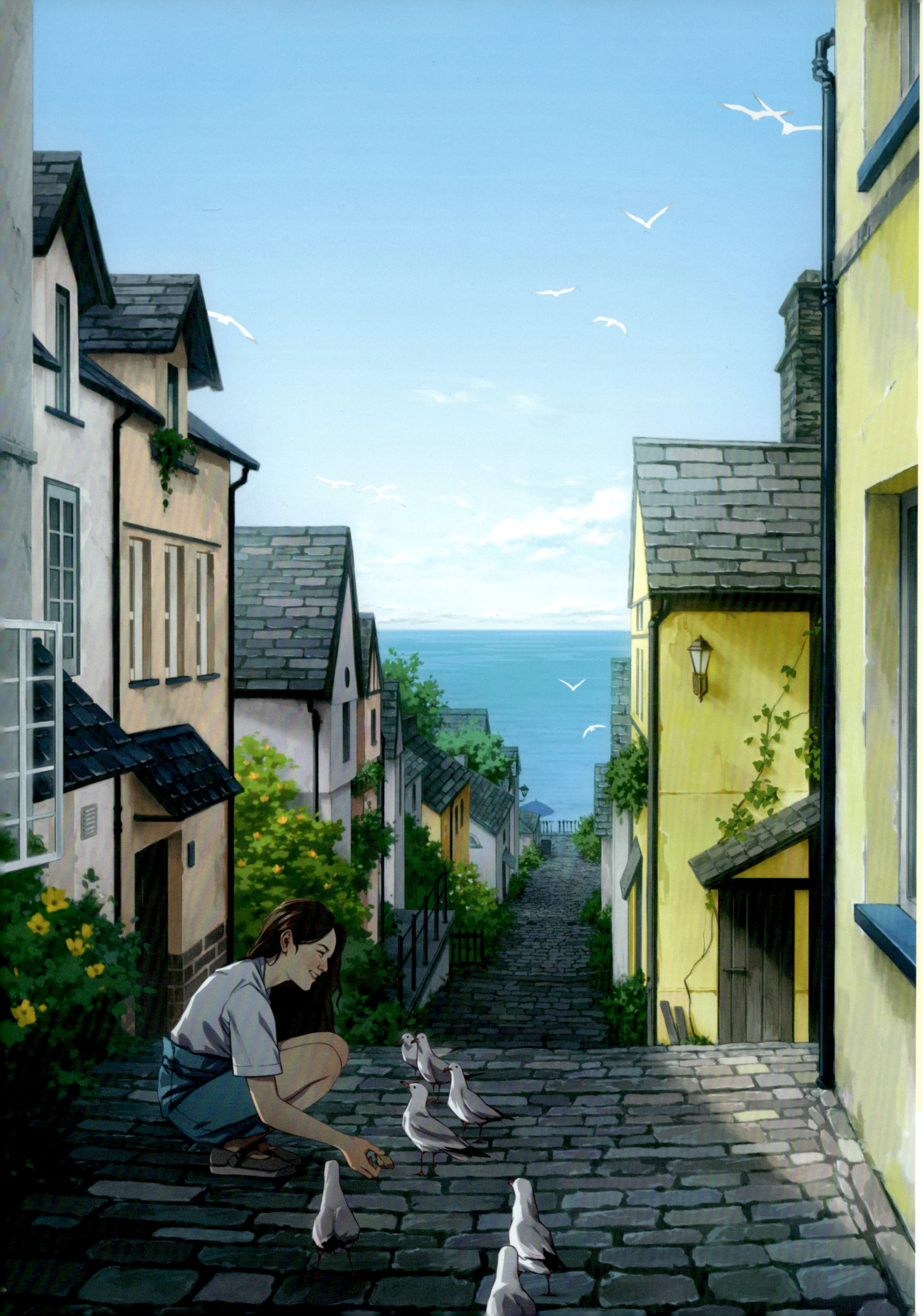

HOW I APPROACH STORYTELLING

For me, ideas and storytelling are inextricably linked. Including a narrative in a work of art, in my opinion, makes it more memorable and engaging. As humans, we are wired to respond strongly to stories, which remain more vivid in our memories – like cautionary tales and fables, for example. The inclusion of narrative allows the recipient to interact with the artwork on a deeper level. Thus, in order to create the emotional impact I'm aiming for, it's essential for me to expand a vague idea into a visual story.

But what makes a story, and when does a picture start telling a story instead of just looking pretty? I believe the fundamental basis of visual narrative is *interaction*: a figure (human, animal, or other) interacts in a visible way with another figure, their environment, or an object. Even simply looking at one's surroundings is a form of interaction.

Furthermore, there is a sense of story when I feel like there is something deeper behind the image that I'm not seeing – like I'm only looking at a glimpse of a whole world that continues beyond the frame. I think a picture tells a compelling story when I don't get the impression that the figures were placed and posed there for me, and instead, they're concerned with their own reality within the image. What breaks the illusion is when they seem too posed and unnatural, like pictures from a catalogue.

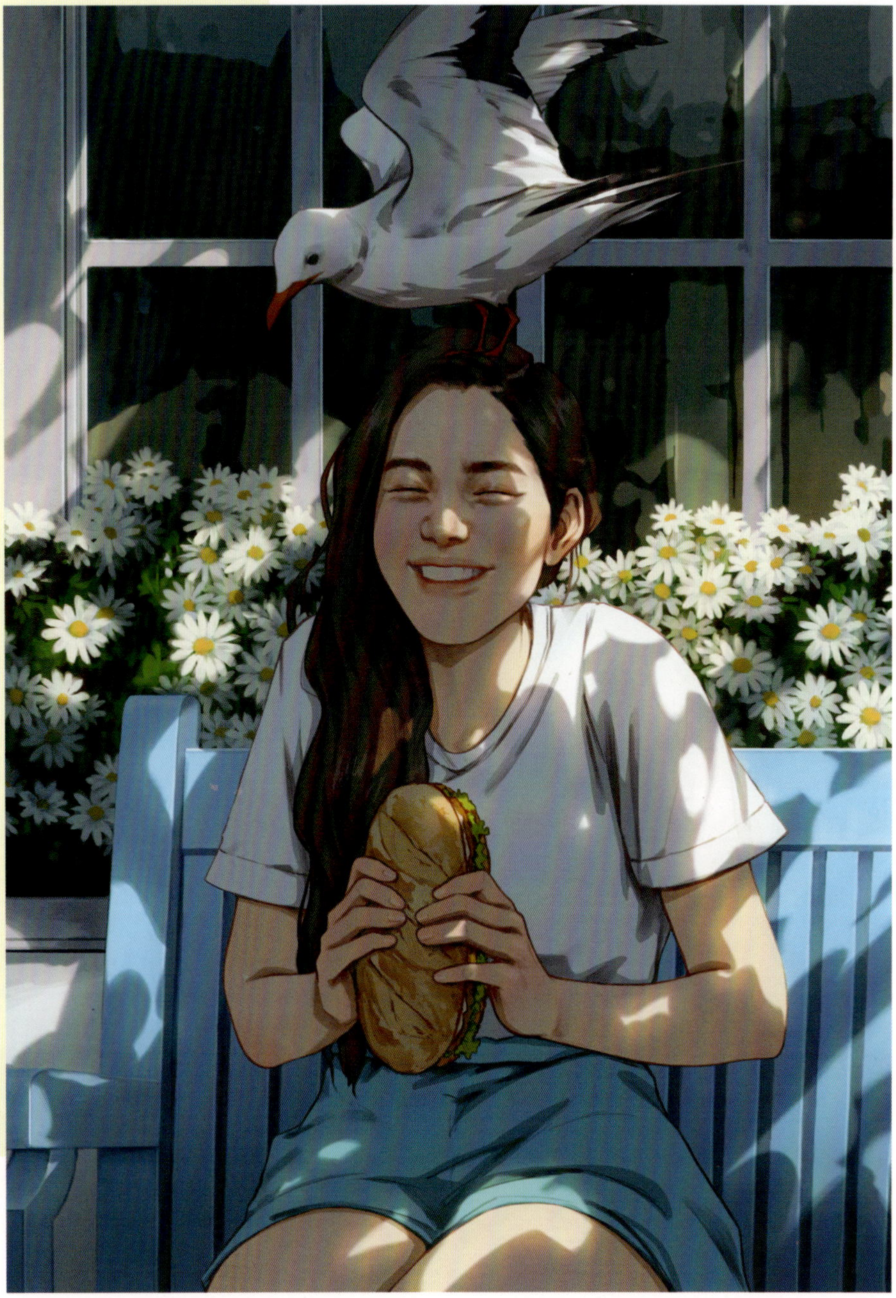

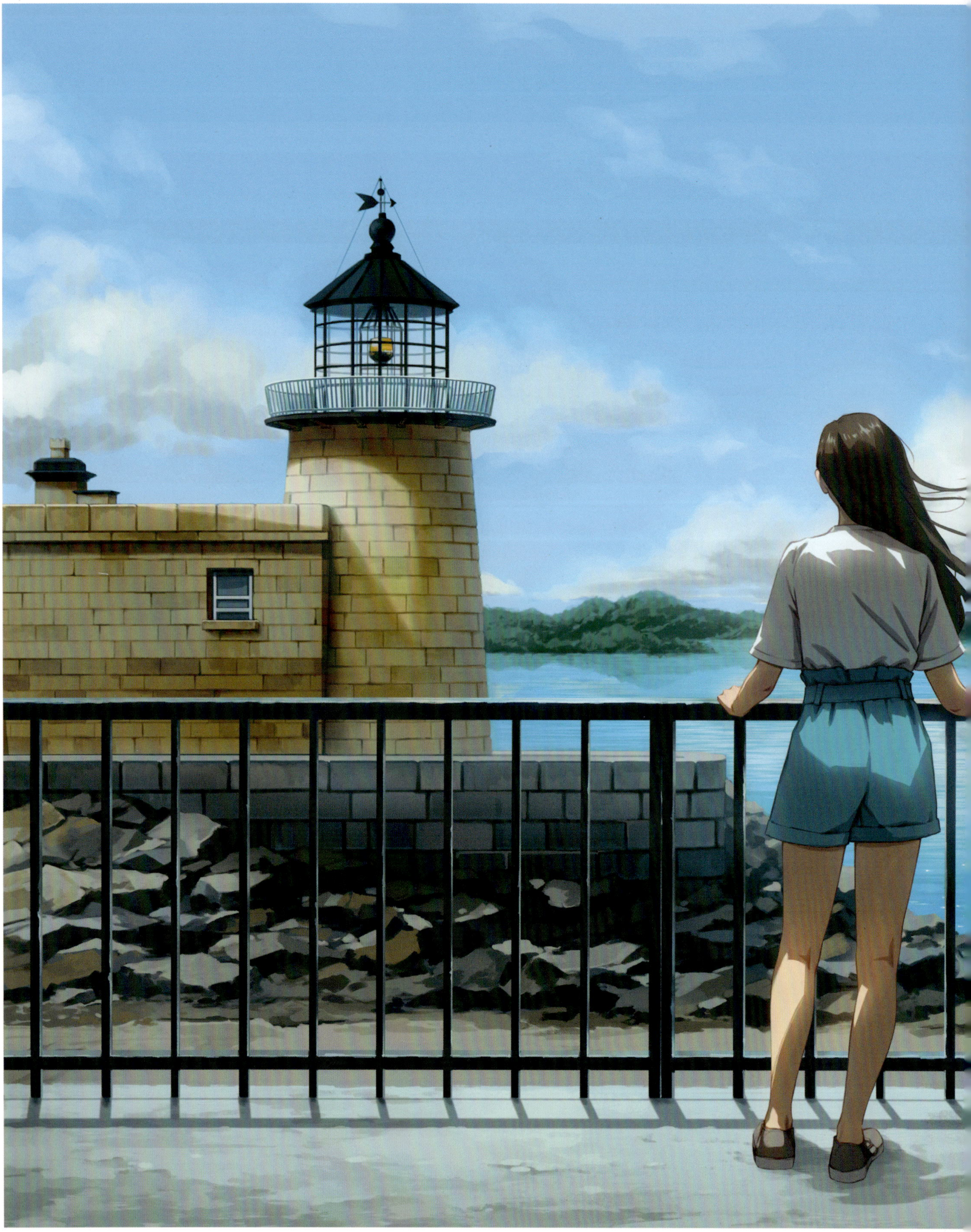

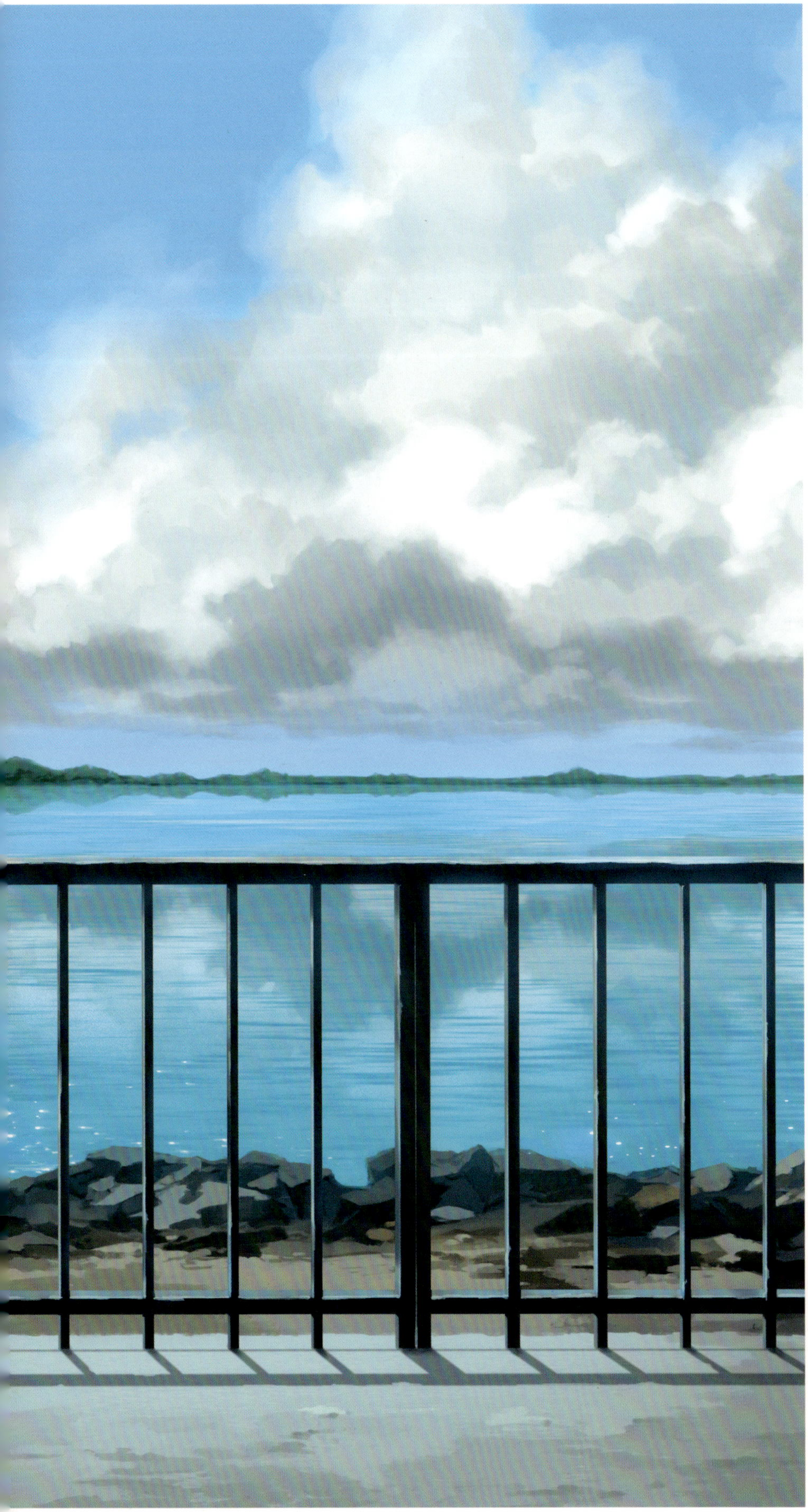

An important guideline for me is cinematic work: my goal is to create images that feel as if they're still-frames taken from animated films with a backstory that the viewer can potentially explore. I especially love slice-of-life moments that celebrate the beauty in the mundane. At their core, these little stories are usually very simple: *A girl lies in the grass and watches a grasshopper; a yawning cat sits in the window of a cottage.* But what makes them unique and interesting is the execution – the choice of elements and details in the scene, and the way in which they are presented. So, I try not to overvalue ideas; I keep them fairly simple and focus on execution instead.

Seaside Town

This is a mini-series of three illustrations, all set in the same coastal town. I wanted to show the same person in different situations throughout the day – like a travel diary

TECHNIQUES FOR VISUAL STORYTELLING

When I come across an idea that interests me, I don't start drawing right away. Instead, I take written notes. I find that if I immediately move on to sketching, the vivid image from my imagination evaporates and quickly gets replaced by scribbles, which don't quite capture the essence and necessary complexity. In order to give myself more room for experimentation, I initially stick to words, and thus further expand the scene. I write down everything that comes to mind and edit later. The following techniques are not necessarily intended to be used in the order presented here. They can be alternated and combined with each other.

TECHNIQUE I: *FREE WORD ASSOCIATION*

This is the most informal method of exploration for me. I simply select a word or an idea as a starting point and write down what comes to mind, such as imagery it may conjure. This way, unforeseen connections are often revealed and my thoughts are able to move in surprising directions. I find the use of symbolism particularly exciting here because it often allows for nuanced representations of themes that are not necessarily what you would expect.

For me, free word association is the best method to fathom abstract concepts and turn them into images. How can I represent concepts like hope, creativity, or loneliness through pictures? This is one of the reasons why I find tarot cards intriguing, because they do just that: they assign concrete representations to these general, vague ideas. But the beauty of it is that each of us has different associations with these concepts, and, accordingly, unique images emerge.

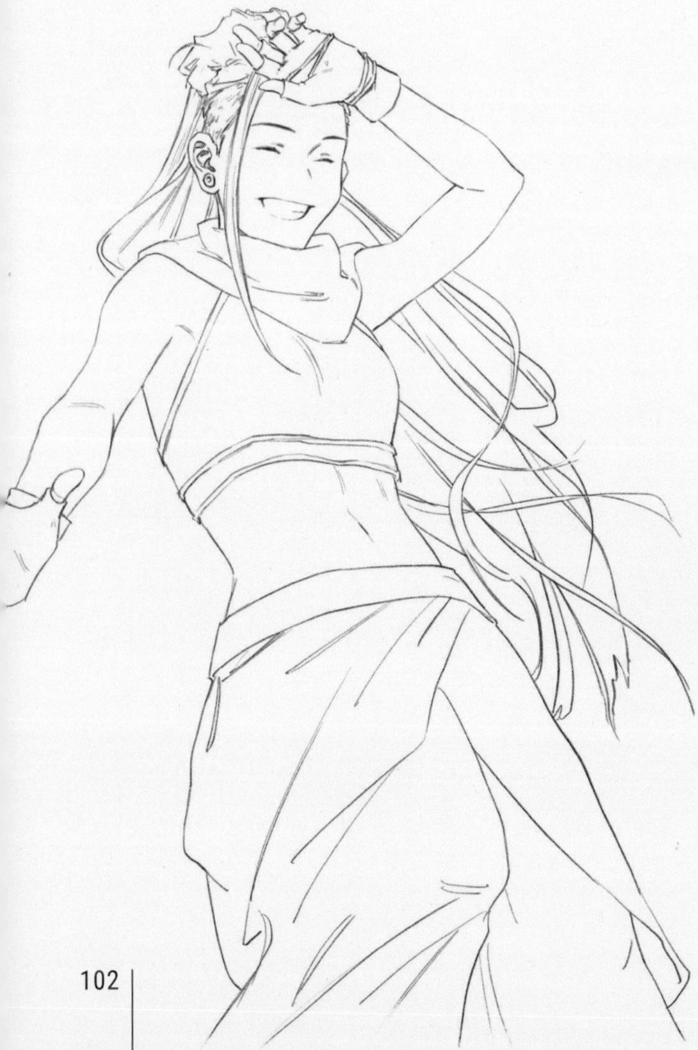

SUMMER

HAZY DAYS AND LATE SUNSETS

EVENINGS

MY HANDS IN THE GRASS

FLICKERING SUNLIGHT

RADIO MUSIC

POPSICLES, HUMIDITY

FANS AND SWAYING CURTAINS

DRIFTING AIMLESSLY

NAPPING

MOSQUITO BITES

THE SMELL OF CHARCOAL

THE SOUND OF CICADAS

RIDING MY BIKE THROUGH EMPTY STREETS LATE AT NIGHT

FREEDOM

ANYTHING SEEMS POSSIBLE

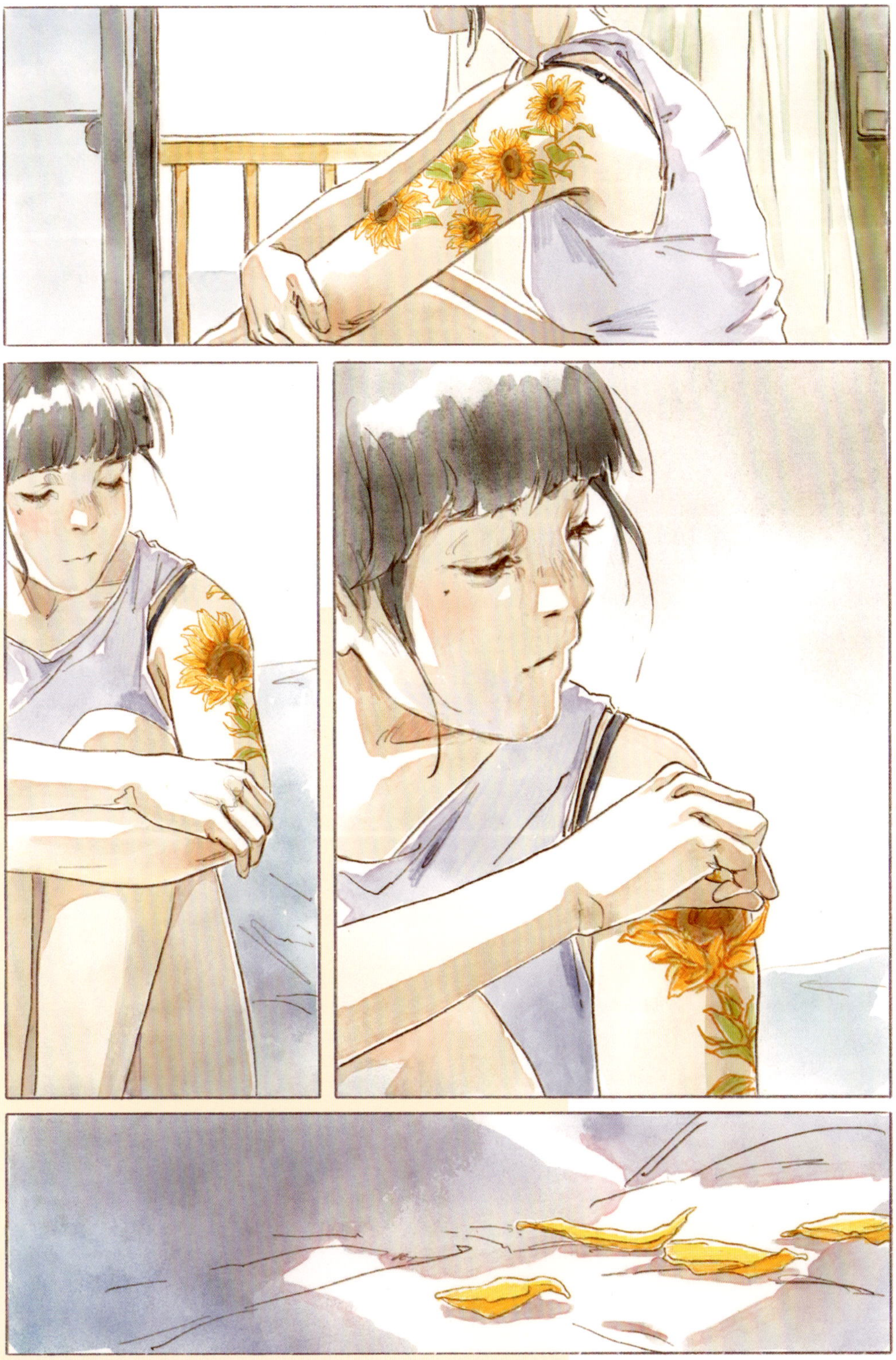

Sunflowers

This page of sequential art came out of a strange idea, and I decided to draw it instead of simply questioning it

LONELINESS

ISOLATION

HOLLOW

DREARINESS

GREY WALLS

A NARROW ROOM

REACHING OUT YOUR HAND BUT FINDING NOTHING TO TOUCH

BLANK STARES

BLUE LIGHT FROM A COMPUTER SCREEN

SOMETHING MISSING

WALKING ALONE AMONG A CROWD

FEELING LIKE A SHADOW

TECHNIQUE II: *ASK QUESTIONS*

The simplest format to think up a quick story is this: ***who** is doing **what**, and **where**?*

Based on this basic construct, specific details can then be added by asking further questions. My goal here is to find the missing pieces and complete the scene in my mind so that it comes to life. A fun way to do this is asking 'what if?'

What if it were a different time of day?

What if the weather changed?

What if it were a different season?

What if the scene were set in the fifties?

What if it were set in my home town?

What if it were set on a different planet?

What if it were set by the ocean?

What if one of the characters were a marine biologist?

What if the characters were deeply unhappy?

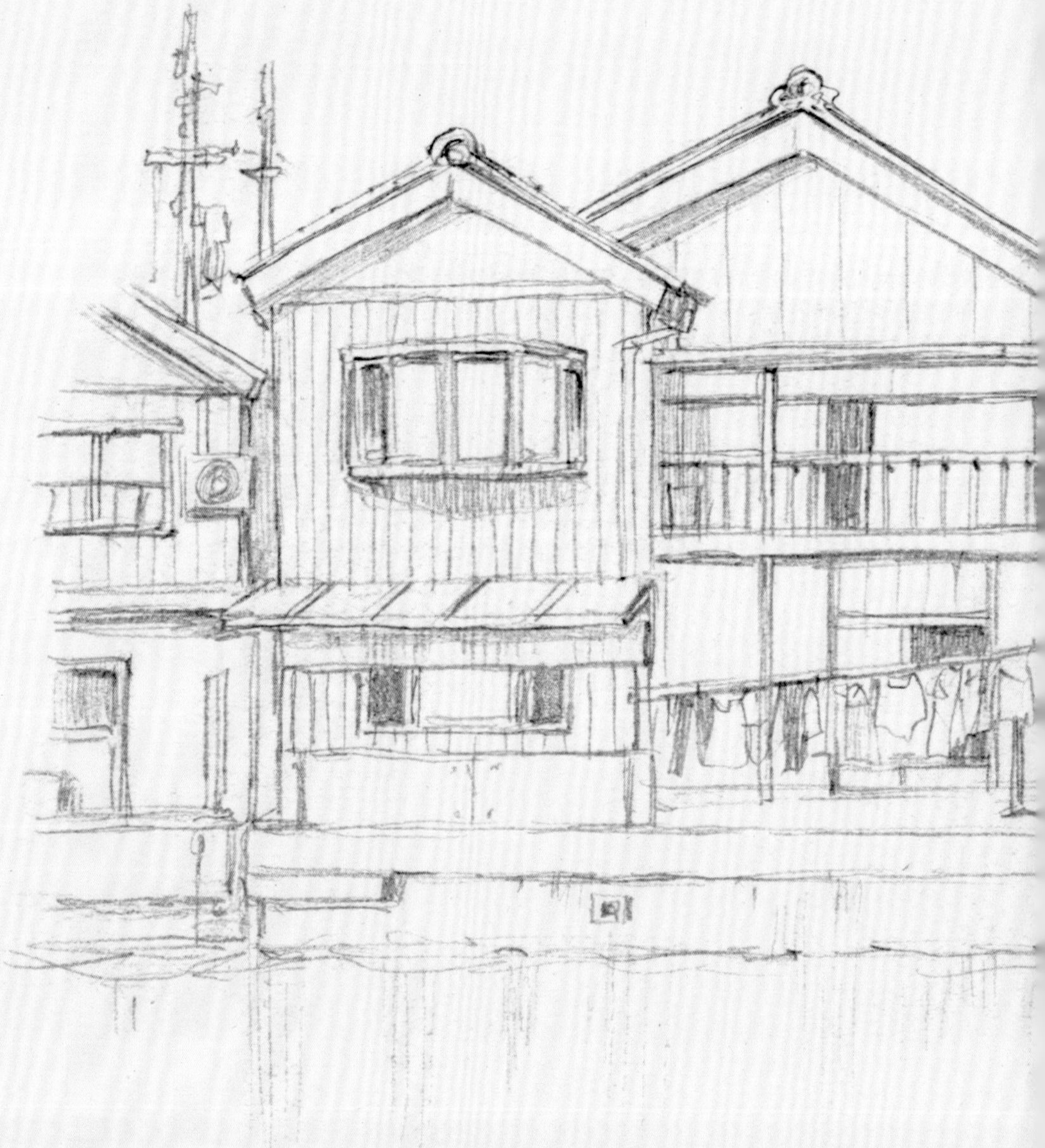

A LITTLE GIRL AND HER GRANDFATHER ARE PICKING MUSHROOMS IN THE FOREST; A COLLEGE STUDENT IS READING A BOOK AT THE LIBRARY

We could go on like this forever.

Once the rough framework is mapped out, it's a good time to note down specific visual details:

What colours do I envision?
What mood? What lighting?
What are some visual attributes of the characters?
What is the environment like?
What point of view do I take as a viewer?

This can include anything I think is important to the story, and if I get stuck at any point, I can think about all the things that I *don't want*, and the things that *wouldn't happen* in the scene. This way I can narrow it down through elimination.

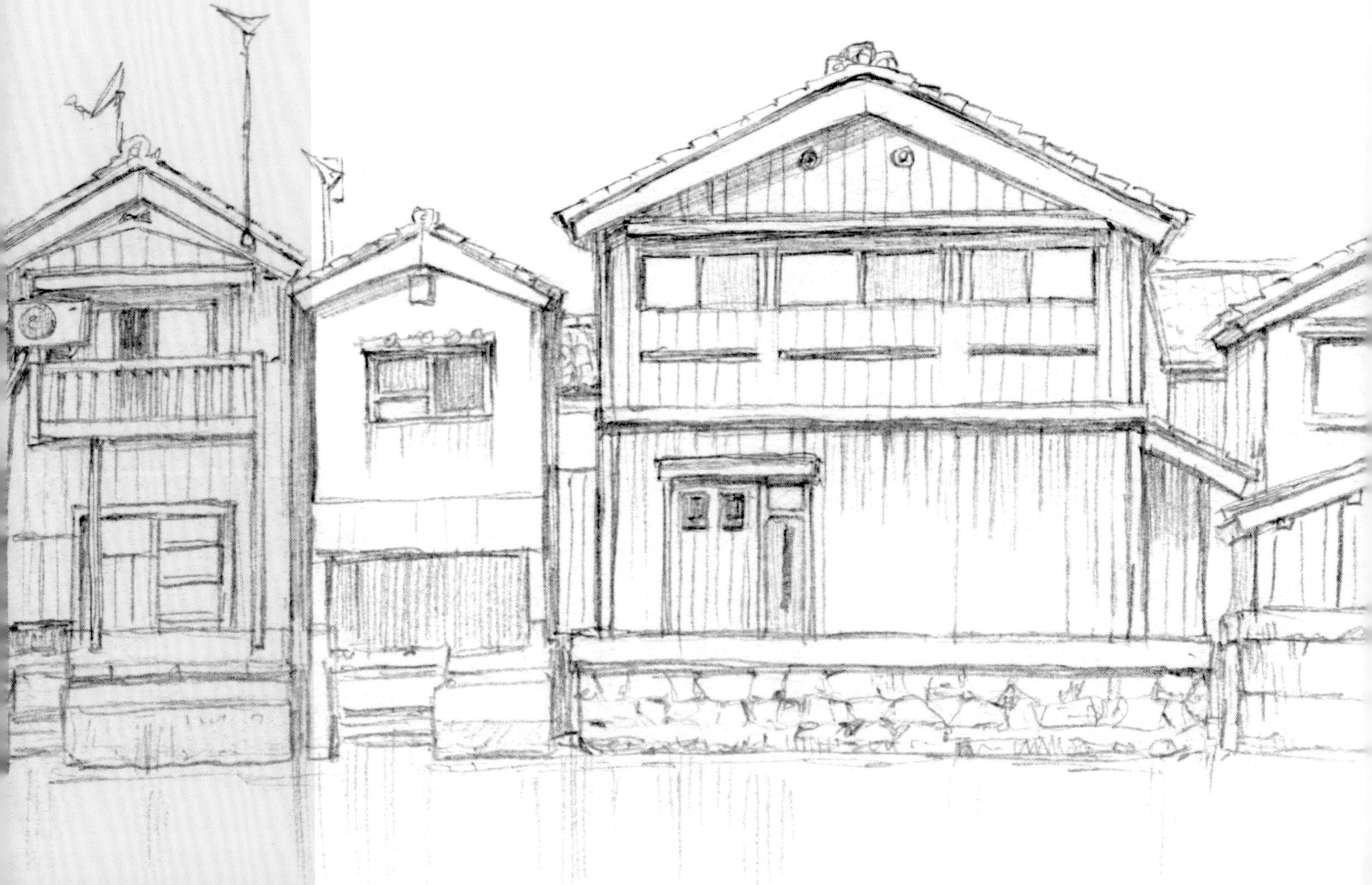

I should mention that it's easy to go overboard and end up wanting to fit three different stories into one image. So, I try to be careful to not confuse the *idea* with the *execution*. The idea remains simple all the way through (**who** is doing **what** and **where**); only the execution is elaborated in more detail. Paintings are not movie trailers and the elements we add should support the core story rather than detract from it.

TECHNIQUE III: *LOCATION-BASED APPROACH*

This method follows a similar procedure to the previous one, except that it only uses a location as a starting point. But I still want to single it out because, for me, it is the most enjoyable one. Simply put, I just pick a location – any place that interests me – and let the story unfold from there: an airport, church, bridge, book shop, and so on.

The reason I like this approach is because a location will often naturally guide the characters' actions. When I imagine a café, I see people drinking hot beverages and eating cakes, reading books, typing away on their laptops, or swapping stories with old friends. Certain locations are so familiar to us that it becomes easy to populate them with characters and stories. The interesting thing is that *my* version of a café will be drastically different from other people's because we each bring our own unique point of view.

This method originated from watching Hayao Miyazaki's films, in which iconic locations often become characters in their own right; they're incredibly memorable. Even if I can no longer remember the plots exactly, the huge bathhouse in *Spirited Away*, or the home of the Forest Spirit in *Princess Mononoke* are still on my mind.

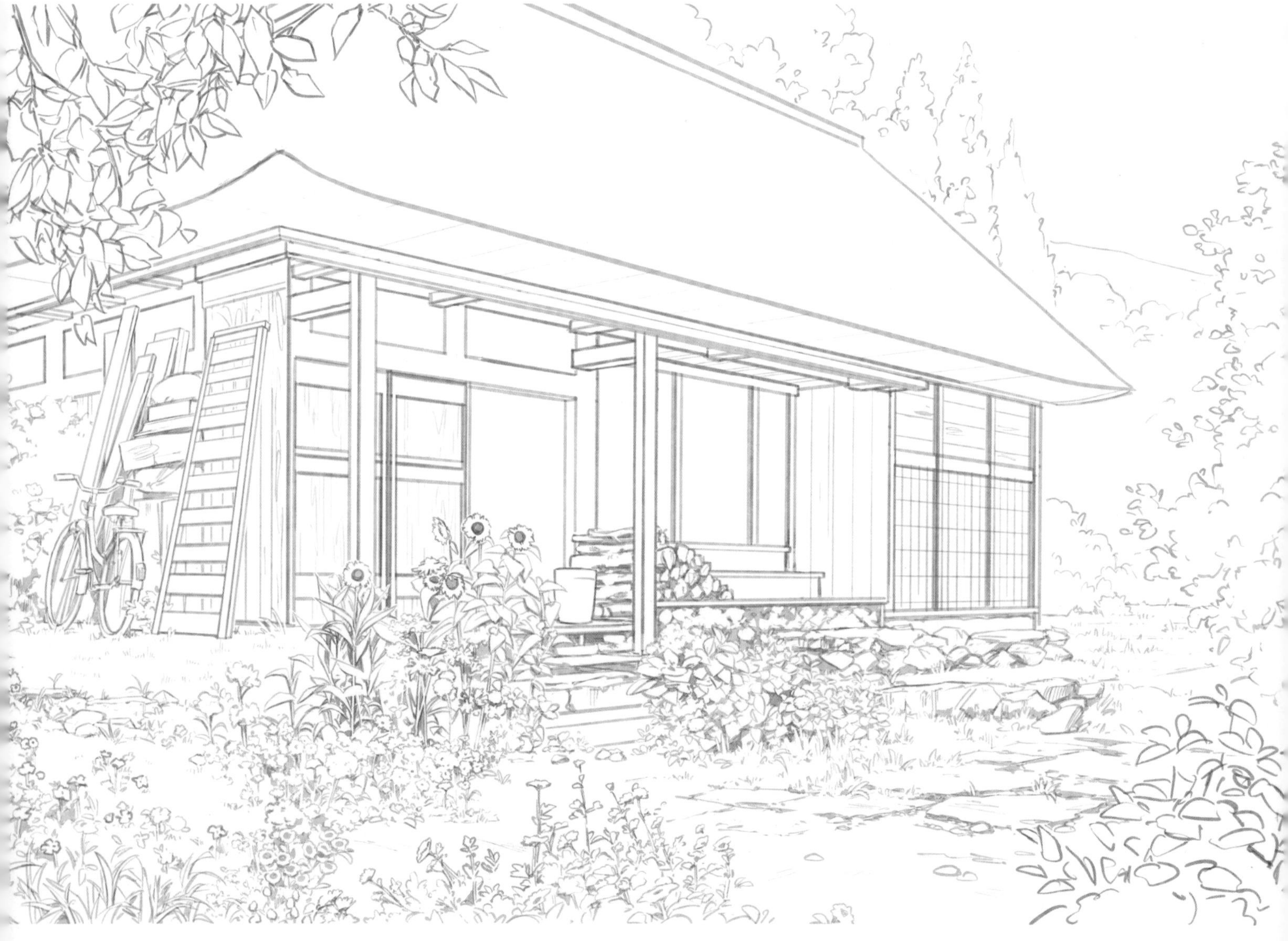

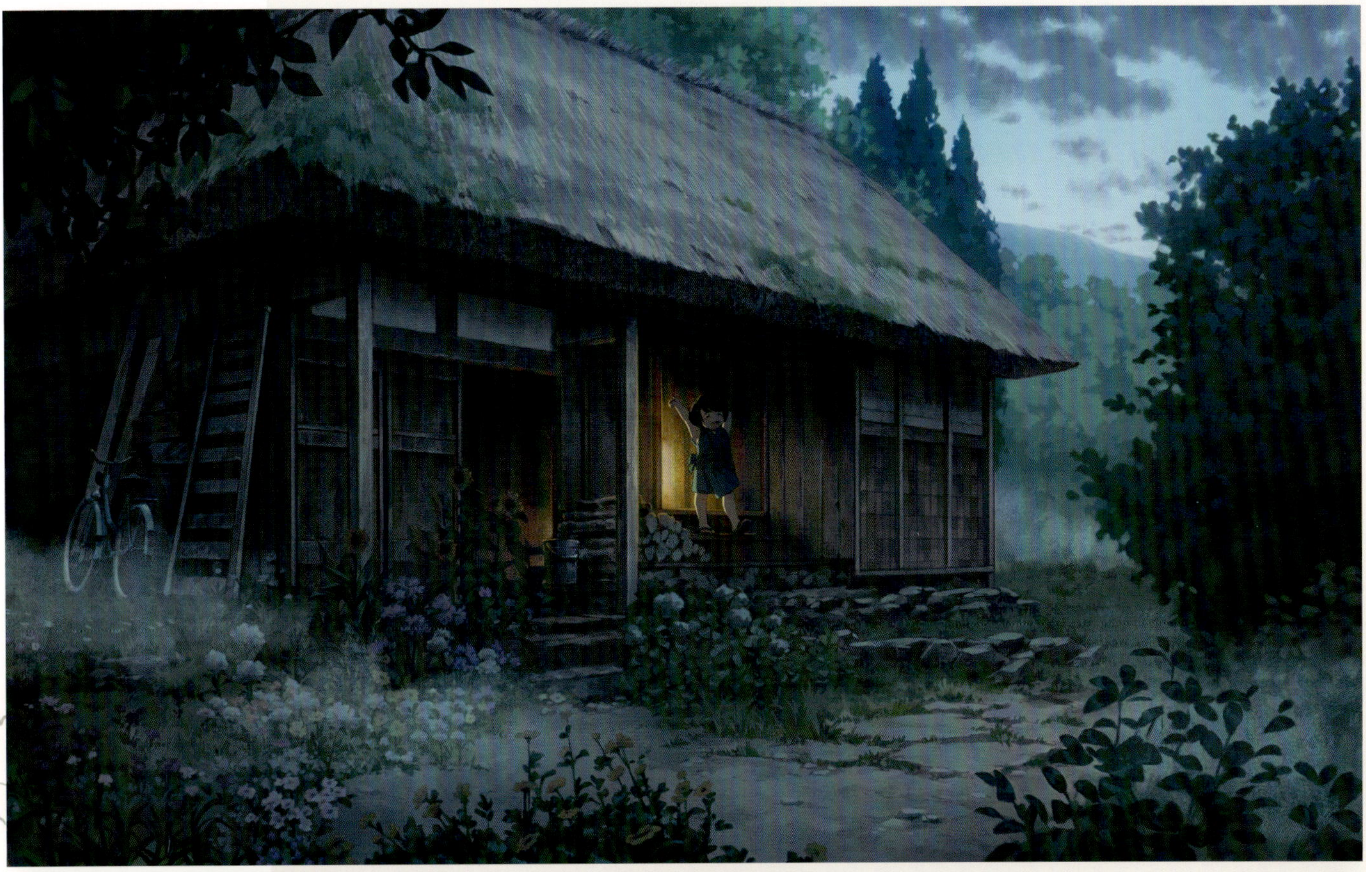

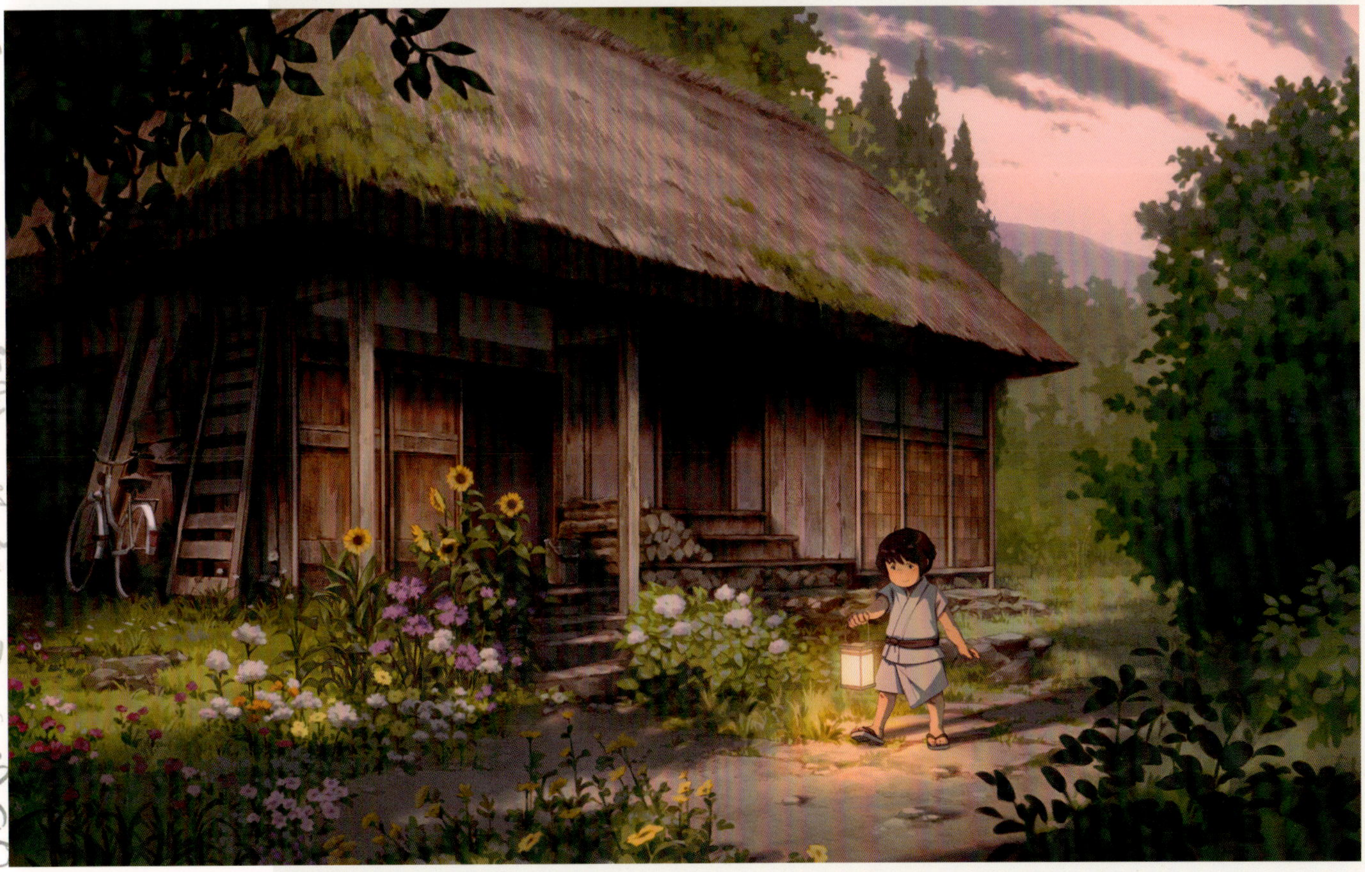

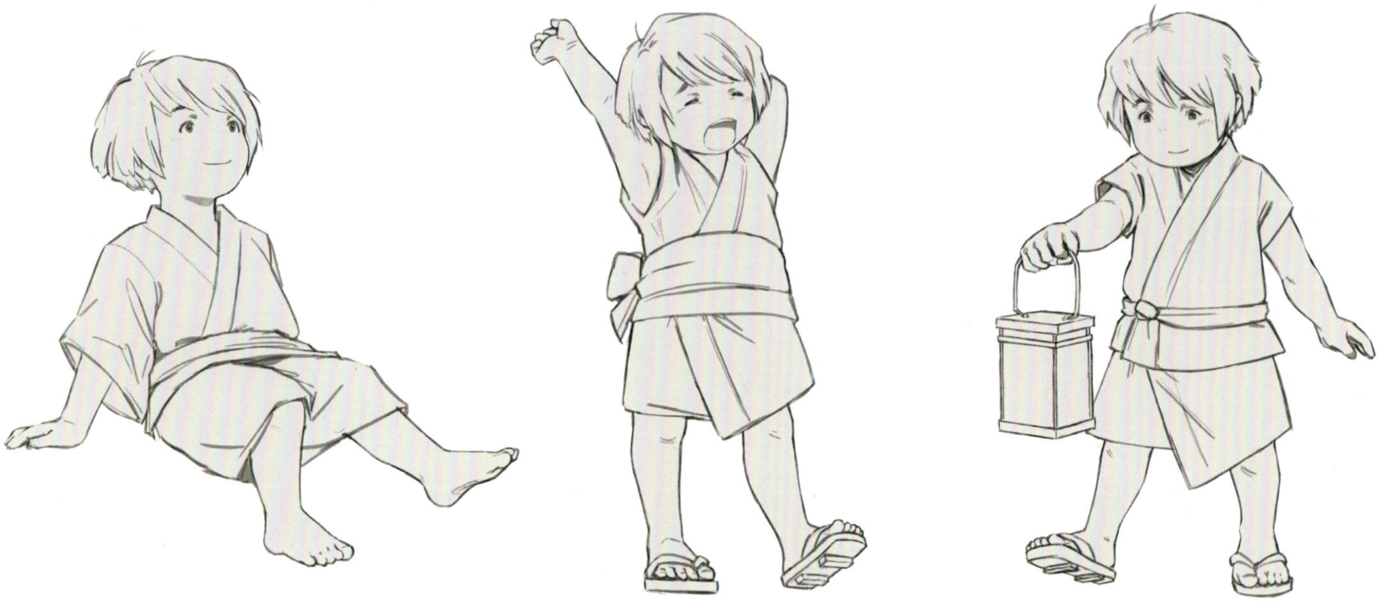

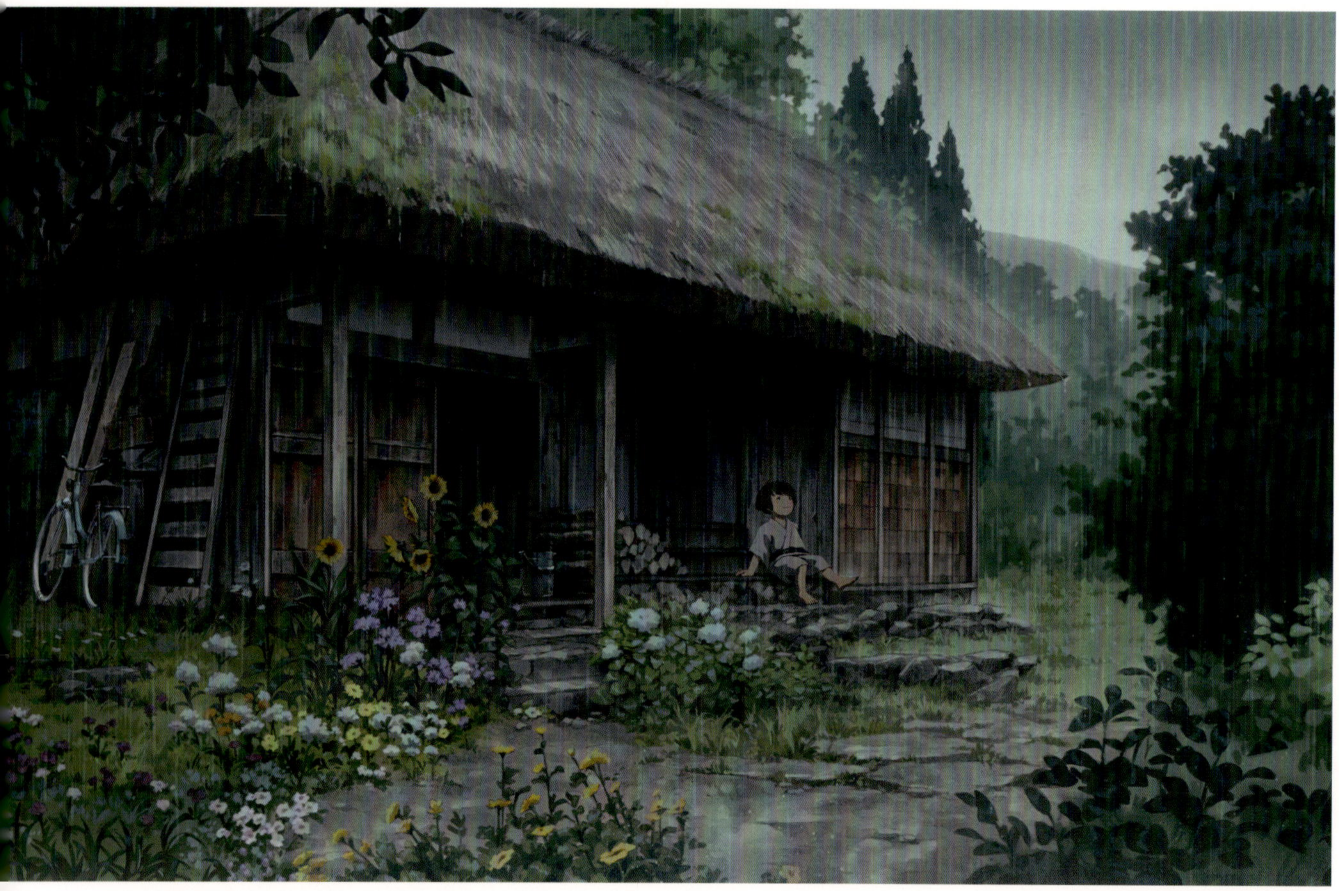

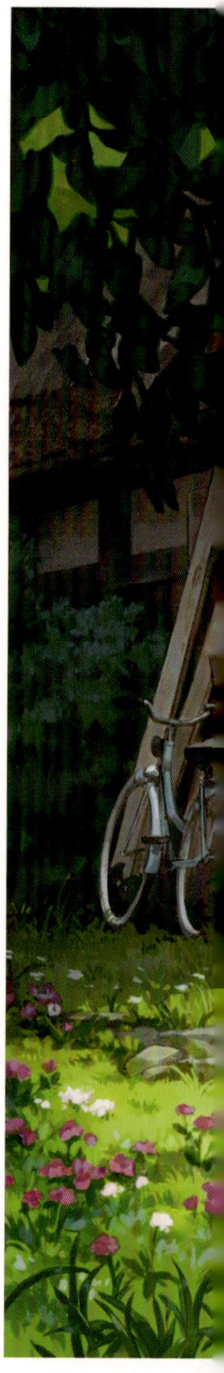

All of these images started with the same location, but they all communicate a different mood and story, primarily through varying colours, light, and the character's actions

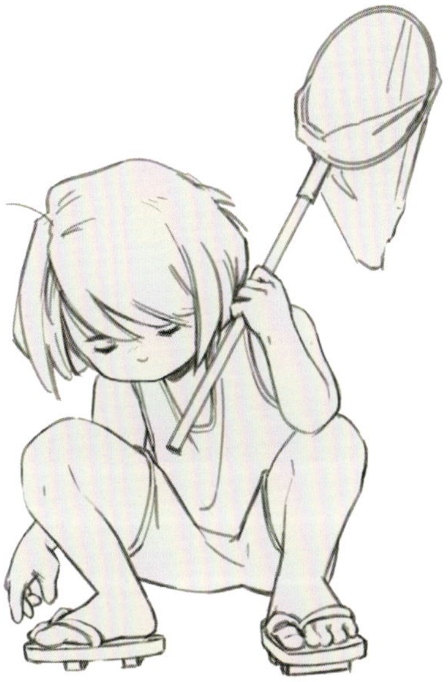

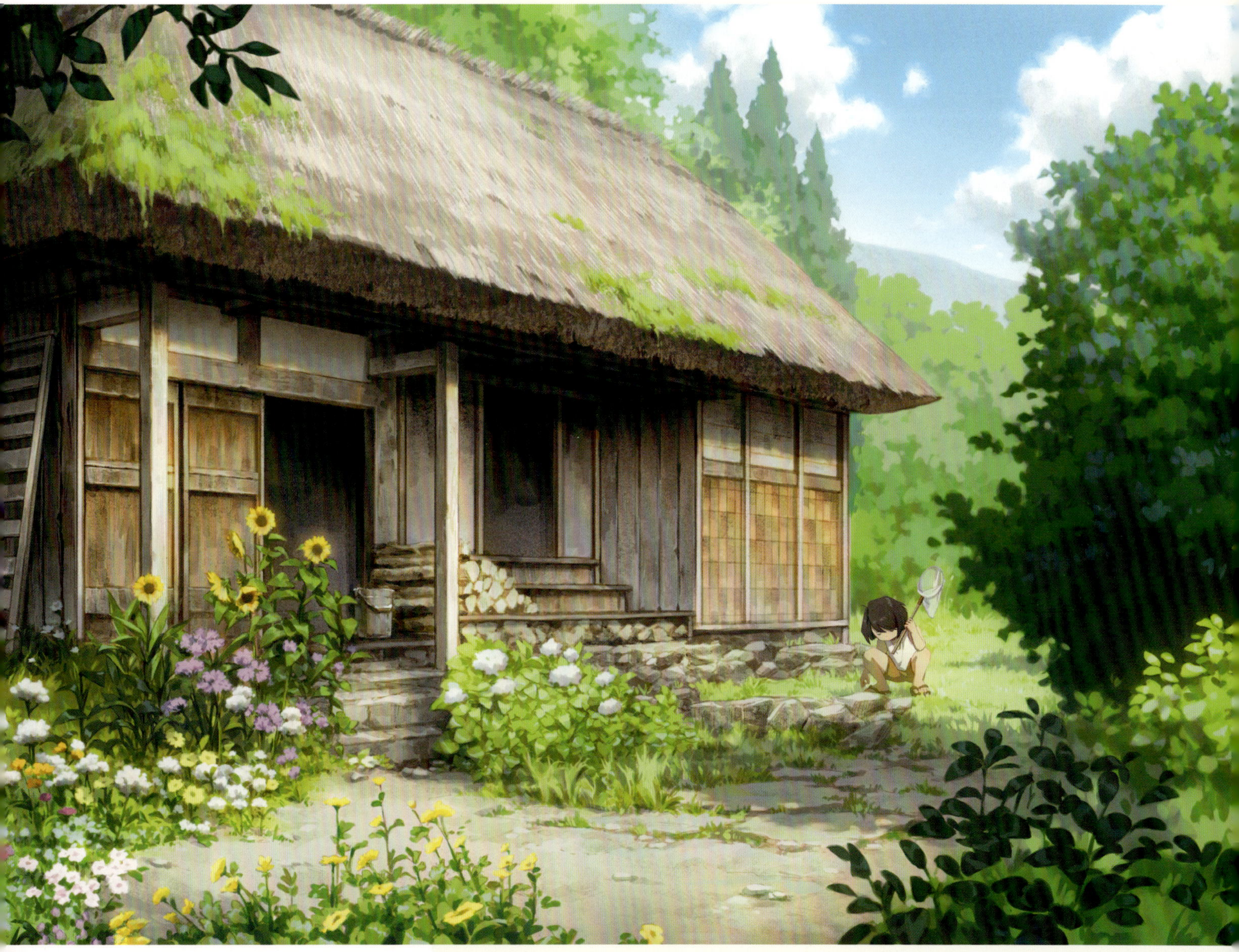

TECHNIQUE IV:
DESCRIBE SENSORY DETAILS

Nothing evokes a certain atmosphere as vividly as smells, sounds, tactile experiences, and tastes. Involving sensory details in our descriptions – aside from what we can see – is a highly effective method for painting word pictures.

Warm/cosy atmosphere:

A crackling fire

The smell of freshly baked bread

Steam rising from a cup of hot chocolate

The rustle of book pages being turned

The soft surface of a wool blanket

Desolate atmosphere:

The rough, brittle surface of rocks

A dusty wind blowing into your eyes

A static charge in the air

Ominous rumbling of thunder in the distance

Thirst

The sharp pain of blisters on your feet

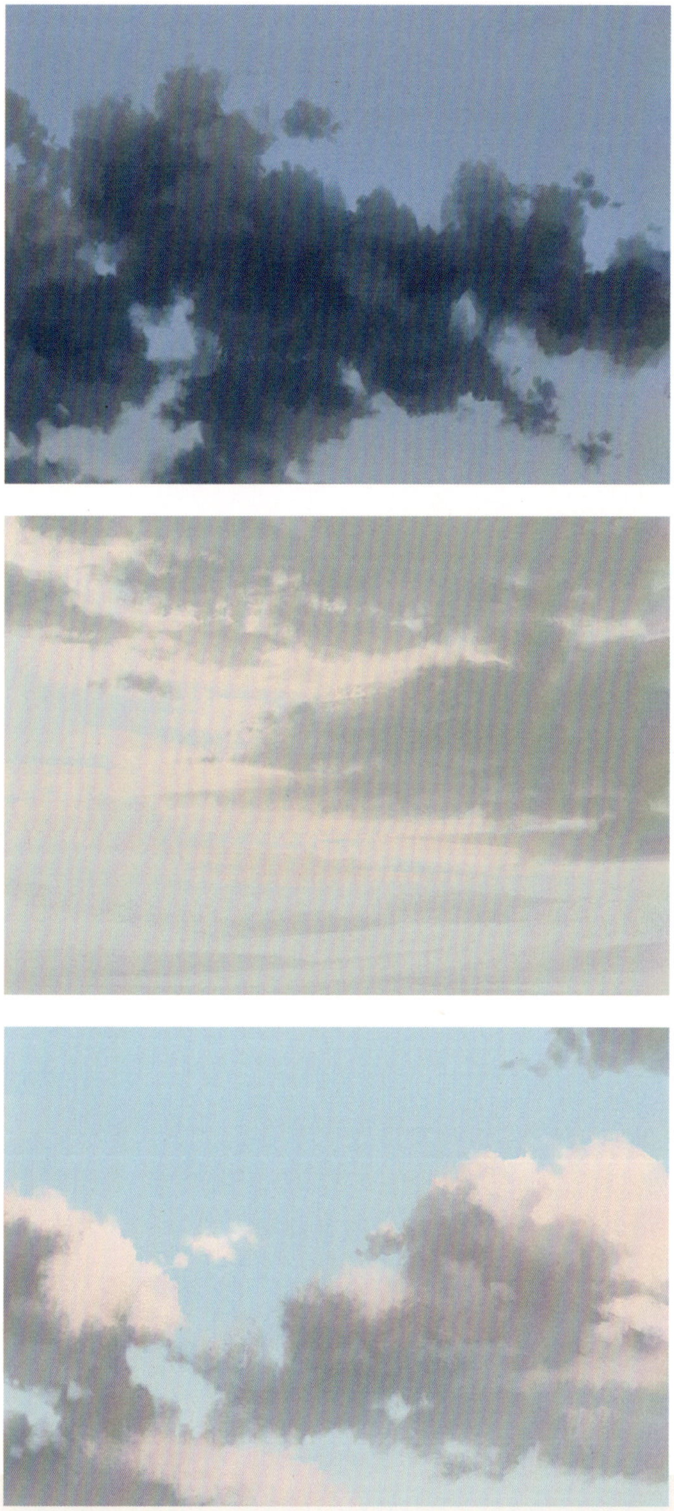

Even though there is no explicit story here, these representations of the sky, with their unique colours and shapes, evoke different emotions

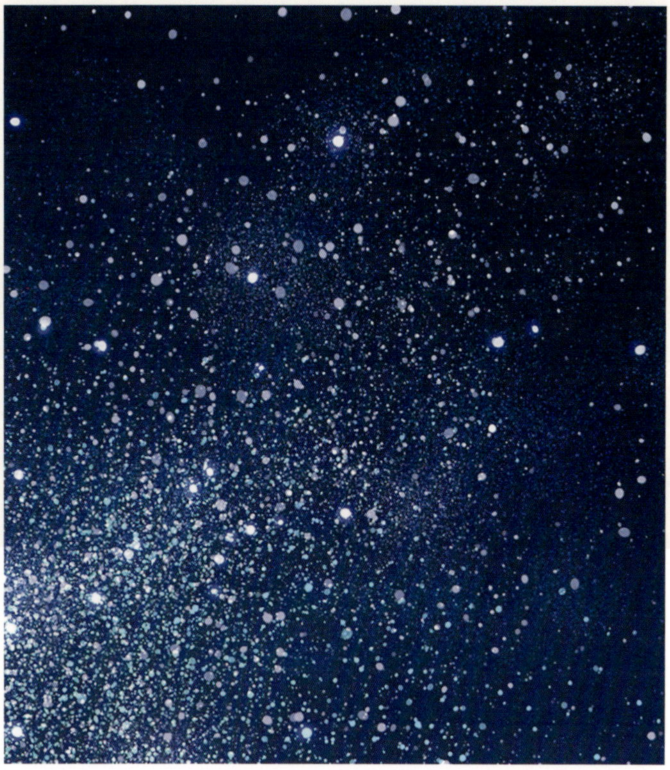

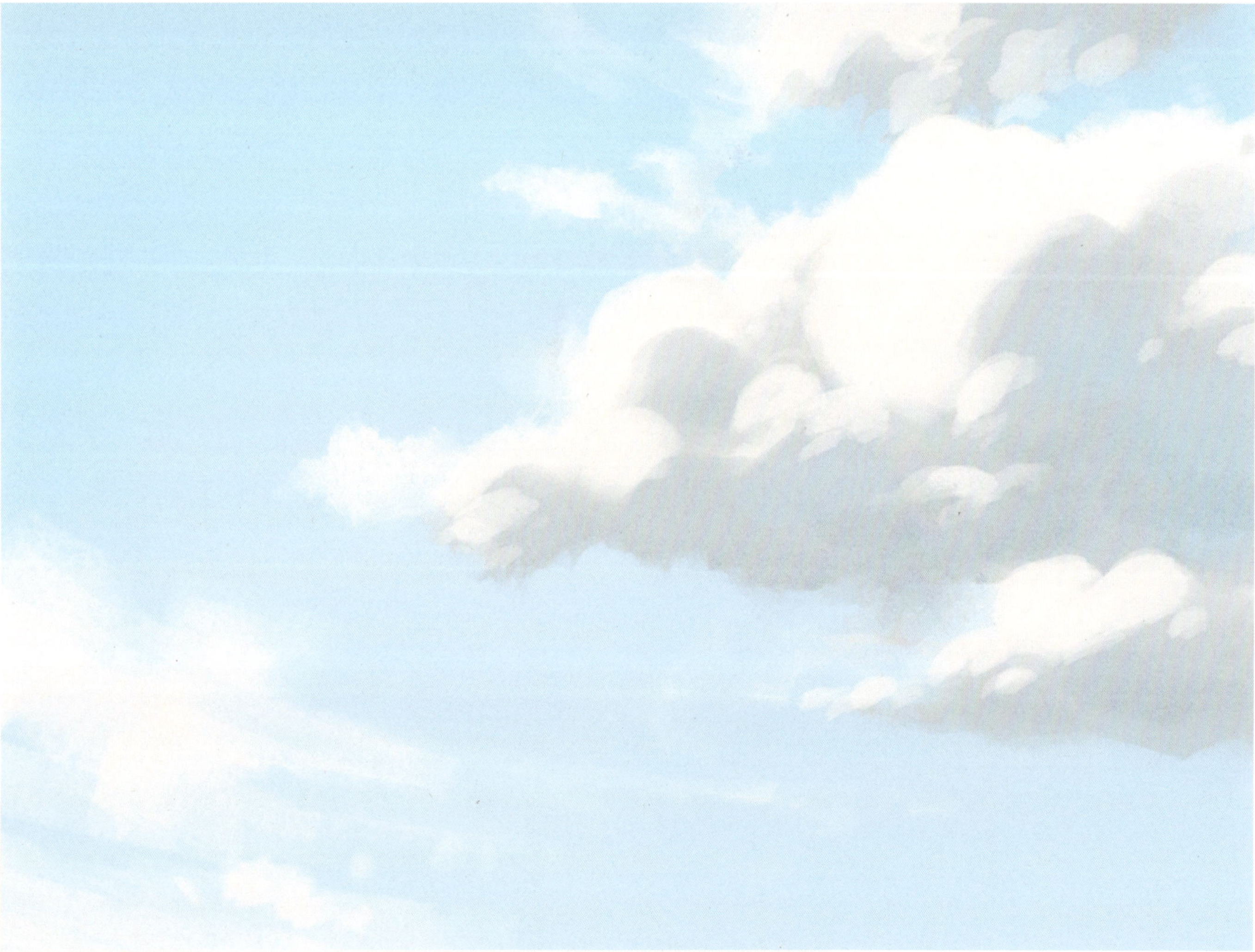

TECHNIQUE V: *THUMBNAIL SKETCHES*

Thumbnail sketches are small, rough drawings that we create to plan the look of our finished artwork in advance – a kind of preview, so to speak. For the sake of simplicity, these sketches are often kept in black and white, with sparse detail. Their greatest benefit is that they allow us to visually plan our painting on a small scale and test whether an idea will work or not. Often, what seems to have incredible potential in our heads then falls apart when we try to put it into practice. But because thumbnails are done so quickly, there isn't a huge commitment involved, so we can work through many variations without spending a lot of time. This way, mistakes are made before the actual painting process so we can avoid continuing with a flawed basic structure. If the sketch doesn't work in its simplest form, more detail and rendering isn't going to fix it.

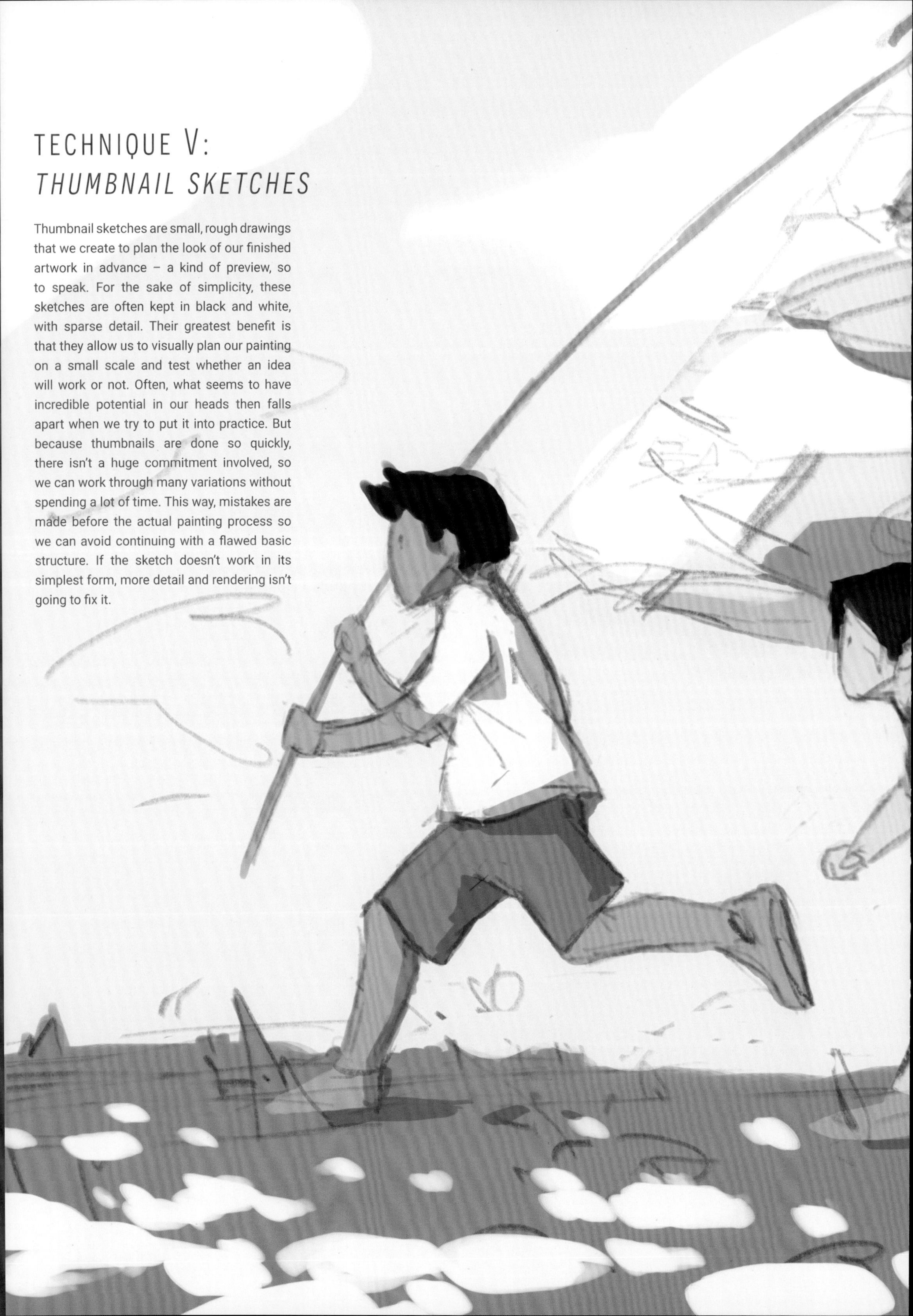

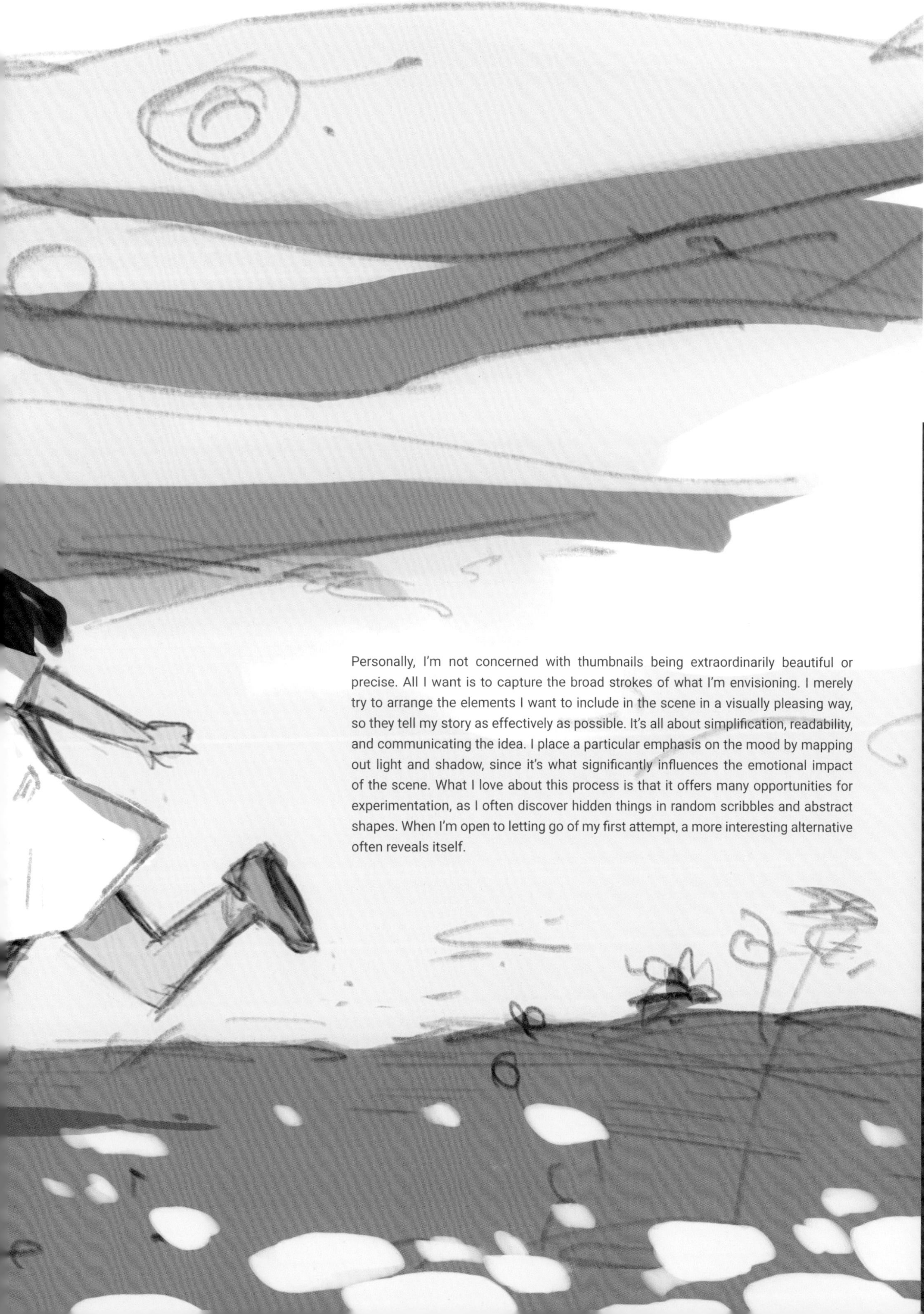

Personally, I'm not concerned with thumbnails being extraordinarily beautiful or precise. All I want is to capture the broad strokes of what I'm envisioning. I merely try to arrange the elements I want to include in the scene in a visually pleasing way, so they tell my story as effectively as possible. It's all about simplification, readability, and communicating the idea. I place a particular emphasis on the mood by mapping out light and shadow, since it's what significantly influences the emotional impact of the scene. What I love about this process is that it offers many opportunities for experimentation, as I often discover hidden things in random scribbles and abstract shapes. When I'm open to letting go of my first attempt, a more interesting alternative often reveals itself.

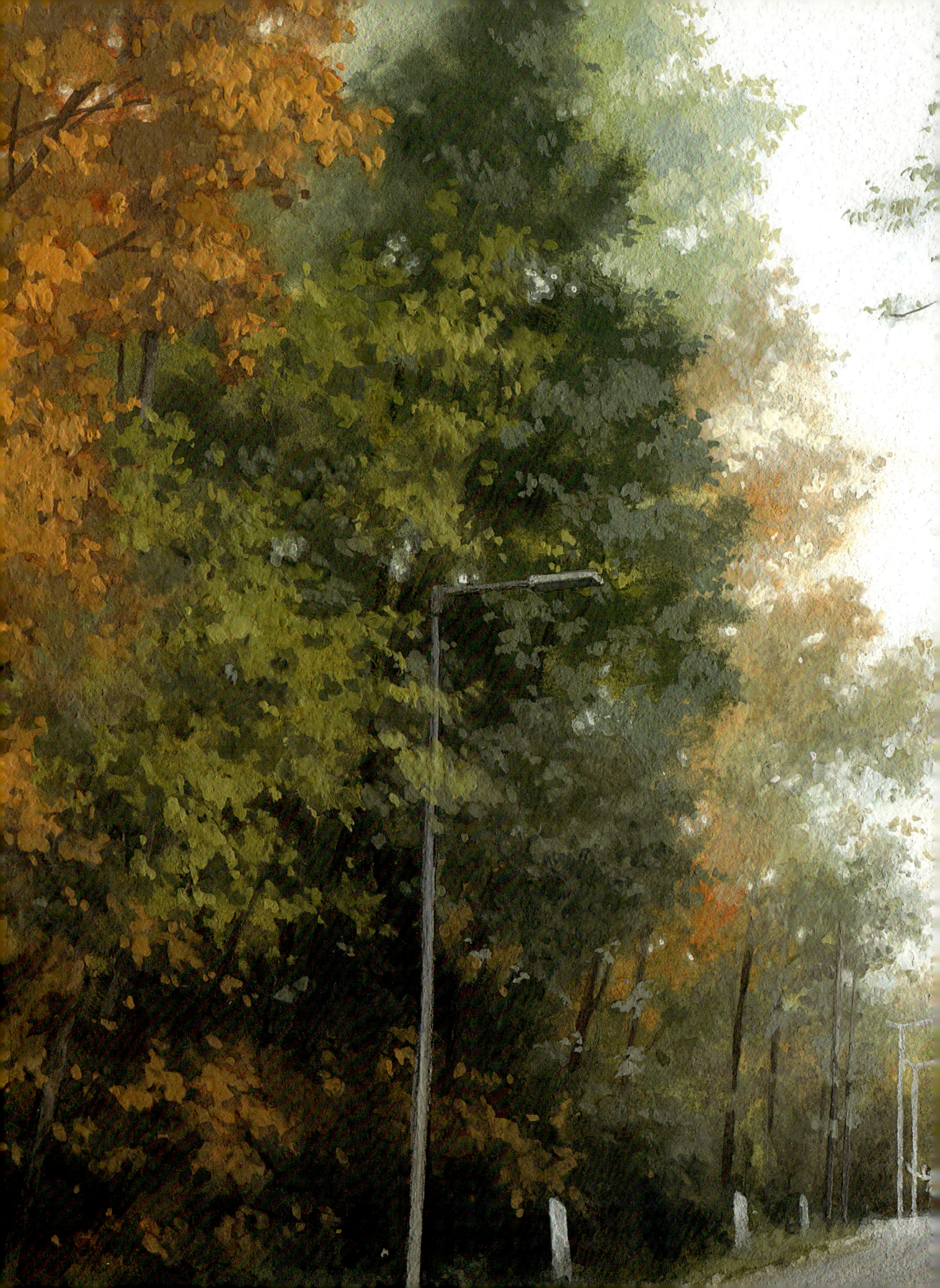

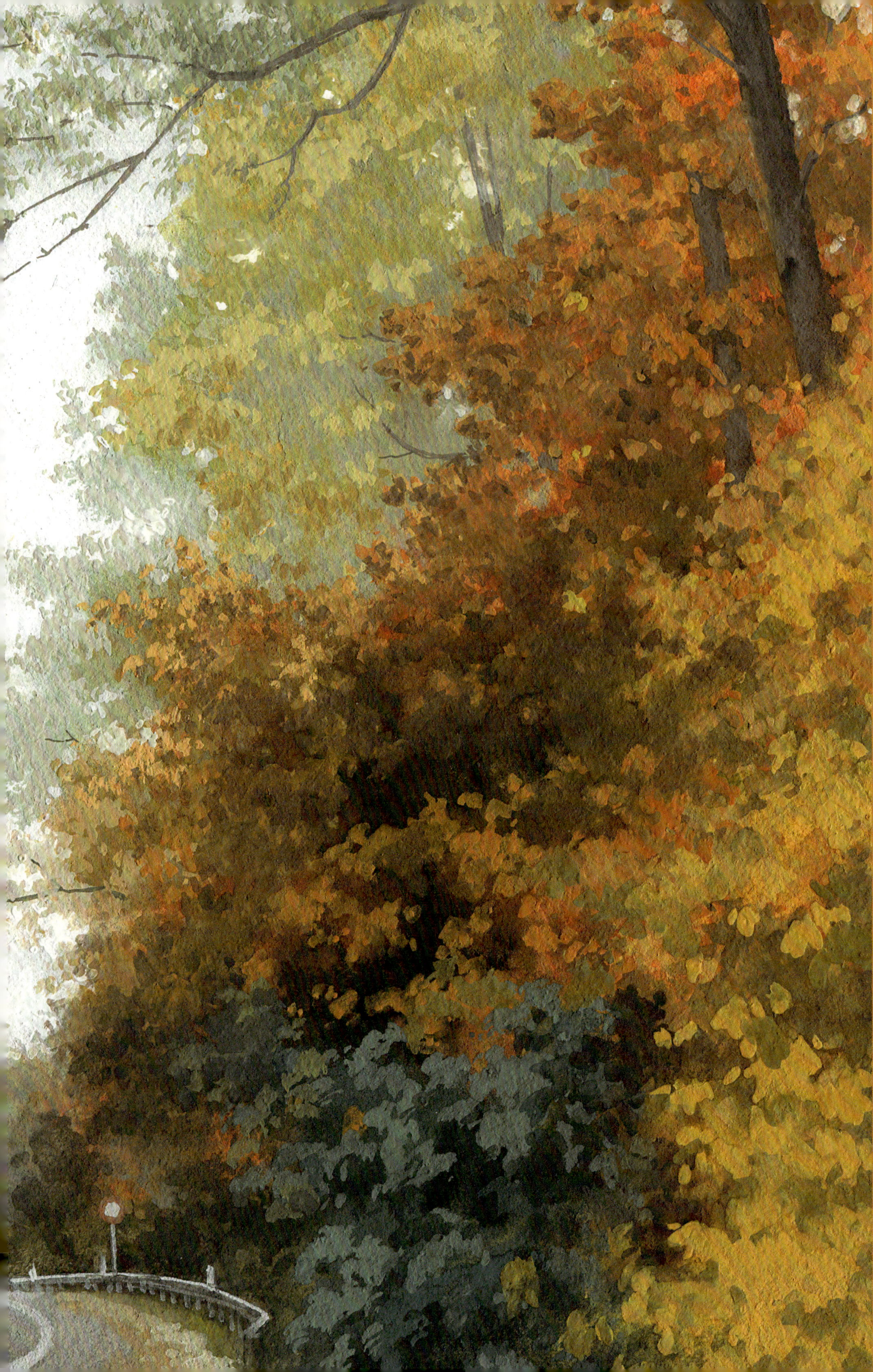

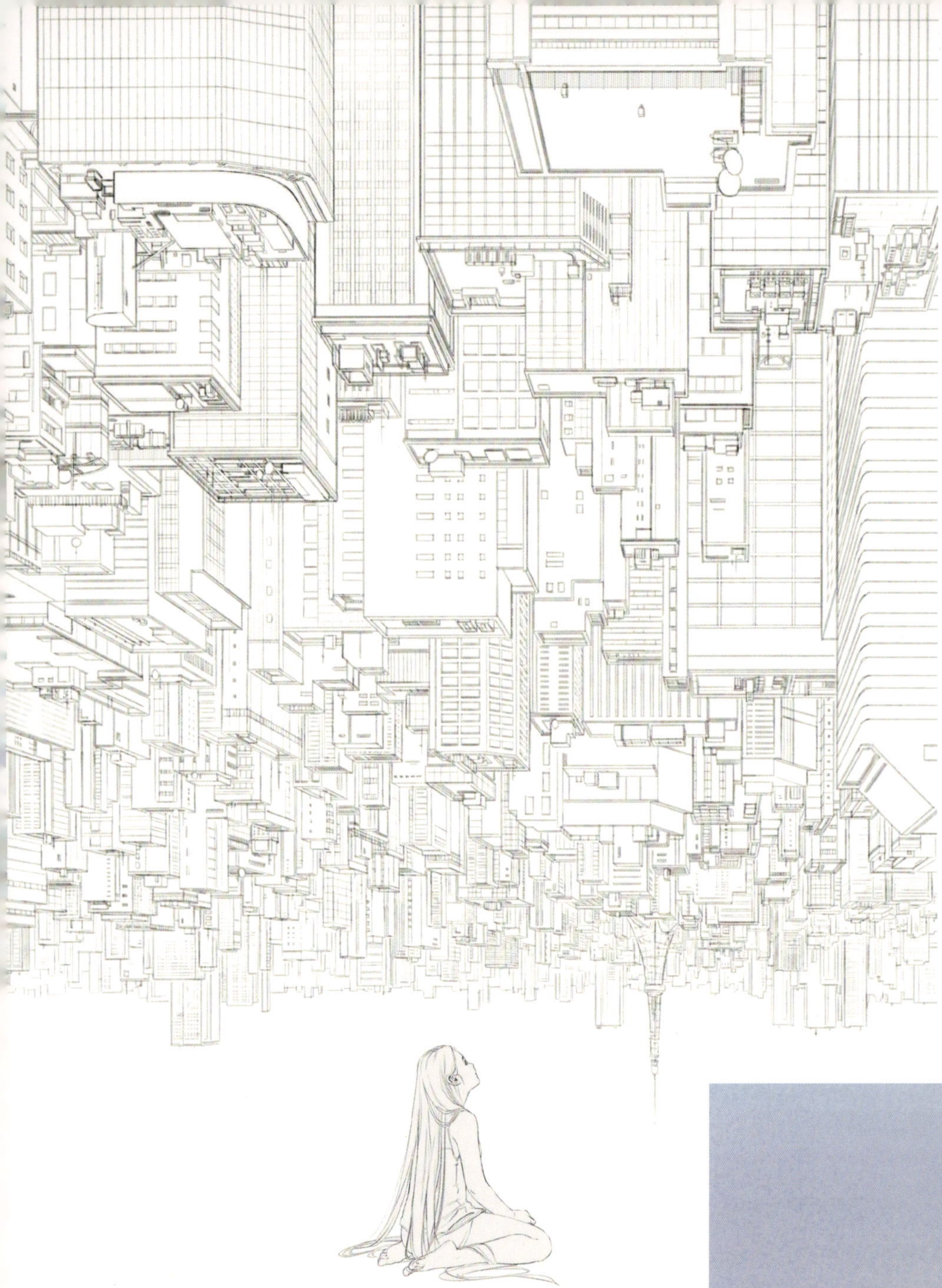

Magic realism is a form of expression that frequently appears in my illustrations. The term is borrowed from literature and describes a style of fiction that, as the name suggests, combines a realistic depiction of the world with magical elements. Generally speaking, stories classified under magic realism involve otherworldly, supernatural phenomena that occur in an ordinarily mundane setting, which causes the lines between reality and fantasy to blur. But unlike writers of the fantasy genre, magic-realist writers do not craft new worlds – they describe our world in microscopic detail and reveal the magic within it. Their narratives are riddled with things that cannot be explained by rational logic and are too strange to believe.

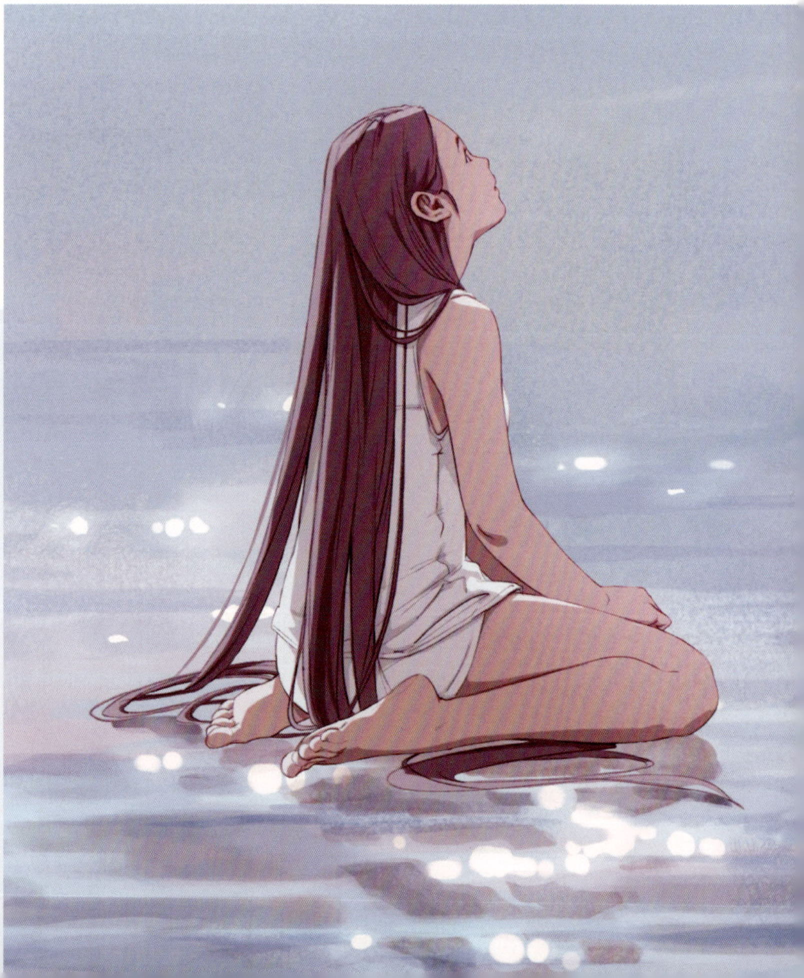

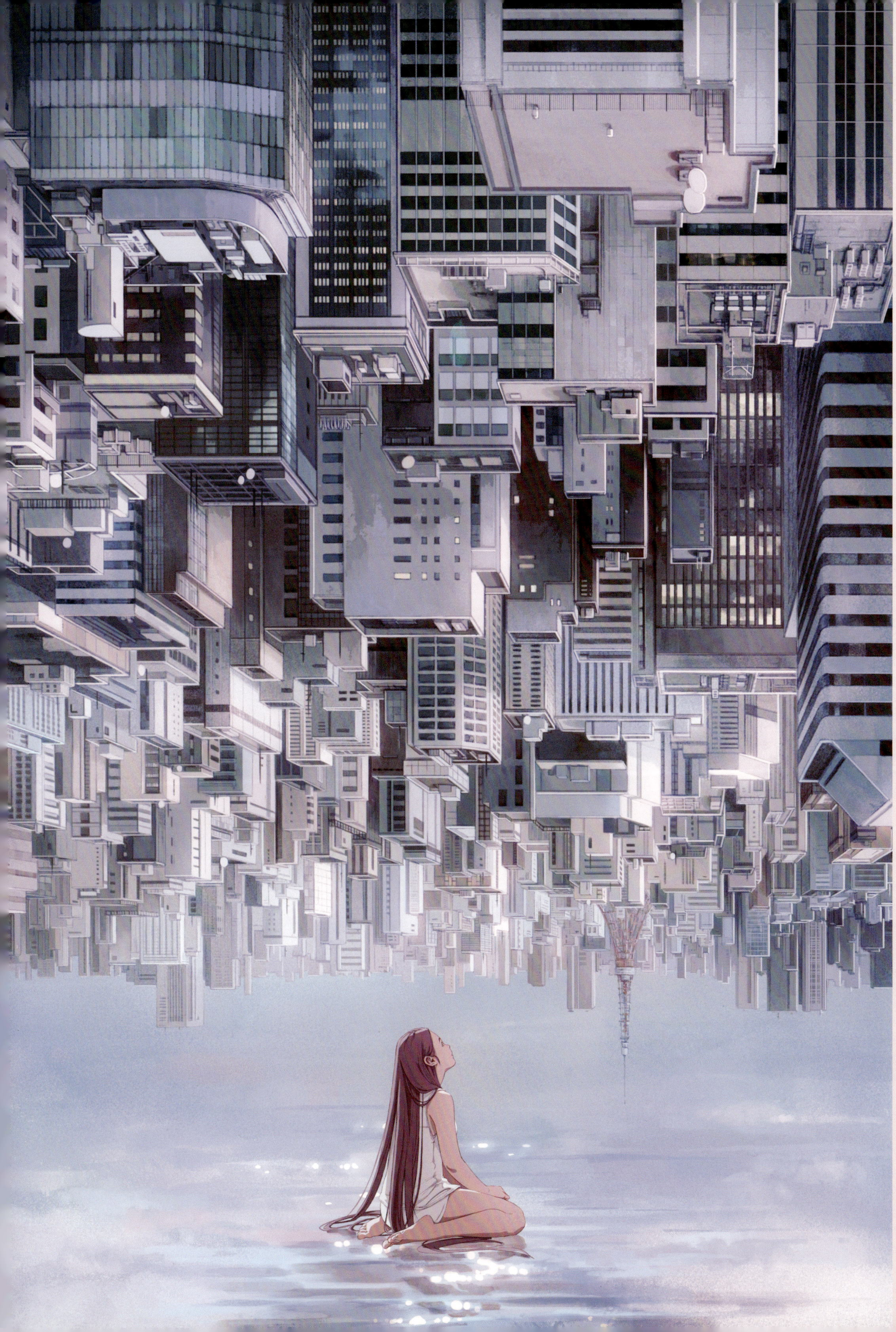

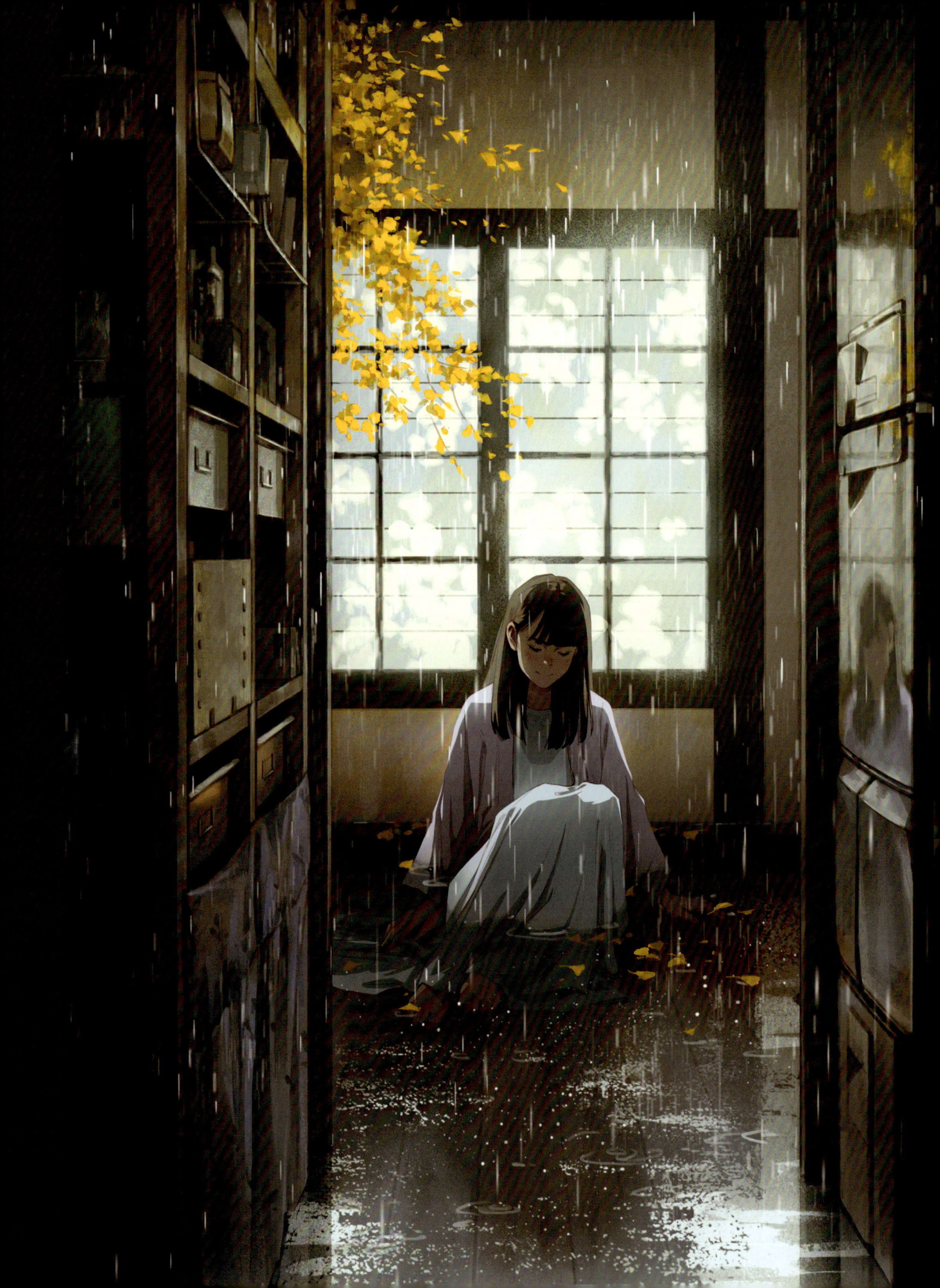

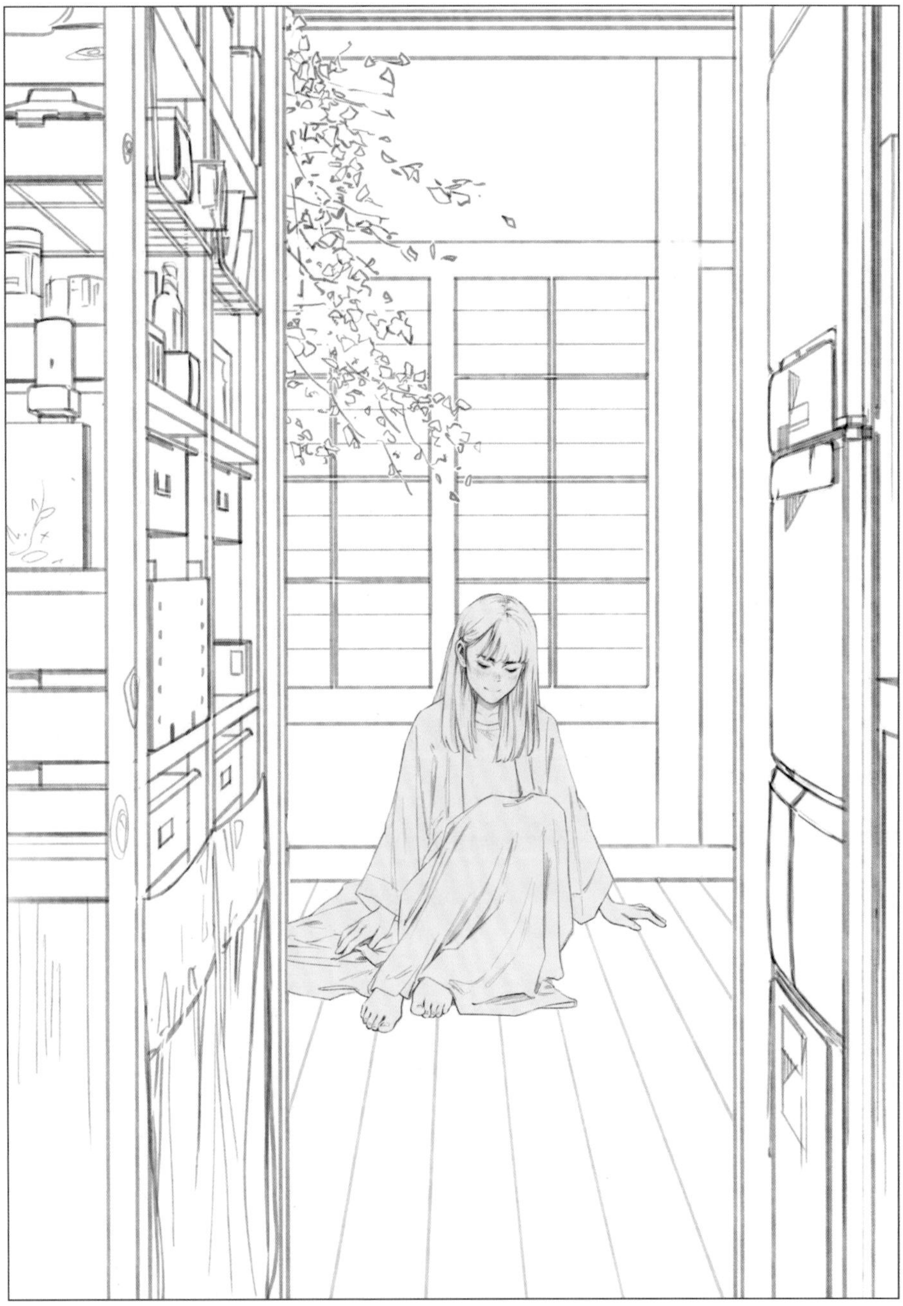

From a visual point of view, it is precisely this combination of the mundane and the strange that fascinates me – it results in scenes that are rooted in reality, but where something is just slightly off. Often, it is enough to move or alter one element in an image to get an unsettling effect: changing the colours or the proportions of a thing, turning it upside down, or placing it where it doesn't really belong. These small shifts bring another layer and 'texture' to the visual language of reality with which we are familiar. In that sense, magic realism expands our vocabulary and provides us with more choices in our creative expression. This often results in pieces of art that are memorable, inspire curiosity in the viewer, and encourage deeper examination.

I also believe that magic realism is a great vehicle for conveying nuanced emotions and thoughts. Therein, we can encode our state of mind and personal experiences without explicitly spelling them out; something deeply personal can be processed in this way and take on a whole new form. Moreover, it is an excellent tool to subvert expectations and to avoid the obvious. There is an exciting element of surprise here, and the visuals that emerge exist at the boundaries, where one thing becomes another and nothing is quite clearly defined.

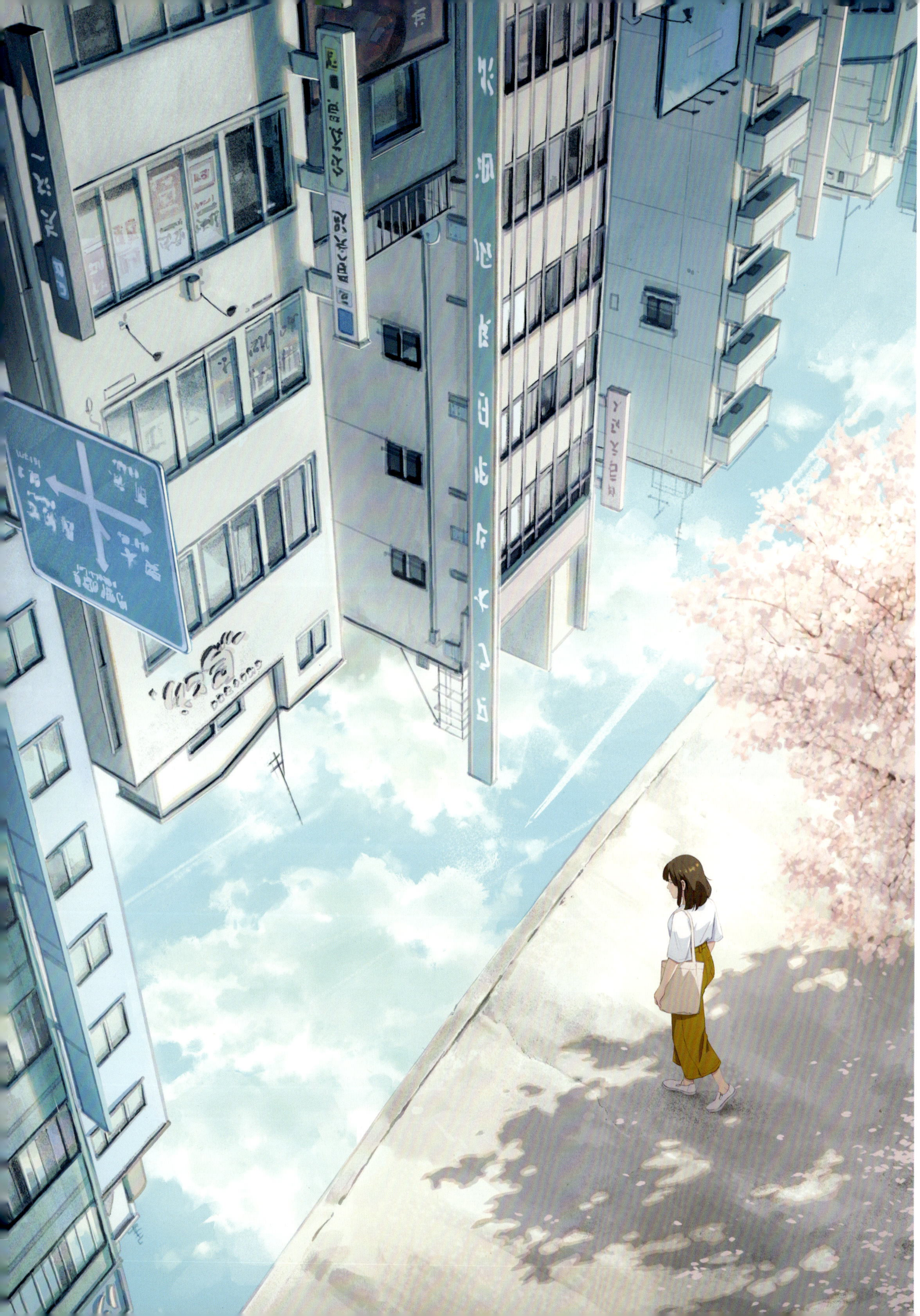

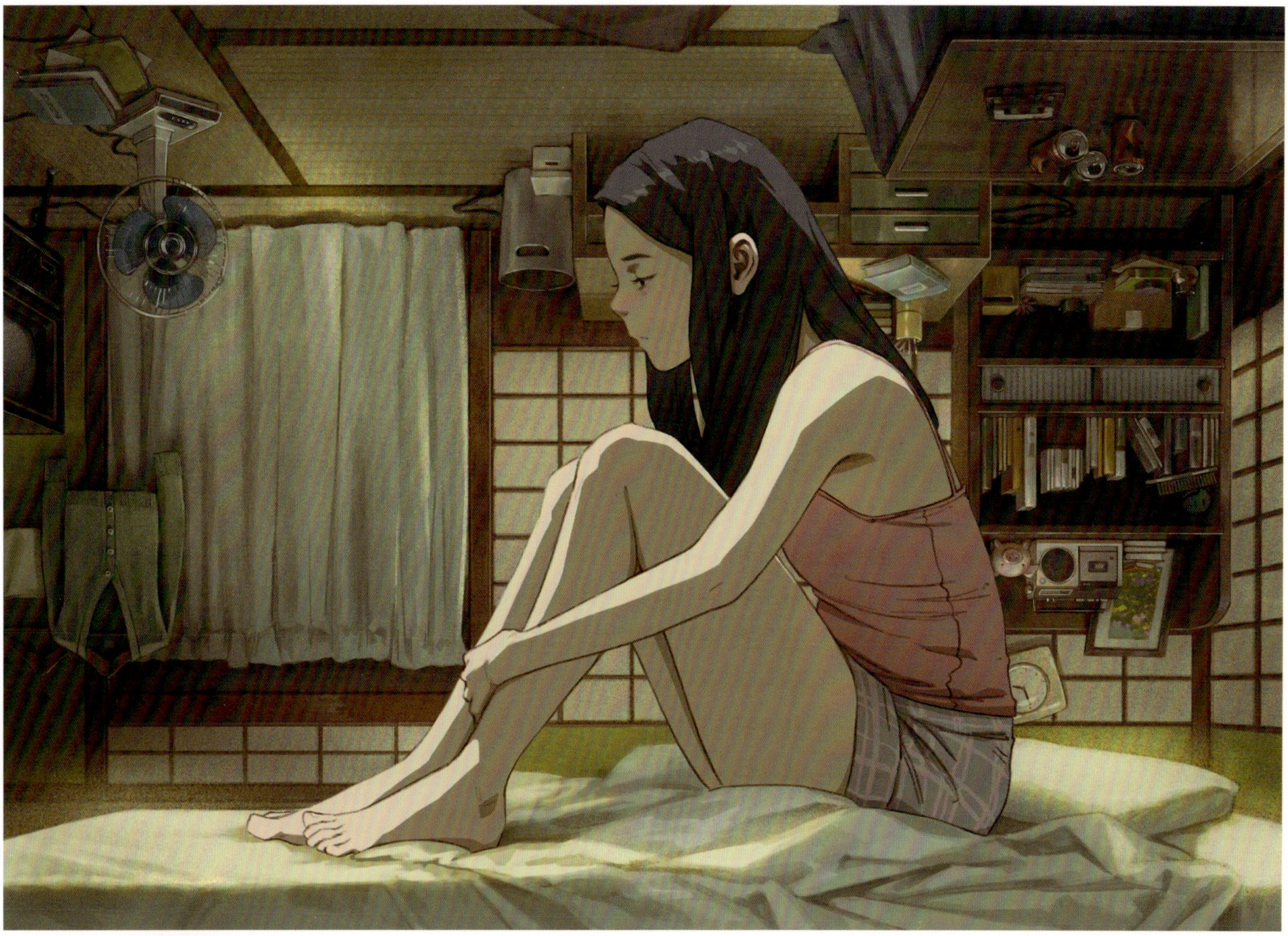

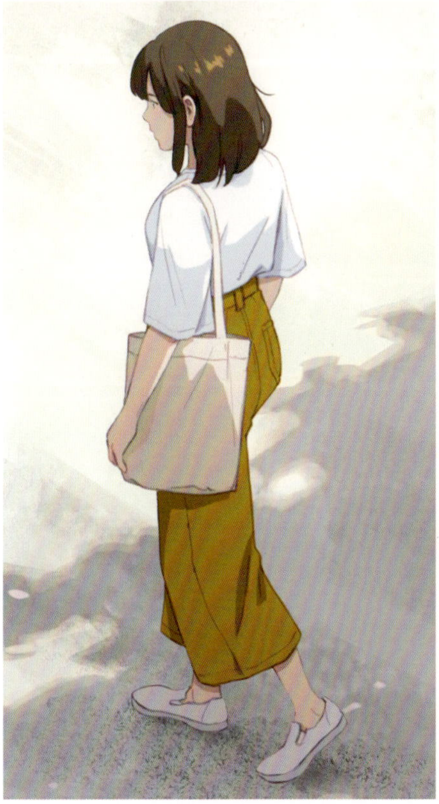

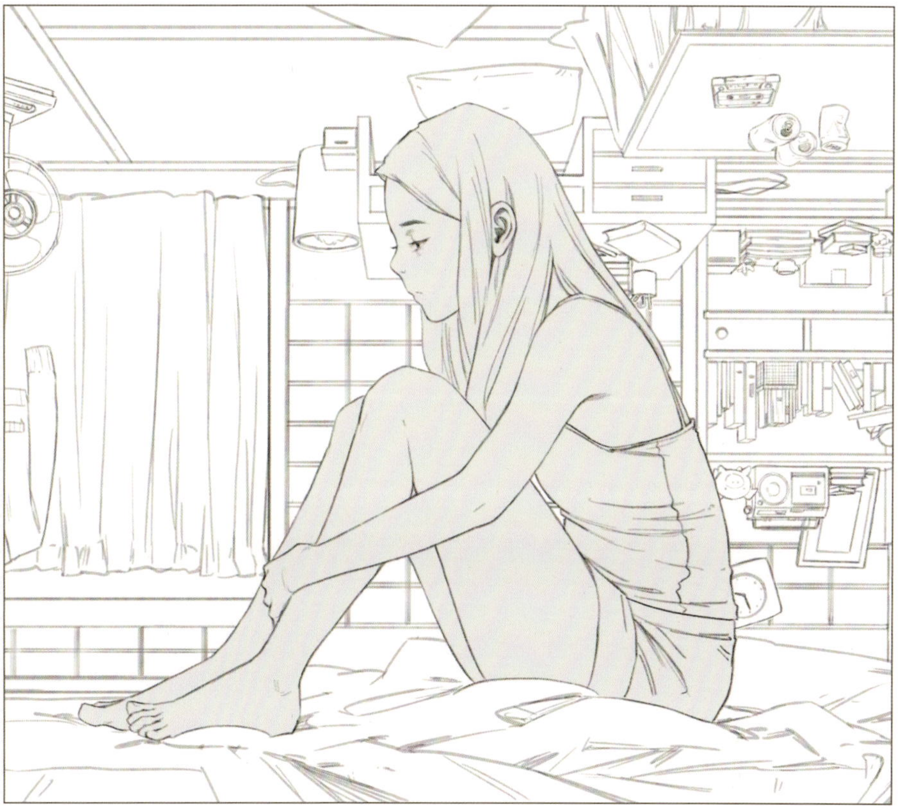

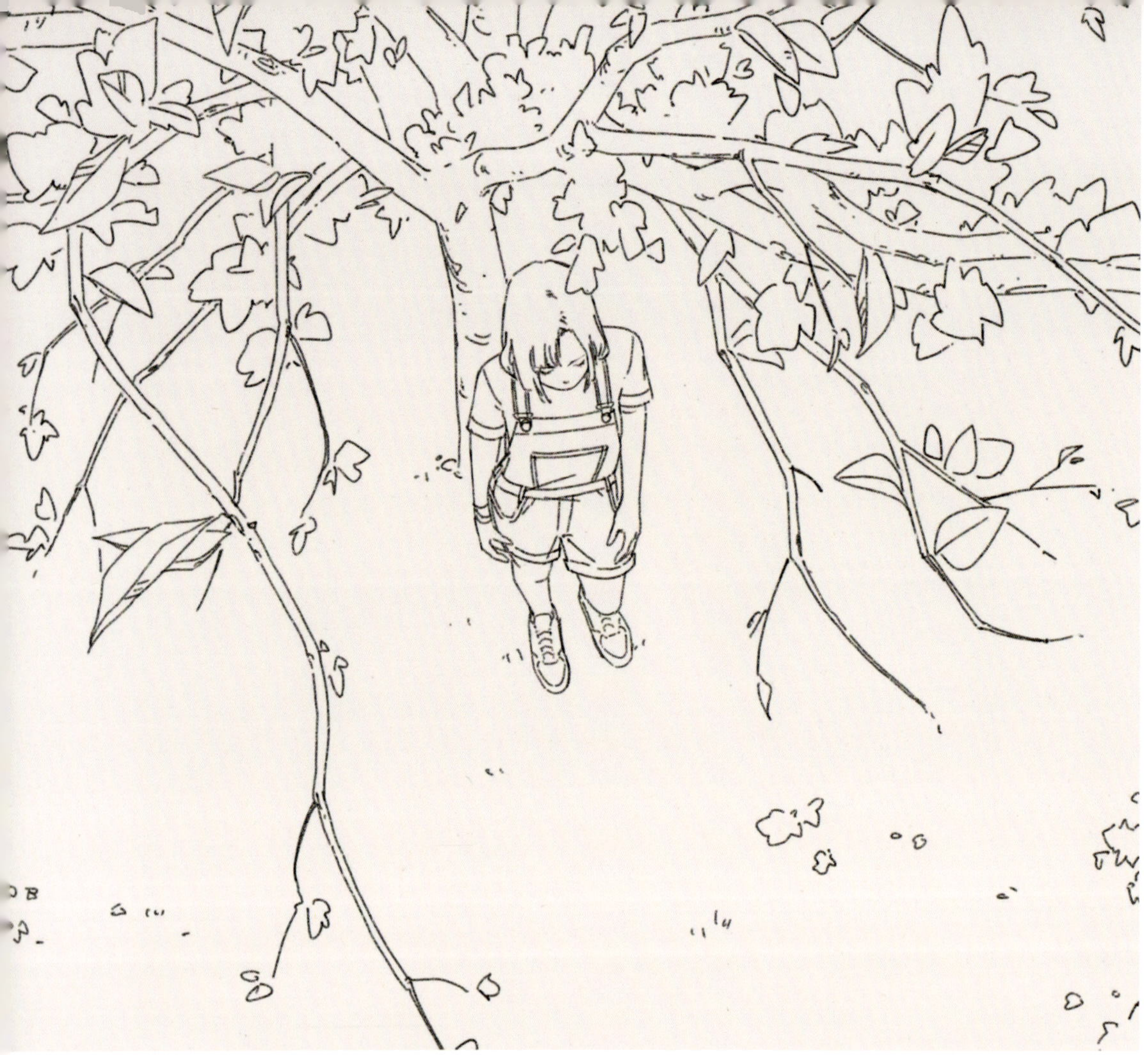

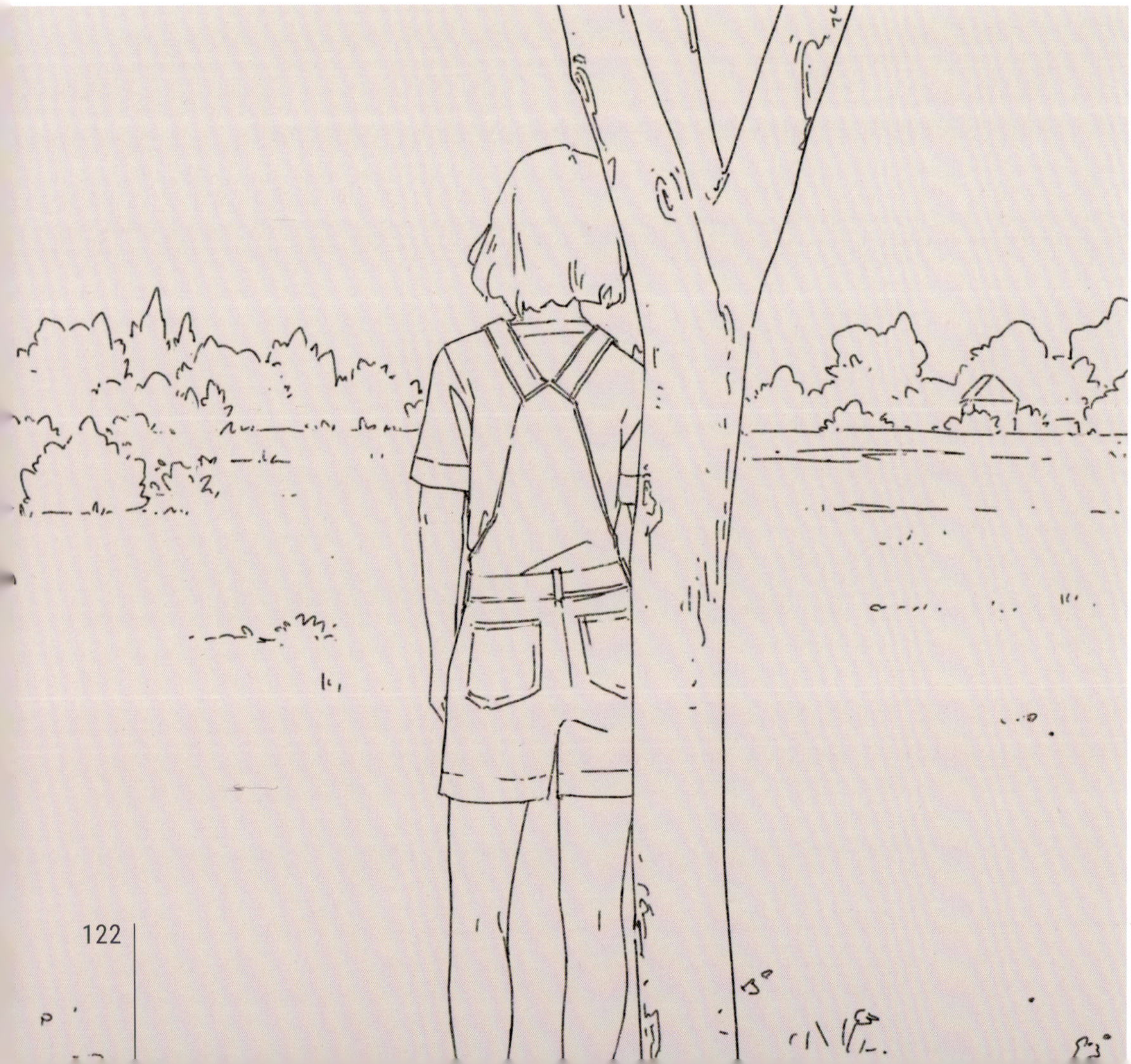

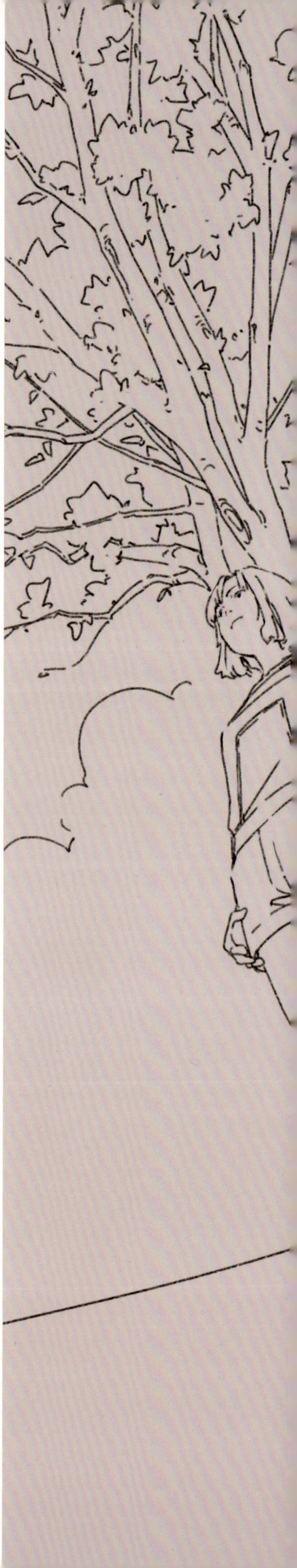

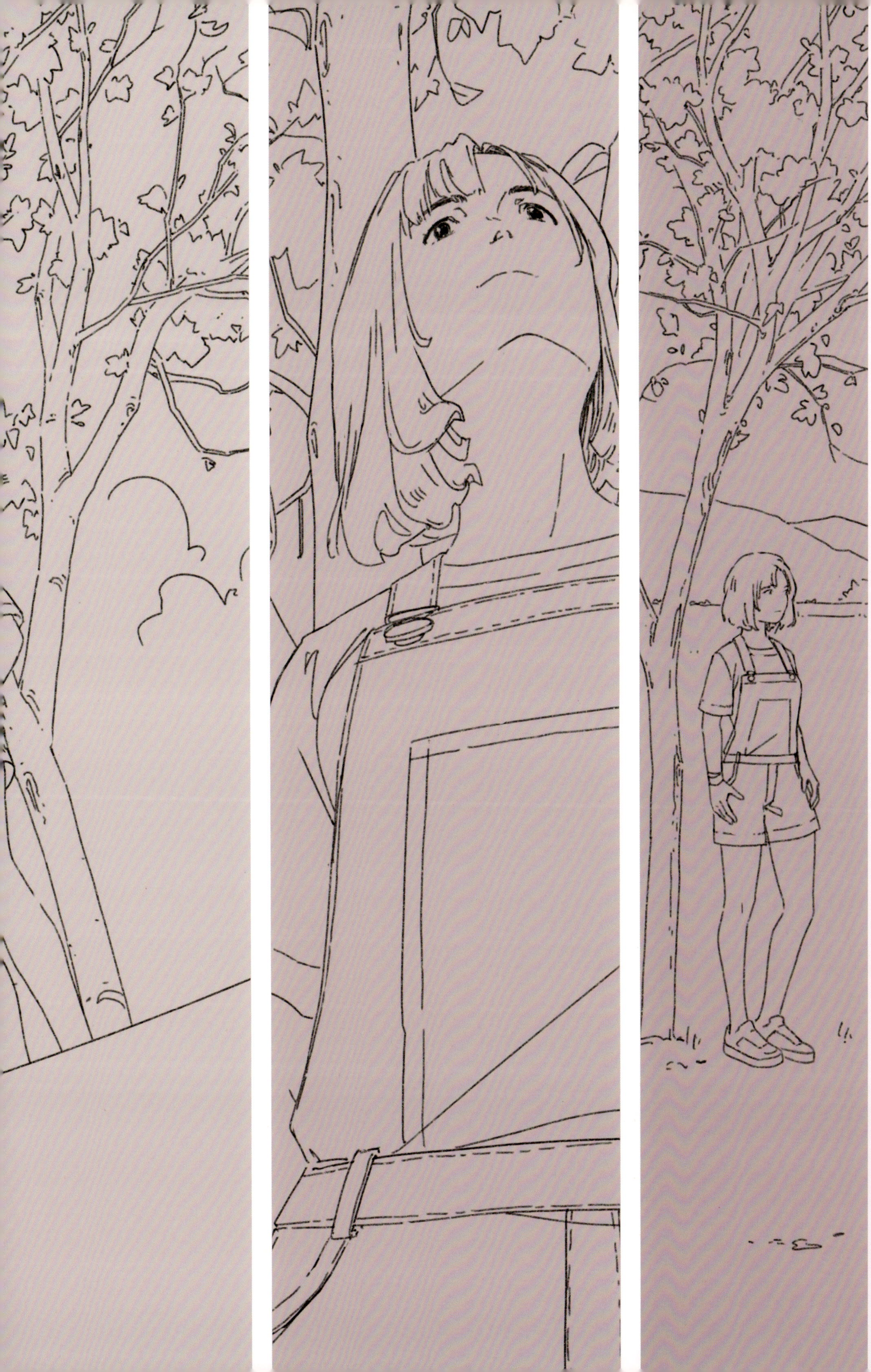

When it comes to evoking emotions through painting, I believe that colour is the most powerful tool at our disposal. My general guideline is 'a line drawing tells you *what* you are seeing; colour tells you *how to feel* about it'. And while that's a good rule of thumb, it's only partly true. Even before colour enters the stage, there are lots of decisions we can make that will drastically influence the emotional impact of any given scene. If we learn to use them strategically, we get to control how the viewer will perceive our painting. The various decisions that go into staging a painting are not unlike those made by a movie director: what's the filming location or set? Where do you position the camera and actors? How can you light the actors and the scene? There is great nuance to crafting an emotional impact, and in this chapter, I will present a few examples, techniques, and tools that illustrate this concept.

TOOL I: PERSPECTIVE & VIEWPOINT

First, let's look at perspective and viewpoint, and how they can affect the emotional impact of a scene. This is not going to be an 'introduction to perspective drawing' or a step-by-step process of how to build a scene in perspective. Those have been covered by lots of other artists far more capable than me. Instead, we will take a look at one specific drawing with a simple idea – a girl standing next to a tree — and see how the emotional quality changes when we alter the viewpoint and perspective, and nothing else. The character's pose and position relative to the tree stay exactly the same in all iterations; it's just the 'camera' that's changing.

One thing that's essential in determining the perspective in a painting is the viewer's role in the scene. Are we looking at the scene as a person of average human height? Or are we standing on a ladder, or lying on the ground? Are we possibly a giant, or sitting on a roof? Or maybe we're a tiny mouse looking at the scene from a hole in the wall? Or are we just in a physically impossible position, like a bodiless presence hovering below the ceiling? The exact same scene viewed through varying viewpoints will look quite different. For easy comparison, and to focus solely on the viewpoint and perspective, the following drawings are stripped down to their bare bones, and only consist of lines.

01 NEUTRAL VIEWPOINT

This is what I would call a neutral viewpoint. Our character is standing next to the tree and we're observing the scene from an average human height, as well as from a longer distance. The set-up suggests that the viewer is a regular person who is standing a bit further away.

How do we know that the viewer is average human height? One perspective rule to keep in mind is this: in any image that follows a standard perspective, the observer's viewpoint/eye level will always fall on the horizon line. It doesn't matter if we're standing on a skyscraper or in a field of flowers, our eye level is always equal to the horizon line. The exception is this: when we tilt our head up or down significantly, looking at the floor or the clouds, the horizon line will slip out of view. But in the case of this specific drawing, we're looking at the character straight-on. It comes across very neutral, casual, peaceful, and some might even say a bit boring. There's no drama or tension in the scene.

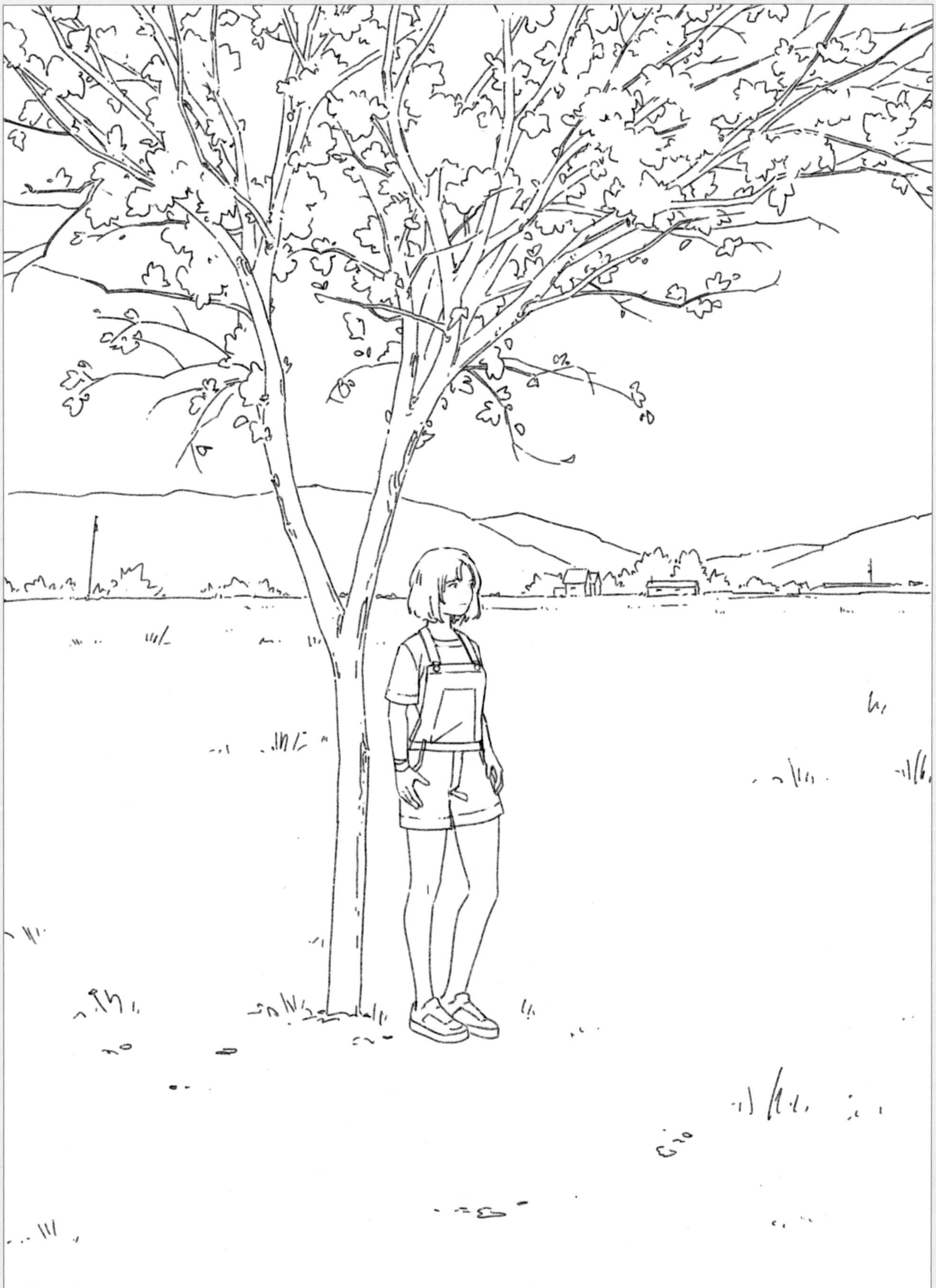

Neutral

We're looking at our character straight-on, from a human eye level, at a safe distance – nothing special here

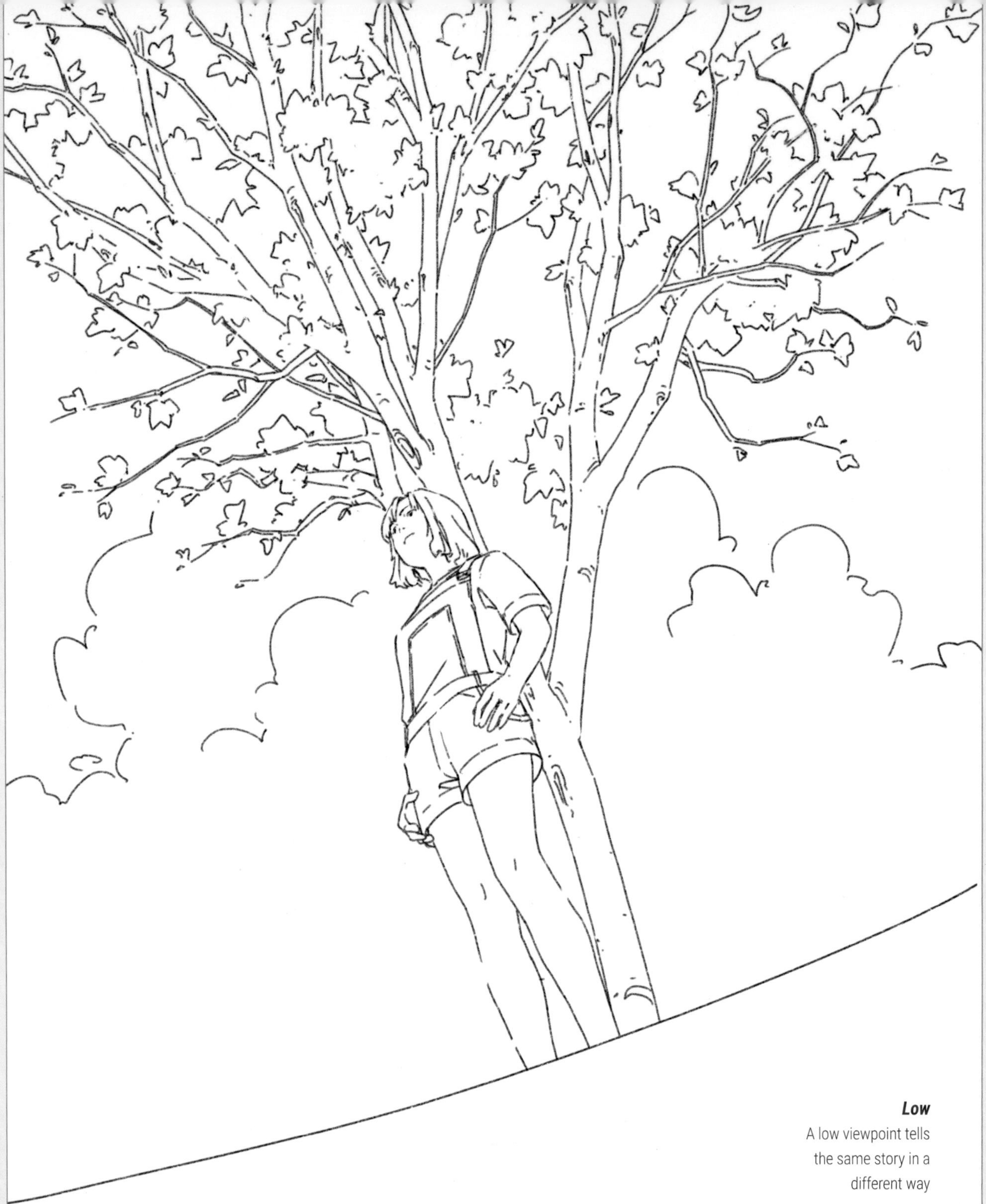

Low
A low viewpoint tells the same story in a different way

02 LOW VIEWPOINT

By moving the viewpoint all the way down, and by tilting the horizon line, we have introduced more tension and drama to the scene. There could be a number of reasons for setting up the 'camera' like this: maybe we want to show a scene from a bug or snake's perspective, sneaking up to the unsuspecting character in an attempt to bite them. Or maybe we want to depict someone as larger than life, and make them appear tall and powerful. This viewpoint also allows us to focus on the sky, to highlight clouds or birds flying above. That being said, it might not provide the most flattering angle for the character, and if you want to highlight their features or clothing, it's probably better to choose a more neutral viewpoint. These decisions always depend on the desired emotional impact, and pulling the right story elements into frame that will best achieve it.

Note: in order to focus on the character, the bottom of the drawing is reduced and simplified. Realistically, there would have been huge blades of grass that covered up a good chunk of the character's legs.

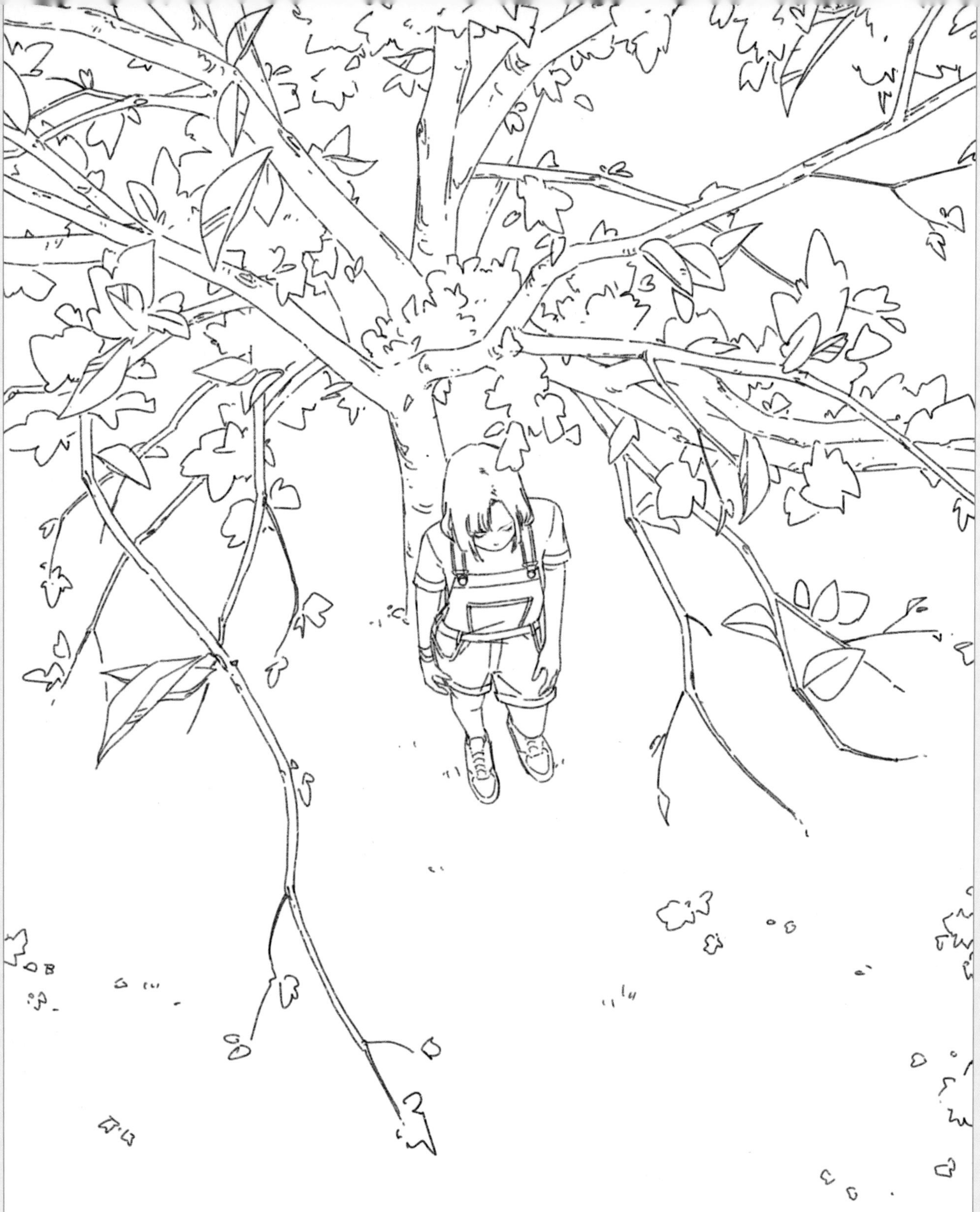

High
The same scene from a bird's-eye view makes the character feel small

03 HIGH VIEWPOINT

Now, by positioning the camera high up in the tree, we take the role and viewpoint of a bird or a creepy observer. Peeking at the character through the leaves gives the story a secretive, voyeuristic quality, like we shouldn't be looking at them because they are clearly oblivious to our presence. The character feels small, exposed, and vulnerable here. This high viewpoint creates a sense of suspense and anticipation of what is to come next, and what is going to happen to the character. Just like in the previous examples, we are further removed from them, watching what's happening to them rather than directly connecting to their emotional state. But in this case, the stakes feel a bit higher.

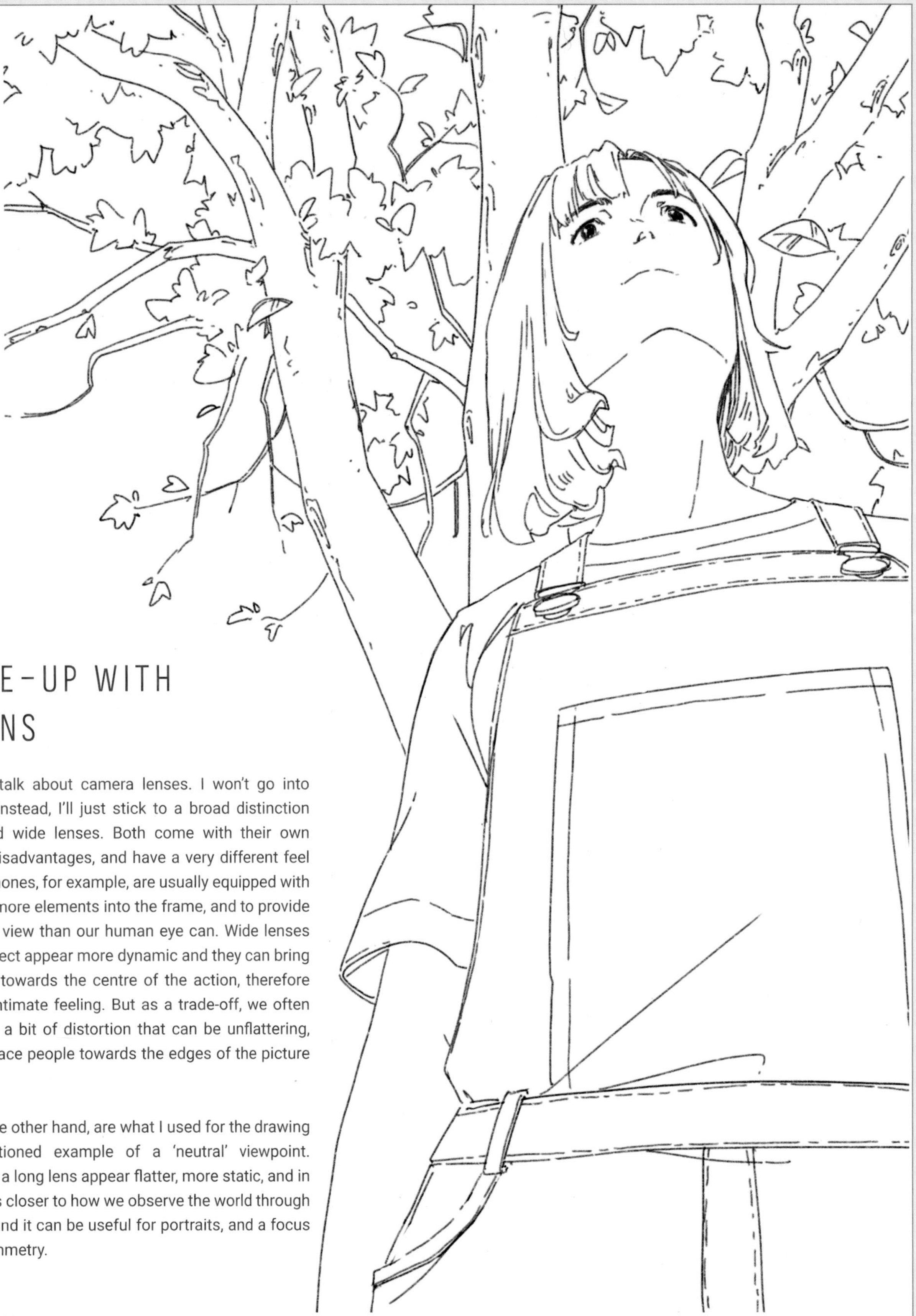

04 CLOSE-UP WITH WIDE LENS

Now it's time to talk about camera lenses. I won't go into too much detail. Instead, I'll just stick to a broad distinction between long and wide lenses. Both come with their own advantages and disadvantages, and have a very different feel to them. Mobile phones, for example, are usually equipped with wide lenses to fit more elements into the frame, and to provide a more expansive view than our human eye can. Wide lenses can make the subject appear more dynamic and they can bring the viewer closer towards the centre of the action, therefore creating a more intimate feeling. But as a trade-off, we often end up with quite a bit of distortion that can be unflattering, especially if we place people towards the edges of the picture frame.

Long lenses, on the other hand, are what I used for the drawing in the aforementioned example of a 'neutral' viewpoint. Photos taken with a long lens appear flatter, more static, and in order. The effect is closer to how we observe the world through our human eyes, and it can be useful for portraits, and a focus on design and symmetry.

Close-Up, Wide Lens

The character's body becomes distorted, and from this viewpoint, in combination with the wide lens, we're almost uncomfortably close

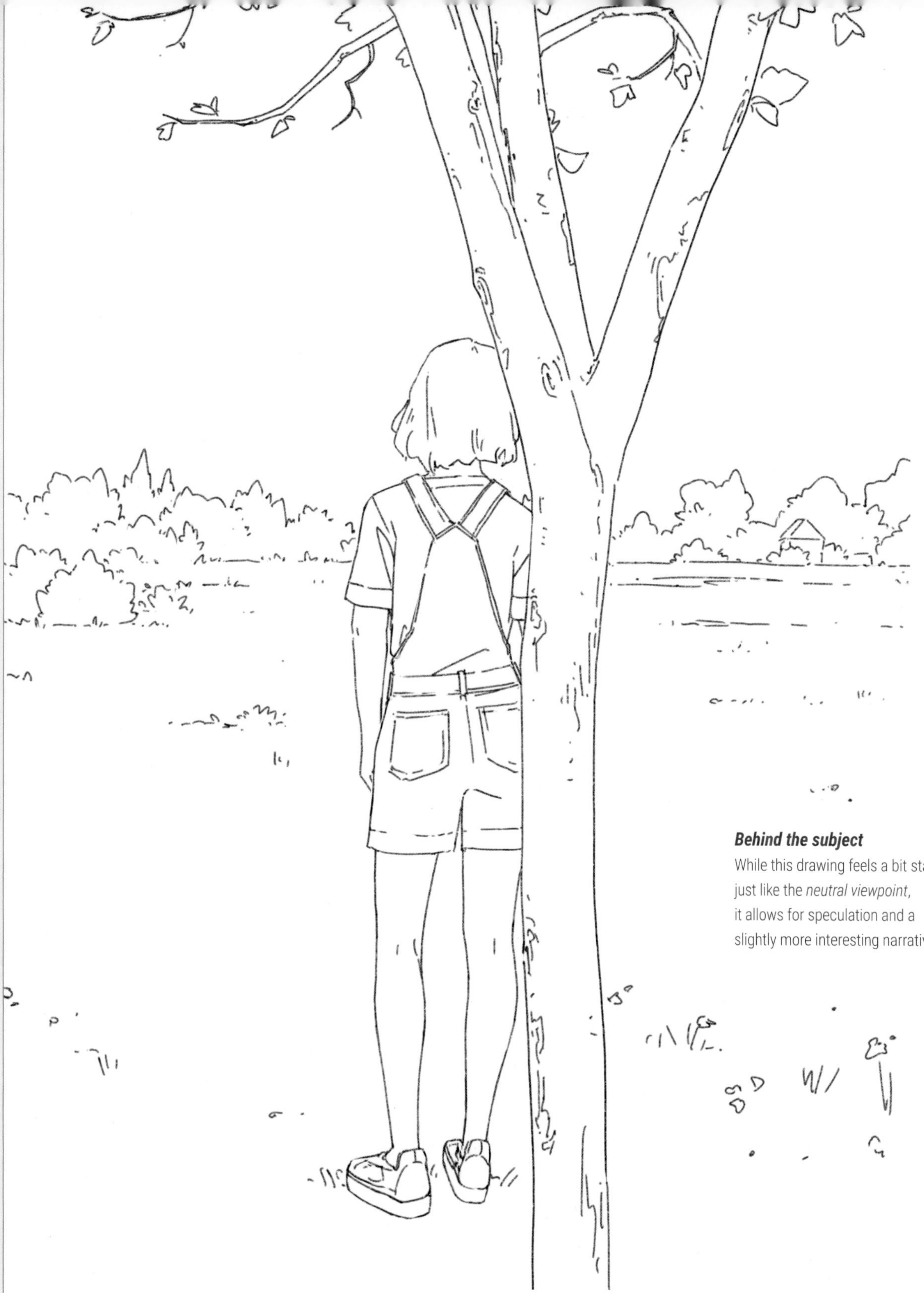

Behind the subject
While this drawing feels a bit static, just like the *neutral viewpoint*, it allows for speculation and a slightly more interesting narrative

05 BEHIND WITH LONG LENS

This scene is viewed through a long lens and at a neutral height, just like the first example. And yet, it feels different. We are positioned behind the tree, slightly closer to the character. It feels like we're walking up to them, about to tap them on the shoulder. They haven't noticed our presence yet, which creates a surprise factor and a sense of anticipation. We don't see the character's face, so we cannot directly connect to their emotional state, and yet, we wonder how things will play out, and how they're going to react. So, it matters where we position the 'camera': not just how high or low the angle is, but also what part of the character we're highlighting, and which one we're hiding.

TOOL II: ENVIRONMENT & SET DESIGN

To comprehensively cover the subject of environment design, we would need an entire book dedicated to it. So instead, just like we did with Perspective & Viewpoint, we will look through some examples, and this time we will examine the role that the location plays for our scenes, and how it can change the emotional impact. To keep it consistent, we're continuing with the same character, this time with a fixed pose and viewpoint. The only thing that's changing is the environment around them.

There are endless possibilities when it comes to selecting or constructing a location for an illustration: are we looking at a natural environment, or an artificial one? What's the climate, flora, and fauna like? What are the weather conditions? Are we indoors or outdoors? Are there architectural elements? If so, what style, era, country, and so on? I could go on and on, and it can get quite overwhelming.

It's therefore useful to consider a few factors that are more graphic-design oriented and abstract, and that provide a rough guideline, regardless of our subject matter. One such factor is shape language: are the elements in the scene elongated and pointy? Or are they round and squishy? Or perhaps they are angular and boxy? All of these will evoke different emotions. For example, rounded shapes will usually come across more friendly and positive.

Another factor to consider is the level of detail: more details and elements in the scene can make it feel more cluttered and oppressive, whereas open spaces allow for more breathing room and a peaceful atmosphere. Furthermore, the directions of lines play a role as well: horizontal and vertical lines feel calm, whereas diagonal lines have a more dynamic quality to them. And finally, how all the lines play together will create a rhythm that can be choppy, or balanced and smooth. If you take these basic principles into consideration, that gives you a good starting point to achieve your desired emotional impact.

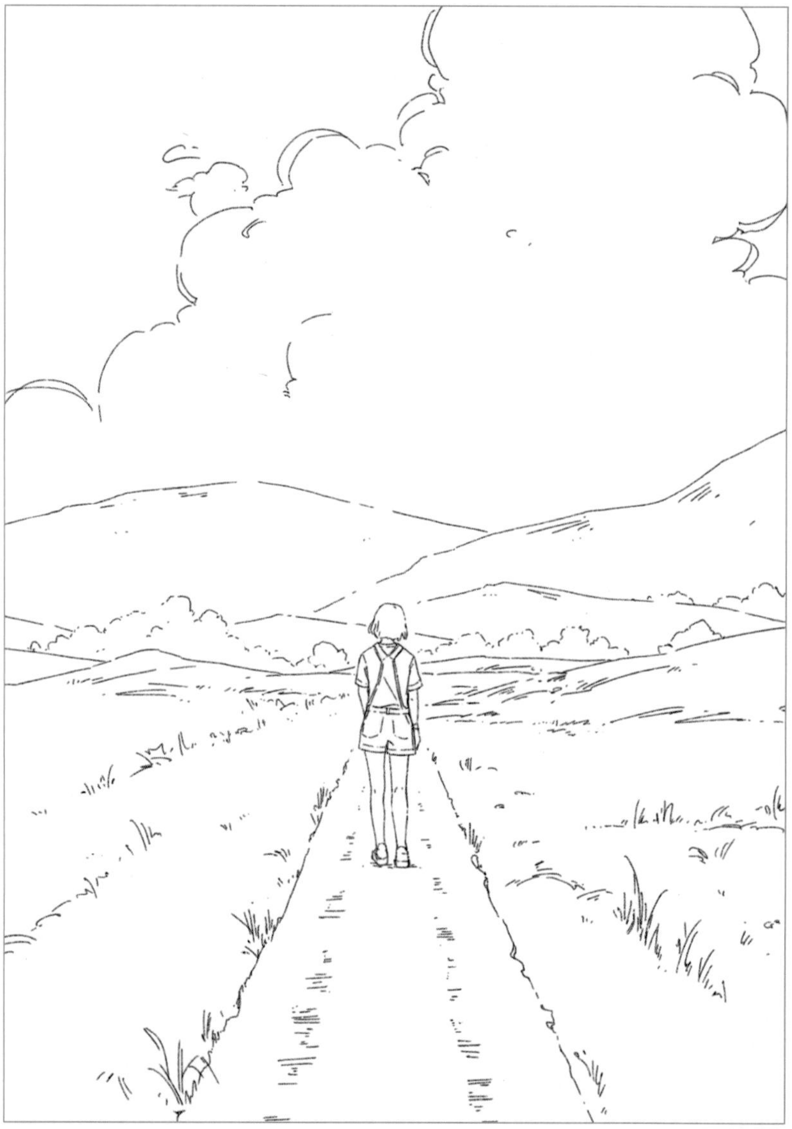

Field

This open field is an example of a very simple, calm environment

01 FIELD

In this example, we're looking at a very simple scene: our character is walking on a path between fields of grass towards a distant mountain range with fluffy clouds in the background. Everything here was designed to support a calm, peaceful atmosphere: the horizontal lines of the landscape, the subtle curves of the mountains, the rounded shapes of the clouds, and the minimal details that provide lots of open space; we can see for miles and miles. And even if there's no colour, it feels like a warm summer day.

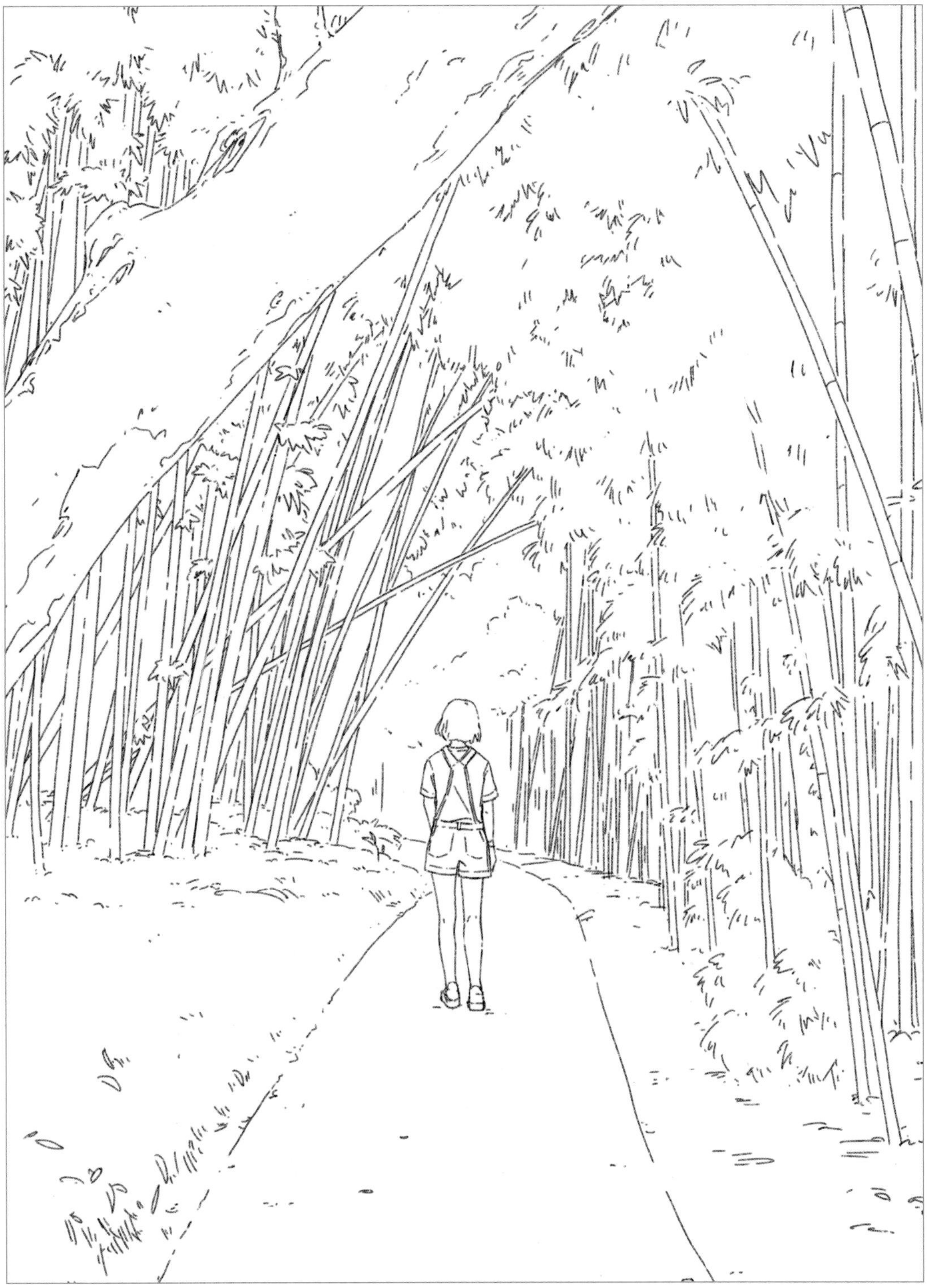

Forest
This bamboo forest has lots of detail, as well as vertical and diagonal lines

02 FOREST

Compared to the previous environment, this one has significantly more detail in just the sheer number of lines being used. There is a mixture of vertical and diagonal lines throughout the drawing, and overall, it feels more closed-off than the previous sketch. We don't have an unobstructed view of what's ahead. And since we don't know what lies within the forest, this scene feels slightly more ambiguous and mysterious, and could easily venture into a dark direction. Since the scene is less open, with the bamboo and the tree surrounding the character, it gives the impression that we're following them into the forest, which makes the scene slightly more intimate.

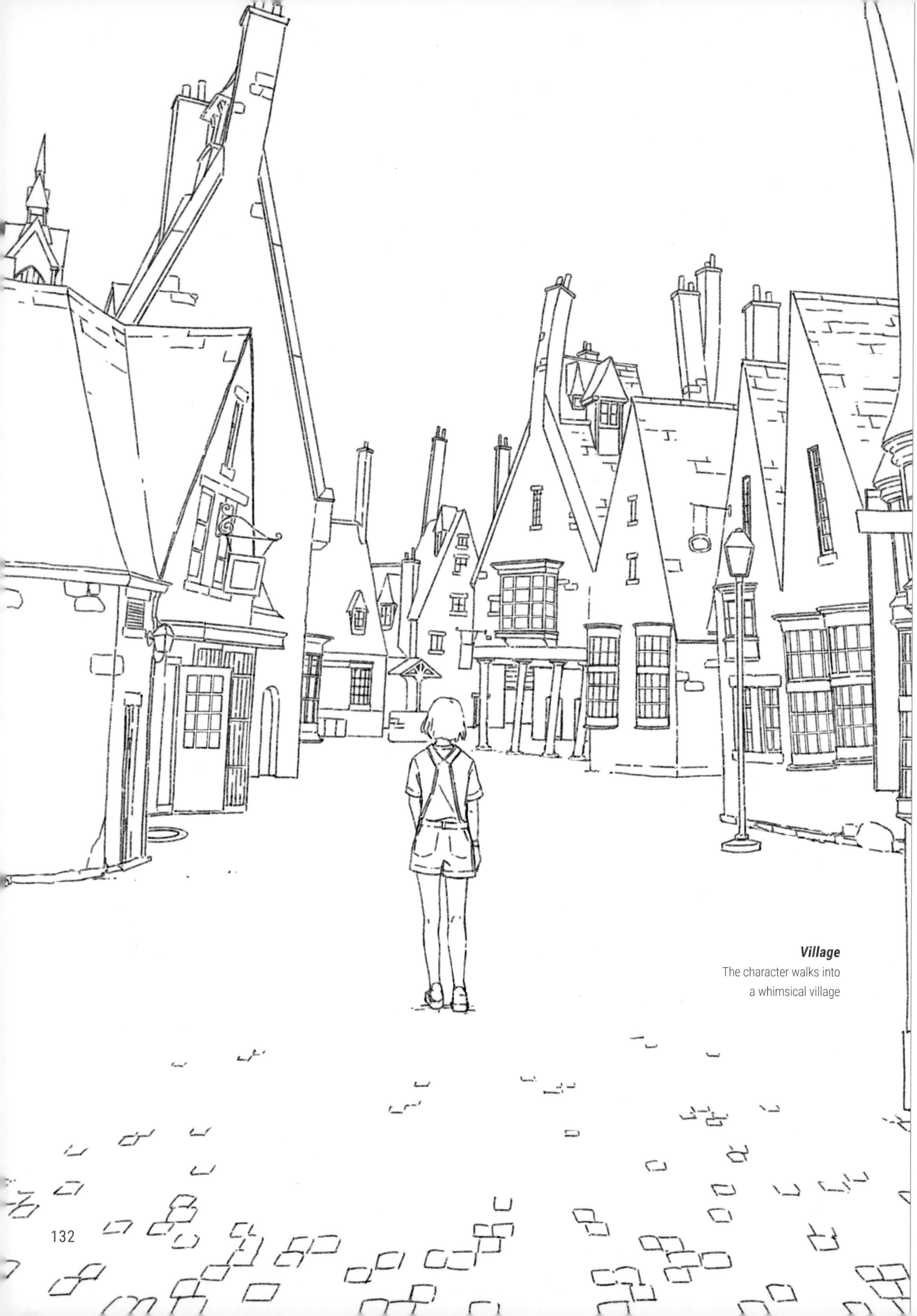

Village
The character walks into
a whimsical village

03 VILLAGE

Just like the drawing of the field, this scene also has lots of open space – to the point where it feels a bit empty. We get the sense that the character is separated from the backdrop and alone here, almost like an outsider in this village. The plaza is so large that a person standing in the middle appears to be lost in all the white space. While the environment looks a bit empty and imbalanced right now, it provides interesting opportunities for light and shadow later on.

From an architectural design standpoint, the houses have unusual, slightly crooked shapes, and give off a whimsical, fairy-tale feeling. As a result, the character design looks a bit out of place here: slightly too modern and dressed for warm weather, while the scenery calls for a moodier, possibly colder atmosphere.

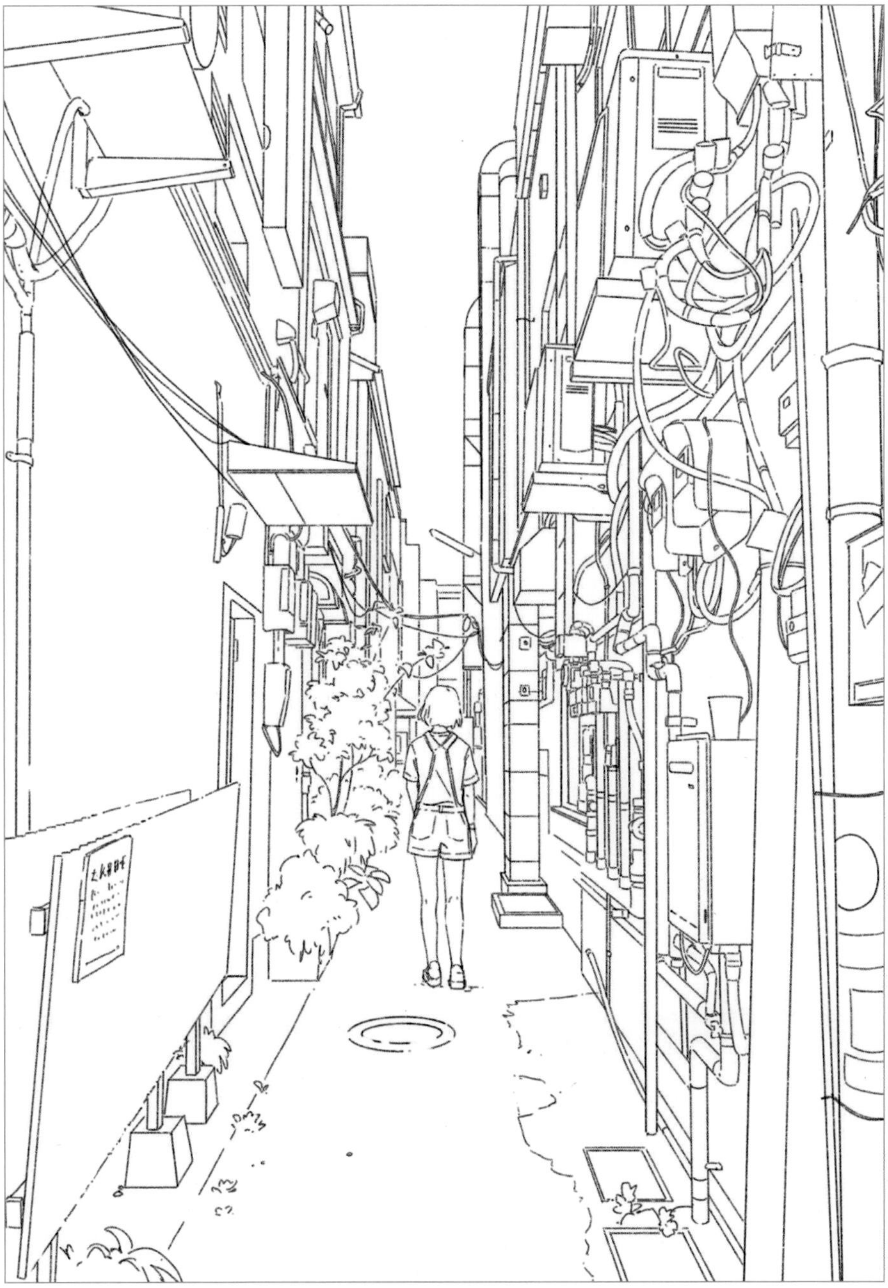

04 ALLEYWAY

In this sketch, the character is walking through an alleyway. The scene comes across as very cluttered and almost oppressive; the space is narrow and dense, and the receding lines point towards the character in an aggressively claustrophobic way. Among all the details, it's difficult to make out the shape of the person, and the character is almost disintegrating into the environment.

For storytelling, this type of scenery could reflect the character's troubled emotional state. An example could be a potential low point in their story in which they're trapped and desperate, having to overcome an obstacle. A busy image is a good metaphor for a busy mind.

Alleyway

TOOL III: COLOUR & LIGHT

Colour is such a deeply personal aspect of painting, and it's where we can achieve the greatest emotional impact. It's what catches our attention, even from a great distance, and what addresses a very primal, intuitive response in us. A lot of it comes down to personal taste: we all have colours that we love, and that make us feel comfortable or uncomfortable. More often than not, this happens at a subconscious level, but to make full use of colour and light for visual storytelling, it's essential to become aware of how we perceive colour, and how it makes us feel. That way, we can utilize it and take advantage of it to convey emotions through art.

Instead of going through the colour wheel and choosing colours in a scientific, systematic way, we'll be looking at a more intuitive, practical approach: letting weather conditions, seasons, and the time of day guide our decisions. By shifting our mindset and running through concrete, real-world scenarios, we immediately get vivid ideas of colour palettes. For example, when we think of the scenario 'thunderstorm', there is a certain image that comes to mind with a very specific mood and colour story. Of course, having a solid understanding of colour theory is immensely helpful here, but it can also lead to over-thinking and missing the mark on the intended emotional impact. So, we're going to keep it simple and look at our whimsical village scene under varying conditions: daylight, sunset, and a rainy day. The following paintings are rough colour sketches and not final illustrations, but they provide enough information to evoke specific moods.

Daylight
This is the village scene on a bright, sunny day

01 DAYLIGHT

A sunny day with big, fluffy clouds is my go-to scenario. It feels happy and optimistic, and the vibrant blue of the sky provides a strong pop of colour that sets the tone for the rest of the painting.

Direct sunlight also allows for an interesting dichotomy and interplay between light and shadow. I like to keep it simple and just divide all surfaces in the painting into 'hit by sunlight' and 'not hit by sunlight', and more often than not, I will make it up as I go, or even purposefully ignore realism in order to create patterns I find appealing. The resulting light and shadow shapes then serve as design elements in the scene. In this particular painting, they break up the ground, which was quite flat and boring to begin with. Additionally, they guide the composition and function as arrows pointing towards the character.

When it comes to colour, I will usually add a blue tint to the shadow areas, and in contrast, warm up the areas that are being hit by sunlight. To maintain harmony, I'll keep the shadow colours close to blue (purple, green, cool grey), and the highlights close to yellow (warm beige, brown, orange, warm green). In this painting, it's not too difficult to create a harmonious colour scheme because the houses have neutral grey hues. That said, I also try to include occasional accents to provide visual interest.

While the palette works together, I think this mood is a bit too cheerful for this particular type of scenery.

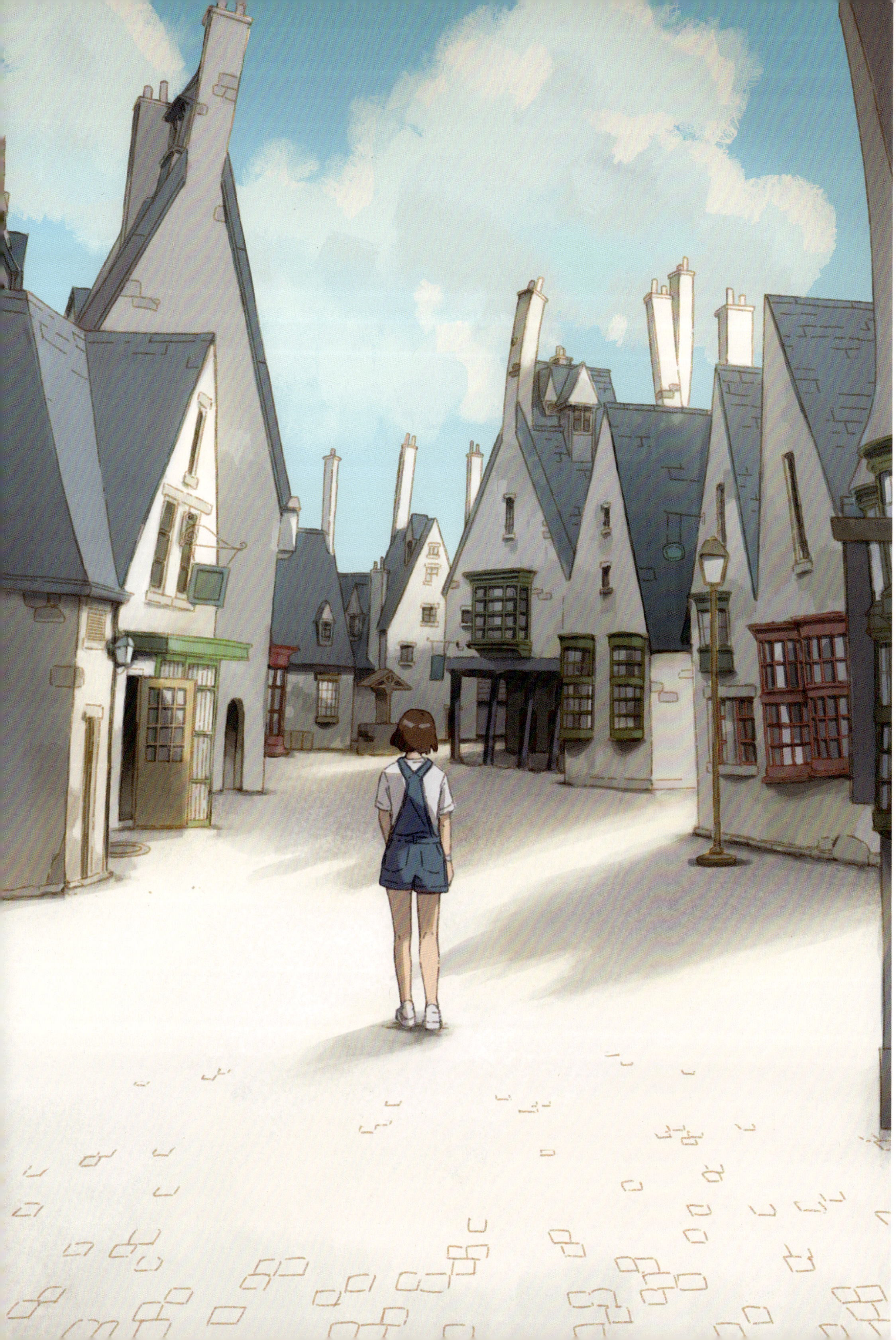

02 SUNSET

The same scene looks very different at sunset, with a warmer colour scheme and long, dramatic shadows. I'm still applying the same principle of dividing the painting into 'hit by sunlight' and 'not hit by sunlight', but the colours have shifted more towards purple and orange versus blue and yellow. My goal was to make the light look blinding and extreme, so I flattened out the sky and made it lighter. With the warm light spilling over the edges of the buildings, it almost has an overexposed effect. I personally prefer this iteration over the daylight version because it suits the scenery much better: the mood feels darker and more melancholic, and the shadow shapes on the ground are far more interesting. Additionally, the character is now fully integrated into the scene.

Sunset
This is the village scene at sunset

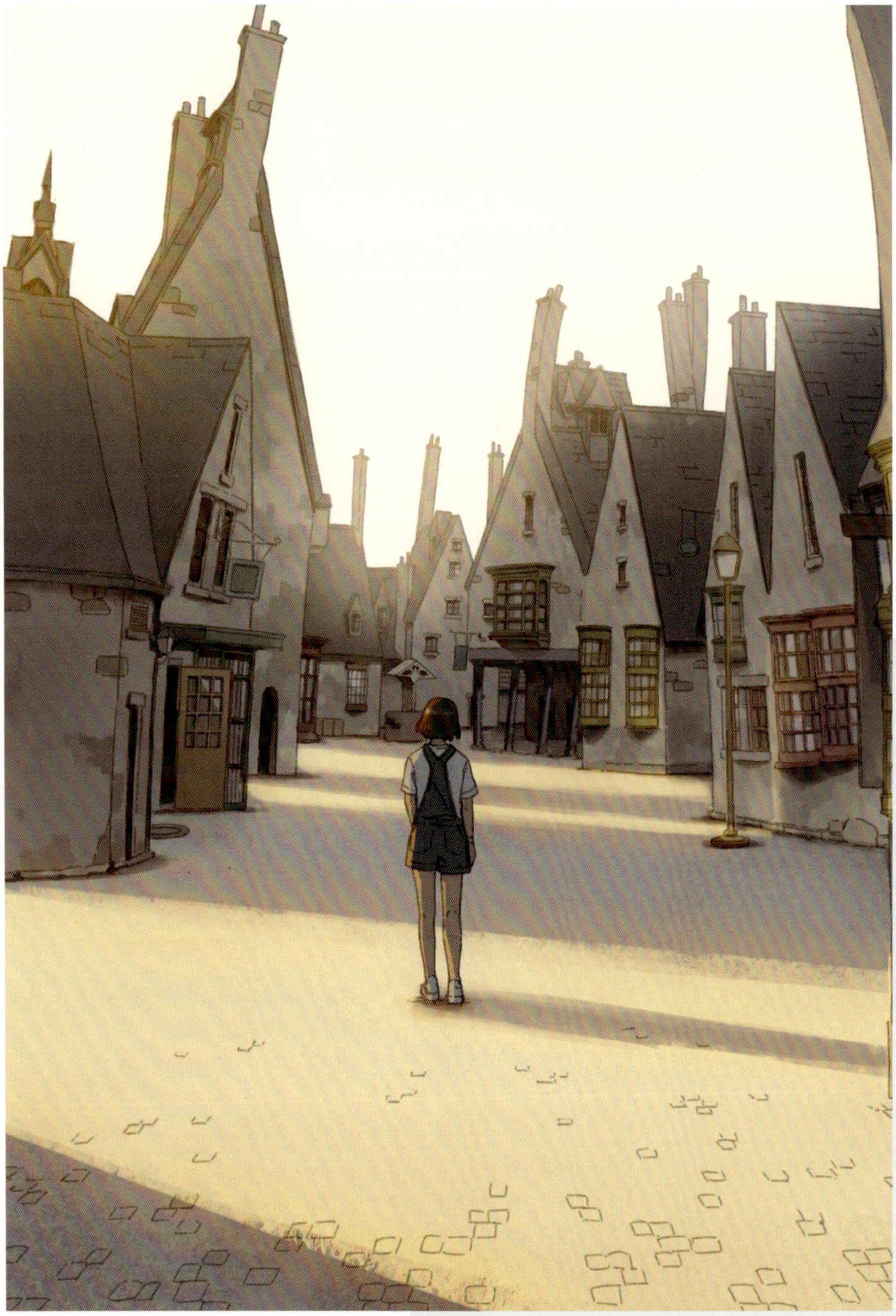

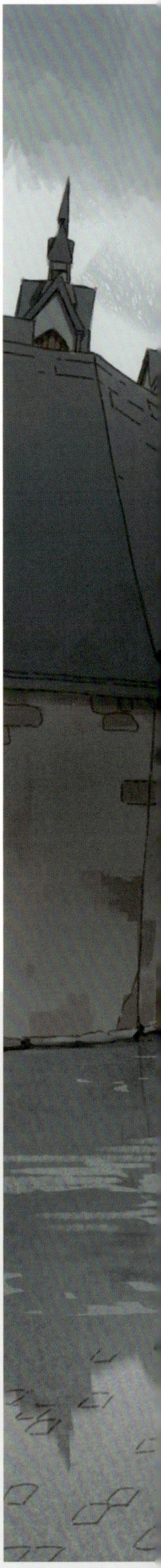

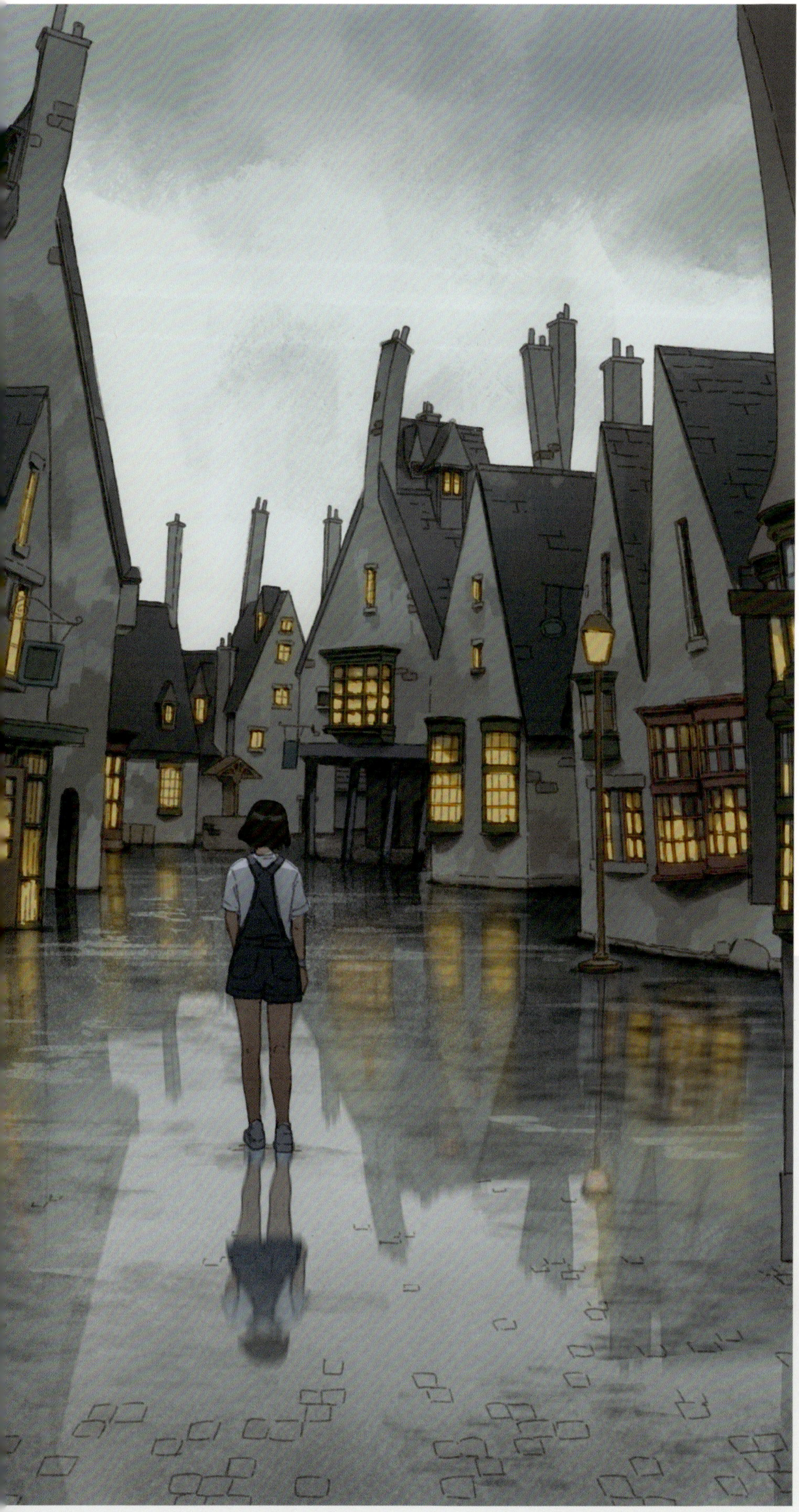

03 RAINY

The last iteration we're going to look at is this moody, rainy scene. Water will turn the ground into a mirror and allow us to play with reflections. That way, we get to turn this boring, flat surface into a feature that's visually exciting!

In addition to the rainy street, I darkened the overall scene just enough to allow for warm light inside all the windows. Narratively, this creates an interesting juxtaposition between warm interiors and the cold exterior, and with the character clearly standing outside, it gives the story a lonely, isolated feeling.

The colour scheme is predominantly grey, with hints of blue and green, but ultimately, it's the orange light that creates accents and variation, pulling it all together. This version of the scene is my favourite because it complements the whimsical but slightly twisted appearance of the place.

Rainy
This is the village on a rainy day

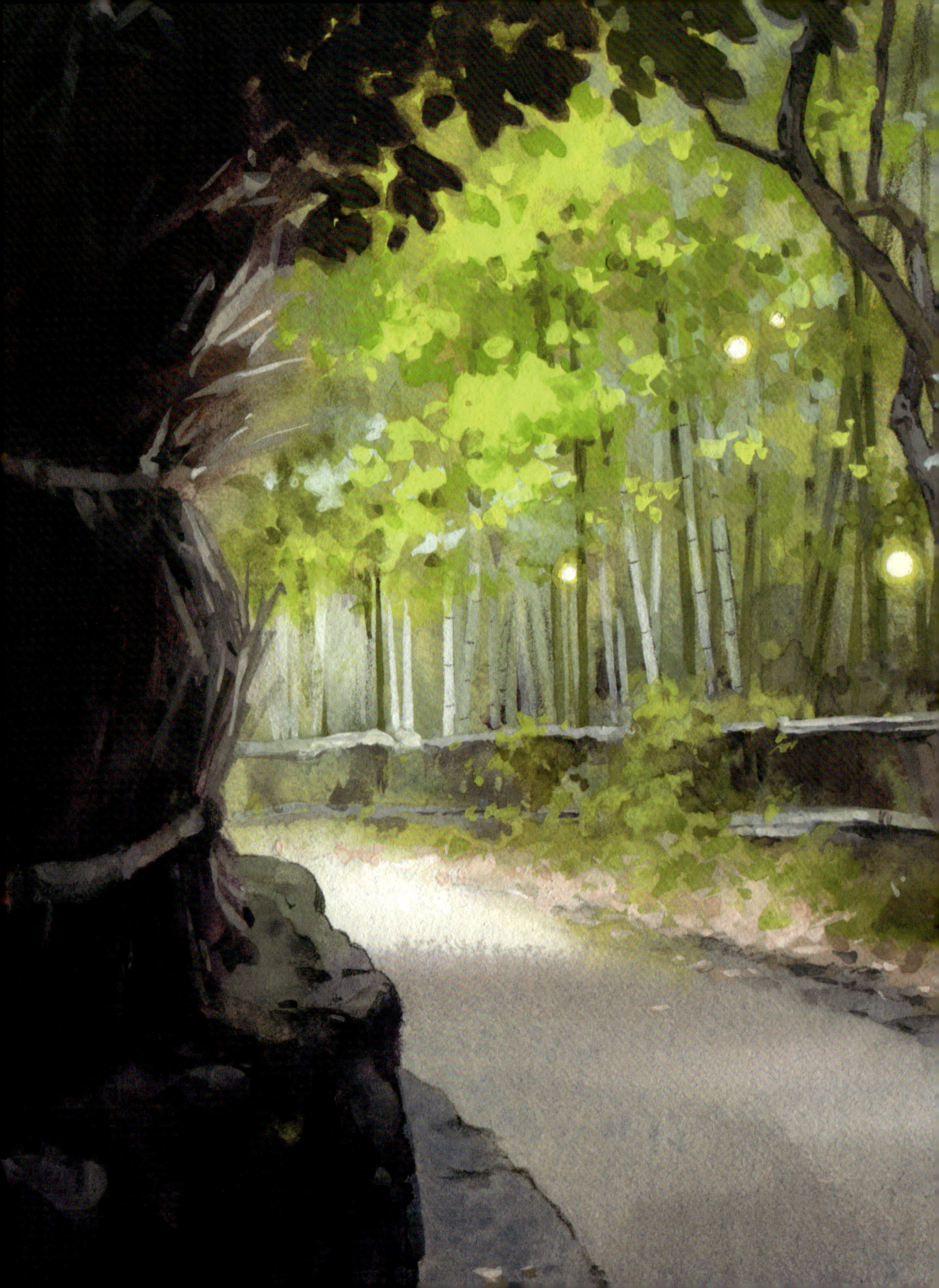

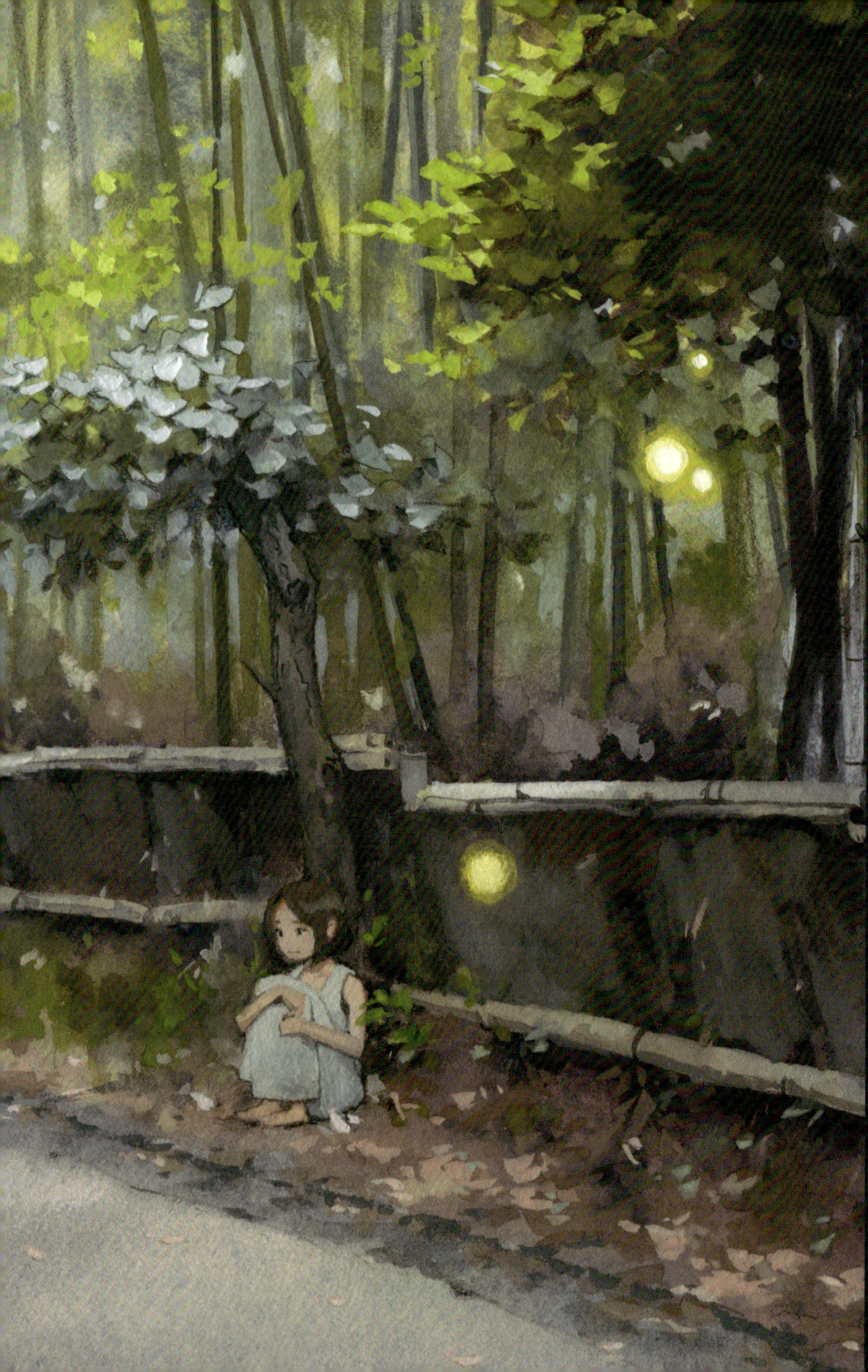

There are many ways to grow as an artist, but reviewing the past year (or month), and becoming conscious of my development and progress, is one of the most helpful practices I can think of – it brings clarity, renewed motivation, and paves the way forwards. I find journaling to be the ideal medium for this, as it allows me to dissect topics, reflect, and answer questions. I sit down to ask myself how the last 365 days have been, what events have had a particular impact on me, and how this has possibly manifested itself in my art. I also compare my paintings with those from the year before to see if I can discern any major differences, new patterns, or trends.

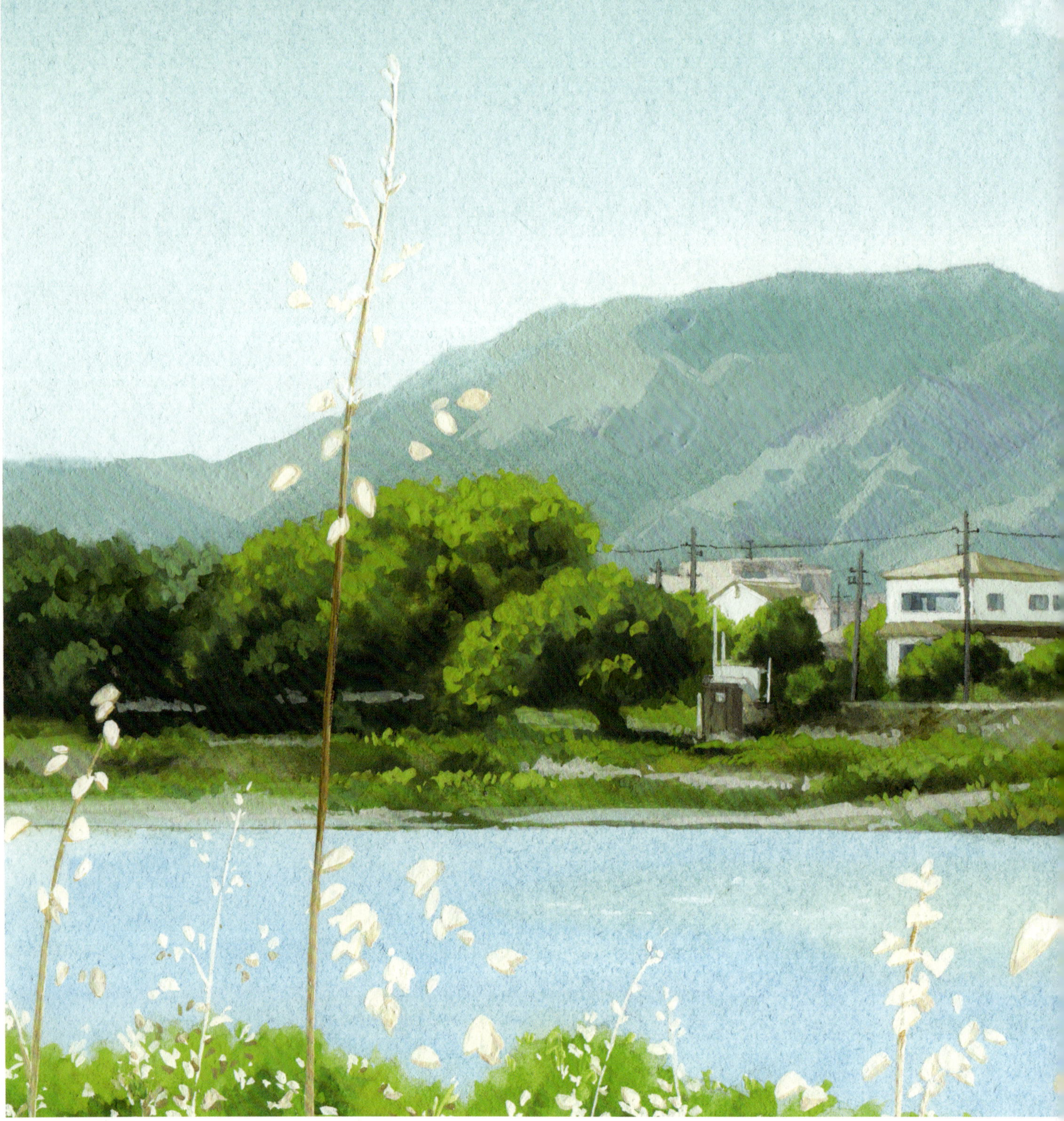

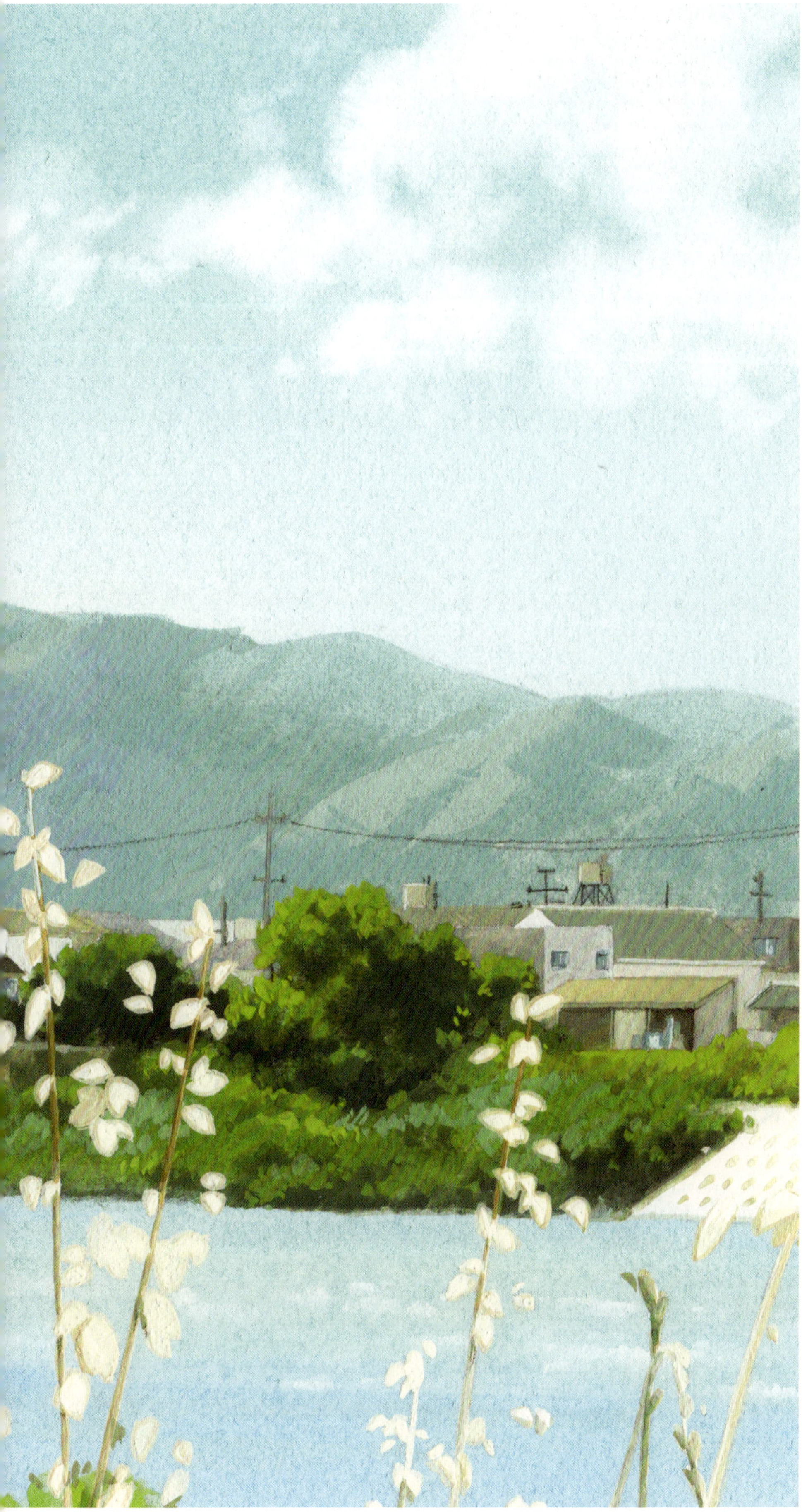

Besides retrospection, another important aspect of my artistic growth is the ability to evaluate art – especially my own. However, this often proves difficult as I tend to be attached to my own creations and cannot adopt an unbiased perspective. That said, there are a few methods that help with this:

I) Step away. As I work on an image, it's important to keep an eye on the overall appearance and regularly zoom out – I physically take a few steps back to judge whether it is working or not. But time apart also helps, especially after I have declared a painting to be finished. Things that previously went unnoticed often reveal themselves when I step away from my work for just one night.

II) Use a checklist. This makes it a bit easier to pretend that I am looking at someone else's painting, as it breaks down the image into matter-of-fact, concrete criteria. I have compiled a checklist on page 149 that lists the various building blocks that make up an illustration in a random order. But I wouldn't get too hung up on it, or try to meet all criteria equally, because there is always a give and take. If I work with more details, my shape language becomes weaker; if I strive for realism, it results in less vibrant colours. So, it always depends on the goal and focus of the artwork.

III) Get feedback. I often ask the people around me – mostly non-artists – what they think of a painting I'm working on, and I usually get insightful responses. People don't have to be artists to recognize that something in a picture looks off, especially human anatomy. But the most important lesson I've learned is this: when someone tells me that a thing in my painting looks weird, they're usually right. But when they give me suggestions on how to solve the problem, they're usually wrong.

By putting these things into practice, I can identify areas for improvement; perhaps my use of light and shadow doesn't yet communicate the desired emotion, or a flawed perspective gives the image a weak structure. These insights allow me to set new goals and consciously work on my shortcomings; they can provide a sense of progression and direction. One crucial skill that should not be underestimated here is to 'learn how to learn'. It's all well and good to set goals, but if I have no idea how to actually achieve them, I'm likely going to struggle. For my own artistic development, studies are the most reliable way to hone my skills and make up for my deficiencies. I have already touched on the subject of studies in the chapter Artistic Voice and presented it as a method of learning from my role models, but it can also take many different forms. The result of a study does not necessarily have to be a beautiful, finished painting. Merely copying something – whether a painting, a photograph, or something else – is not the goal here. It's about analysing, taking things apart, and extracting useful information. Ideally, the study should provide me with new insights, and the way to get there is highly individual. I often take notes next to the image I'm studying and add little doodles, sample colours, and paint swatches; I also trace or circle elements to analyse their relationships and composition.

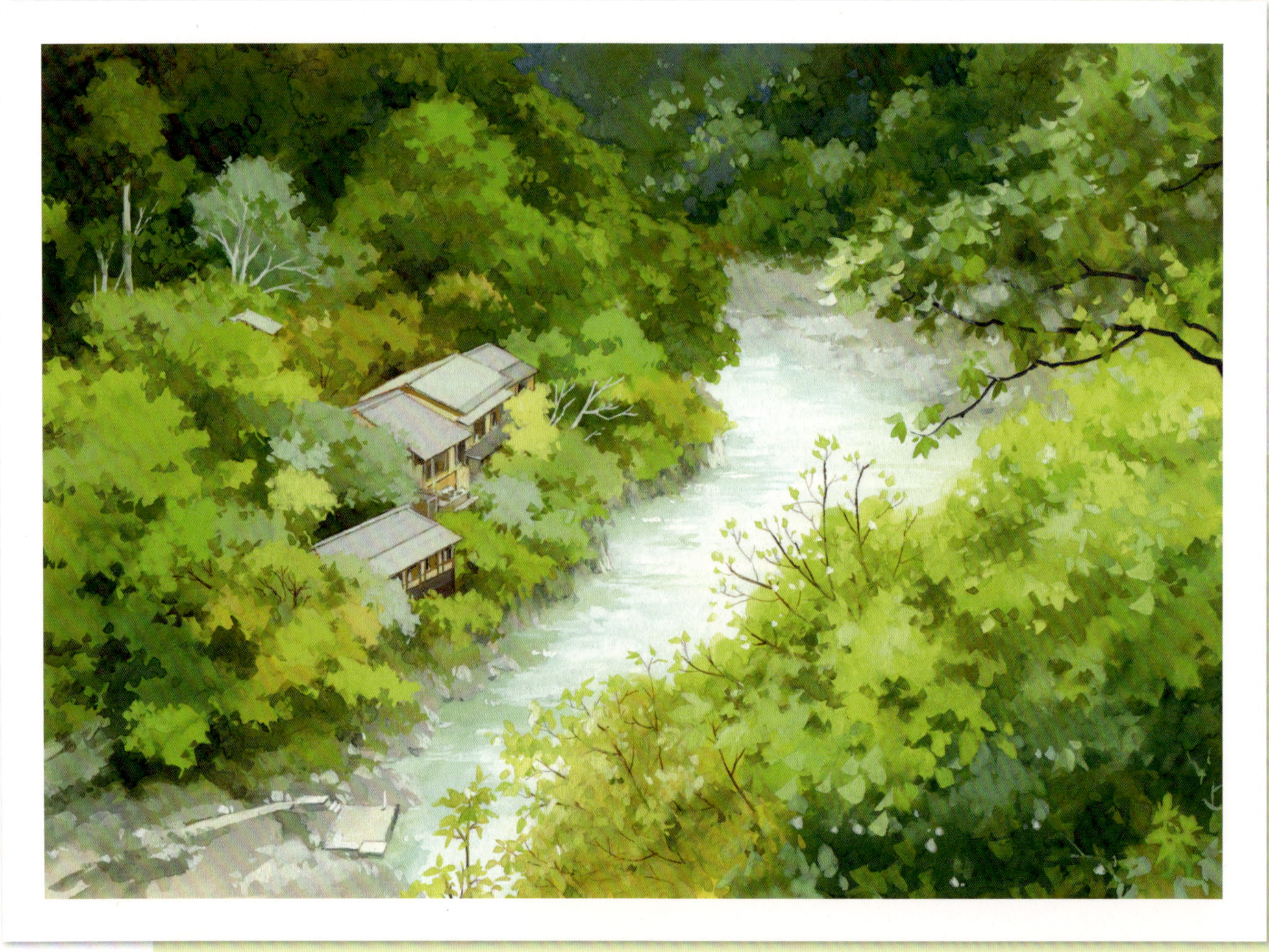

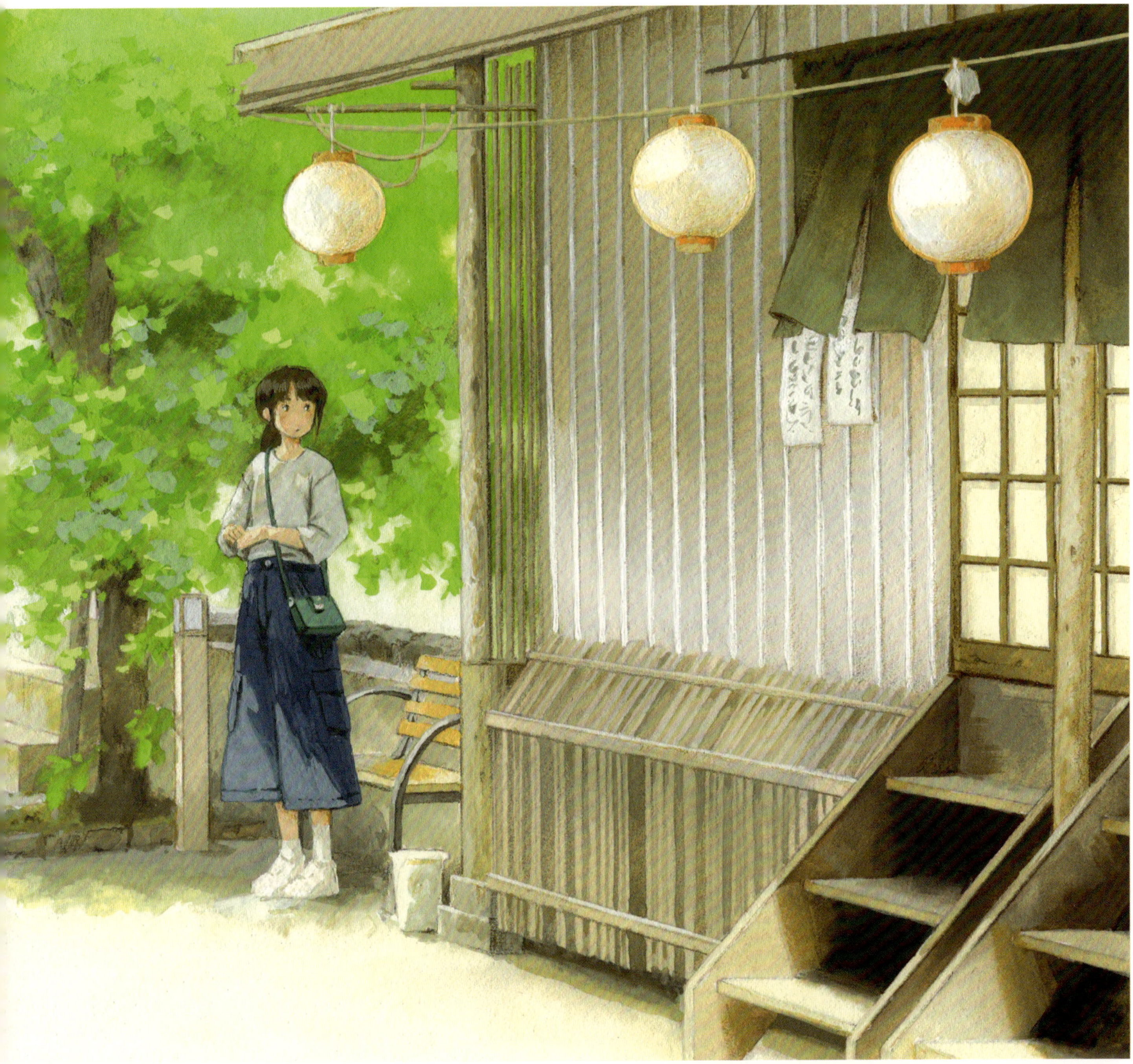

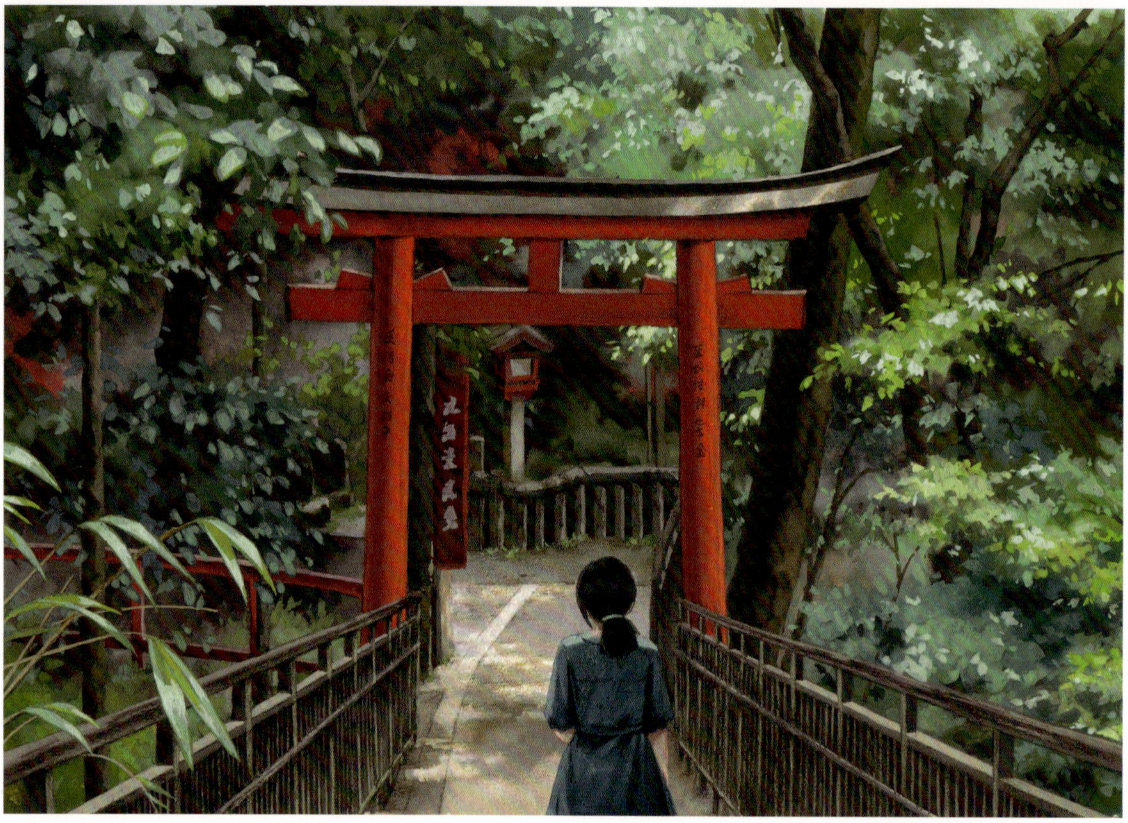

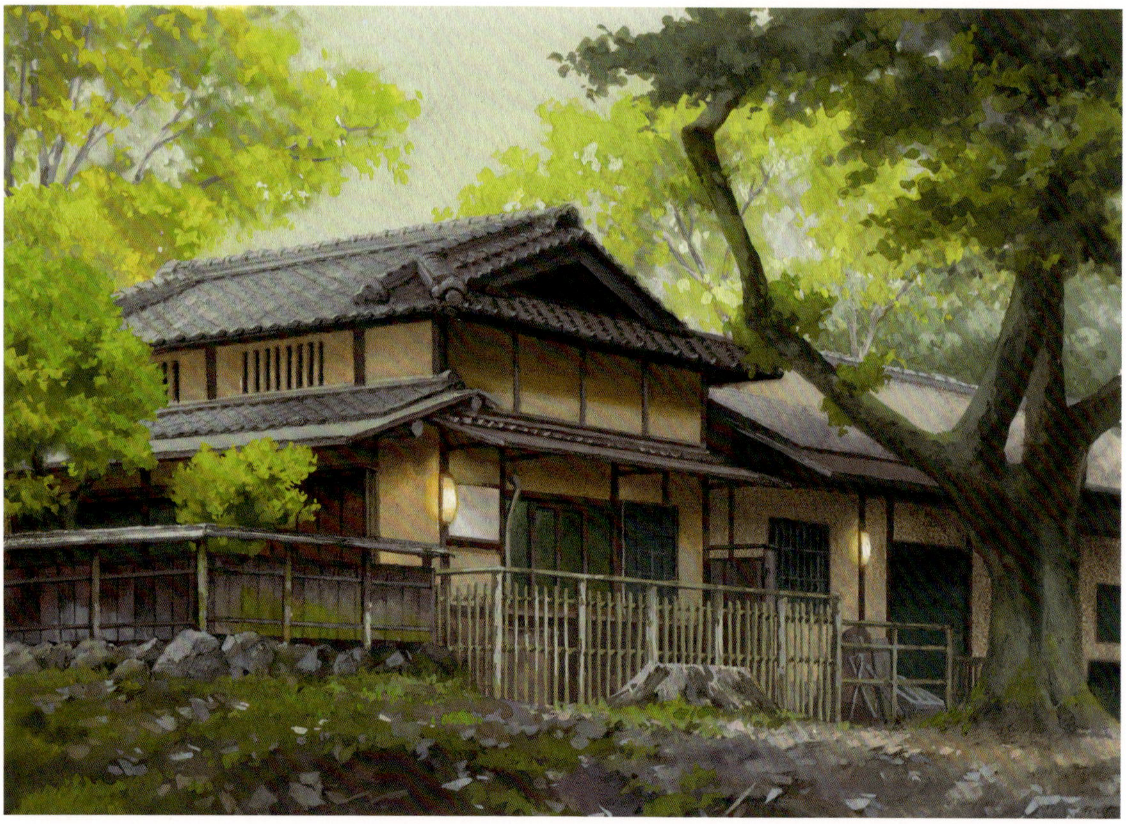

As far as I'm concerned, there are no limits or rules to this, and anything is allowed that helps us better understand things and actually retain the information. For example, to get comfortable with perspective, I often recommend that people trace photographs, especially of interior scenes, until they develop an intuitive sense of the prevailing angles and lines. It is also particularly important not to do studies simply for the sake of doing studies, but to select material that makes sense for our own work. John Singer Sargent, for example, was an incredible painter, but since I'm currently not aiming for realistic, painterly portraits, it makes less sense for me to study his art. However, if painterly portraits *were* my intention, I would proceed as follows: I would start with an analysis of one of his paintings (taking apart colours, simplification, stylization, and brush economy) and then make as accurate a copy as possible based on these criteria. The next step would be to transfer or apply what I have learned: I would now find a photograph or a living model, and try to paint them, ideally, as Sargent would have.

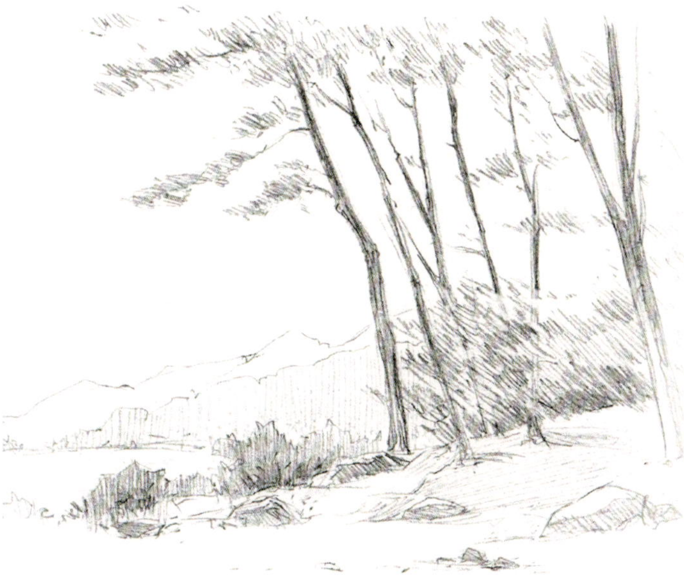

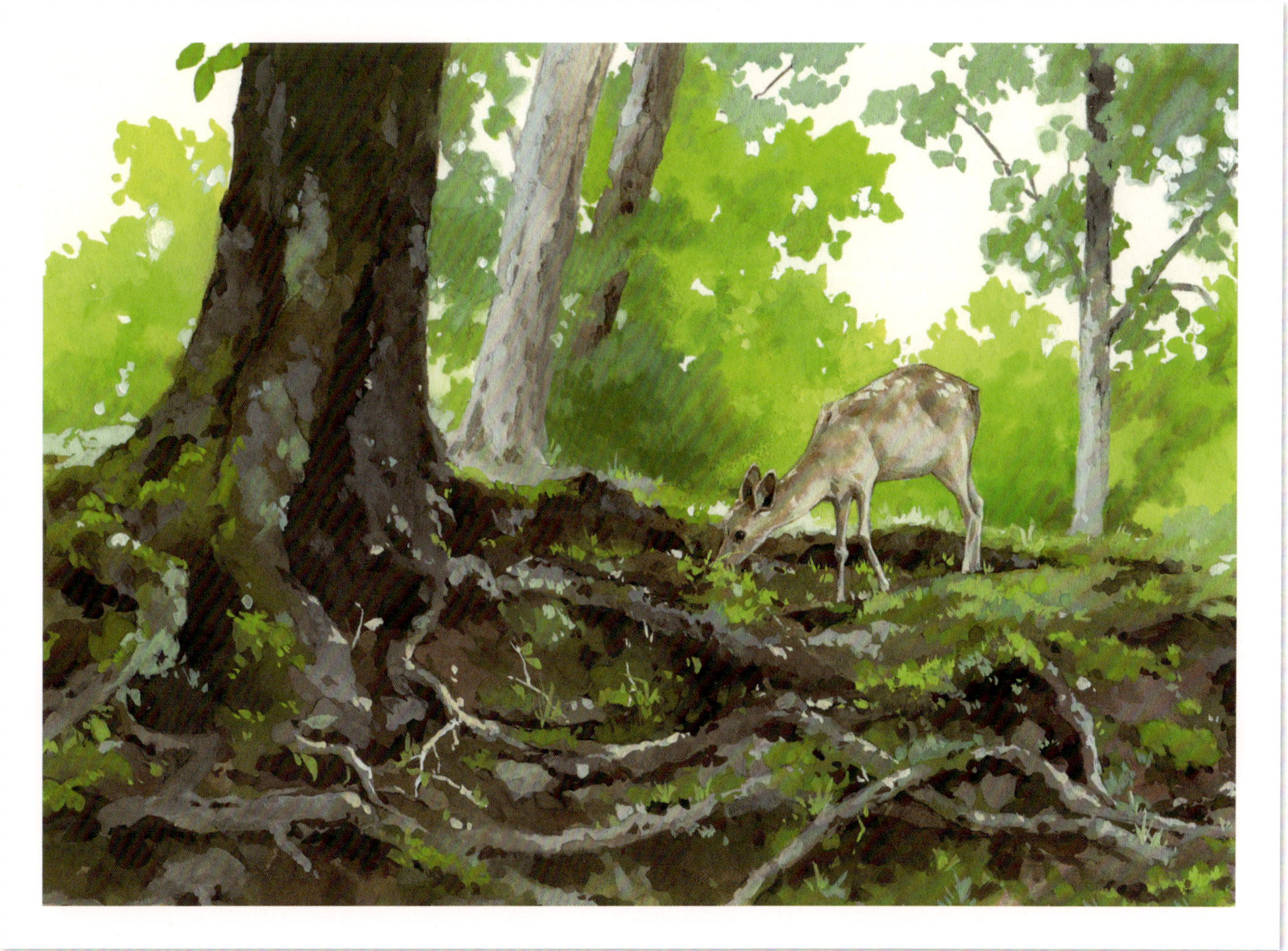

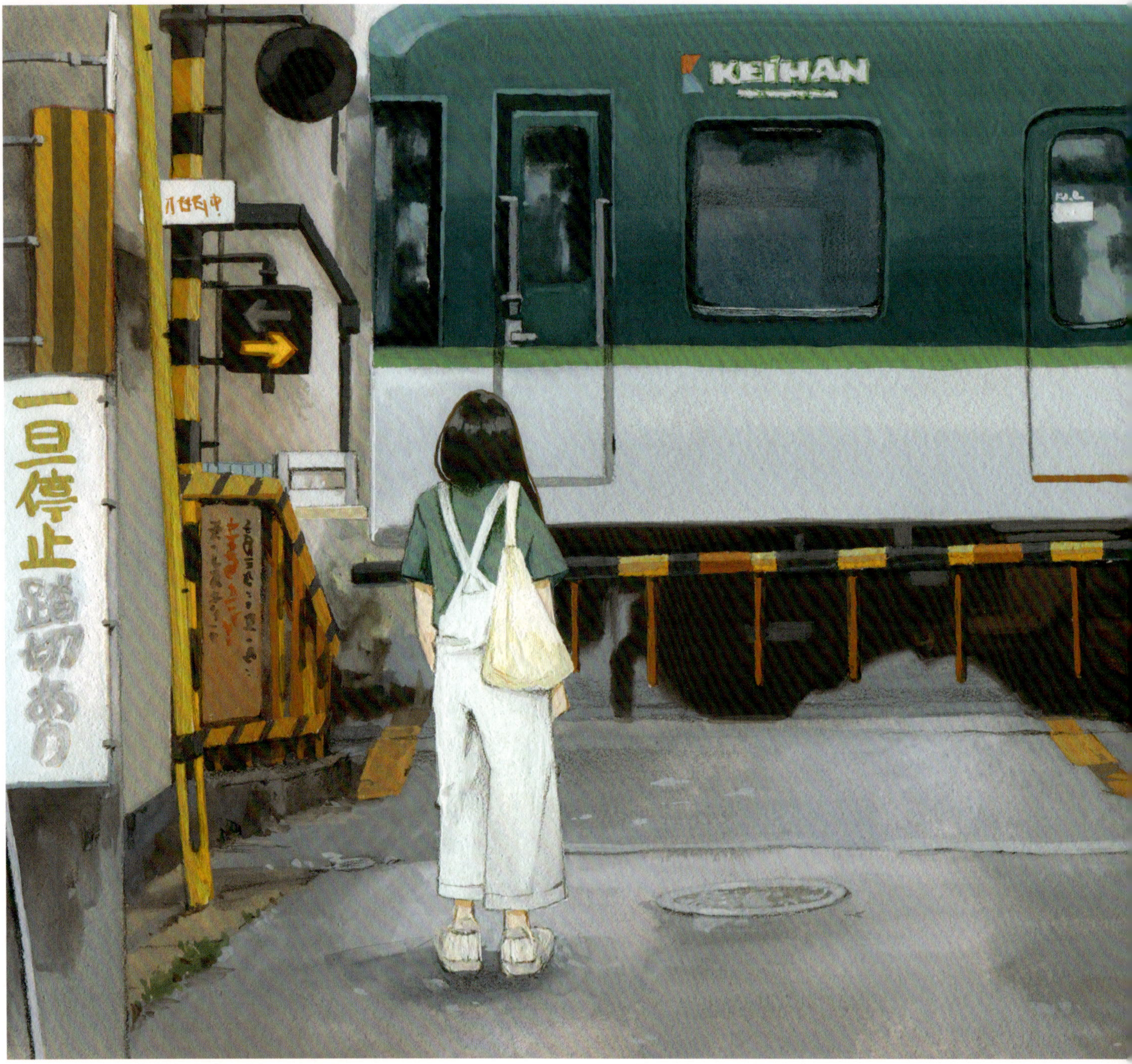

Continuing to develop as an artist is something that feels natural to me. I thrive when given the opportunity to learn new skills, and if I don't challenge myself, I get bored easily. Change is a part of life. Nothing ever stands still, and I think the same is true with art. On this topic, Nick Cave comes to mind once again, for he mentioned in an interview that with every new album he releases, he wants people to re-evaluate whether they still like his music; he always delivers something new. I like this sentiment of constantly reinventing yourself and being able to surprise both yourself and others. Be it in art or in life, I enjoy pushing boundaries and exploring places I haven't seen before. I am convinced that expanding my skill set can open new possibilities and take my artistic career in unexpected directions.

Currently, I am working on my ability to paint traditionally with gouache, and, who knows, maybe one day it will lead to an exhibition or something entirely different I can't even foresee. So, when I feel like I'm stagnating, I look around and explore a new medium, or get inspired by disciplines outside my area of expertise: film, graphic design, fashion, architecture – there's a myriad of things to discover and learn, as long as I stay curious.

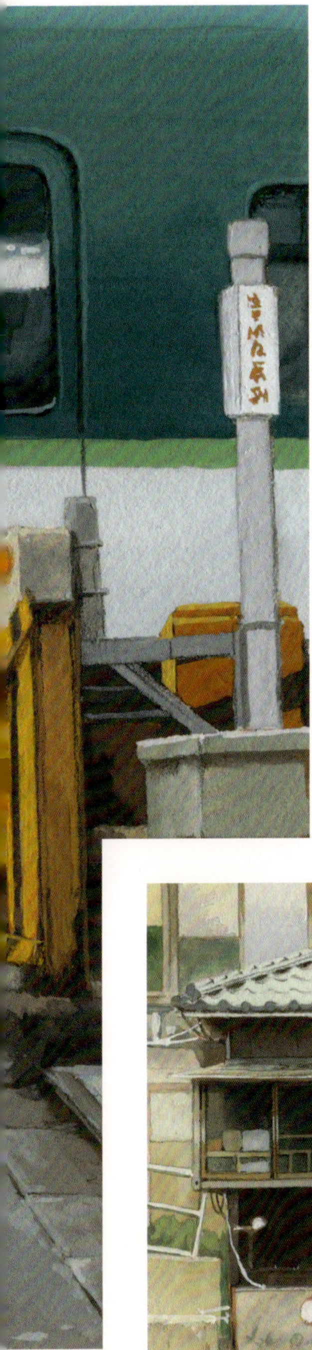

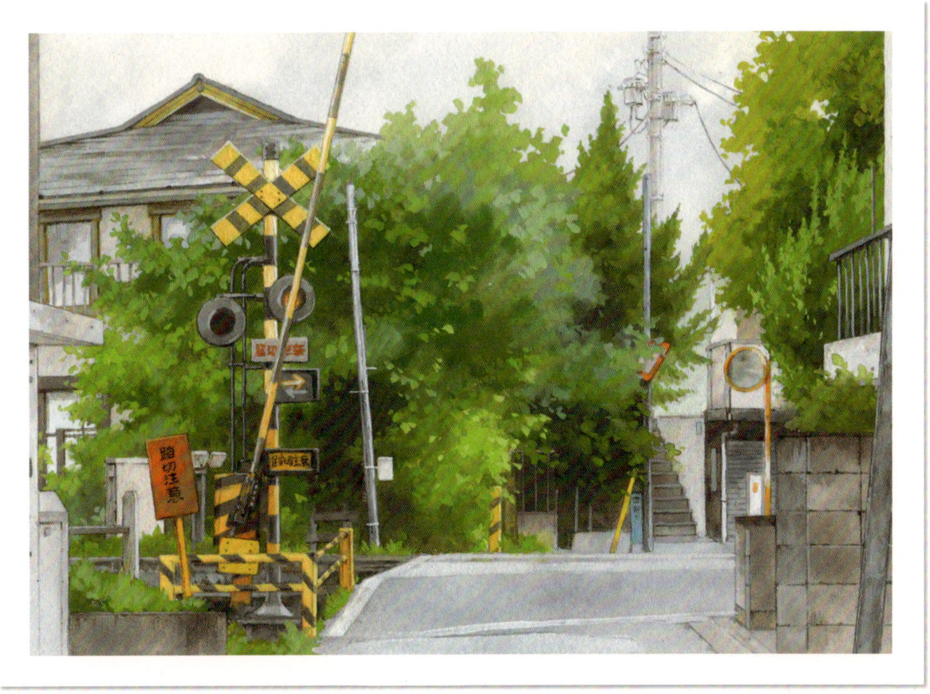
踏切注意

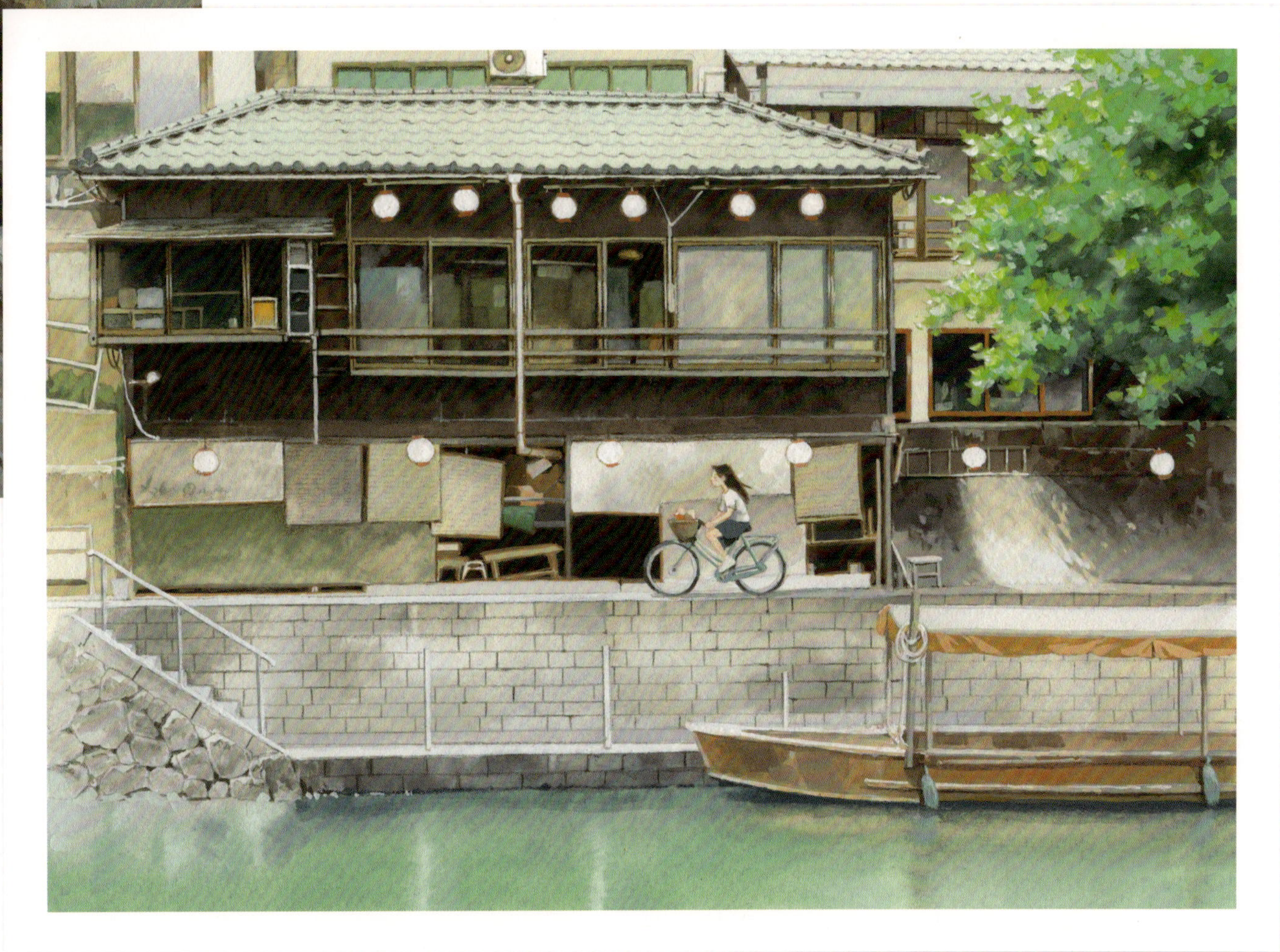

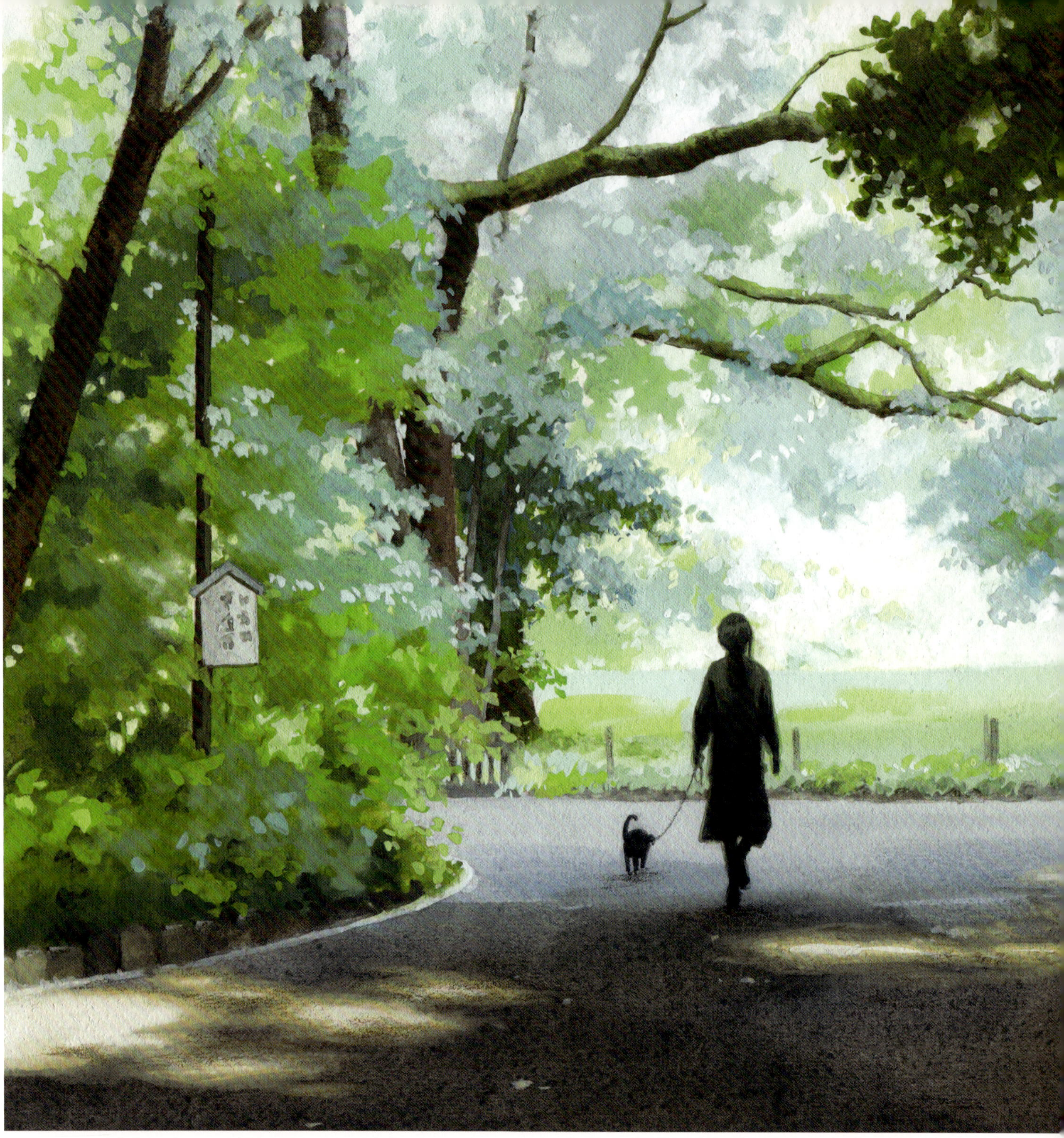

GUIDING QUESTIONS:

- Where do you find inspiration?
- What has made a lasting impression on you in the past year, in terms of your life and art? What about it was significant?
- When you look at your artwork from last year, what patterns or trends can you see? Do any new motifs emerge, and if so, what are they?
- What do you want to focus on in the year ahead, in terms of your life and art? What areas can you identify in which you want to grow?
- What is something you would like to have more of in your life? What would you like to have less of in your life? What would you like to let go of, or eliminate?

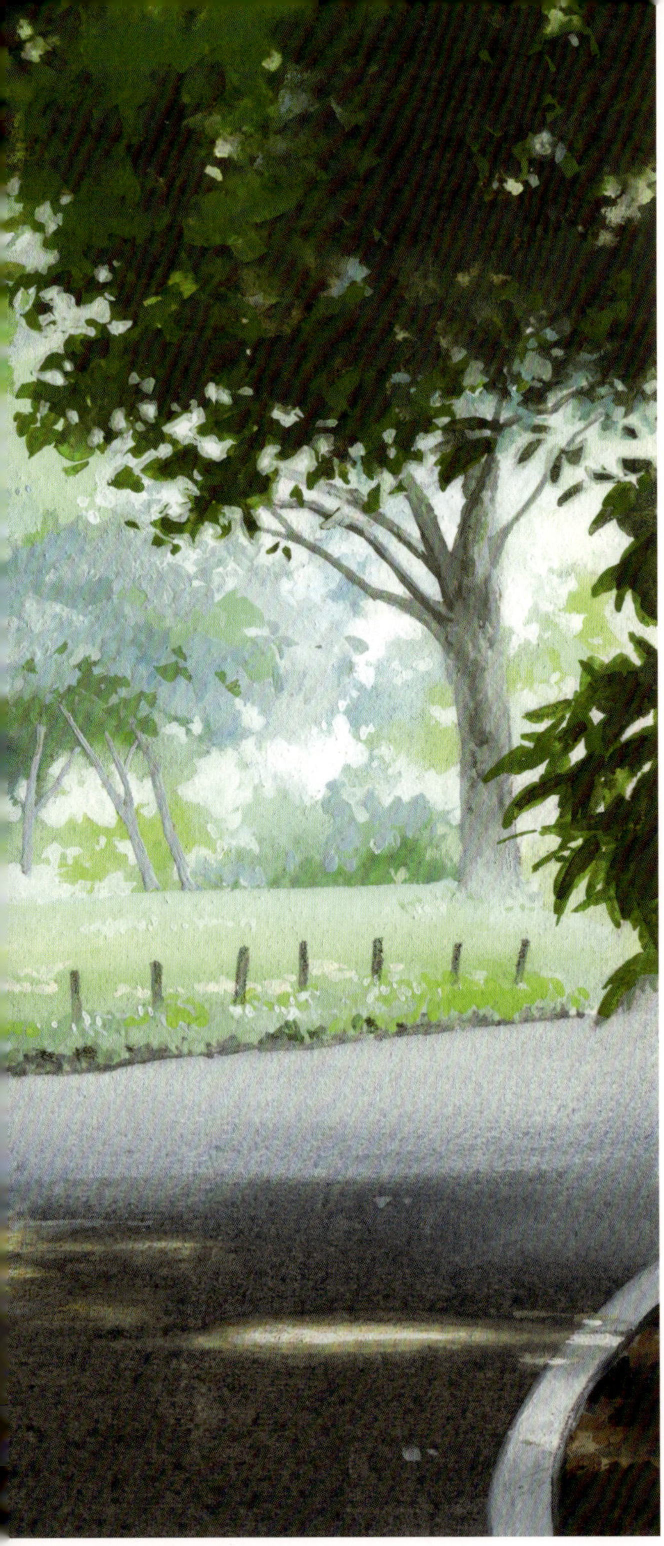

SELF-EVALUATION CHECKLIST FOR PAINTINGS

☐ Perspective: Do all elements share a common horizon line? Is the character's perspective consistent with the environment? Do you have a clear grasp on what you see from above or below? Are the vanishing points placed too close together or too far apart?

☐ Character: Is their design intentional and appropriate for who they are? Does their body language support the story? Is the anatomy correct?

☐ Set design: Did you put enough care and consideration into the design? Is it serving its purpose for the story? Is there too much or too little detail?

☐ Colour and light: Is the colour scheme appropriate for your story? Could it be more or less saturated? Does it look balanced? Is there a juxtaposition of harmony and contrast? Could certain areas be emphasized or toned down? How do light and dark colours play together? Did you use colour to draw attention to the main areas of interest? Is the lighting believable? Do you have a clear grasp on the light source(s) you're working with? Does the lighting support the story? Does it draw attention where you need it? Could there be more light or shadows throughout the scene?

☐ Proportion: Are the elements in your scene well-balanced? Do the major masses have the right amount of variety to serve the story? Should they be more even or more varied? Can you push their relationship to one another?

☐ Tangents (tangents occur when elements in the image unintentionally touch or intersect, causing a disruptive effect): Are there any tangents that distract the viewer? Could elements be moved further away from or closer to each other?

☐ Cropping: Is the crop emphasizing the story? Is there something that doesn't serve a purpose and can go? Is there something distracting that has to go? Can a different crop make the scene more interesting? Does the subject have the right amount of room around them to tell the story?

☐ Depth: Does your painting feel dimensional? Are there elements overlapping each other?

☐ Focus: Is the eye moving around the page in the way you intend it to? Through composition, contrast, colour, and light, were you able to bring attention to the main subject? Is there something that is distracting from it? Can you knock back certain areas and bring others forwards?

☐ Detail: Is there enough visual interest throughout the piece? Have the different surfaces been given enough attention or does anything feel sloppy? Could there be more or fewer details in certain areas? Does anything feel too smooth or too rough?

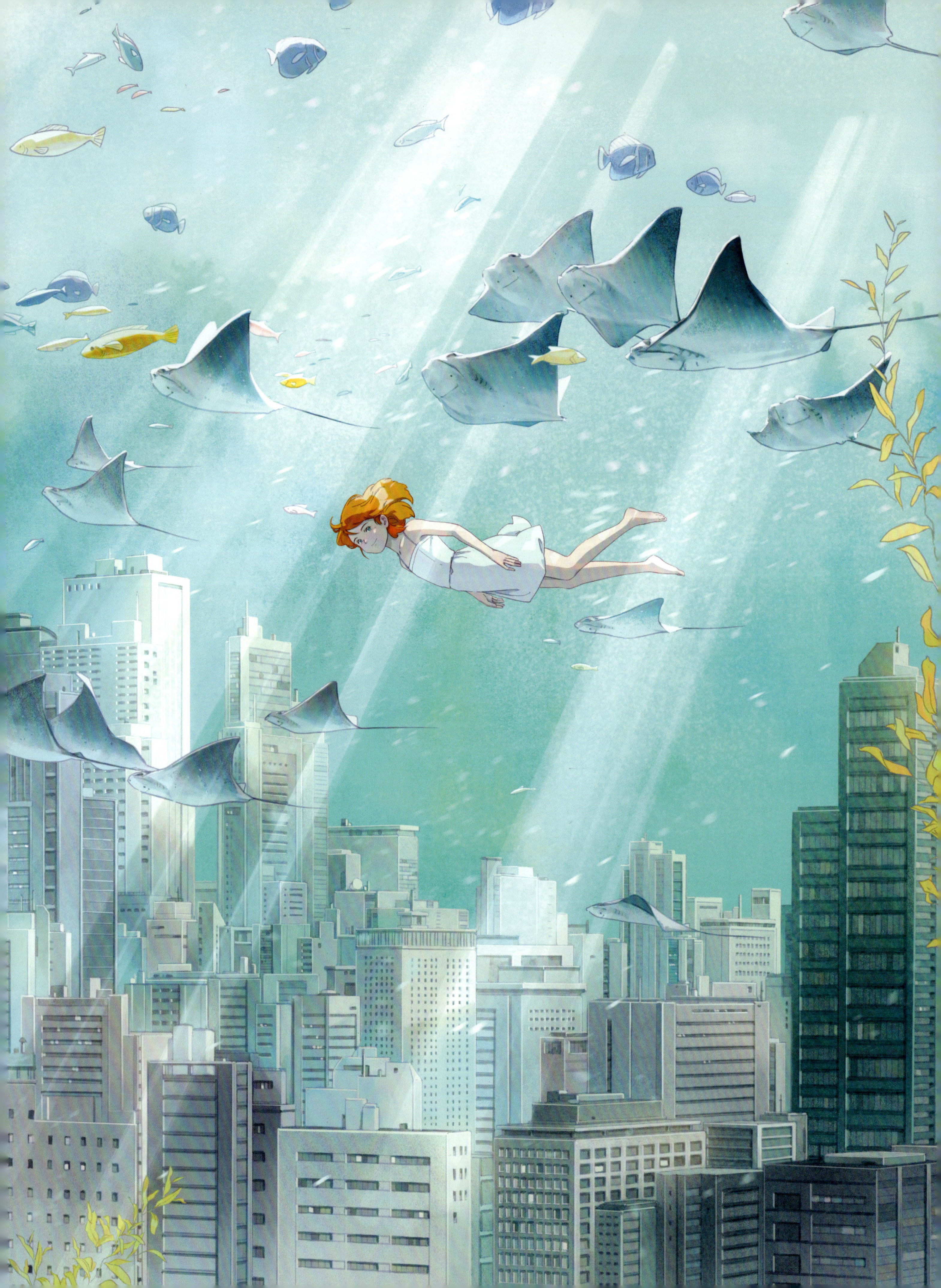

When I woke up on the morning of 20th April 2020, I was practically shaking because I was so anxious, knowing that my book *Komorebi* would be launched on Kickstarter on the same day. I had never worked on such an ambitious project before, and I had no idea how the book would be received. So, I rounded up a small group of good friends to help keep me company, and together we experienced those tense seconds as the campaign went live. Four years have passed since that day, but I still remember my nervousness and how comforting it was not to be alone at that moment. And this theme runs through my entire artistic career: I couldn't have done it alone.

Although I paint my illustrations on my own, quietly and secretly in my little room, it has always been the people around me who have enabled me to continue working as an artist. If it weren't for the support of my partner, my friends, my local art community, my followers, and my publisher, there would be no sequel to *Komorebi*. And even though my hands are getting sweaty thinking about the Kickstarter campaign for this second book, I know that I have people who believe in me and who are looking forward to *Luminescence*, and that puts my mind at ease. I'm so proud of the community we've built together, and this book is not just a collection of my art; it's a testament to the power of a supportive community. I'm so grateful that every day, I get to paint, and learn, and be inspired by the people around me, and I plan to continue until you're all tired of me.

Thank you.

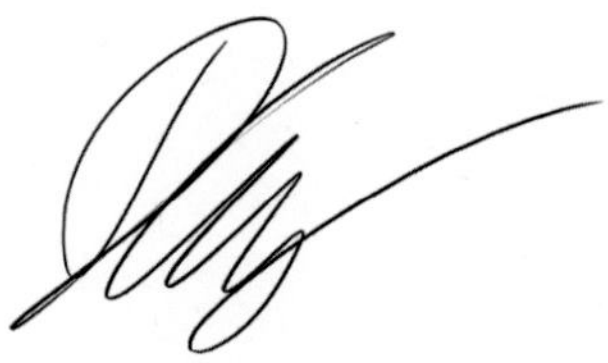

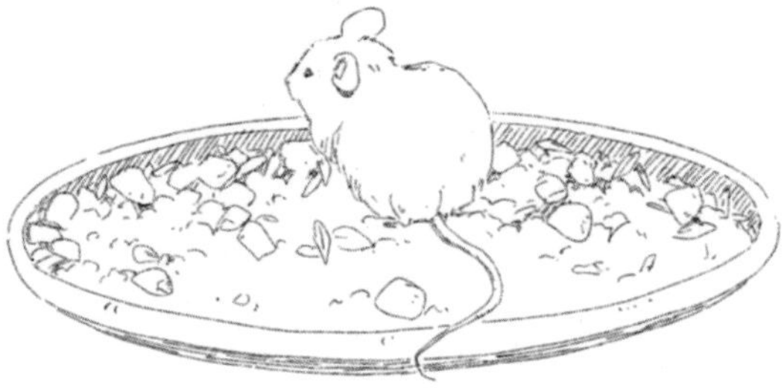

3dtotal Publishing

3dtotal Publishing is a trailblazing, creative publisher specializing in inspirational and educational resources for artists.

Our titles feature top industry professionals from around the globe who share their experience in skillfully written step-by-step tutorials and fascinating, detailed guides. Illustrated throughout with stunning artwork, these best-selling publications offer creative insight, expert advice, and essential motivation. Fans of digital art will enjoy our comprehensive volumes covering Adobe Photoshop, Procreate, and Blender, as well as our superb titles based around character design, including *Fundamentals of Character Design* and *Creating Characters for the Entertainment Industry*. The dedicated, high-quality blend of instruction and inspiration also extends to traditional art. Titles covering a range of techniques, genres, and abilities allow your creativity to flourish while building essential skills.

Well-established within the industry, we now offer over 100 titles and counting, many of which have been translated into multiple languages around the world. With something for every artist, we are proud to say that our books offer the 3dtotal package:

LEARN • CREATE • SHARE

Visit us at store.3dtotal.com

3dtotal Publishing is part of 3dtotal.com, a leading website for CG artists founded by Tom Greenway in 1999.